AF443695

5.00

PAINT THE
CHANGING SEASONS
IN
PASTEL

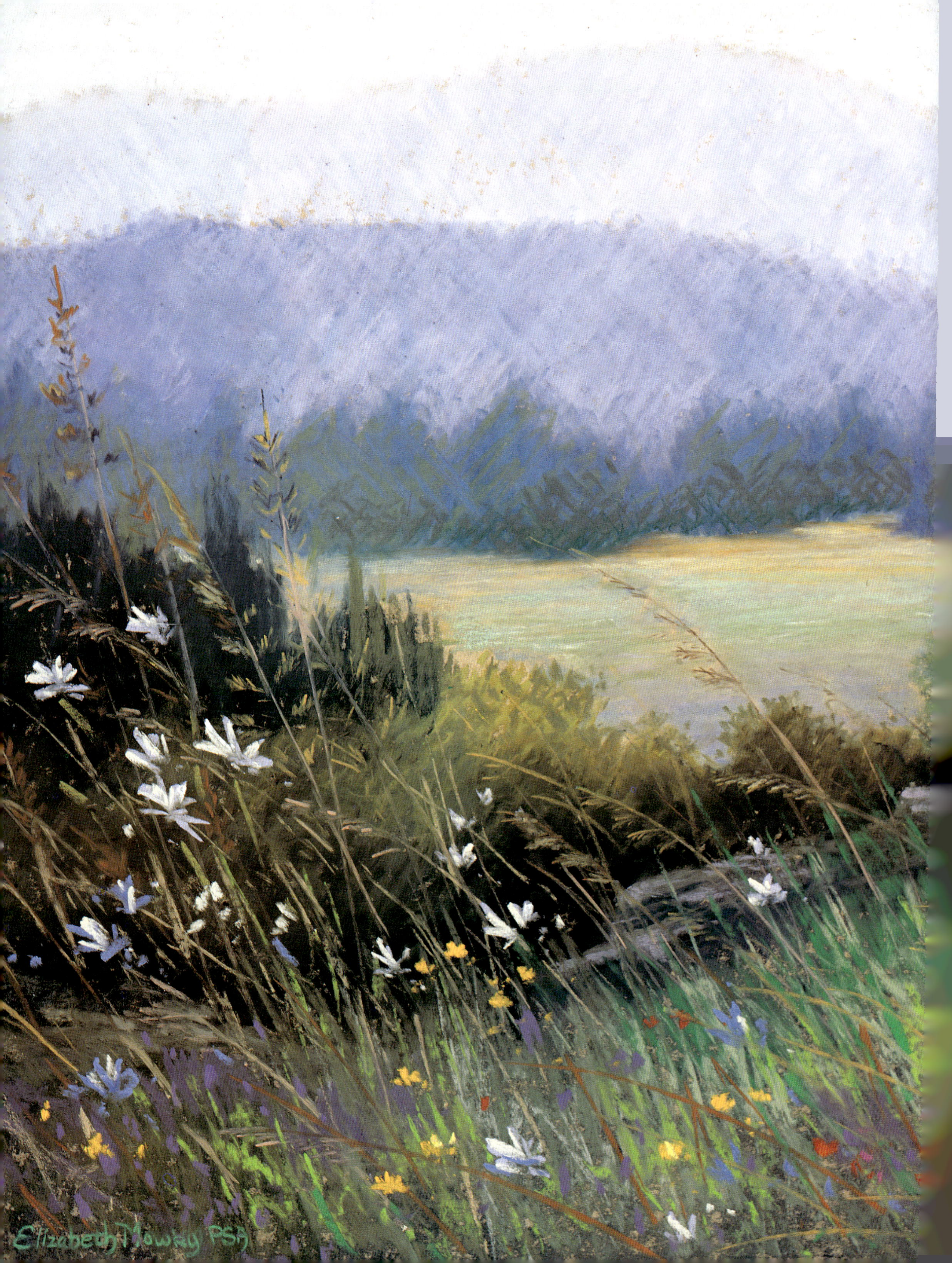
Elizabeth Mowry PSA

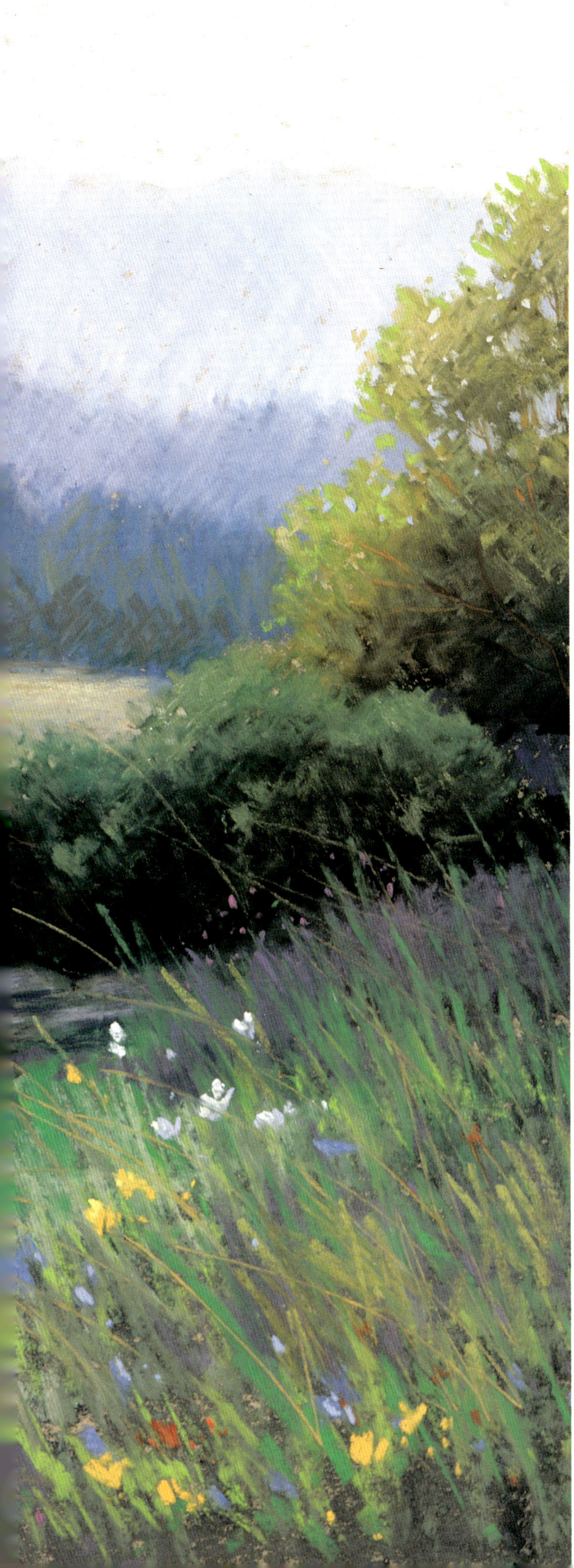

PAINT THE
CHANGING SEASONS
IN
*P*ASTEL

Elizabeth Mowry

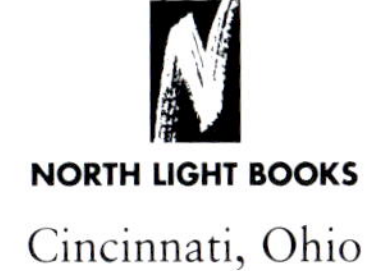

NORTH LIGHT BOOKS

Cincinnati, Ohio

About the Author

A Master Pastelist of the Pastel Society of America, Elizabeth Mowry teaches at the Woodstock School of Art in Woodstock, New York. She has worked exclusively in pastel for the past ten years and, during that time, has been a consistent award winner in many national juried exhibitions and competitions. Elizabeth resides in upstate New York between the Catskill Mountains and the Hudson River, which are the subjects of many of her landscapes.

Paint the Changing Seasons in Pastel. Copyright © 1994 by Elizabeth Mowry. Printed and bound in Hong Kong. All rights reserved. No part of this book may be reproduced in any form or by any electronic or mechanical means including information storage and retrieval systems without permission in writing from the publisher, except by a reviewer, who may quote brief passages in a review. Published by North Light Books, an imprint of F&W Publications, Inc., 1507 Dana Avenue, Cincinnati, Ohio 45207. 1-800-289-0963. First edition.

98 97 96 95 94   5 4 3 2 1

Library of Congress Cataloging-in-Publication Data

Mowry, Elizabeth.
  Paint the changing seasons in pastel / text, Elizabeth Mowry.
     p. cm.
  Includes index.
  ISBN 0-89134-574-4
  1. Pastel drawing—Technique. 2. Landscape drawing—Technique. 3. Seasons in art. I. Title.
NC880.M72 1994
743'.836—dc20   94-11698
                                                     CIP

Edited by Kathy Kipp
Designed by Brian Roeth

METRIC CONVERSION CHART

TO CONVERT	TO	MULTIPLY BY
Inches	Centimeters	2.54
Centimeters	Inches	0.4
Feet	Centimeters	30.5
Centimeters	Feet	0.03
Yards	Meters	0.9
Meters	Yards	1.1
Sq. Inches	Sq. Centimeters	6.45
Sq. Centimeters	Sq. Inches	0.16
Sq. Feet	Sq. Meters	0.09
Sq. Meters	Sq. Feet	10.8
Sq. Yards	Sq. Meters	0.8
Sq. Meters	Sq. Yards	1.2
Pounds	Kilograms	0.45
Kilograms	Pounds	2.2
Ounces	Grams	28.4
Grams	Ounces	0.04

Dedication
To my mother,

For a very early introduction to the quiet plea-
sures of gardens and the outdoors, and then for leaving the back gate open so that, as a child, I could
explore nature with the freedom that had so much
to do with why I paint today.

And in memory of my dear father,

Who told me that I would be able to do anything
I tried,

and I believed him.

Acknowledgments
With heartfelt gratitude —

To my children, Jennifer, Albert and Andrew, for
their love,

To Richard, for his deep understanding and support of my quest for harmony and personal excellence,

To all of the wonderful people connected with the
Woodstock School of Art,

To Phyllis, Elizabeth, Mathew, Carol, Eva, Rosemary and all of my dear friends for their help and
encouragement,

And to my students, for insisting that this kind of
book had to be written.

I also wish to thank Annie Schley Ross for the field
box construction design, and Alexander Casler for
photography and for patiently teaching me what I
needed to know about taking slides of my work.

Finally, I wish to thank my editors, Kathy Kipp,
Rachel Wolf and Greg Albert, graphic designer Brian
Roeth, and all of the people at North Light Books
for having faith in my vision of this book from the
start and for their expertise in putting it together so
beautifully.

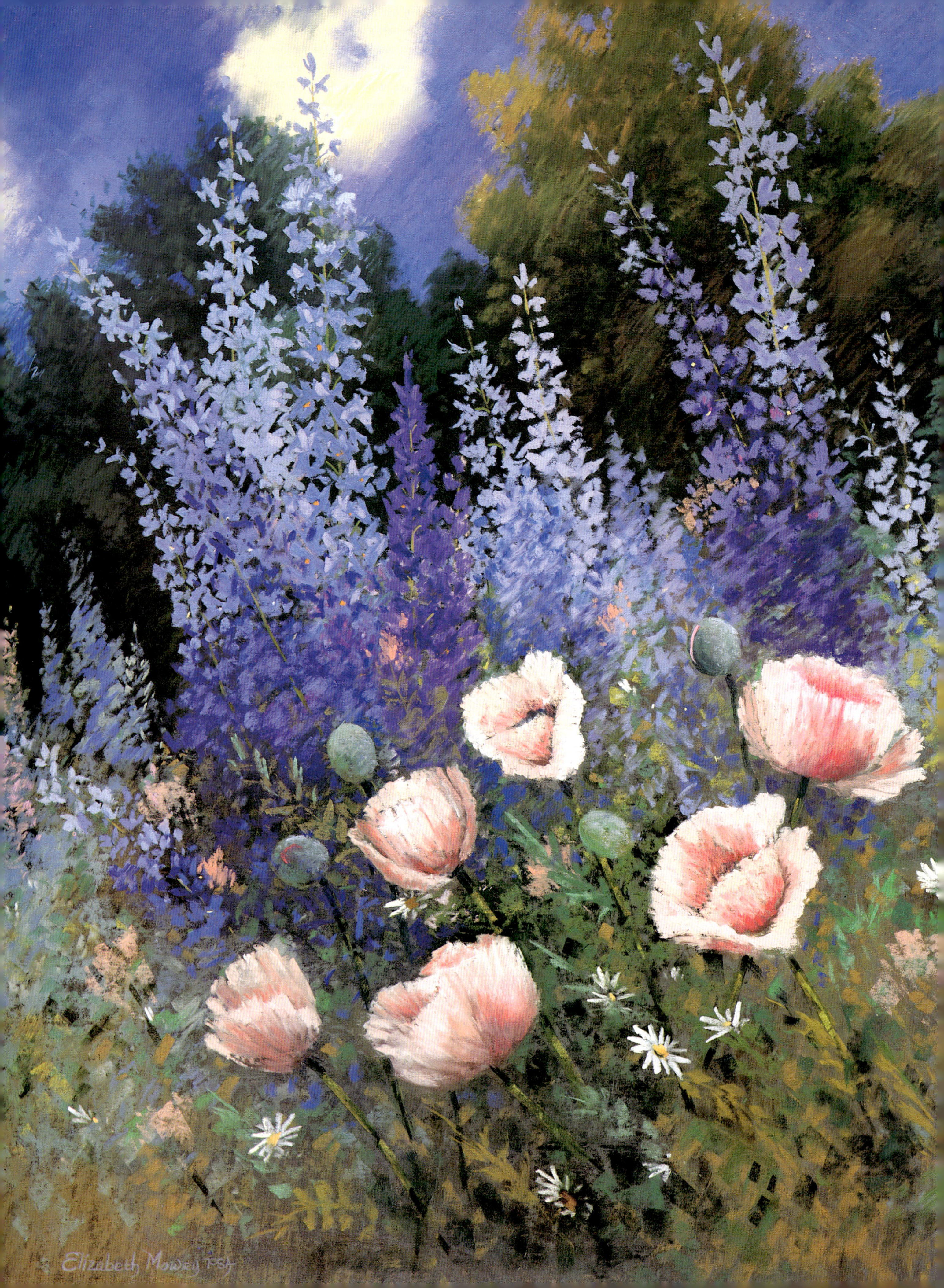
Elizabeth Mowry PSA

TABLE OF CONTENTS

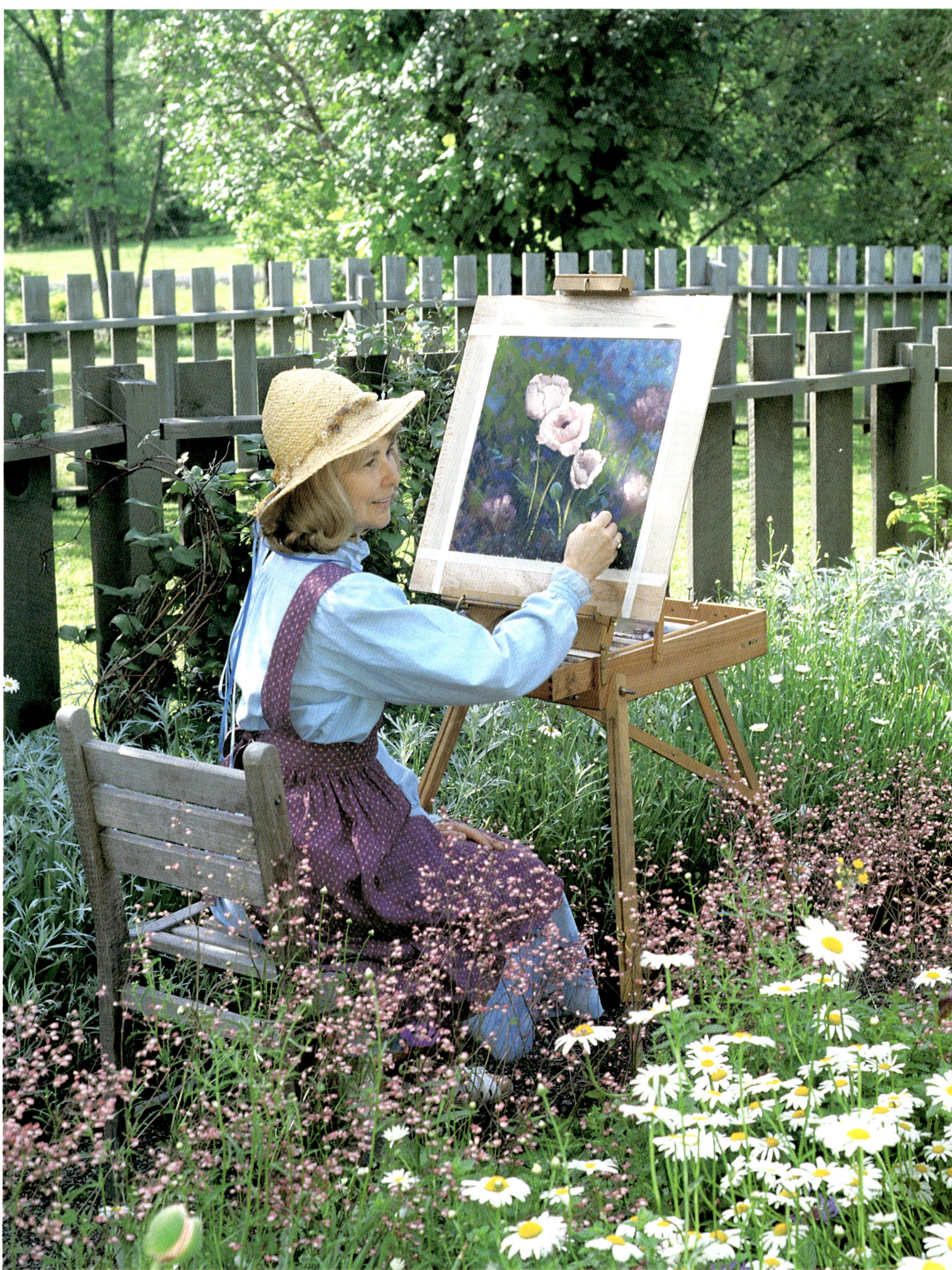

The author at work in her garden.

INTRODUCTION

The enduring harmony of nature's landscape, even as the seasons change, has evolved over the years as the abiding source of most of my work. Nature was my first teacher. I learned about it by being in it, day after day, season to season, accepting all that was offered. I was enticed by its beauty, humbled by its surprising exceptions, and gently nudged to look more and more carefully at its intricacies, until eventually, I began to see. But nature is a silent teacher, a wordless, open book.

In my respectful communion with the outdoors as a youngster, there were no labels for what I was learning. I could see that hills in the distance were smaller and less distinct, and when it was time, that was how I painted them. Today there are formulas for almost everything, including one for expressing distance by using cooler colors, smaller proportions and softer edges. In this book, I wish to share what I have discovered to be worthwhile after years of assimilating and sorting, as well as the results of those early silent conversations between nature and my soul.

Many students who enroll in my classes, already having a foundation of basic skills, want to know how to begin a thoughtful and sound departure that will take them beyond the rules. In this book, you will find guidelines to a sensitive and perceptive approach to painting; all of the pastel techniques that I use; and a painting philosophy that embodies, with equal importance, common sense as well as poetic personal vision.

I have divided this book into five parts, one for each season plus a general introduction to pastel to help you get started. At the beginning of each season, you will find material culled from my nature journal—"paintings in the mind" that suggest what to look for at a particular time of the year as you make a connection with your subject matter. My own creativity is limited by personal meaning. I believe there is, or should be, something that calls us to paint a certain place or subject; some reason we choose one view over another when many are accessible. The text of the book will invite you to follow the thought patterns that lead to selection of subject, color and mood. It is important to remember that it is the total response of *all* of the senses that constitutes the emotional essence of our paintings.

Within the following chapters, I focus on skills specific to pastel—not isolated strategies, but *applied* techniques—in demonstrations and examples that show the relationship between the technique and its place within the finished work. Additional studies show a simplified approach to some singular aspect of nature. Color selection, use of materials, value and composition are blended into each season's approach to painting nature.

I hope some of the special pastel techniques that I use will help you in your work, and perhaps some of what I have learned so laboriously by trial and error will save you some time. But most important of all is that you will witness seasonal *impressions* being translated into personal *expressions*. Know with certainty that you can do the same.

Each of us sees differently. Personally, I feel compelled to paint what I know best. My activities in my gardens, in my kitchen and in my studio are so closely entwined that they spill into and enrich one another. While nature supplies shape and movement, light and shadow, sound and scent, what we create with them depends on what lies within ourselves. Our feelings about life, our memories and longings, our fears and deepest joys influence how we perceive all that surrounds us. This book shows that how we see translates directly into what and how we paint.

The most memorable image is one that strikes a chord in the heart of another over and beyond being faultless, for a painting can be technically correct and have little impact. The purpose of this book is to encourage a blending of your emotional response to nature's seasons with your ever-growing mastery of pastel painting skills. Only then can we expect to paint pastels that are more than ordinary and, as they should be, more than words.

Elizabeth Mowry

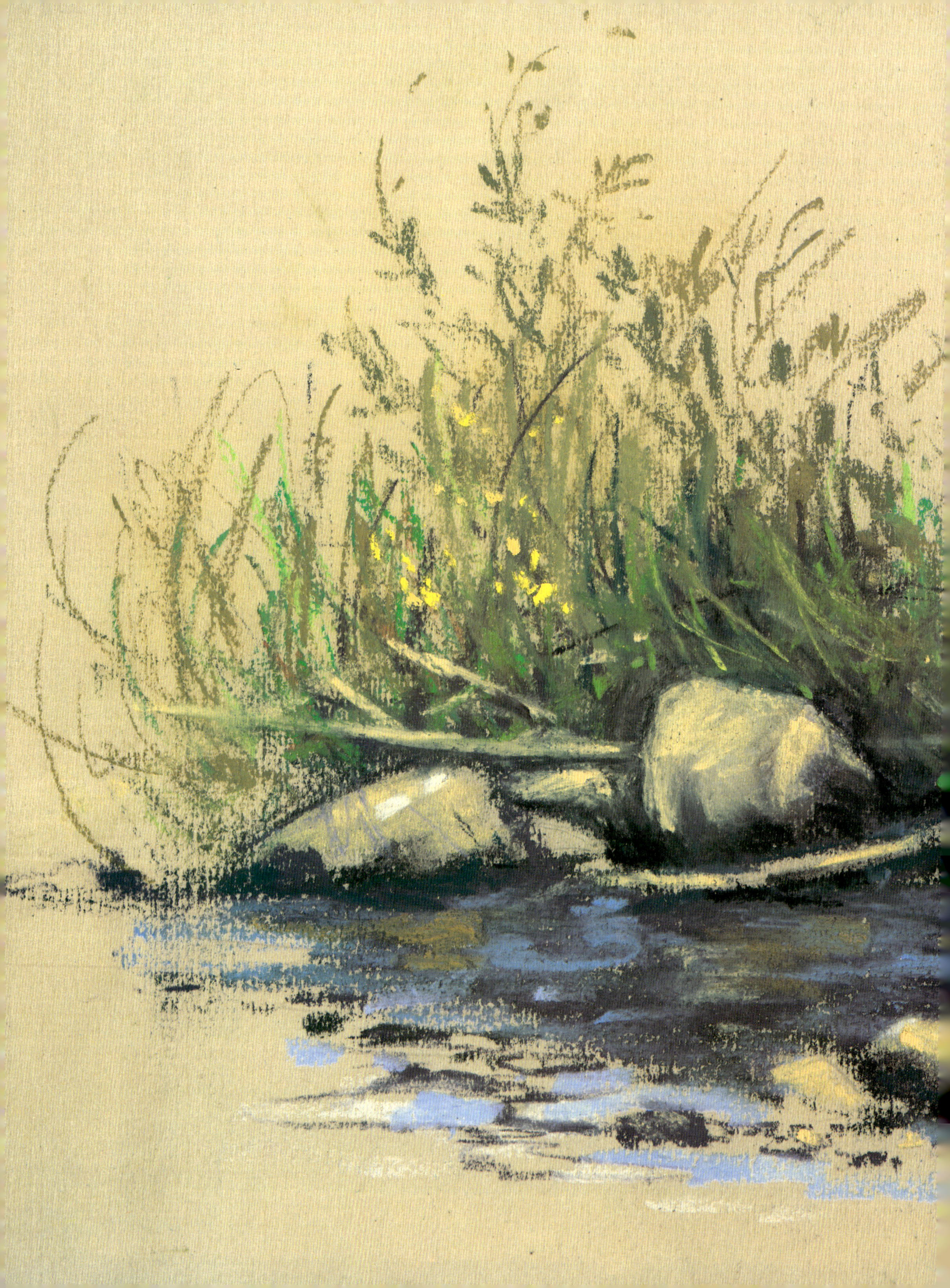

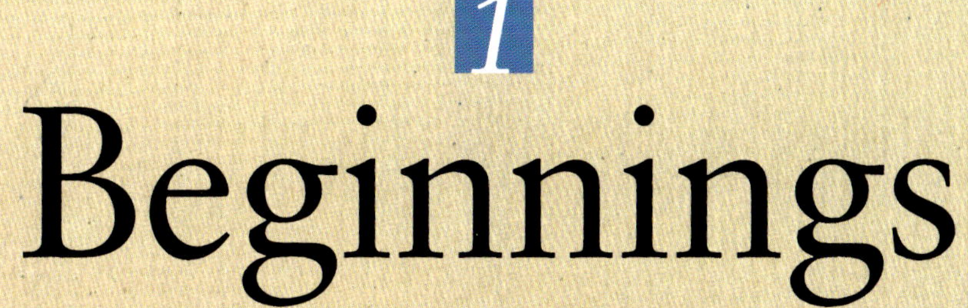

1

Beginnings

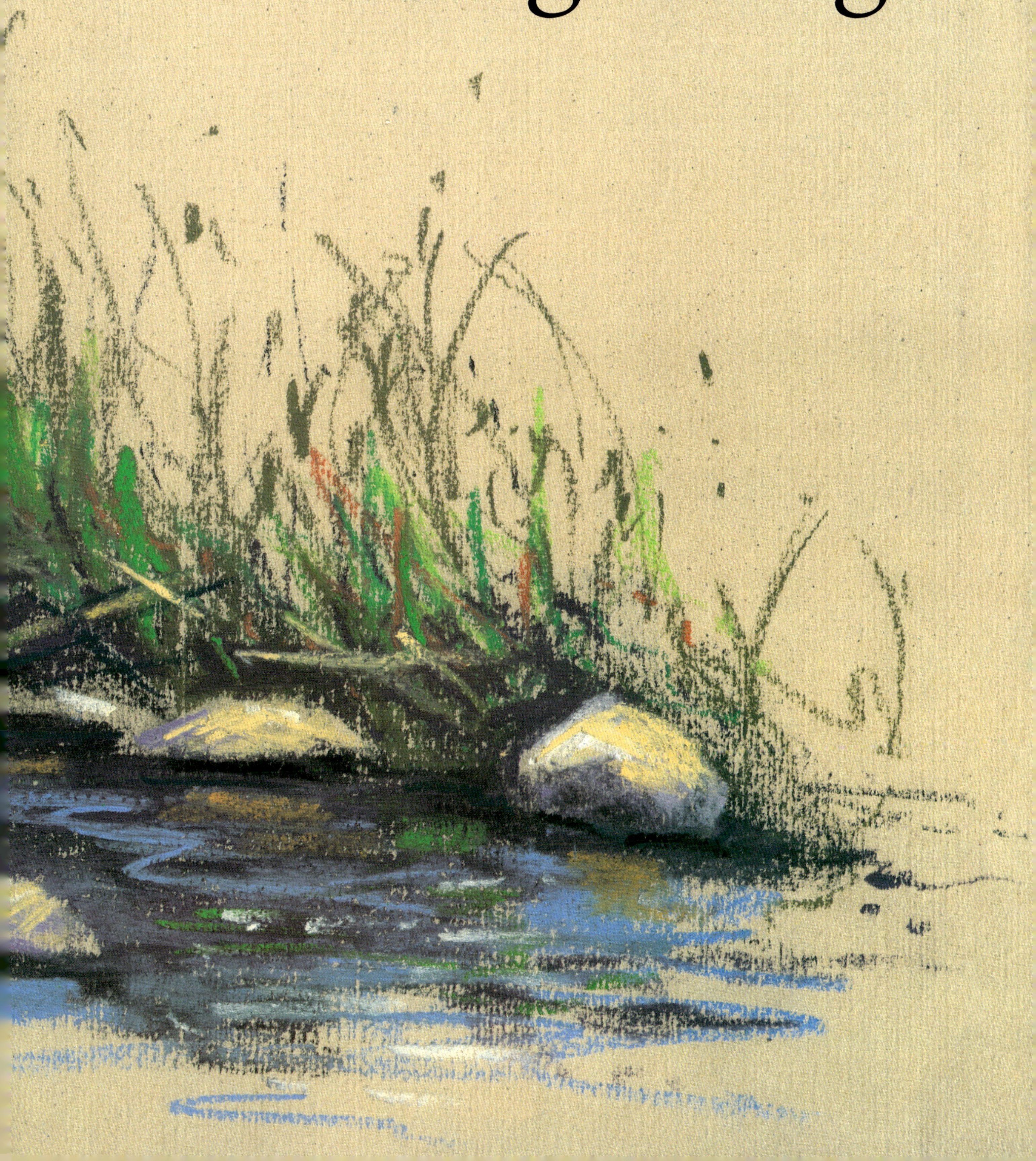

NOTES TO THE BEGINNING PASTELIST

For those of you new to pastel, I hope that you will not be intimidated by the term *technique*. A reassuring definition according to Webster tells us that technique is simply "an artist's special method of execution used to obtain a certain result." In this book, I will show you the methods that work for me, and I will be right alongside to lend encouragement. Beyond that, you will find that (1) the process of actually painting; (2) the learning that occurs from trying; and (3) attempting to paint the same or a similar subject better with what you have discovered is all there is to learning a technique. In short, mastering technique comes ultimately from doing it. You can watch someone else do it, you can hear about it and you can read about it to enhance your understanding of the procedure; but you learn it from the processing that occurs in your brain as you perform the motor skill of doing it, even if poorly at first.

Before attending a class, or even attempting a painting, spend some time making friends with your pastels. Examine and handle the tools of your new medium, and try using the pastels on a few different recommended surfaces. Get a feel for holding them, and notice what differences in applied pressure will make in the resulting marks or strokes on your surface. Practice a light touch, but don't be afraid of your pastels or reluctant to break them into pieces to get the stroke shapes that you want.

Try to abandon the notion that you need a formula for everything you try in pastel. There are many, to be sure, but early dependence on formulas will stifle your exploration of pastel and your creativity. Every artist is different; every artist's work, then, if it is honest, will be different as well.

My suggestion is that at first you get down your idea in any way you can with whatever materials you have. Then, over a period of time, begin to work at getting your idea down cleaner (less buildup), more directly (less fussing) and quicker (knowing beforehand, to some degree, what you are after). At the same time, your work will become more expressive as you become comfortable with the medium, and it will begin to exhibit the sparkle inherent to pastel.

BIRD NEST
Pastel on sanded cloth
7" × 9"
Collection of Rosemary Thibaut

Here's an example of a simple image pulled out of a dark space with pastel pencils in just a few colors. Attempting small studies such as this will help you develop facility with your materials. First, side stroke a spot of dark color on your surface for the shadow. Free strokes of gray, ochre and dark brown pencils weave the nest.

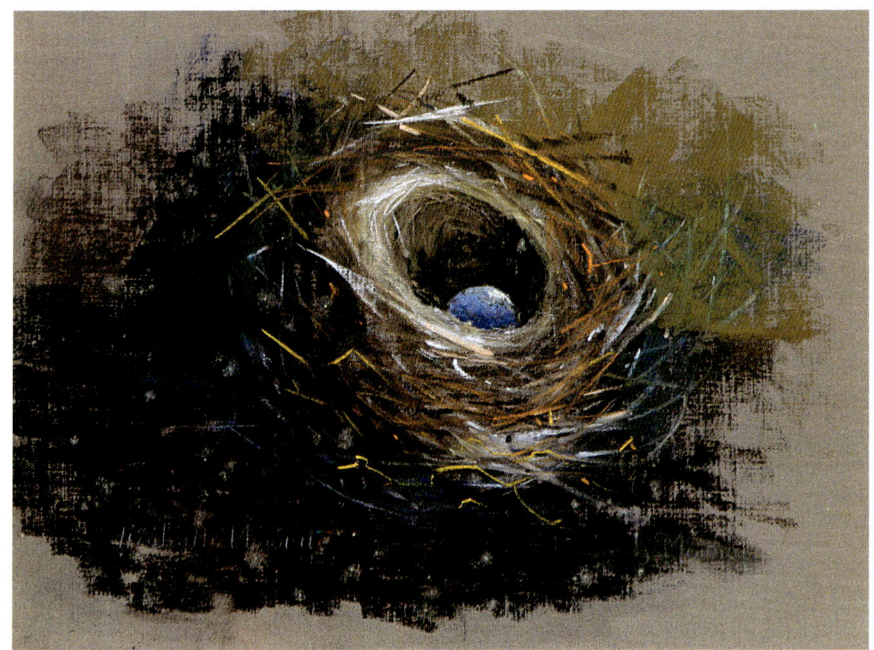

Here within the same painting, broad and bold painting strokes create a dialogue with the linear drawing strokes. Stroke variation can often strengthen the compositional design of your painting.

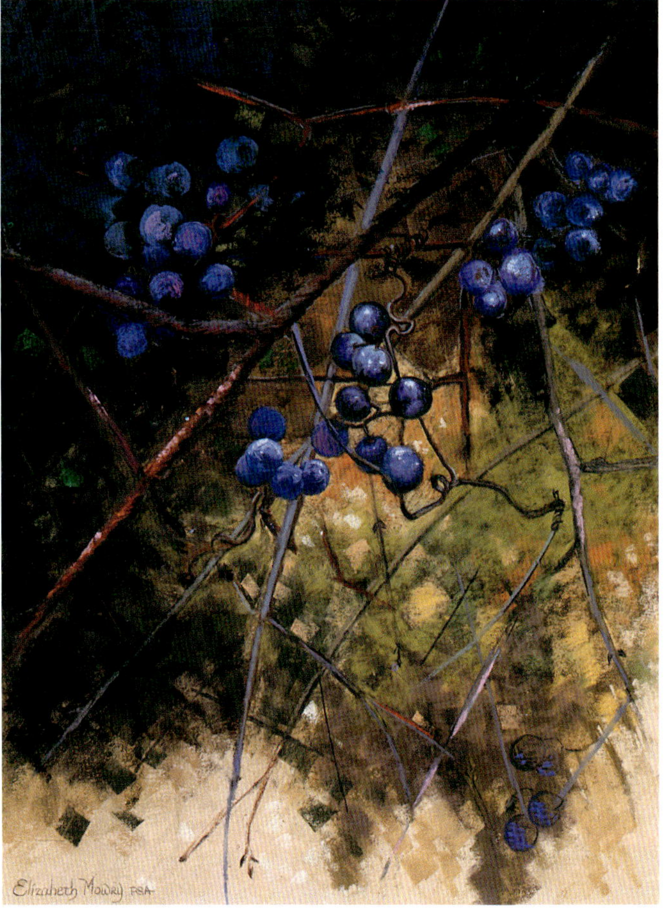

SKETCHING WITH PASTELS

Pastels or pastel pencils can be used as a drawing medium where the end result is a sketch or finely finished drawing that involves very little layering and a minimal background—in other words, a vignette. You sketch in the subject you are interested in and pastel does not cover the entire surface of your paper or go to the edges.

Sketching with pastels may appeal to some people because there is no need to make judgments as to whether to put the background in first or tuck it around the center of interest later.

With sketching, you get accustomed to your pastels gradually. You will need a good-quality paper, your pastels, and some blending stumps or totillions. (Through-out this book, because it is about painting—and particularly, painting landscapes—you will notice that I do not encourage the use of fingers to blend color, because in landscapes, other methods of blending usually give better results, as you will see.) However, when you sketch on paper or a smooth surface, you may frequently need to use your fingers as an extra tool for obtaining softened effects.

PAINTING WITH PASTELS

When used as a painting medium, pastel is stroked across an abrasive surface in layers, and it completely covers the painting ground. Put a color layer onto a practice sheet and cover it with another color layer, allowing some of the first layer to show through. See how layering can cause your colors to vibrate? Keep adding more color layers. Learn what each surface you work on looks and feels like when you have filled its "tooth" to capacity. What happens after that? You will find that additional pastel falls off most surfaces and they begin to feel slippery. This is probably the most important experiment you will ever do. When your painting surface no longer holds the pastel, you have discovered the pastelists's equivalent of the oil painter's or watercolorist's "mud," or as I think of it, "the point of no return" in a painting.

Many pastelists use a combination of drawing and painting techniques in their work, and the combinations may change with each pastel. (See *September Patterns,* above.)

BASIC STROKES

Here are some exercises that you may find helpful, particularly in your pastel painting approach to nature:

Exercises 1, 2 and 3 may be useful in learning to paint water with pastels.

1. Fill a circle with closed strokes. Closed strokes occur when one stroke is placed directly next to or overlapping the previous stroke.

2. Fill a second circle with open or broken strokes. Open or broken strokes have space around and between them. They may be sporadic or in a pattern.

3. Fill a third circle with open strokes placed over a layer of closed strokes.

Exercises 4 and 5 may be particularly helpful in understanding blending and painting skies. Use soft pastels in sky areas because they blend easily.

4. Make a color strip showing a graduated order of color. This is actually a value scale. Keep the values separate.

5. Blend your color values into one another to show a smooth gradation from top to bottom and from bottom to top. Do this by pulling some of each of the colors into the color directly above and below it with your pastels. Any two or more colors can be blended in this manner on an abrasive surface on which there is ample pastel. No fingers are necessary.

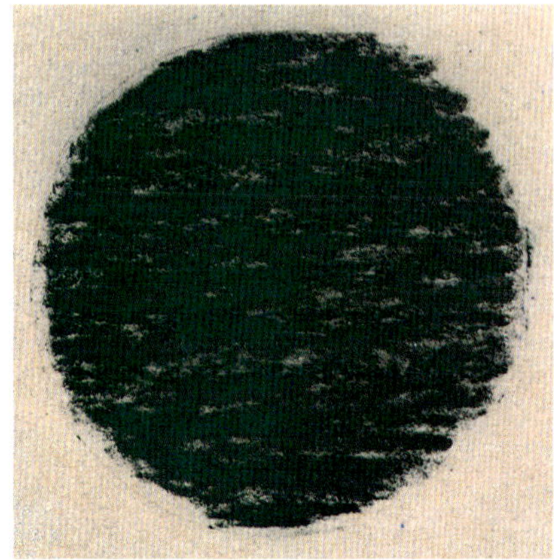

1. Closed stroke

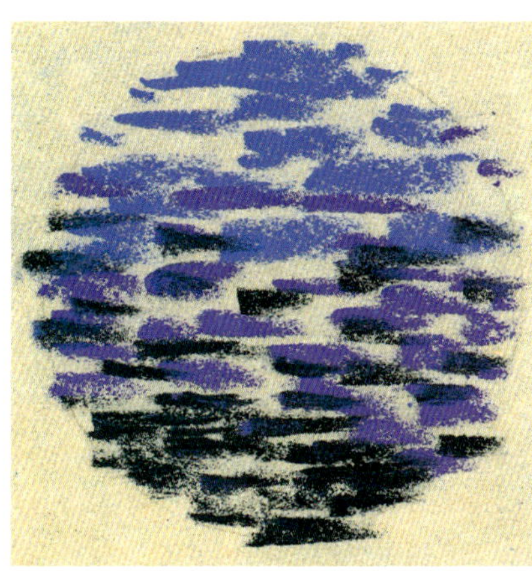

2. Open (or broken) stroke

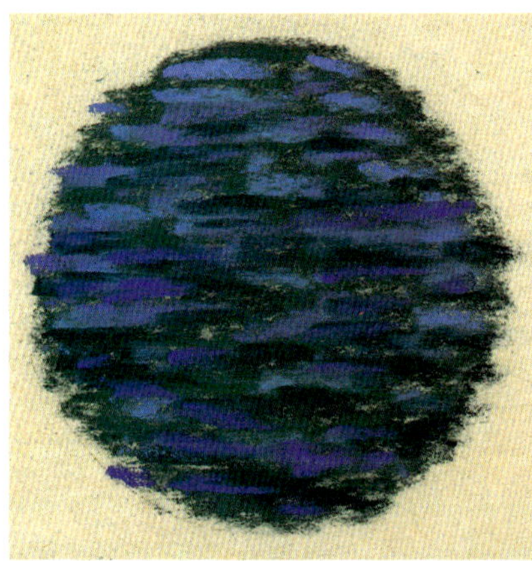

3. Open (or broken) stroke over closed stroke

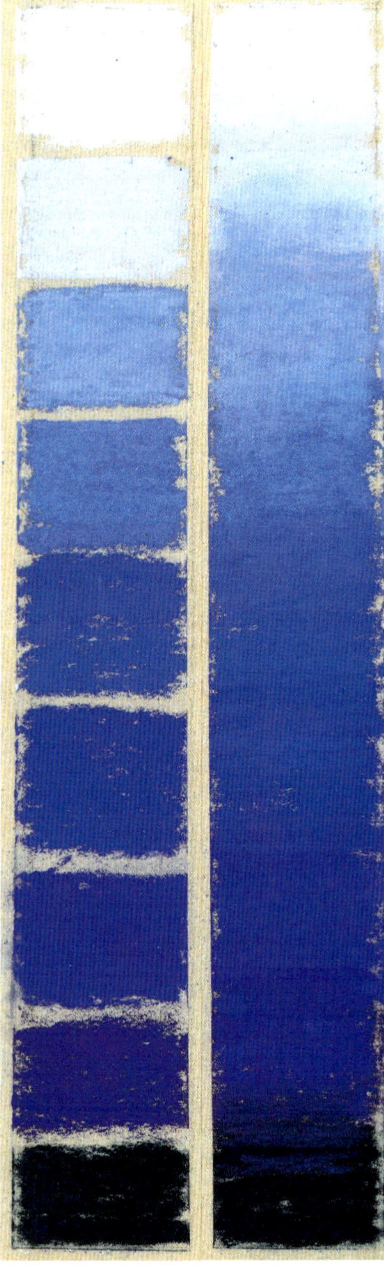

4. Graduated color/ value patches

5. Blended color/ value patches

Exercises 6, 7 and 8 may be useful when you wish to put in a background that suggests growth or foliage.

6. Use a pastel piece on its side and pull it over a large area evenly and lightly. This is called a side stroke, which is a good way to put in a first layer of pastel in your painting; it can be done with soft or hard pastels.

7. Use more side strokes of same-value colors. When you squint, they will nearly blend together.

8. Using side strokes again, in many directions, use different value colors.

6. Side stroke

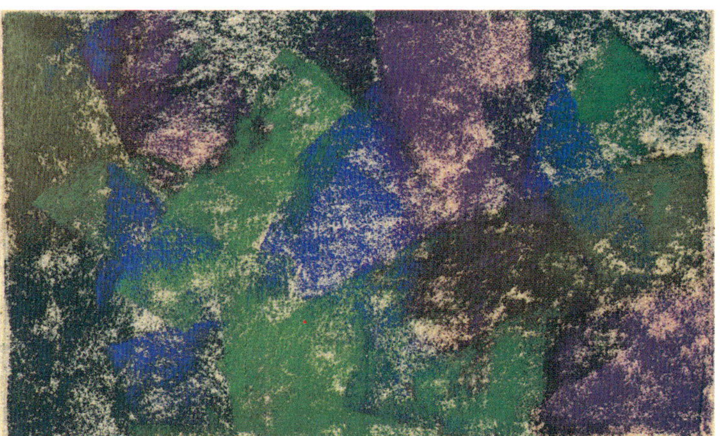

7. Side stroke using same-value colors

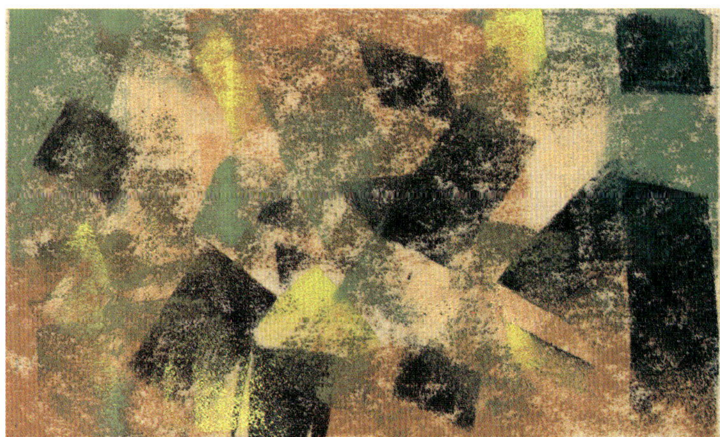

8. Side stroke using different-value colors

Exercises 9 and 10 show a versatile pastel stroke that is useful in all types of pastel painting. It is commonly referred to as crosshatching. Use it to put life back into areas that become overblended and appear lifeless.

9. Fill a circle with crosshatch strokes using the same color in two directions.

10. Fill a circle with crosshatch strokes using a few colors in several directions.

11. Exercise 11 is useful in representing man-made landscape shapes such as barns, fences or other hard-edged objects when a crisp, sharp demarcation of color is desired.

12. Exercise 12 may help you discover how the soft edges found in distant mountains, hills and clouds are achieved. Layer some colors onto your pastel surface. Where the colors meet, blur the edge with a blending tool called a *tortillion*, or a discreet, light pat or push with the finger. (A tortillion or blending stump is a hard, rolled-paper cylinder, the point of which is used to spread or blend pastel.) For example, if you have a horizontal mountain line, the push will be vertical, across the line to soften it. Usually it is more effective to push parts of a line and leave other parts intact (lost and found edges).

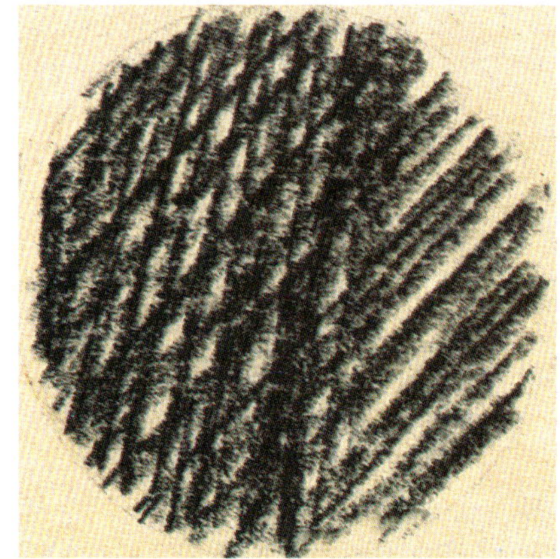

9. Crosshatching

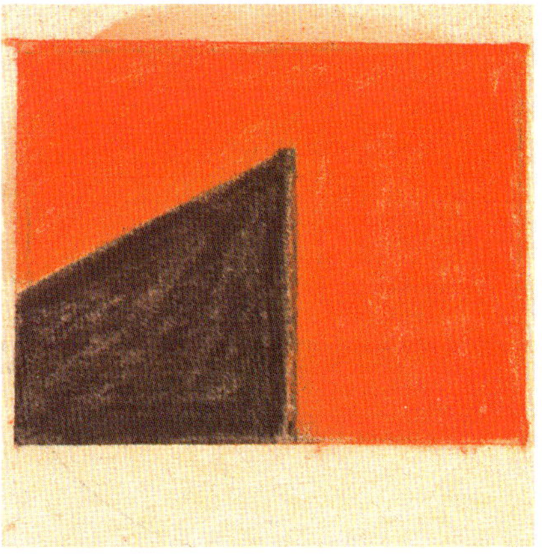

11. Hard edges

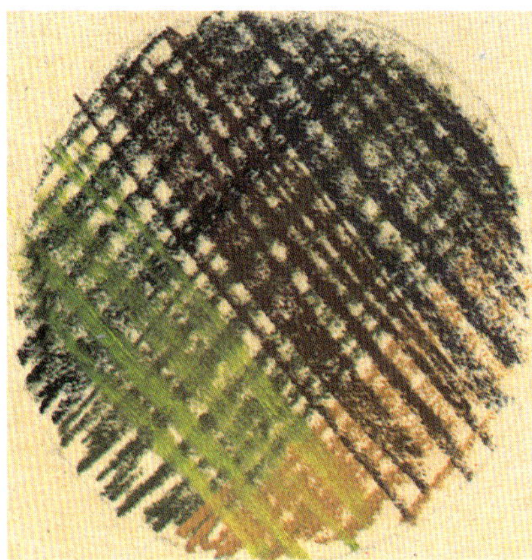

10. Crosshatching using different colors

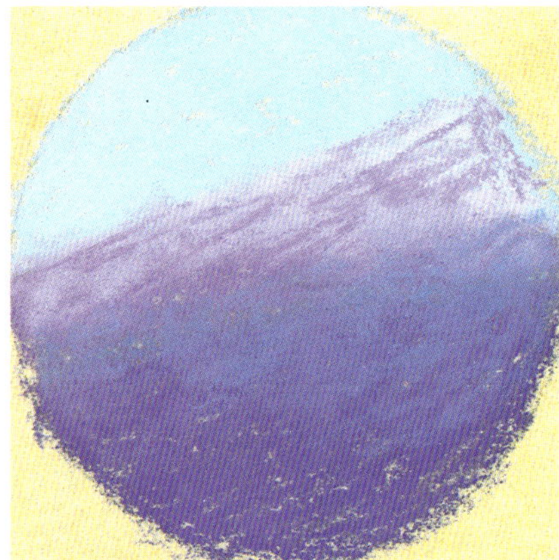

12. Soft edges

13. Exercise 13 shows a diagonal "scribble" stroke that can be made with either pastels or pastel pencils to represent grasses. Hold your pencil farther away from the point than you usually do for free and expressive movement.

14. Exercise 14 demonstrates two different approaches to putting objects or natural component shapes into your landscape. To make a shape, you can draw it and fill it in. This is a method that starts first with a line. See the circles on the left, below.

Approaching the same circular shape from the opposite direction (right to left on the example below) would begin with an approximation of the shape itself (far right). The shape becomes refined and ad-justed by the colors that eventually surround it and push into it. This approach is helpful for putting foliage groups into trees.

The stroking exercises described above will give you a jump start at getting your pastels to do what you want to happen. What you gain from putting in some quality time that combines motor activity with intense focus of attention is yours always, to use and to build upon. And it is best to spend this time early on. In that way, when you are working on a painting out in the field, you can work spontaneously and with feeling. Otherwise, the struggle with basic techniques will, no doubt, inhibit your creativity, and it may understandably affect the quality of your work.

And finally, remember that observation is a large part of an artist's life. Even when you are not painting, you are still an artist. Observation does not stop. It continues, and with awareness, it quickly expands. Sometimes paintings will result, and at other times they will not. However, the mind stores the information that you can focus on, making it retrievable when it is needed. Make use of your heightened observation (1) before you paint to find your composition, (2) throughout your painting process as you make the comparisons between your subject and your work, and (3) finally, after you paint for critical evaluation.

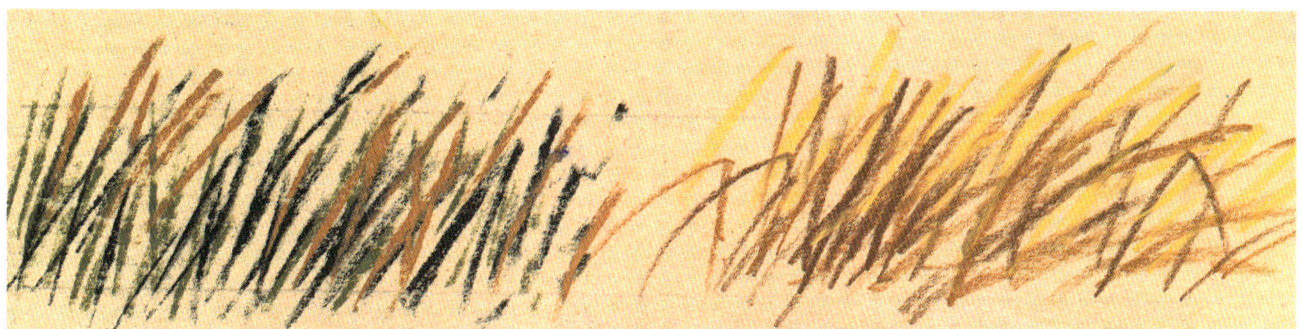

13. Scribble stroke

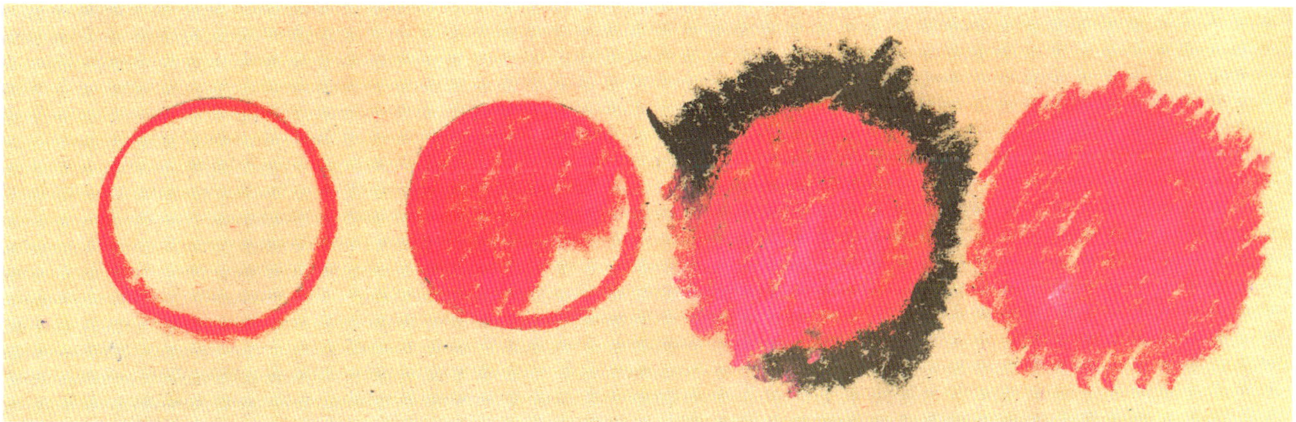

14. Two approaches to shape

Line to shape ⟶ ⟵ Approximation to shape

PAINTING SIMPLE SHAPES IN PASTEL

Small-scale exercises are excellent for learning about form, light, strokes, backgrounds and making adjustments throughout your painting process.

Beginning with a few simple shapes and using a single stick of color, you can build confidence as well as familiarity with your pastels as you gradually change flat color shapes into modeled ones. Notice where the light on the objects comes from and how it affects the color of the objects. Light also throws part of the objects into shadow and, under light, the objects themselves cast shadows. Next, adding even a minimal background gives the objects a setting. Then, final all-over adjustments, including highlights and a few details, bring your subject to life. Remember: Keep it very simple at first.

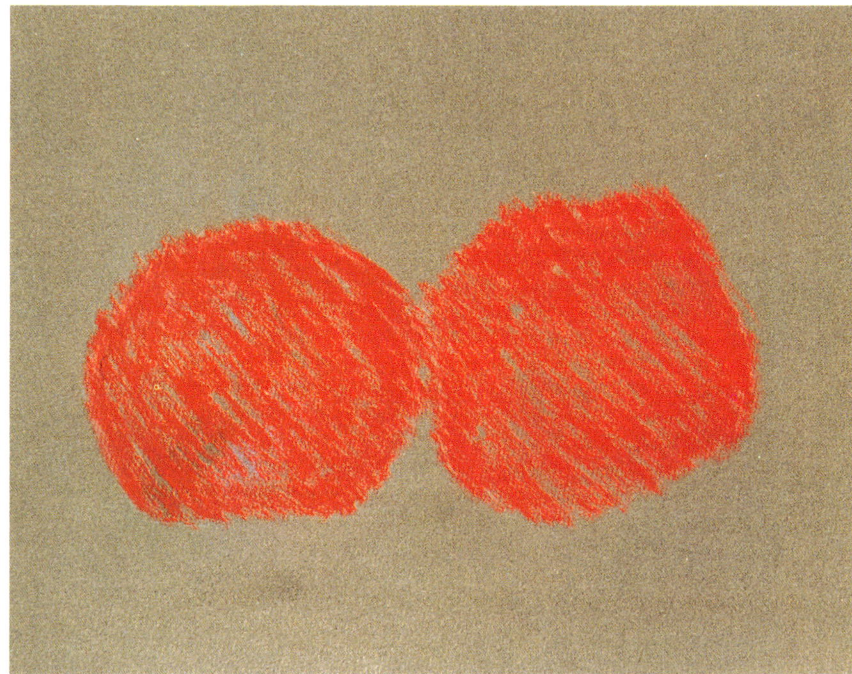

Step 1 Sketch the Shapes
Here, on a 7" × 9" piece of charcoal-colored La Carte surface, I sketch in the approximate shapes of two pomegranates using the tip of a medium red, soft pastel in diagonal strokes.

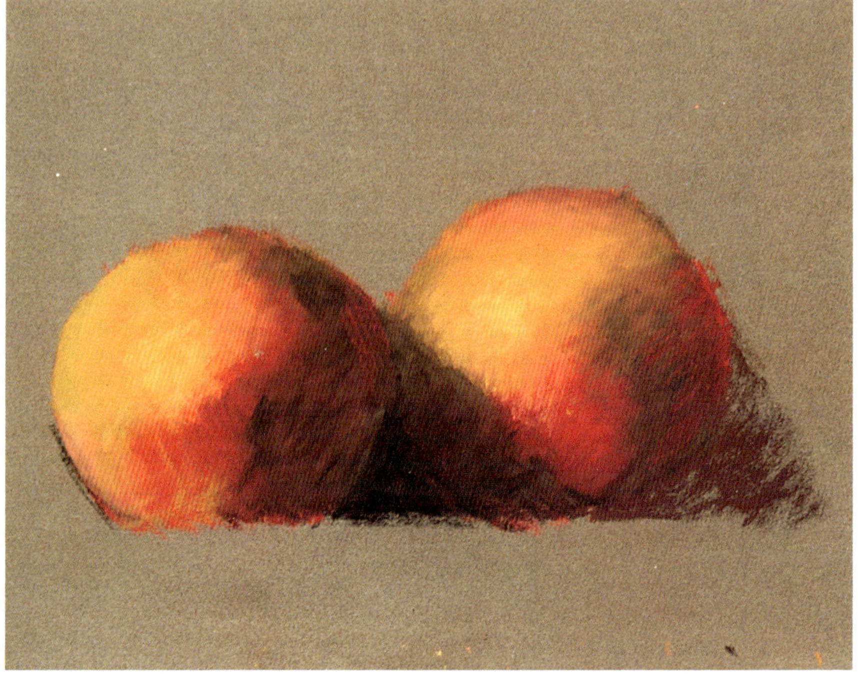

Step 2 Add Light and Shadow
Now I literally put some light on the subject to achieve form. The source of light is from the upper left, so I make that part of each pomegranate appear lighter with a color change to yellow and ochre, which I apply with a crosshatch stroke on top of the red. I pull each color into the color next to it so that the color transitions blend gradually. The lower right of each pomegranate, which gets less light, is made darker with lower value, dark red-brown. At this point, I stroke in the cast shadows as well.

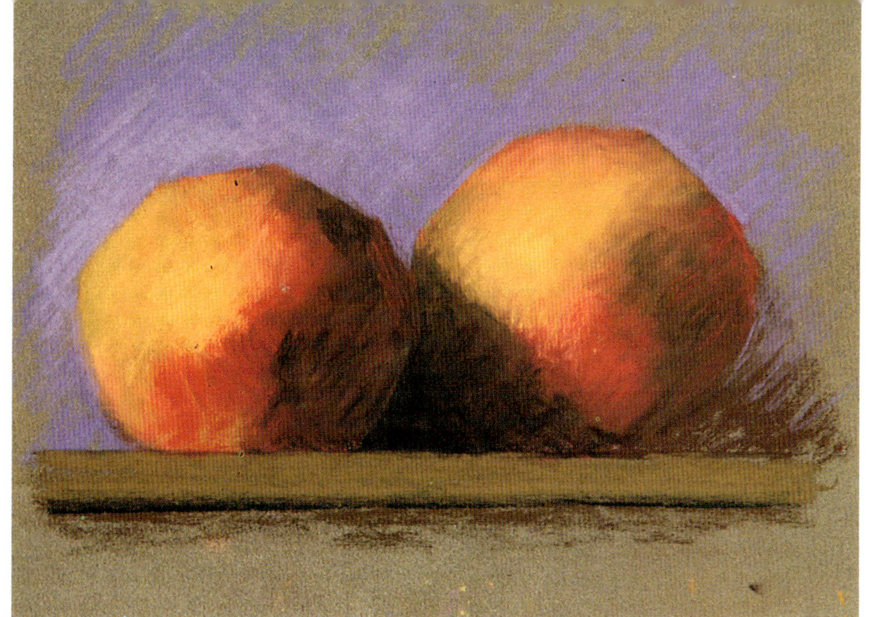

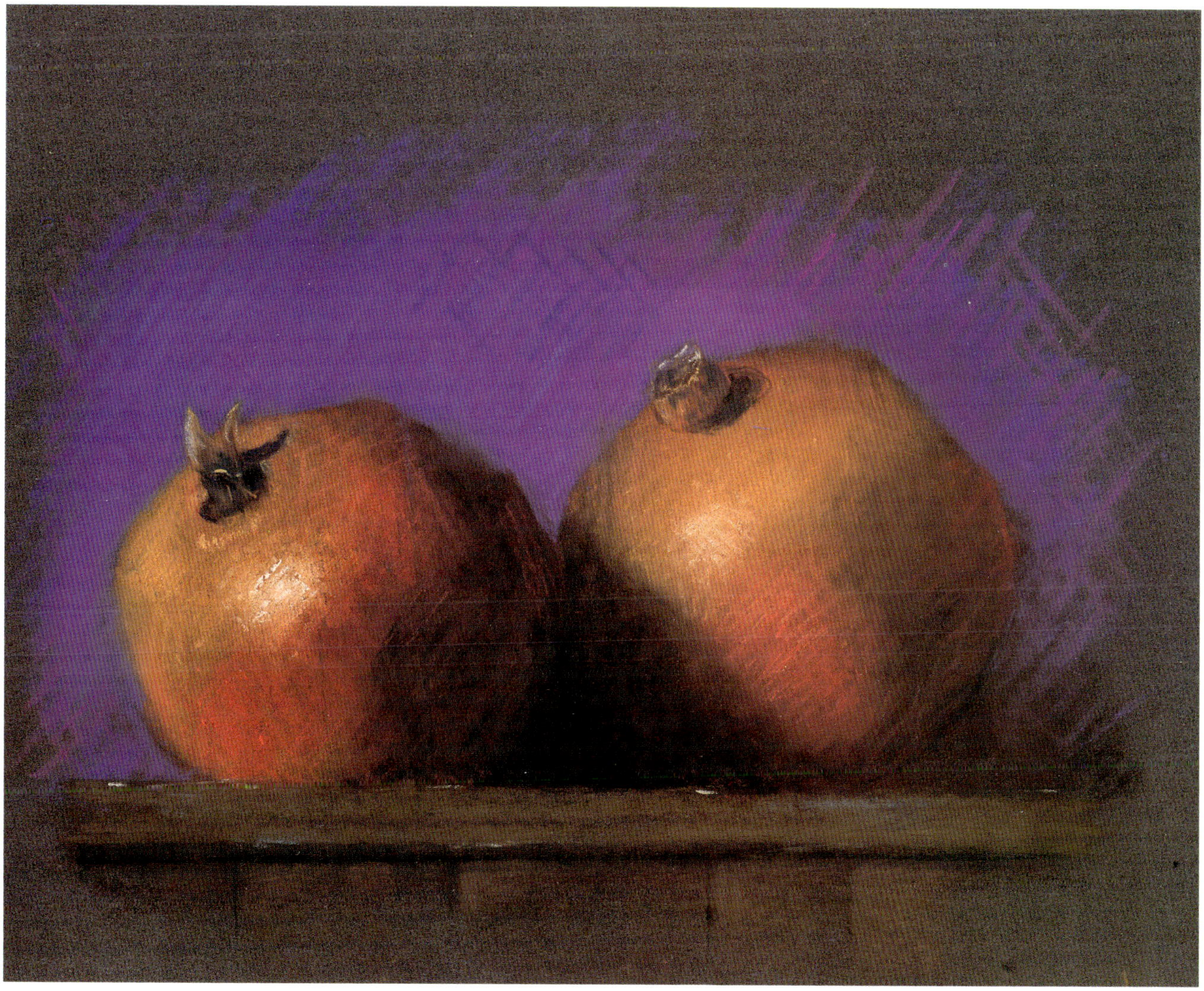

Step 4 Make Final Adjustments
Finally, after a short break, take a fresh look at your work to find where adjustments are needed. In this case, I heightened the lighted area of each pomegranate with a lighter (higher value) yellow. I freshened up dull areas with crosshatching. Details at the top of each fruit are drawn in using pastel pencils, and I warmed up the background by crosshatching some red-violet over the blue-purples.

PAIR OF POMEGRANATES
Pastel on La Carte
7" × 9½"

NOTES TO THE ADVANCED PASTELIST

When I paint a scene for the first time, the painting is often quite literal. I use what skills I have to interpret what I see the best I can. As I explore the same place through additional paintings, I am released from the literal interpretation, and my work becomes more expressive through variety in composition, light and color. I feel liberated in the sense that I then enjoy experimenting with different times of the day, different seasons and even different weather conditions.

The direction of our painting, as we examine the same place at different times, will grow more inward. When we know the landscape intimately, our mind crosses over and beyond *what is* and becomes free to explore adventuresome color, fluid movement or expressive pastel application.

As in the little scene above, which captivated me with its simplicity as I drove home from taking my son to his first term at college, I often feel a need to paint a scene more than once, or even many times. It is as though I am coaxing nature's secrets to unfold. The resulting circular effect is that my own awareness expands. This is simply a matter of intensifying my focus to a point where I see not only seasonal but monthly changes, then weekly, and even daily ones. The revealing and unraveling of nature's tiny intimacies is extremely up-

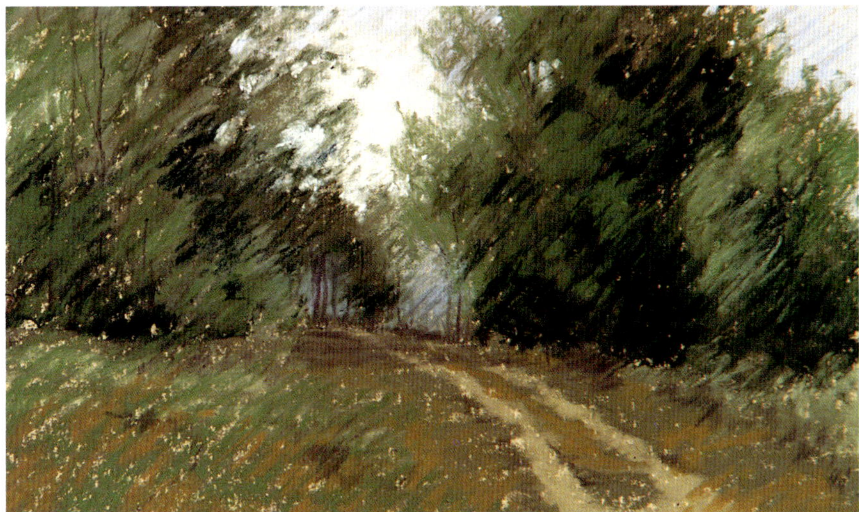

This pastel interpretation was done at the scene the first time I saw it. I had not been looking for subject matter at the time, so I used the materials I had handy to simply get the information down. On a piece of sanded paper, I recorded the view using soft pastels in loose, open strokes, being faithful to the greens that were there. I was mainly interested in the subtle value relationships.

PATHWAY, MAINE
Pastel on sanded board
6½" × 10"

lifting, and I regard it as a solemn gift. The ideas that occur at this level of attention and awareness are deep and fundamental, and many times, abstract. Pursued, they have the potential to influence our work and our lives.

At the beginning of each following college year, I would look for this same little scene. The simple beauty remained over the years, always calling to be painted. Although weather and time of day were different each year, I began to feel a sense of comfortable familiarity and a growing maturity of vision.

When painting the landscape that you know well, visualize the scene according to your accumulated experiences in that place; determine a mood along with the

colors you will use to achieve it; and then throw the gauntlet of challenge at your own feet. In so doing, you unlock the gate to adventure. This is where you draw on memory and emotion as well as a sturdy file of information lovingly collected. This is where you push the edge of what you know toward what you hope yet to achieve. It takes courage, but it is always an exciting adventure.

I think that the most masterful paintings are able to convey to the viewer the same spiritual feeling about a subject that was experienced by the artist. Monet's haystacks and his cathedral paintings are examples that come to mind, as well as the sunflowers loved so well by van Gogh.

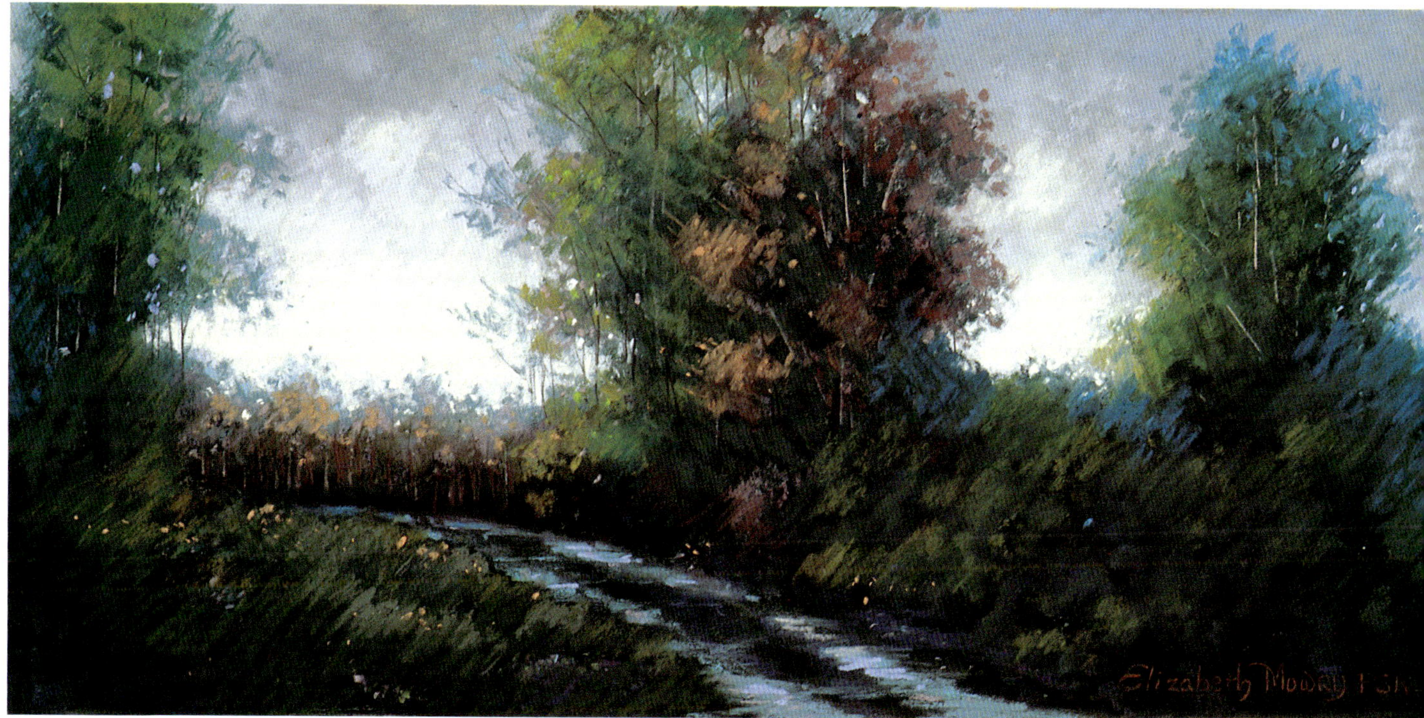

This second interpretation opens up the view more on the right, uncentering the pathway. I was already familiar with the forms so I felt more receptive to the light in the sky after a shower. Freed from the literal, I pushed the foliage colors by introducing soft blues and reds. The use of loose strokes with the soft pastels blends the colors and adds interest to the painting without disrupting the harmony.

LANDSCAPE LIGHT
Pastel on sanded board
9″ × 18″
Private collection

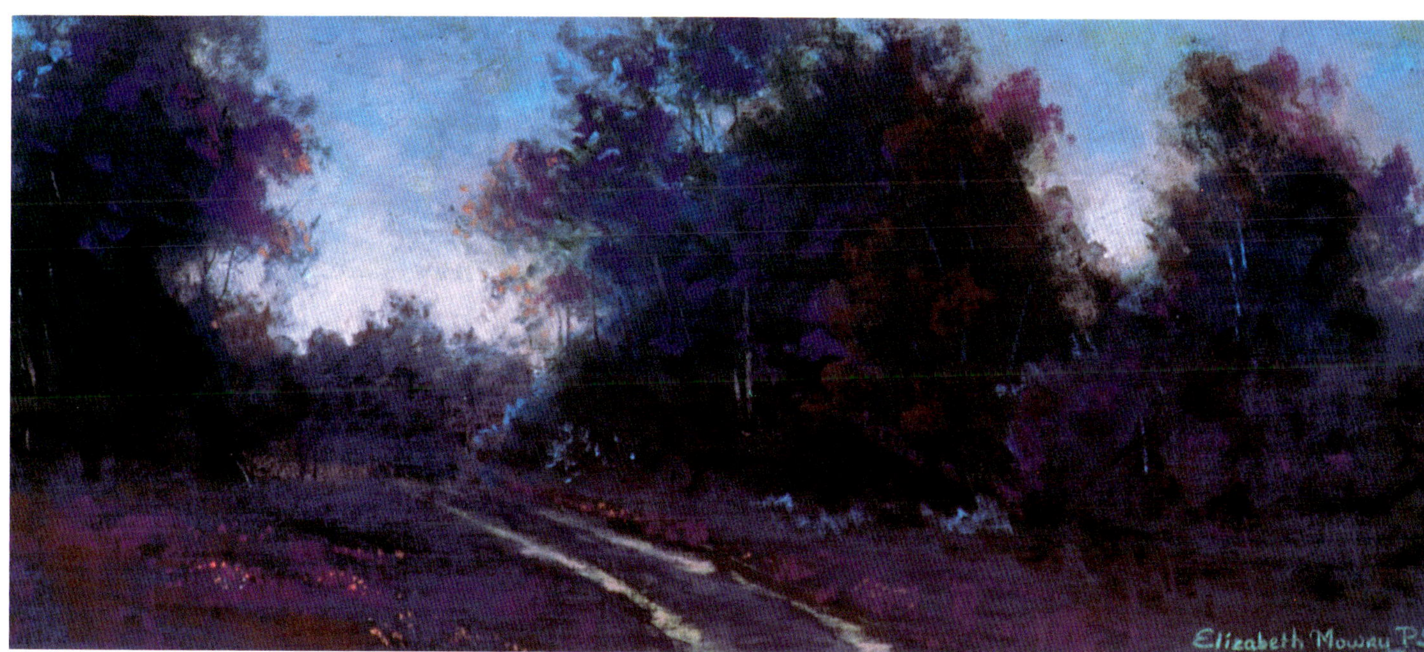

In this third interpretation, I was completely free of the reality of the scene. It was time to joyously play with the simplicity of light and dark space, choosing colors with utter disregard for the literal. I used purples for distance, and low-value reds, greens and purples for the shapes against the pink-and-gray of the sky. The stroke, using all soft pastels, is predominately diagonal except at the foliage edges and the path.

END OF DAY, MAINE
Pastel on sanded board
9″ × 18″
Private collection

ABOUT MATERIALS

Substantial differences among the various brands of pastels and pastel surfaces require some thoughtful experimentation before making a serious investment in your pastel supplies. Instructors who advise students to try a varied sampling are not evading questions. This is truly the only way that you can find what you like to work with and on best. What works adequately for some artists may fall short of being the very best for you. Style of painting, subject matter and your personal vision of the desired result in your work may influence your preferences in materials. Even individual temperament, which can affect the quality and pressure of stroke, may be a consideration. By trying a variety of pastel materials, you will avoid locking yourself into a commitment to tools that are less than optimal for you.

The ever-growing list of new materials available to the pastel artist today makes any attempt at a comprehensive evaluation virtually impossible, even in books devoted to the subject. So keep in mind that what follows is only an overview of materials I use or am in the process of trying.

SOFT PASTELS

My hodgepodge assortment of soft pastels, acquired over the years, now consists mainly of Sennelier and Rowney, but I continue to purchase and use individual Rembrandt pastels as well as those made by Grumbacher. Once a year, while I am in New York City, I stop at New York Central Art Supply and treat myself to a few handmade dark greens and purples and blues by Townsend. For use in my studio, I have a large set of soft pastels and several smaller sets. I prefer to replace and add to my supply by purchasing single sticks of color. (I have tried a popular brand of even softer pastels, but their butter-like consistency did not work well for me.)

It is important to have a comprehensive selection of pastels. Some instructors even insist on a minimum number; the reason for this is to reduce the frustration that occurs when students do not have the adequate range of pastels necessary to take advantage of the instruction being given.

Once you find some brands of pastels that you like to use, save up for one of the larger sets and, after that, buy single sticks of color. You will find that muted colors are more suited to landscape than the bright colors needed for still life. Frequently purchasing beginner's sets may add to your total number of sticks, but this plan gives you too many duplications of colors deemed basic by manufacturers.

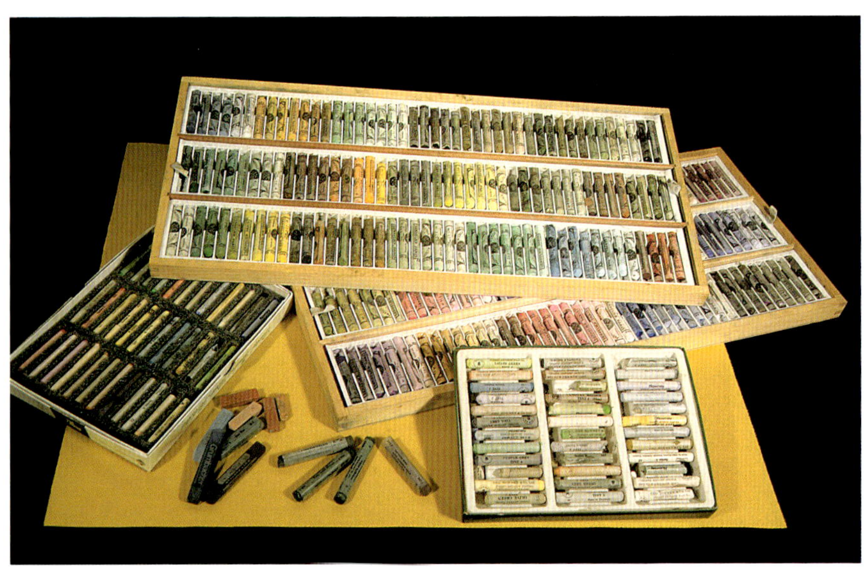

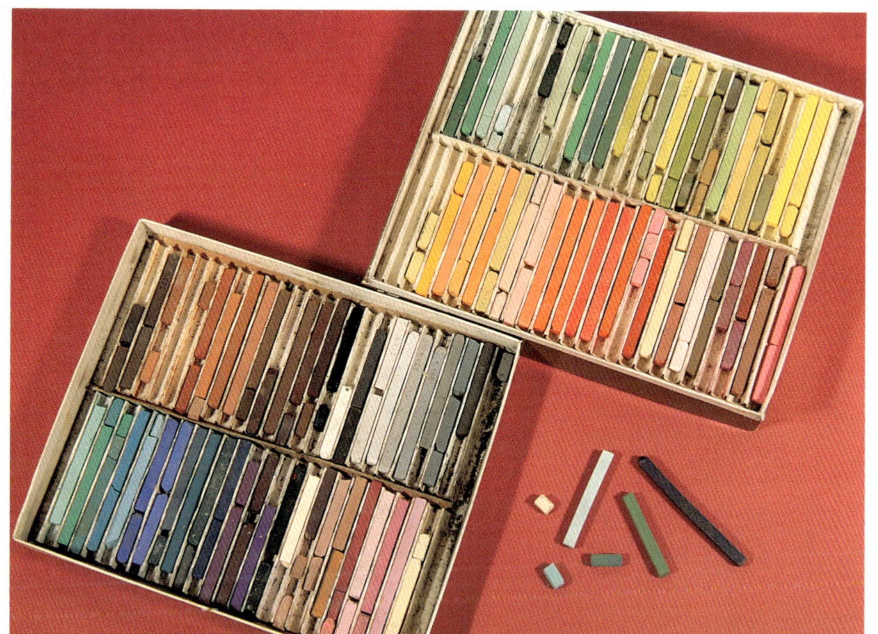

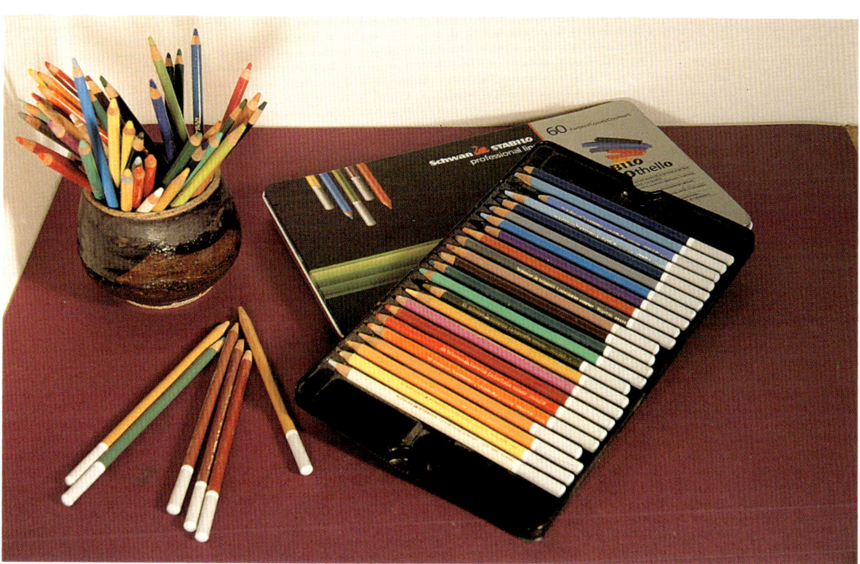

How many cadmium orange mediums do you need? What you want to begin to accumulate after a large, basic set are more unusual colors.

HARD PASTELS

The hard pastels I use are the popular Nupastel. I find that working with the edges of short, broken pieces of these harder pastels gives me the crisp stroke definition that I frequently use in my work. The edges of Nupastels can be freshened on a sanding block.

PASTEL PENCILS

Carb-Othello pastel pencils by Stabilo are my choice in pencils. They fit into a standard sharpener, being the same diameter as a regular pencil and feel comfortable in my hand in the many positions in which I use them. To sharpen pastel pencils, I use an electric sharpener in my studio, and a tiny twist sharpener outdoors. (Clinique's eyeliner pencil sharpeners do not break the pastel inside the pencils, and I am sure there must be others.)

PAPERS AND SURFACES

Sanded pastel paper has an abrasive surface, sometimes referred to as grit, or *tooth*. When pastels are stroked across this granular surface, the color becomes embedded in the tooth of the sanded paper. Made by Ersta Starcke and imported from Germany, this buff-colored, sanded paper was the surface recommended to me when I first began to use pastels, and for a long time, I used it exclusively. It comes in fine and extra-fine grit, in 22″ × 28″ sheets. I prefer the fine grit. This paper is also available in rolls for large work, but without drymounting, the pieces cut from the rolls tend to curl. Unless you need the larger size, the sheets are more convenient. Although it is not acid free, this paper is nevertheless very popular with pastelists.

Water tends to damage the grit of the paper, but from Albert Han-dell I learned to darken or tone the lightness of the buff-colored sanded paper by brushing diluted, turpentine-based wood stain (the undisturbed thin liquid at the top of the can) over the surface and allowing it to dry thoroughly. This keeps the small depressions that make up the tooth of the sanded paper open so that subsequent layers of pastel will adhere. *Summer Lilies* (opposite) is an example of work done on a background that was completely toned.

Partially toned surfaces can be prepared in the same manner. You will then stain only the areas where you know you will want dark values in your painting. A value sketch will tell you where those areas are. Dark walnut or Jacobean diluted stain by Minwax gives rich, dark tones, whereas American Cherry produces a warmer tone. *Winterset Raspberries* (opposite) is an example of work on a partially toned surface.

Another approach to obtaining large areas of low value on a light surface such as the sanded paper is to do underpainting. Here, you apply color to your surface with hard pastels that will not clog the tooth of the paper, and brush the pastel into the surface using a poly-foam brush that has been dipped into Turpenoid. The polyfoam brush does not leave lint or brush hairs on your surface, and gives an even distribution of color. Allow the surface to dry thoroughly. *Iris and Daisies* (opposite) demonstrates this procedure.

All pastel papers have a grainy or abrasive texture that provides adhesion for dry pigment, though sometimes this can barely be felt by passing one's hand over the surface. Since there is no liquid to help penetrate the color into the paper

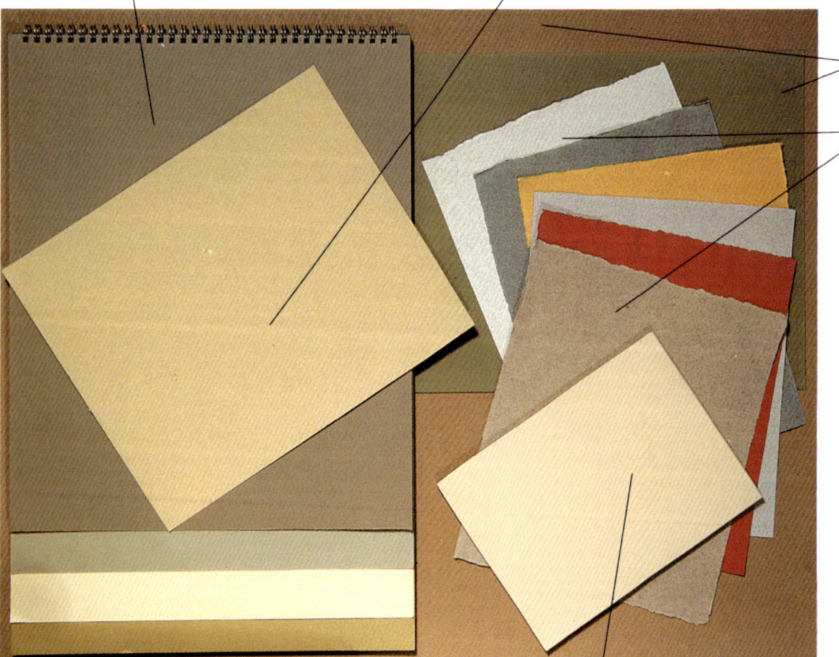

Daler Ingres pastel papers

Ersta Starcke sanded paper

Sennelier La Carte Pastel

Larroque Bergerac Pastel

Windberg pastel panel

Pictured here are the pastel surfaces that I use. Because I am satisfied with the quality of these surfaces, I don't hesitate to recommend that you try some of them.

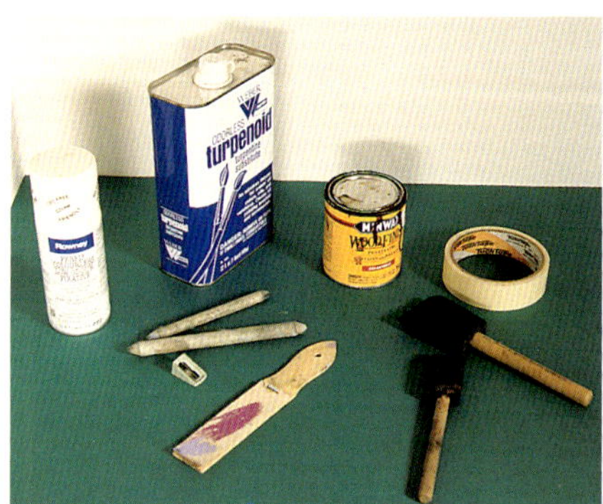

Some useful supplies include stain, polyfoam brushes, tortillions, Turpenoid (an odorless turpentine substitute), sharpener, masking tape, sanding block and fixative.

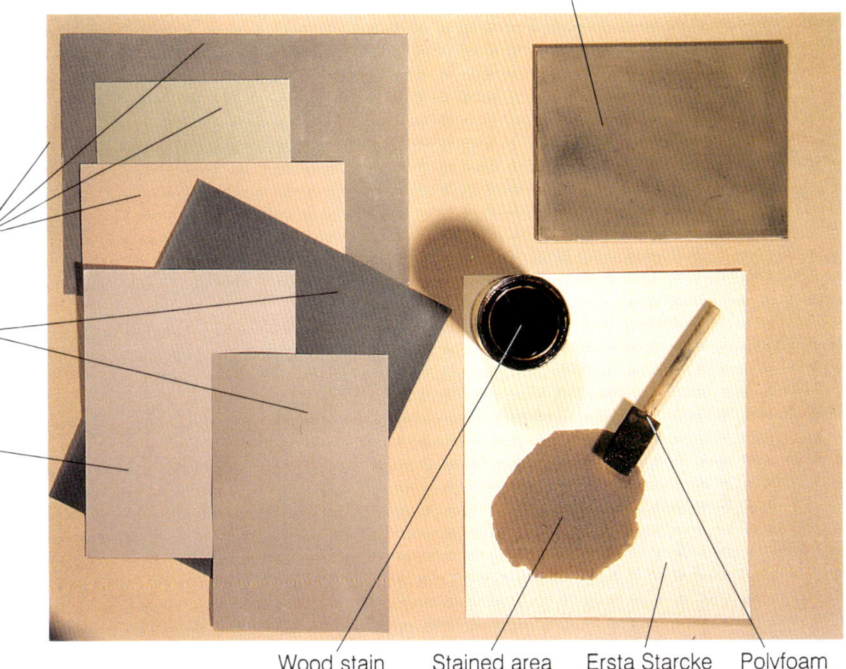

Here is a comparison of medium/dark value surfaces and stained light surfaces. Pictured on the left are some unaltered surfaces of medium to dark value. On the right, I have stained areas of two different light-colored surfaces.

La Carte Pastel in earth, charcoal, green and Van Dyke brown

Sandpaper and sanded cloth (from the hardware store)

Daler Ingres Pastel paper

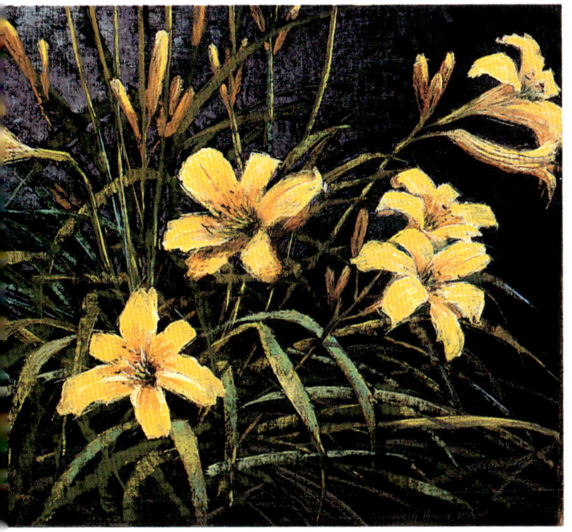

SUMMER LILIES
Pastel on toned
sanded paper
18″ × 21″

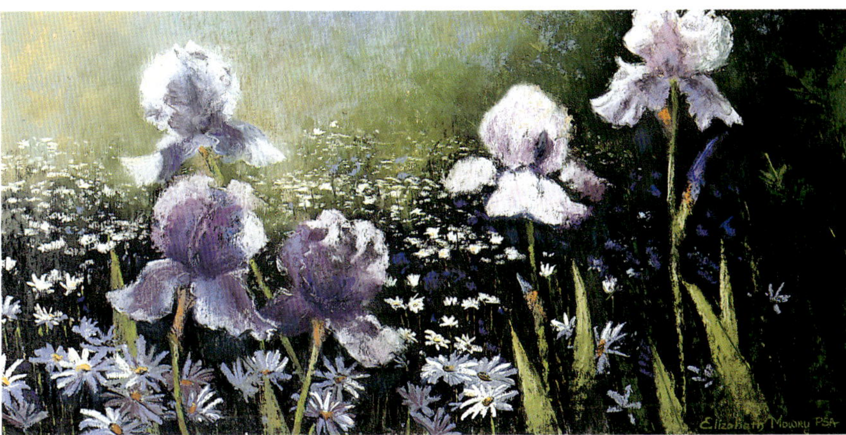

IRIS AND DAISIES
Pastel on underpainted sanded board
11″ × 21″

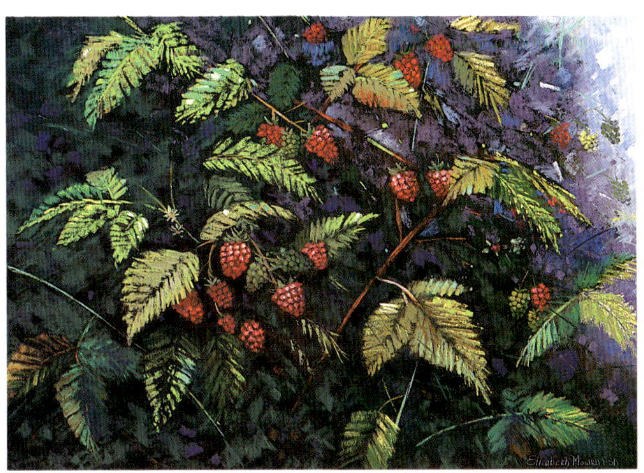

WINTERSET RASPBERRIES
Pastel on partially toned sanded paper
14″ × 19″
Collection of Dr. C.R. Webb, Jr., and
Andrée Webb

as in watercolor, the granular texture is essential to a pastel surface. Smooth surfaces cannot hold much dry pigment; therefore, the pastel artist looks for a surface with a grit or tooth that suits his own style of work, much the way a watercolor artist selects paper from many brands and types to suit his watercolor style.

For sketching and drawing with pastels, I found the Daler Ingres pastel paper to be a superior surface for pastel. It has excellent holding quality. Made by Daler-Rowney, the spiral pads have eight subtle colors of paper, all beautiful. *Edge of the Stream* (top right) is a painting done on this paper.

For a free, loose application of pastel with a soft-edged look, the handmade papers by Sennelier called Larroque Bergerac are exciting to work on. These papers are available in colors designed to complement pastels. See *Springtime Layers* (right).

When you are painting with pastels, and layering as well as backgrounds must be considered, La Carte Pastel by Sennelier may be a surface you will enjoy using. This is a pH neutral board with a slightly abrasive, uniform tooth for dry media only. It is available in 19½″ × 25½″ sheets in fourteen colors. This surface is well received

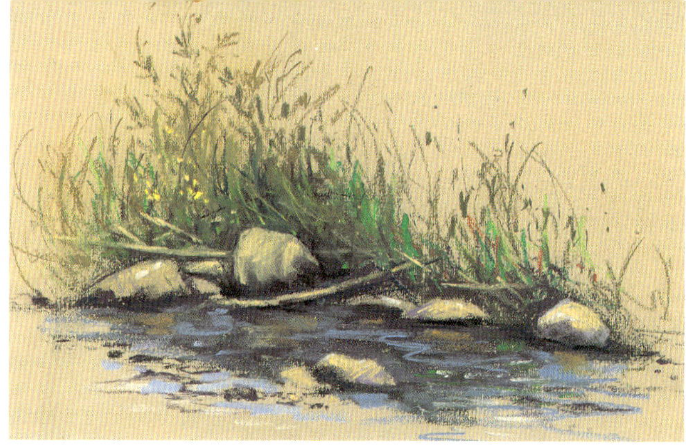

EDGE OF THE STREAM
Pastel on Daler Ingres paper
9″ × 12″

SPRINGTIME LAYERS
Pastel on Larroque Bergerac paper
7″ × 12″

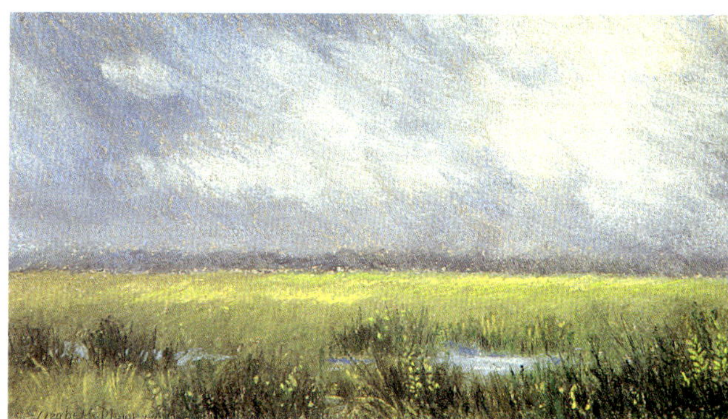

GOLDEN HILL
Pastel on Sennelier La Carte
5½″ × 9½″

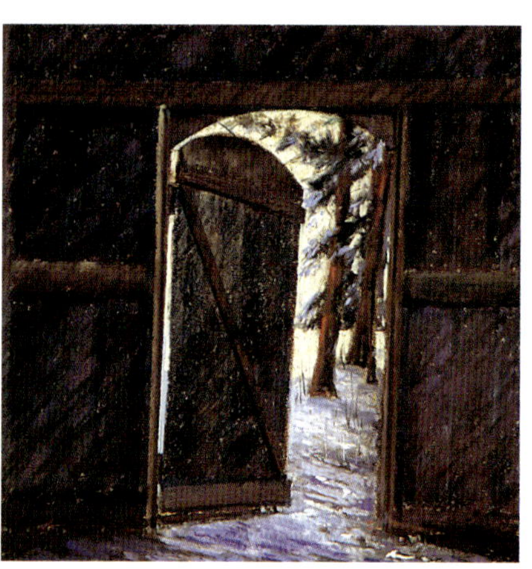

WILDERSTEIN GATE
Pastel on sanded cloth
8″ × 8″
Collection of Raymond and Linda Caddy

MORNING SLOPE
Pastel on Windberg pastel panel
8″ × 16″

by students in my classes. *Golden Hill* (opposite) was done on La Carte Pastel.

Windberg, Inc., supplies a durable pastel panel with a marble dust finish on untempered hardboard. It comes in standard sizes and in several colors, including sand, gray and green. The surface texture holds multiple layers of pastel. *Morning Slope* (opposite) is an example of a painting done on Windberg Pastel Panel.

I have also used several types of abrasive cloth, including one called pastel cloth, which is white and can be purchased in rolls and stretched like canvas, and a dark-toned sanded cloth made by 3M Company, which is frequently stocked in 9″ × 11″ sheets by hardware stores. Both have a cloth rather than a paper backing. *Wilderstein Gate* (opposite) was done on sanded cloth.

FIXATIVE

If your work has a tendency to become muddy because many layers are superimposed, you can apply a light spray of fixative between some layers and then work again when the fixative is dry. A final, or next-to-the-final-layer, spray of fixative is also helpful when paintings will be in transit, or which will remain unframed, and therefore without the protection of glass. Although not an avid fixative user, when one is required, I use the colorless, low-odor Perfix by Rowney.

FRAMING

Having two large collies with bushy tails, and a limited studio space, I find that I tend to frame my work soon after it is completed. Because of this habit, and my almost-always forgotten signature, my accommodating framer has de-

vised a way for me to easily remove and reinsert my work into its frame, by using tab-screws that can be turned, instead of brads.

In this way, my work is protected, yet I still have the opportunity to make adjustments after a period of distancing objectivity. This is such an important part of my work process, and sometimes it takes months before enough detachment from the work enables me to make dispassionate judgments about the final touches.

THE FIELD BOX

Field box is my name for an old berry-picking carrier that my friend Scrappy and I found very useful many years ago when painting outdoors. I have continued to use it simply because I really haven't found any method I like better for getting my supplies to a painting site.

When I set out to paint the landscape, all the supplies I need are in my field box or my day pack. I have moist towelettes, some small, sturdy painting surfaces, a folding seat, insect repellent, sunscreen, a small blanket, sometimes a sweater, and always a lunch. In the field box, I carry all of the pastel supplies I need to do near-finished work outdoors. The legs on the box keep it off the damp ground, and the removable cover protects the pastels in transit and in case of rain. Under the cover, my materials are in usable order so that there is no need to spend a lot of time setting up at the painting site.

The compartments of my field box are filled as follows: (1) the pastels I am using on a current painting; (2) blues and purples; (3) yellows, pinks and oranges; (4) browns, siennas and ochres; (5) greens; (6) neutrals; (7) pastel

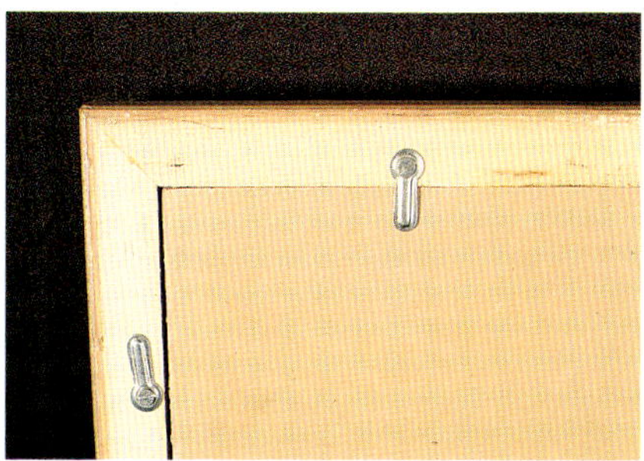

Tab screws can be turned aside for removal of work from its frame.

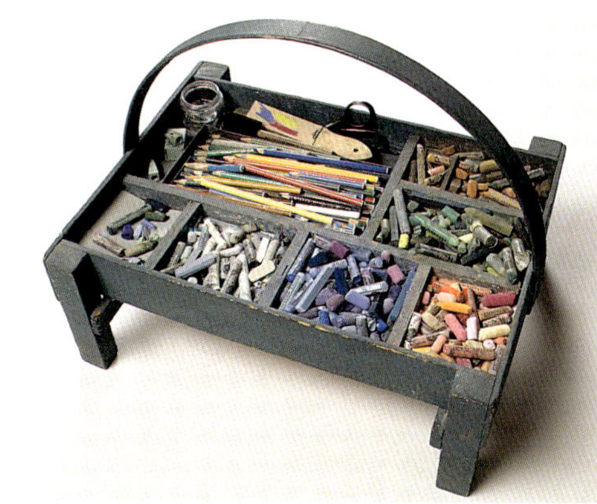

My field box holds all of the pastel supplies I need to do near-finished work on location. Sturdy legs keep it off the ground, and under a removable cover my materials remain in usable order, which eliminates setting up each time I move on to a new location.

pencils, scissors, tape, screwdriver, kneaded eraser, blending tortillions, Turpenoid in a small jar, a polyfoam brush, a sanding block and a small sharpener.

Berry boxes of this type may be difficult to locate now, so I asked a friend to draw up a pattern and construction plan for the box I have. There are many other means of getting supplies to a painting site, and what works for one artist does not necessarily work for another. But if your heart is set on having your own field box, you can make one using the list of materials and instructions provided in the back of this book.

KEEPING A NATURE JOURNAL

Keeping a nature journal can be a satisfying experience for anyone. For an artist whose chosen subject matter is nature's changing landscape, keeping a journal is not only rewarding, it is also an invaluable source of personal discovery.

It does not matter what part of the country, or even what country you live or work in, or how your seasons differ from those elsewhere. What is essential is that you tune in to what is happening where you are, which, in turn, enables you to draw from what you know best.

Each day, I take a break from what I am doing and enjoy a walk nearby, up the roads and paths I know well, or through the woods and fields close to my home. I'm gone only between twenty minutes and an hour, yet I always notice some small change from the day before. When I return to my studio, I usually make a cup of tea and sit down to quietly write as little as a single sentence centered on the next blank page in my journal, and then date the entry.

Once in awhile, I make a sketch of something I've seen or brought back. Sometimes, I will research a flower or a leaf in my guidebooks, but most often I record just one observation. This time has become a poignant ritual in my day. It constitutes "falling in love" with the day before me if I am out in the morning, or bidding farewell to the afternoon if

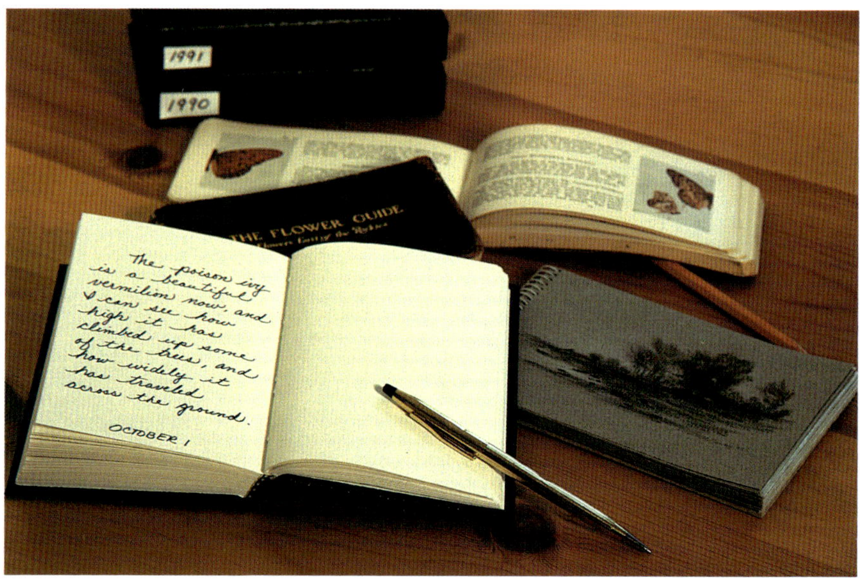

My own journal-keeping has become a daily habit over a period of many years and has evolved from extensive to joyously simple. I like using the common 4″ × 6″ black sketchbooks, which also happen to fit easily into a day pack or a jacket pocket.

I'm out later. At either time, it confirms the joy of learning and embraces what nature has to offer when we take time to see deeply. Some random sample entries look like this:

- *April 9, 1992* — This morning I saw a single yellow violet near the stream now overrunning its banks.
- *June 22, 1992* — The air is fragrant with the heavy scent of the catalpa blossoms, which have begun their summer snowfall in the breeze.
- *September 11, 1992* — For the past several days, the field of loosestrife has been at its peak, and the "purpleness" is breathtaking.

The purple of the loosestrife that took my breath away was transformed into a meadow of

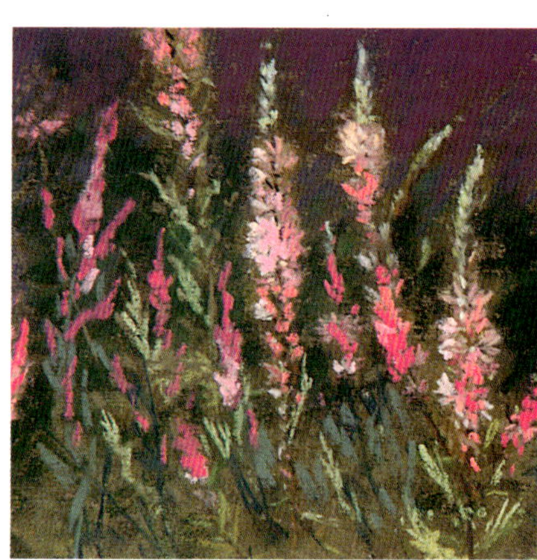

Loosestrife, a tall, common, invasive plant found in marshy areas, is scorned by farmers and sought out by artists for its rich color. As with Alaskan fireweed, it colors entire fields with purple.

goldenrod only weeks later. Did it happen suddenly? No, but then nature doesn't wait for us to notice. It changes such a little bit each day, but with steadfast certainty and the sureness and power of a steamroller. While the loosestrife dulled with the autumn rain and the last of the purple disappeared with the summer butterflies, the goldenrod had heightened inch by inch, forming yellow-green buds, and then the familiar flower heads. The color increased until one day it, too, became overwhelming. The changing is continuous. When we happen to notice it depends upon how closely we pay attention.

SUGGESTIONS FOR KEEPING A FIELD JOURNAL

1. Savor and enjoy this endeavor rather than allow it to become a task.

2. Use a blank book without pre-dated pages. Instead, enter and date each entry as you go along. It is forgivable to skip days at a time. Other discoveries may be longer and require more space.

3. Be specific. (Depending on your experience outdoors, initial entries may be more general.)

4. Focus on different elements each year. This will occur effortlessly because when you recognize something you have seen before, your mind will build upon it. In this way, your knowledge will com-
pound until you feel confident to draw on it.

5. Allow your journal entries to revolve meaningfully around the work you are doing at the time. What we know enters into what we do. So when you paint nature's changes in pastel, you will connect with those who have experienced the same discoveries about nature that you have.

HOW A JOURNAL CAN HELP YOUR PAINTING

1. A journal is personal. By paying attention to nature's changes in *your* location, you can add a personal and knowledgeable element of depth to your work.

2. Keeping a journal enables you to view the seasons as more than four separate, static divisions. When you have finished your journal, you hold a year of minute changes that *you* have noticed, but it adds up to a full year. The concept of the year as a changing, evolving whole becomes significant.

3. You become adept at matching landscape components accurately with each season in your area when you wish to add something that is not at the scene where you are. For instance, if you wanted to paint some wildflowers in a painting of a field, by referring to your journal, you could add a variety that is appropriate for the time of the year and the region you are depicting. Even if you are merely suggesting the flowers in your painting, it is better to suggest some that actually do bloom at that time. Otherwise, the distracting jolt of sensing something not quite as it should be makes it less possible for a knowledgeable viewer to appreciate the work. In a spring scene with blooming apple trees, the dandelion would be a better choice for a foreground flower than autumn's goldenrod.

4. You will begin to see the larger, consistent patterns of each season, as well as more specific variation.

5. A deeper understanding of the progressions of seasonal change could result in more painterly work, because you will not have to rely on being at the scene every minute. You will learn to use the large shapes, make color notes, and then work with confidence in your studio. Once you have the information you need from the scene you are painting, it is often helpful to turn away from it at some point. If the concept of the painting can be improved with changes, you can make them objectively. Leaving the scene before completion of your painting, or just turning toward a different direction, also allows more room for expression of the painter to enter the work; by remaining at the scene for too long, you may succumb to the temptation of filling space with unnecessary detail.

WinterSpringSummerAutumnWinter

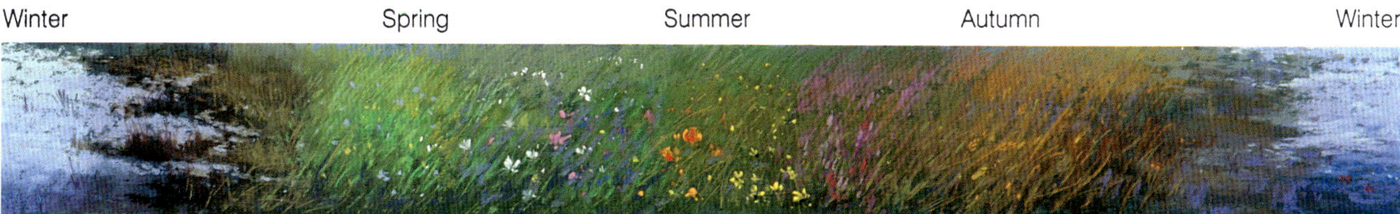

Beginning at the left, this earth study shows changes that occur as the year gradually progresses through the twelve months in my area. Every 2½ inches equal one month, until the yearly cycle completes itself.

THE YEAR
Pastel on sanded board
3½" × 30"

USING THE CAMERA AS A TOOL

Painting at an inspiring location on a beautiful day is what artists dream about, but ideal conditions are not always possible. Instead, rain, chill, wind or distance, among other things, may prevent painting at the scene. Having a file of photographs allows you to compose paintings and to paint regularly.

By its nature, the camera lens is an easy-to-use viewfinder, especially outdoors, because it effectively blocks out everything surrounding the lens opening, and thereby eliminates distraction.

As you evaluate what you see through your camera lens, ask yourself the following questions:

• Am I after the large vista here? Or do I want to zero in on part of the scene?

• Does a horizontal format suit this subject? Would a vertical format be more interesting?

• For this scene, do I prefer a low horizon? How about a very high one?

• Are the negative spaces in the scene pleasing?

These questions require the decisions that strengthen your compositional skills. Then continue:

• Is the main object too central? Or is the view too symmetrical?

• Does my eye follow a strong line in the landscape, such as the slope of a hill, and then go out of the picture? Or does a landscape line go to the corner and become trapped? Being aware of a composition with drawbacks does not prevent you from using the subject, but it helps you to see where changes could improve it.

• And finally, ask yourself, "Does this make sense?"

With your camera, you can purposely put your scene out of focus in order to clearly see the large shape relationships without the distraction of detail.

You will soon find that the qualities that make an excellent nature photograph are not necessarily the same ones that make a good painting. Nature photographers look for detail. Painters should look for contrasts—in value, edges, color and shapes. If your photos lack contrasts, adjust your paintings to strengthen them.

Always avoid using photographs that someone else has taken. They do not represent your experience, so no personal connection exists. When you use photographs *you* have taken as just one source of reference for your paintings, or to jog your memory of a sense of place, you are using your camera as a tool rather than as a crutch.

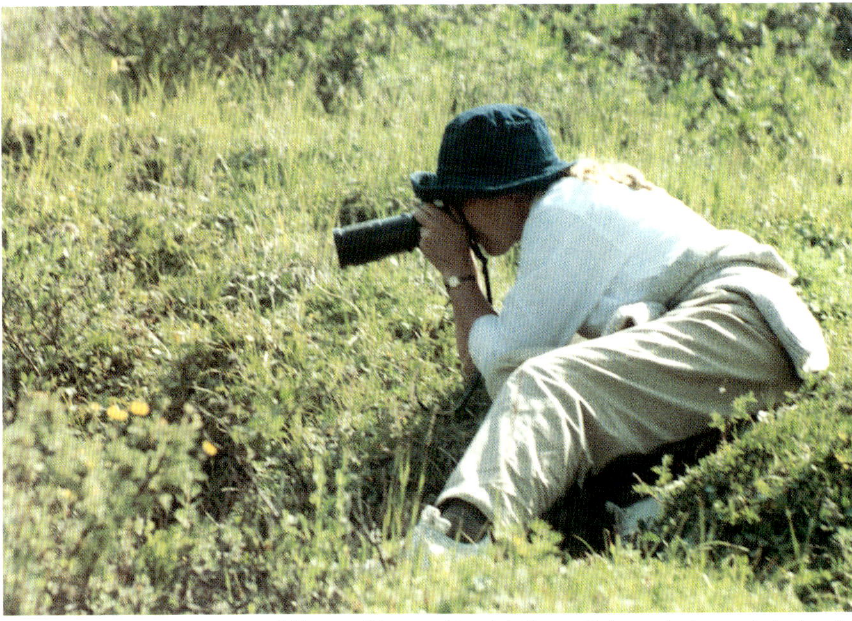

Tracking down an Alaskan wildflower. No need to pick them. Take a photograph instead. (Photo by Richard McDaniel)

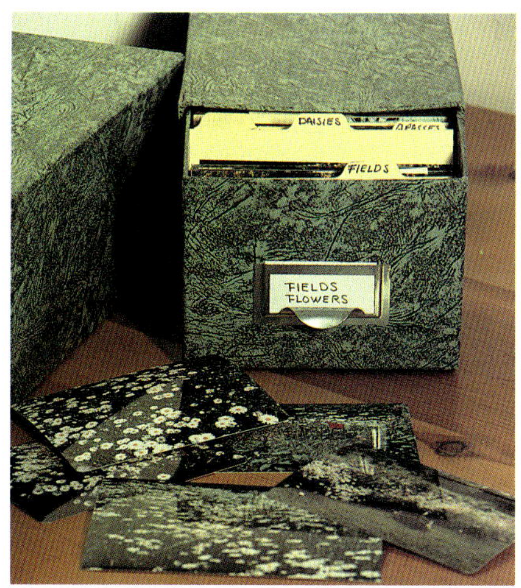

The file boxes for my photographs are divided by subject matter.

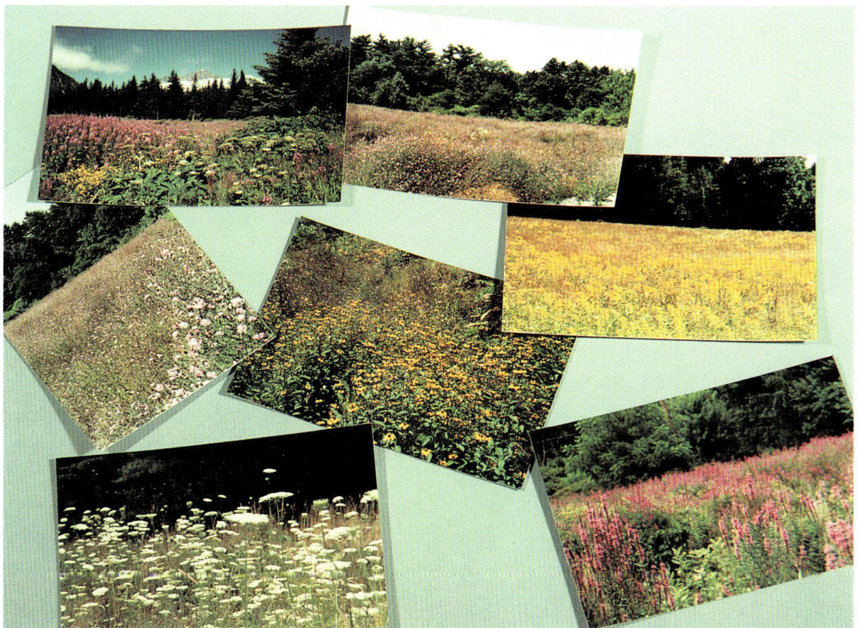

Here are some photographs from my file in the section on Fields, specifically Summer Fields. They include Alaskan fireweed, Queen-Anne's lace, common loosestrife, goldenrod, ironweed and black-eyed Susans. These are useful in reminding me of the intense visual impact of summer wildflowers en masse.

KEEPING A FILE

I use two 5″ × 7″ × 15″ file boxes to store my photographs. They accommodate the usual 3″ × 5″ and 4″ × 6″ sizes easily. I group the photos by subject matter, such as clouds, fences, outbuildings, barns and fields. I date each on the back so I know what time of the year it was taken.

Suppose I wanted to paint a foreground of daisies, and it is wintertime. I look under *Wildflowers*, at a section of photographed daisies. I find one showing distant daisies in a field that illustrates how they group in clumps. Another photograph shows close-up daisies with some in shadow. In still another, it becomes clear what other wildflowers bloom at the same time, so in my painting, if I chose to do so, I could add other flowers as well. I even have a photograph of drooping daisies in the rain. All were collected casually and enjoyably over a period of time, and filed.

Building a file is helpful, but the main purpose is to deliberately zero in on a specific landscape component. My file is a priceless source of information simply because it is of places and subjects that I have personally seen. As I browse through my files, evoking memories of places I've been, that too, influences my work, whether I refer to the photographs or not.

THE COLOR STUDY

aking a color study is a no-nonsense method of quickly getting a lot of valuable information into a small format. I use soft pastels for the broad areas and then finish with pastel pencils. When a color study is not successful, I can brush it out and use the surface again, without having invested a great deal of time. A study is exactly what the word implies: a place for learning through experimentation and risk. Taking the opportunity to do small color studies keeps yourideas separate rather than dissipated, and the larger paintings you do from them maintain a stronger impact.

There are two ways to use a color study, each for an entirely different reason:

1. When your intention is to stick closely to reality as you paint on location, you can make a color study to record the patterns of light and shadow before they change. The study becomes an accurate reference if you must retreat indoors because of time or weather. The color study gives you not only values, but color as well, and quickly.

2. Color studies are also useful when your purpose is to recreate the scene differently, the intent being *not* to paint reality. In this case, you might want to be at the scene for ambience of place, but you may just as well prefer to be in your studio.

For the advanced pastelist, who has been observing nature closely for some time, this second method of using the color study is an exciting way to work.

COLOR STUDIES HELP MAINTAIN FOCUS

Once you abandon the color reality of a scene, then what? There are so many possibilities. You will be faced with the challenge of deciding on one of many interpretations. You can work out individual studies of the same scene before doing a large work having no singular focus. When more than one idea is calling for attention when you begin a pastel, you might be tempted to use part of one idea, part of another, etc. Sometimes when this happens, you discover that you have invested precious time and energy into not only a muddy concept, but a muddy pastel as well.

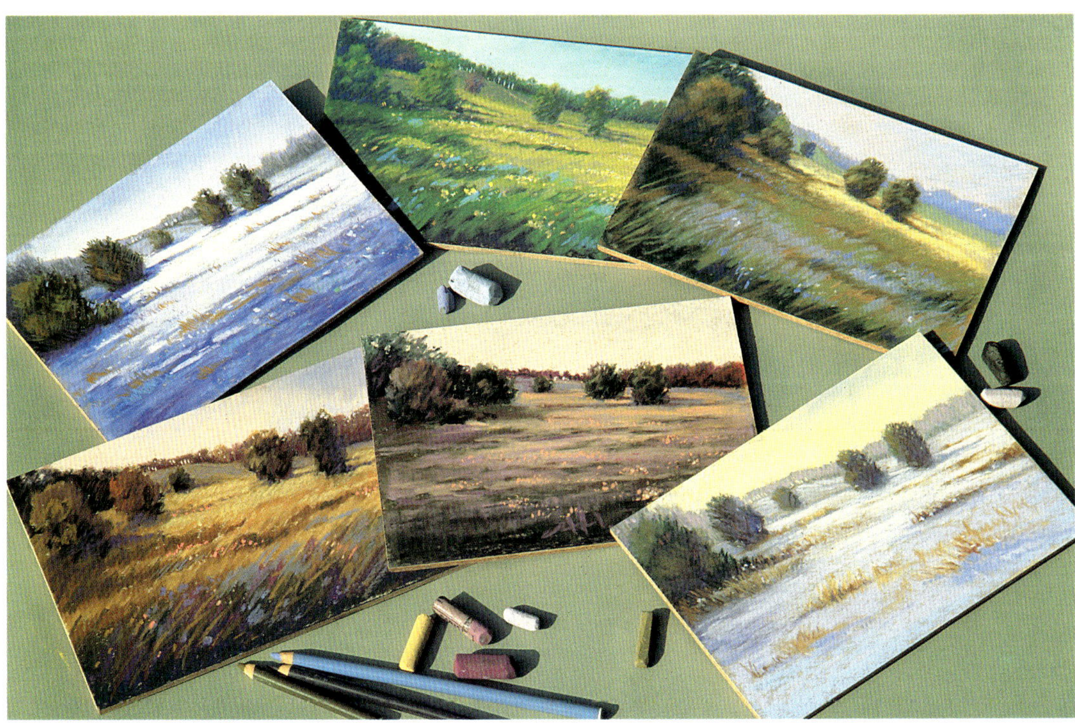

Here are six color studies of a favorite place, each 5″ × 8″, from the same viewpoint. Each one has a distinct seasonal focus and energy.

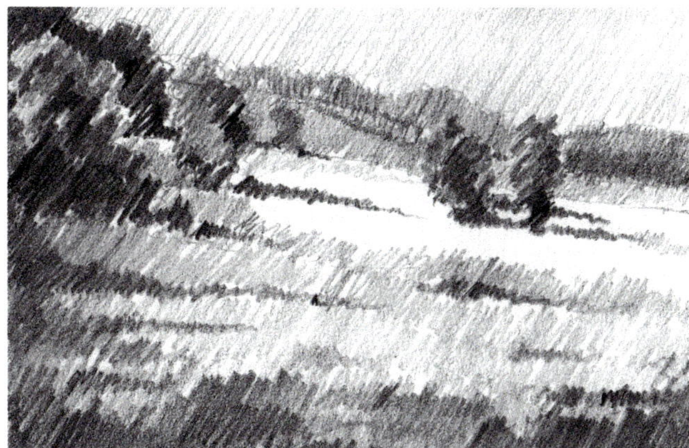

Pencil sketches help us to see values. With correct values, any color palette is possible.

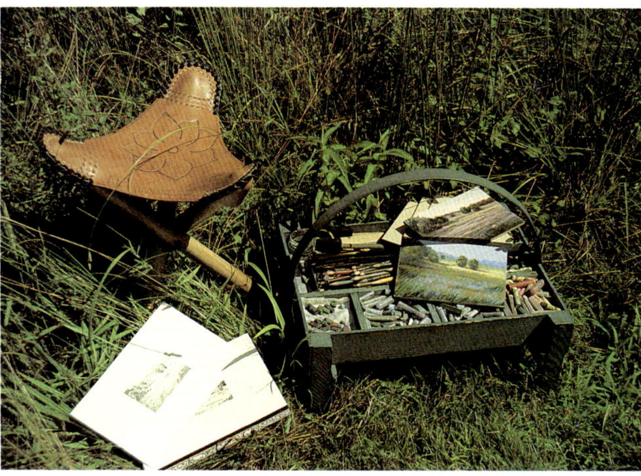

LIMITING THE SCOPE
Small value sketches and two small color studies help me to focus on the part of the scene that interests me most at the time. Focus is extremely important in all outdoor work.

I find that my work is more powerful if I pursue a single line of clarity and strength. Small color studies make it easier to decide which I wish to elaborate on in a more ambitious painting. Setting up several possibilities side by side can make visual sorting out direct and objective. In this way, I can keep my full-scale paintings clean and fresh, which, in my view, is a very desirable attribute of pastel.

An additional bonus to making color studies is that you have miniature reminders of the special places you have painted and loved long after your paintings are owned by someone else. And, based on your studies, possibilities remain endless for future explorations of seasonal color.

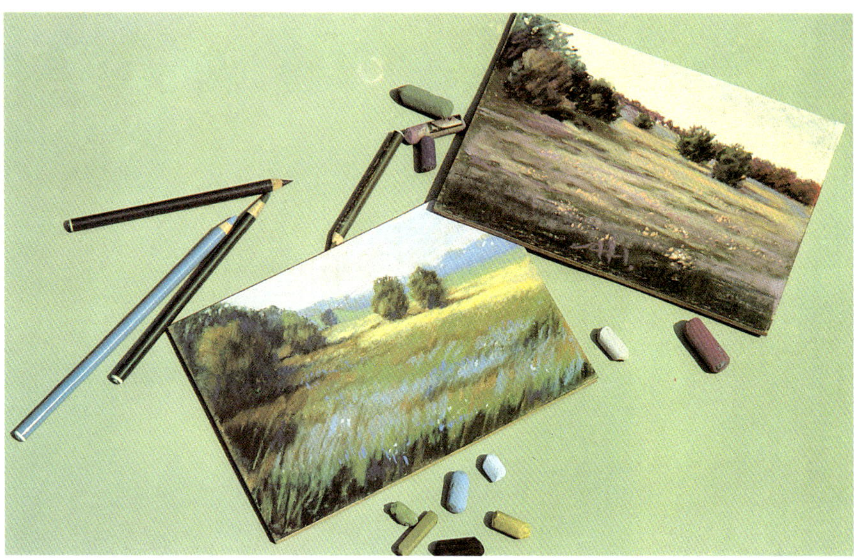

SETTING THE MOOD
Back in my studio, but still under the spell of this beautiful place, I review the two spontaneous color studies. Working out color on a small scale helps keep my pastels "clean." Once I decided to use the study on the left for a larger painting, my mind was free to let the mood of the other one go, knowing that having the study, I could use it at some other time (which I did). Again, my focus was directed.

SURFACES FOR SMALL COLOR STUDIES

Many of the new sanded panels can be cut to size, but when I want to work on sanded paper for my studies, I first have a sheet dry-mounted onto plywood with a meltable plastic barrier called Fusion 400 between the paper and the board. Then I have this surface cut into shapes and sizes that I like to use, such as 5″ × 5″, 5″ × 8″ and 5″ × 9″.

You could also use a photo mounting spray to mount a sheet of sanded paper to 100 percent museum rag board. Roll it flat with a rolling pin or squeegee, and then cut to the sizes you wish to use.

I take several formats in my day pack each time I go out to paint. Having a sturdy surface to work on makes it possible to travel without a cumbersome drawing board. In case of rain, a piece of tracing paper between two painted boards that are face-to-face and held firmly together with a rubber band works just fine.

PAINTING FROM A COLOR STUDY FOR UNIFIED COLOR

This field is on the property of one of the famous estates that line the Hudson River, namely, the Vanderbilt Estate. Although open to the public, the acreage is so vast that solitude is seldom infringed upon.

I know this place well. In all seasons, I have hiked up the far hill, through wild strawberry, summer nettle, slippery mud and snow. By painting from my color study, away from the detail of reality, I can use the form and the light of nature, and then add a sense of personal mood and color in my interpretation.

When you find a place that you love, go back often and paint it again at another time. Painting the same place in different seasons, or under different weather condi-

tions, or even at another time in your life, can be not at all constraining, but the most rewarding experience you could ever have.

Because the undulating contours of the meadow in this scene would have been lost in overhead light, I chose morning to go out to do the sketches and studies. As the sun rose to the left, the shadows of the surrounding landscape gave shape and compositional strength to the simplicity of the field. The interplay of cool shadows and warm dried grasses set up a rhythmic horizontal movement across the subject that took on additional momentum as it moved from the middle of the field into the foreground.

Preparatory steps for paintings vary according to the subject and

the intent. In this painting, color decisions for the large areas were already worked out in the study. I spent the time I needed to establish the subtle color relationships in the background because these set the tone, and I related all strokes, color and value to that small area. This is one way to achieve a harmonious effect in a painting. I saved the detail for last and found that I needed very little. The blue and purples that were chicory and ironweed to me could be lupine or clover to someone in Maine or Alaska or Texas. Working from color studies takes you away from specifics. The point is that in some paintings where the landscape is of a nonspecific nature, suggestion is more powerful than detail.

Color studies of The Meadow *in all four seasons.*

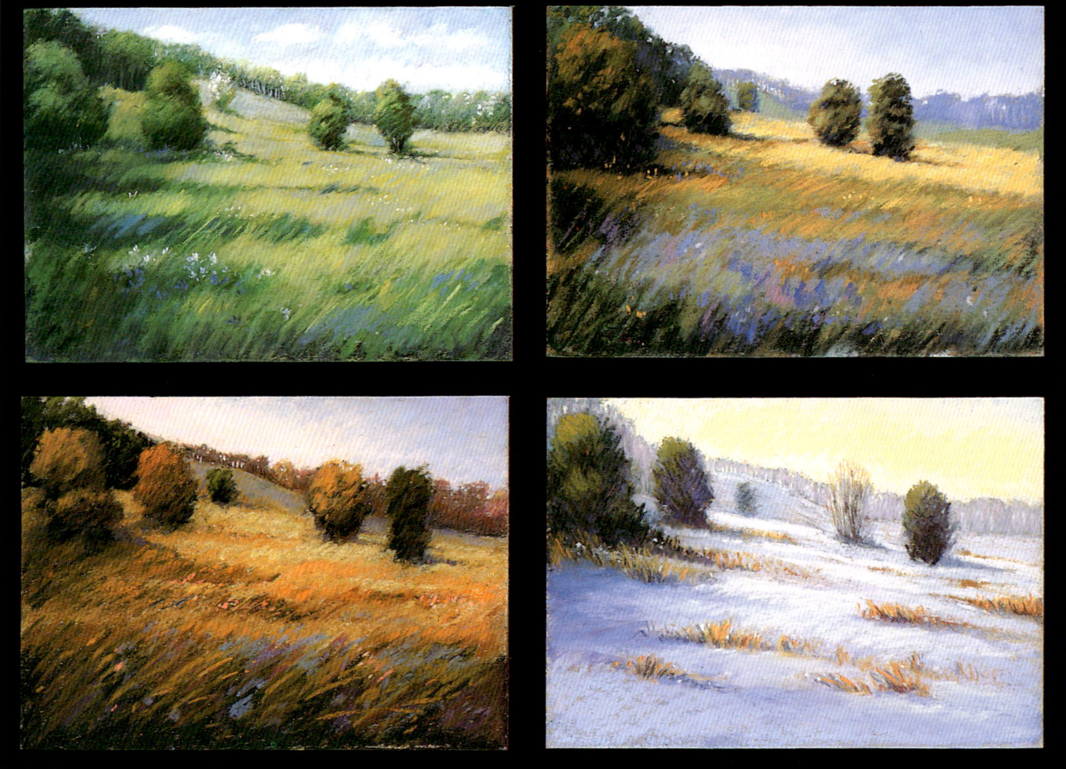

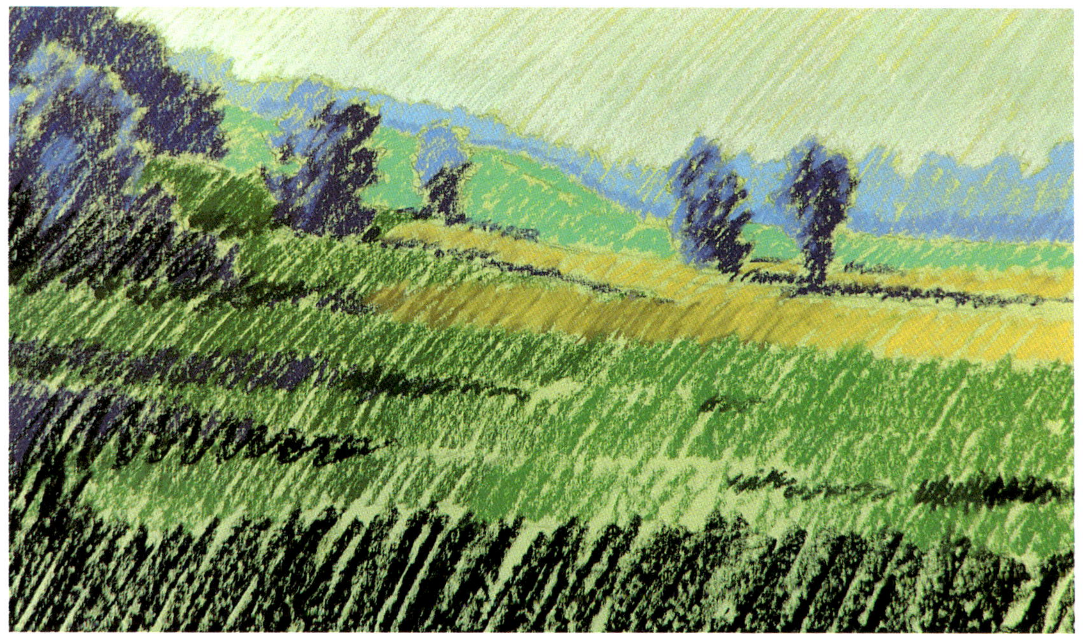

Step 1 Establishing the Large Value Masses
After a minimal sketch on my sanded ground, I lay in the first layer of color with open diagonal strokes using soft pastels. As in the color study, the sky sets the tone for the summer haze effect I want in the background. I apply cool purple and green soft pastels in open strokes to the shadow areas, and warm ochre soft pastels to the sunlit pattern across the field. Attention to color distribution keeps this simple landscape quiet.

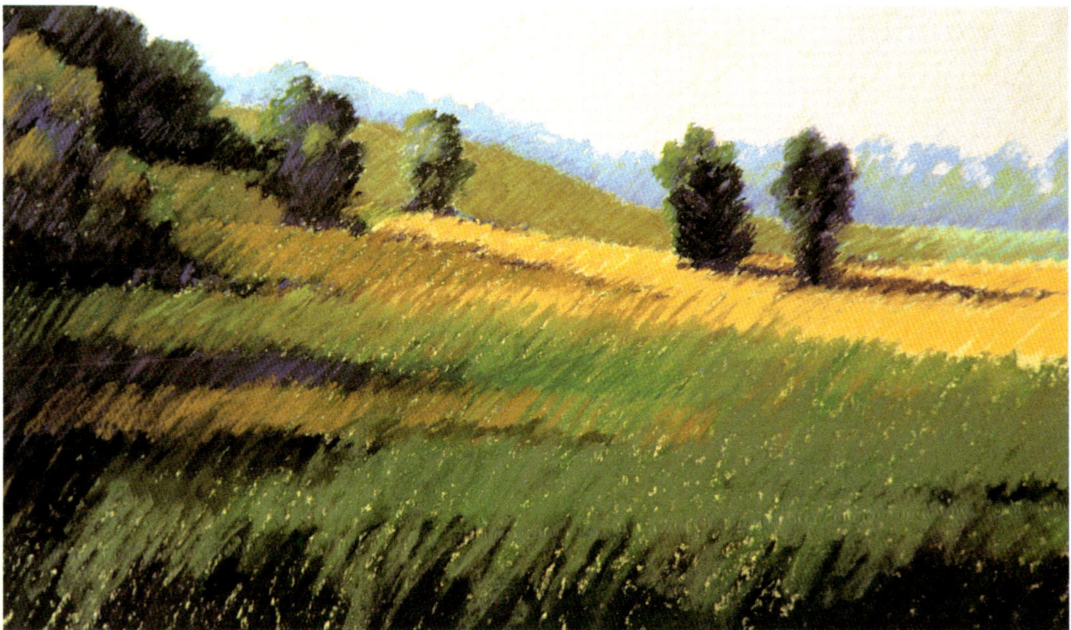

Step 2 Refining the Shapes
To minimize texture in the sky, I close up the stroke in that area with mauve and blue pastel. In the remainder of the painting, traces of the first layer of color show through subsequent layers. The soft pastel begins to fill the tooth of the paper. With deliberate strokes of warm and cool color, I shape the trees and the shadows across the grasses.

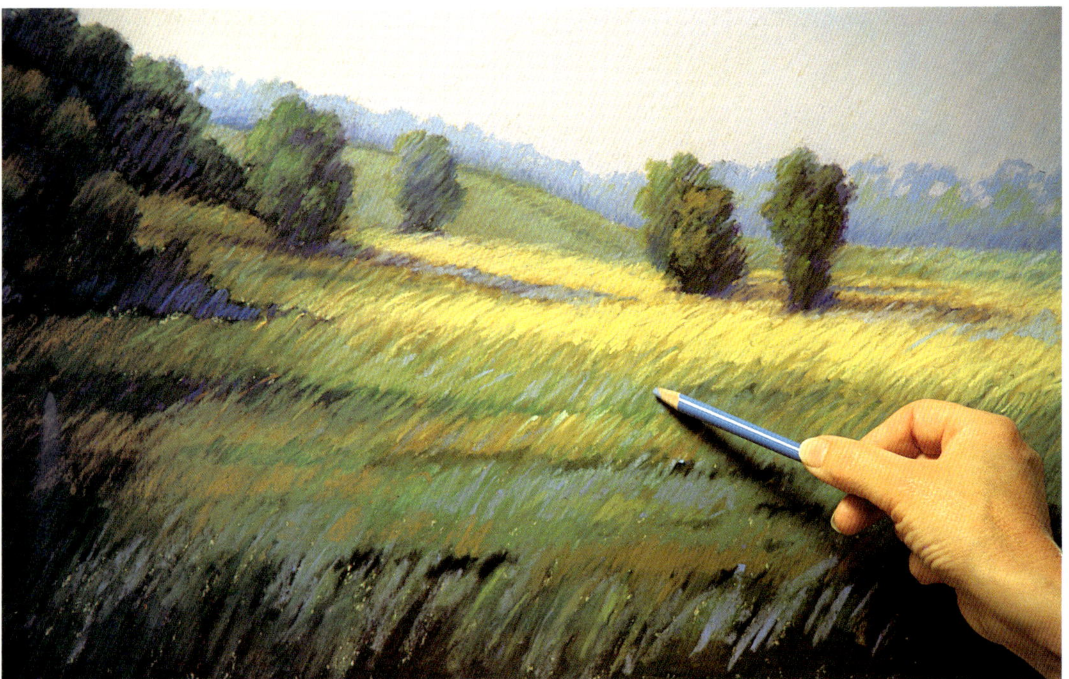

Step 3 Unifying the Color

The field, having been prepared with color, is now ready to catch the morning sun on its grasses, which I apply with a higher value yellow pastel. Then, lightly scumbling a blue pastel pencil through the background hill, trees and grasses, I harmonize the color and soften edges. As I approach the foreground, pencil is exchanged for several values of blue pastels, and heavier pressure is applied in some places, leaving more color behind than the pencil. This step ties all the colors together, giving the painting a sense of serenity.

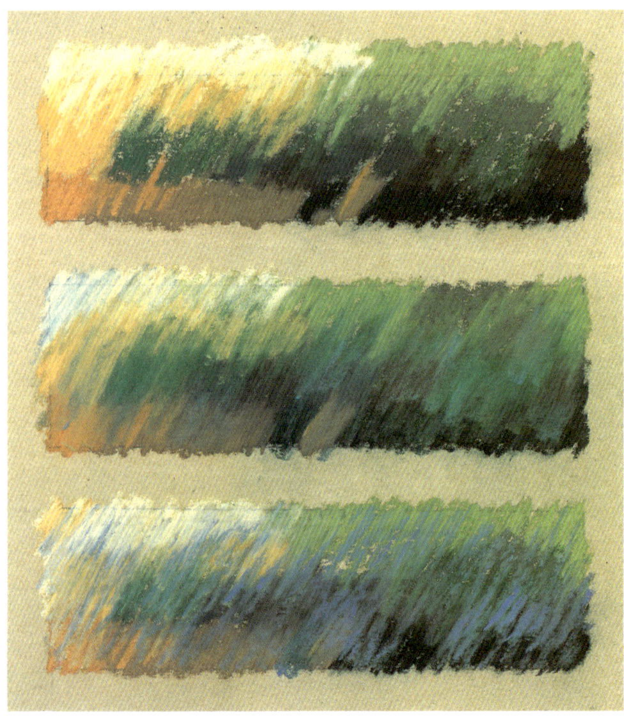

These sketches show in more detail the technique I used in The Meadow *to unify the color areas in the field grasses. All three rectangles were covered in the same manner with strokes of soft pastels and pastel pencils. Sanded paper is the ground.*
A. Pastel strokes alone.

B. Here a blue pastel pencil is scumbled through the area in the same direction as the applied pastel. The movement of your hand should be rhythmic, with the pencil sometimes touching the paper, and sometimes not.

C. Here, blue soft pastel is used instead of pencil. Hand pressure can be varied depending on the desired effect. With practice, the pencil or pastel will become an extension of your hand and mind and do its own dance upon the paper with interesting results.

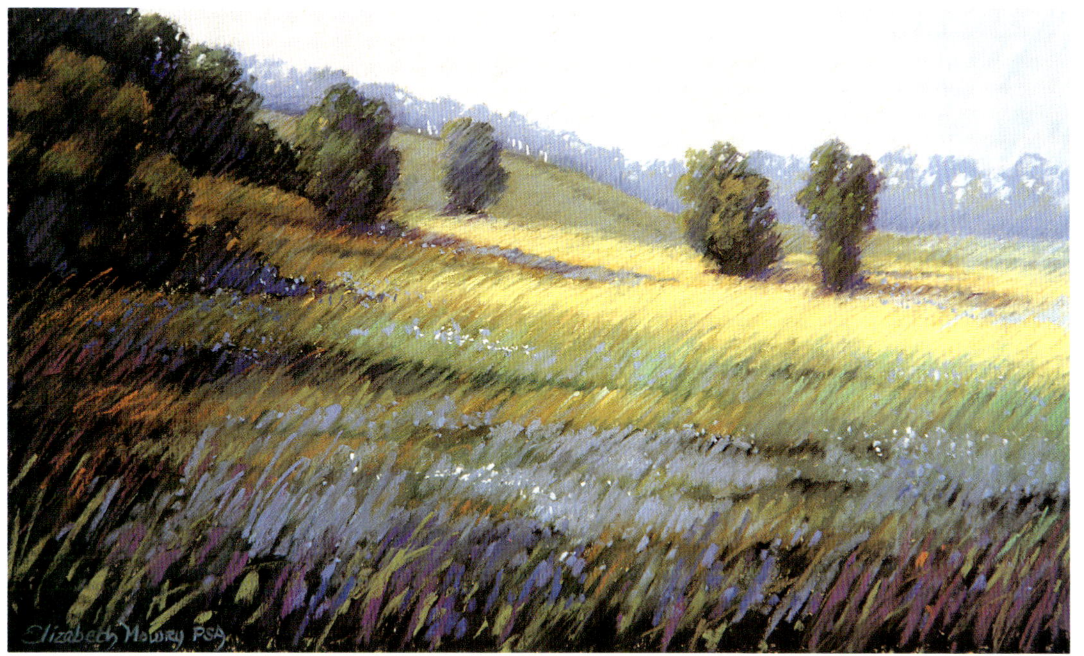

Step 4 Final Details

Now is the time for sky holes in the background trees and detail in the foreground grasses. I use red-violet and some sienna as a color surprise in several places in the foreground. Finally, I add delicate hints of field flowers such as blue chicory and the abundant purple ironweed. Mood, paired with a simple landscape that has no distracting specifics, is an invitation to viewers to fill the space with their own thoughts and yearnings.

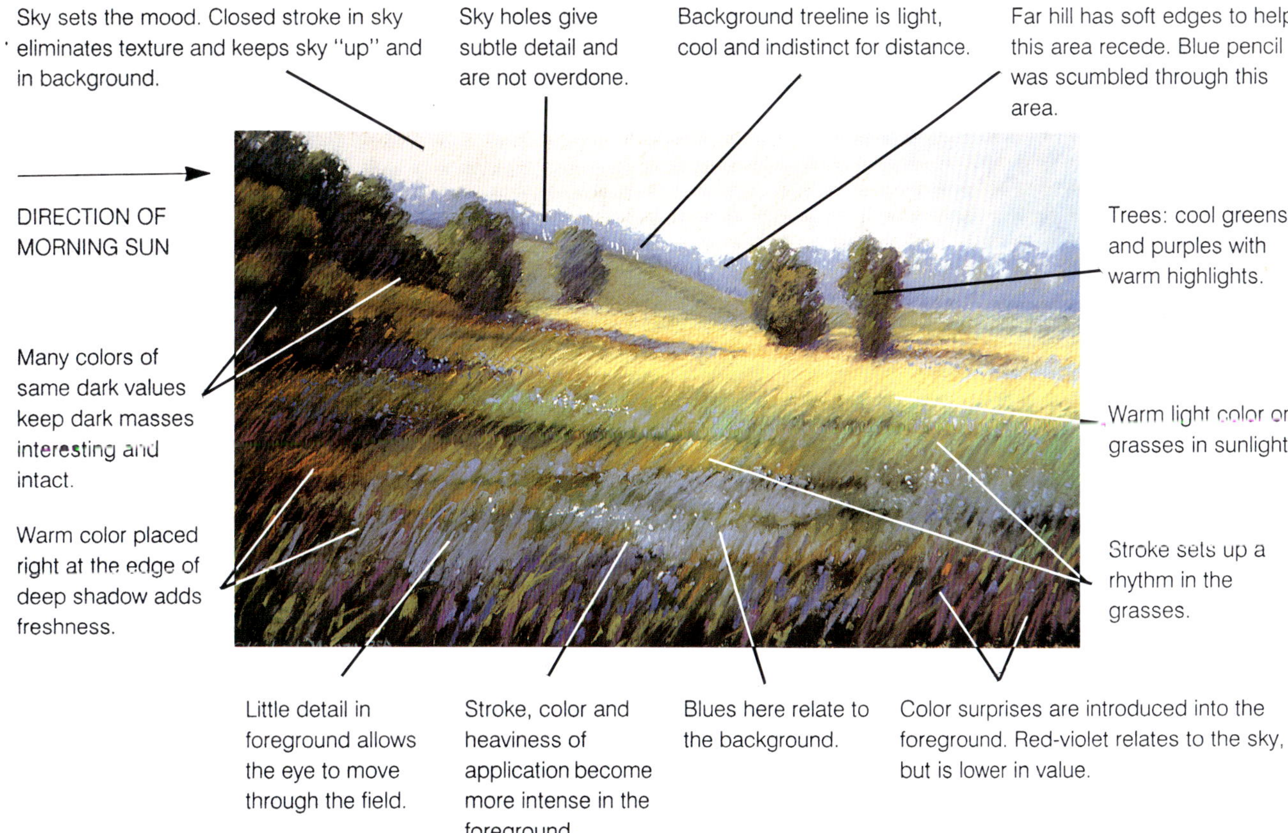

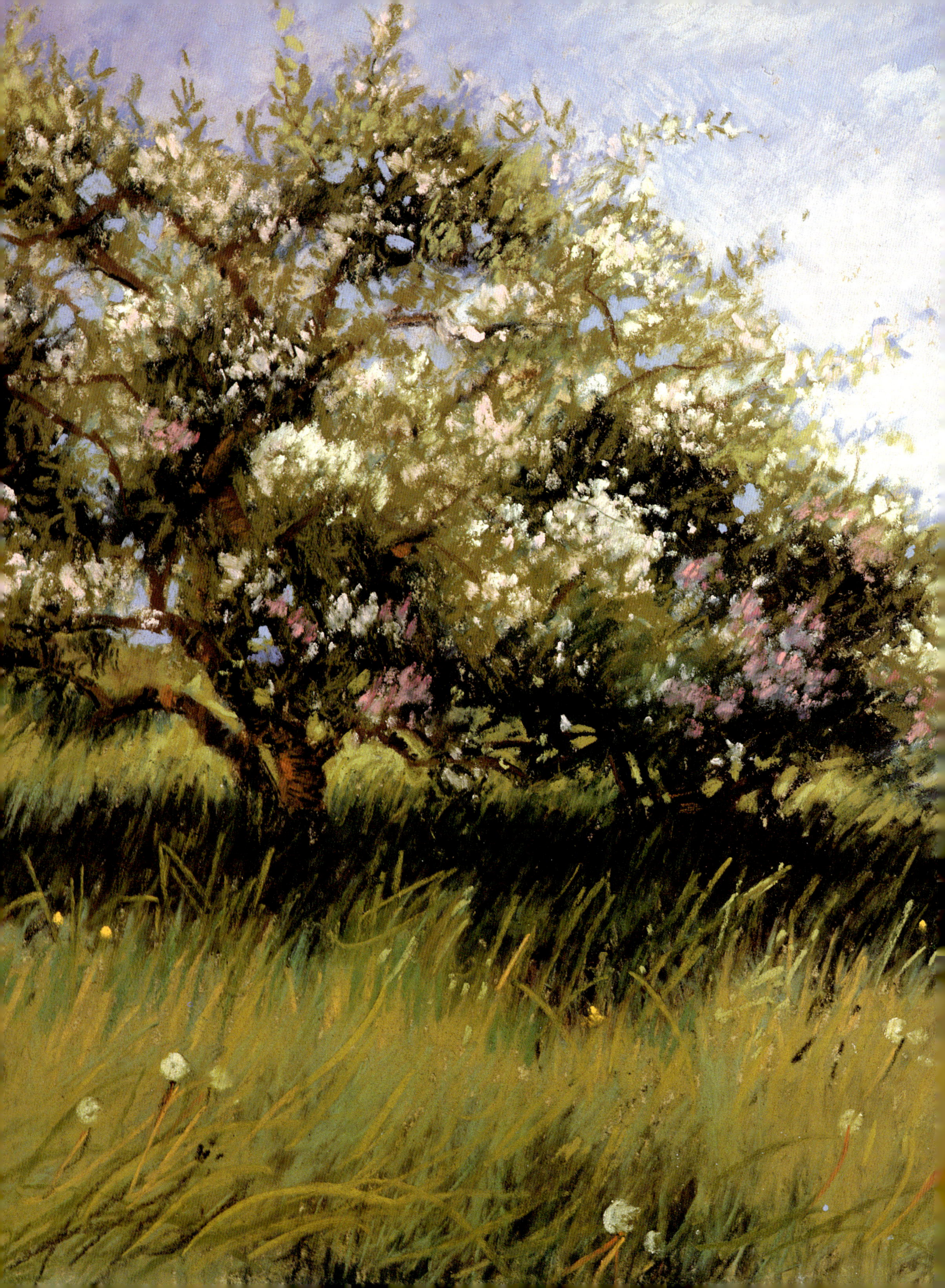

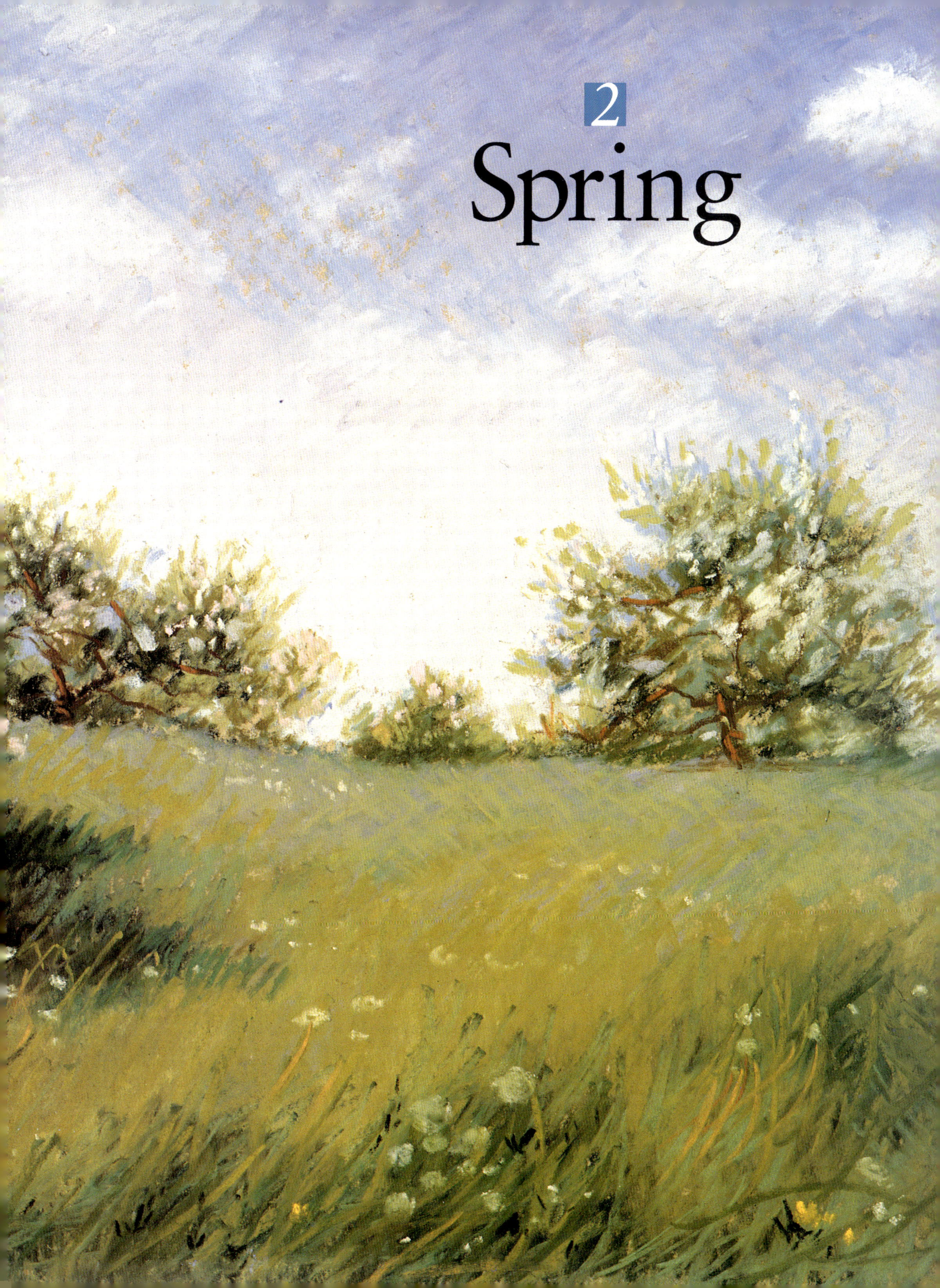

2

Spring

A RESPONSE TO SPRING

O ut from under matted brown leaves, the first snowdrops and marsh marigolds herald the season. Spring is a new beginning, a good time to begin an acquaintance with nature, or rekindle an old one, because at first, changes happen gradually. Unlike the botanist, we are not required to classify or categorize what we find. We are free to sketch and paint outdoors whenever the weather permits, or to simply witness and absorb the onset of nature's evolving cycle. Sometimes ideas for paintings will occur, and other times they will elude you only to show up later in the backgrounds and foregrounds of your work.

The first signs of spring can be noticed when you look down toward the wet, warming soil. The grass is greening, the tender skunk cabbage glistens in the wetlands, ferns uncurl and the year's first flowers awaken. Brilliant reflections in the water collected by muddy pathways and roads strike jewel-like contrasts to the rain-soaked earth. Above ground level, budding bushes and shrubs host returning birds that sing and call to one another even before dawn.

When you look off toward a wooded hillside, you will see florescence, the beginning of bloom that so delicately transforms winter's gray deciduous tree line into

warm pastel tints of green and pink, and the willow's yellow. Only a week or so later, the leaf buds on the trees burst dramatically into green, and you will see geese returning across the warming sky.

By the time the leaves reappear on the trees, growth has escalated to a degree that is impossible to record. It closes in, laying claim to the open spaces of winter. Shadows fill out as well. By mid-May, the moist, warm air carries the heavy scent of flowers and grasses, and butterflies and insects add to the activity. Changes in form multiply. Cirrus clouds sweep the sky above us. Newly ploughed mounds of earth

MARSH MARIGOLDS
Pastel on sanded paper
8″ × 9½″

Marsh marigolds are one of spring's earliest surprises and are found in the wetlands among the muddied brown leaves and earth. Emphasis, through detail, is on the flowers, with the deemphasized background tucked in afterwards with loose side strokes. This is a strong example of pairing the specific with the suggested.

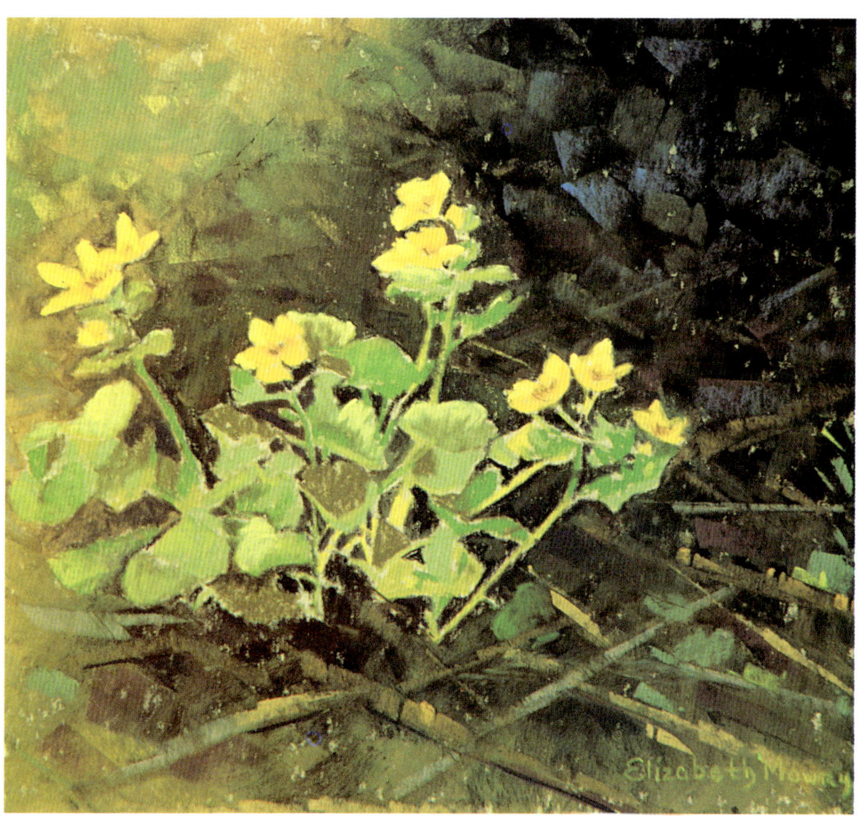

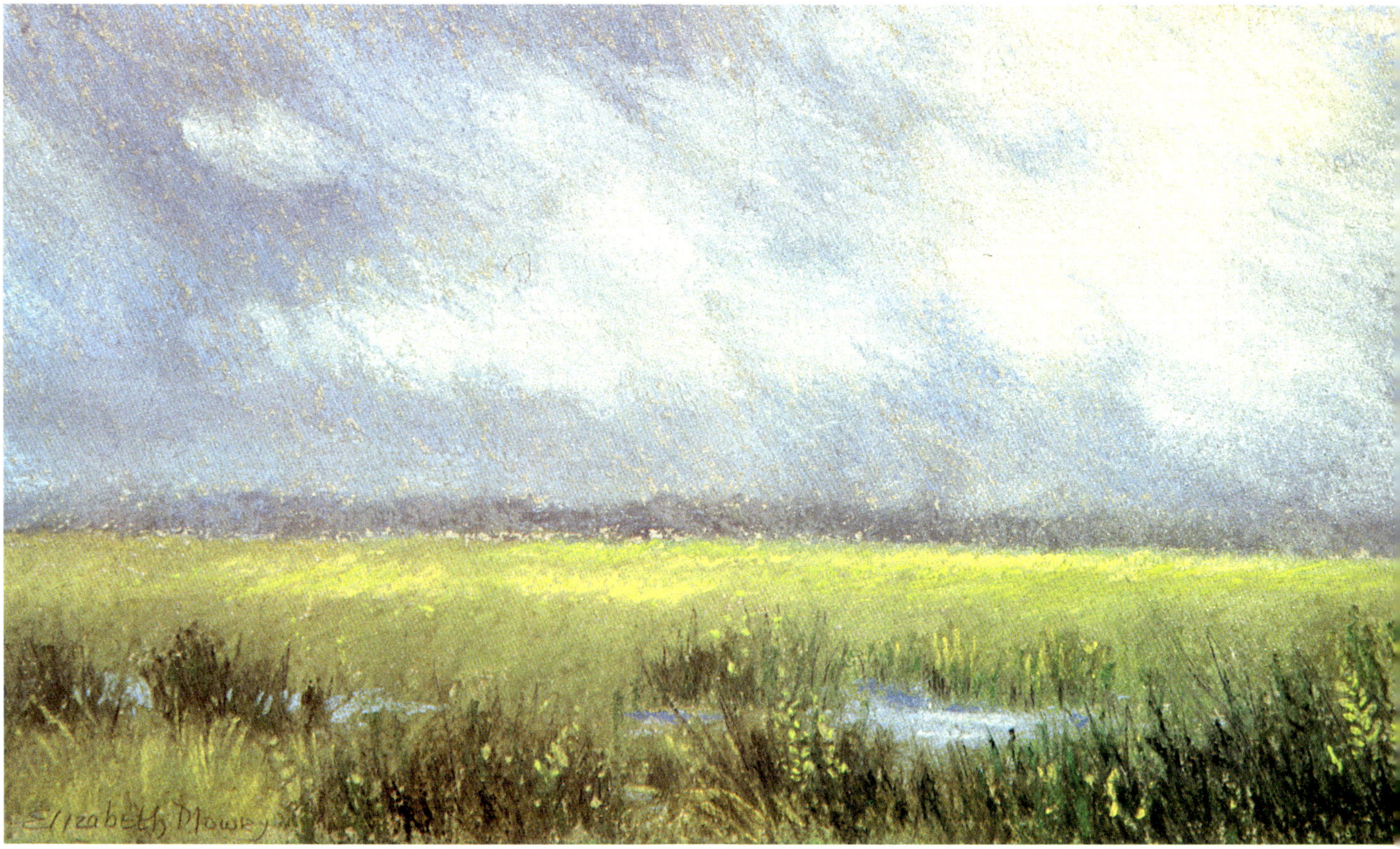

SPRINGTIME LAYERS
Pastel on Larroque Bergerac paper
7" × 12"

New young greens under the rapid movement of a typical sky make
this study an allegory for spring.

freshen the grayed fields, and winter's bare branches round out with blossoms. Notice how the violets and bluebells, the jack-in-the-pulpit and trillium spread over the woodland floor. Where humans have claimed their space, lilacs and forsythia soften weathered barnsides. You may even catch a glimpse of turtles socializing on sun-warmed logs that jut out of a quiet, moss-edged pond. And in the evening, a hearty chorus of peepers will call their hypnotic, one-note finale to the day.

Spring's optimism colors the landscape, and our paintings, too, fill again with the color we have longed for.

In Springtime Layers, *the palette consists of six pastels, but high, middle and low values do exist within it. The colors are shown from top to bottom as used, and intermingled on the surface of the paper.*

HINTS FOR BETTER SPRINGTIME PAINTINGS

Together with the landscape's saturation of new color, spring's multiplicity can be disquieting to the senses. Throughout the winter, you have looked deeply into the landscape, searching and pulling out what you needed for your paintings. Now the landscape is inundated with growth and color, and it is necessary to change tactics. Instead of searching, you will engage in an intelligent sorting out.

Much of the time, weather now permits you to paint outdoors, where keeping a focus becomes critical. Being literally surrounded by subject matter can be unsettling to even the advanced painter; if you are a novice, you may feel bewildered by foliage or a moving sky above you, the colorful growth beneath you, perhaps some water to your right, or a barn or orchard to your left. It is all there, all real, and it may all be interesting and paintable. The most difficult task is to choose a focus. Inability to focus can destroy your chances of painting a successful landscape even before you begin.

USING A VIEWFINDER

Simple as it is, making and then *using* a viewfinder can be most helpful in finding a focus. Instead of cutting a centered square from a piece of cardboard for a viewfinder, discover the advantage of using two L-shaped pieces for the same purpose. In that way, you can change the format of your view

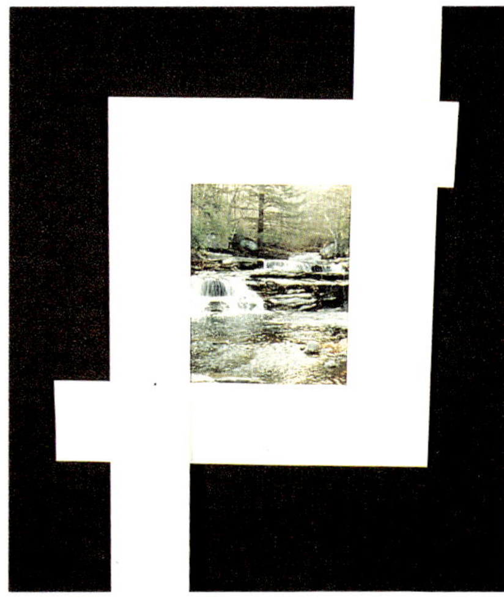

Here, the two-piece viewfinder marks a vertical format on a photograph showing the path of a tumbling stream. By including the background's falling water, which is important to the "story" of the water movement, the falls in the middle ground seem pushed too close to the edge on the left.

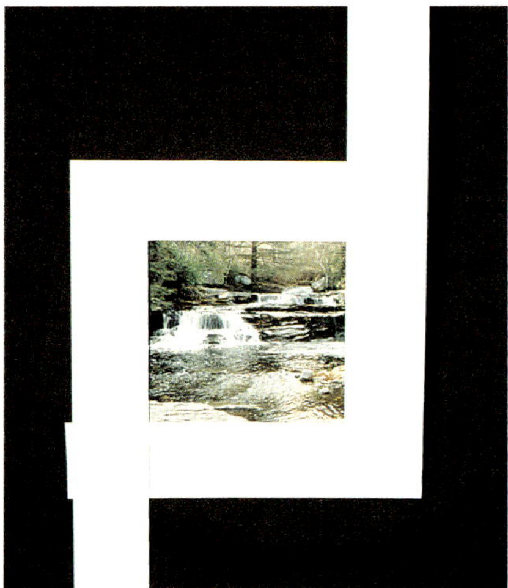

Moving the L-shapes of the viewfinder into a square format improves the position of the waterfall in the middle ground, but there is still a lot of distracting water movement in the foreground.

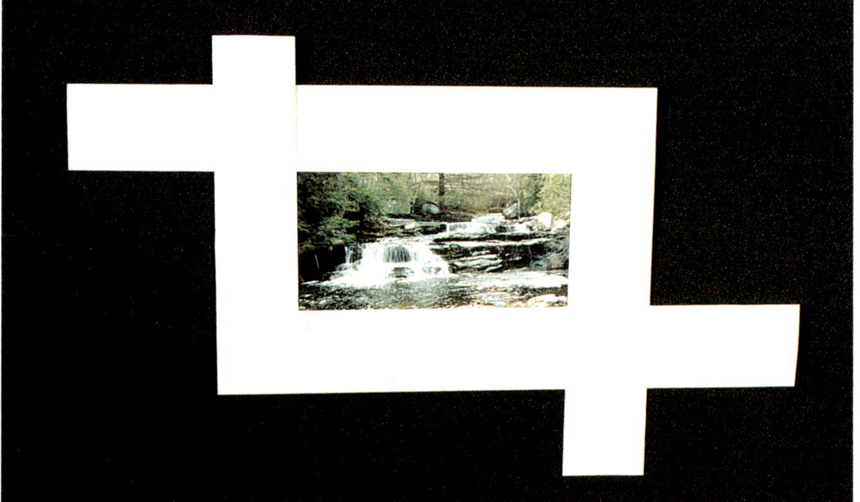

This horizontal format now puts more space on the sides of the subject and excludes the foreground distraction. The emphasis is now on the center of interest.

Trees and shrubs are left dark and undetailed, leaving emphasis on the garden.

Lots of color repetition keeps the painting quiet. Strength in reserve.

Dark-stained background contrasts with light spring flowers. Contrast gives strength.

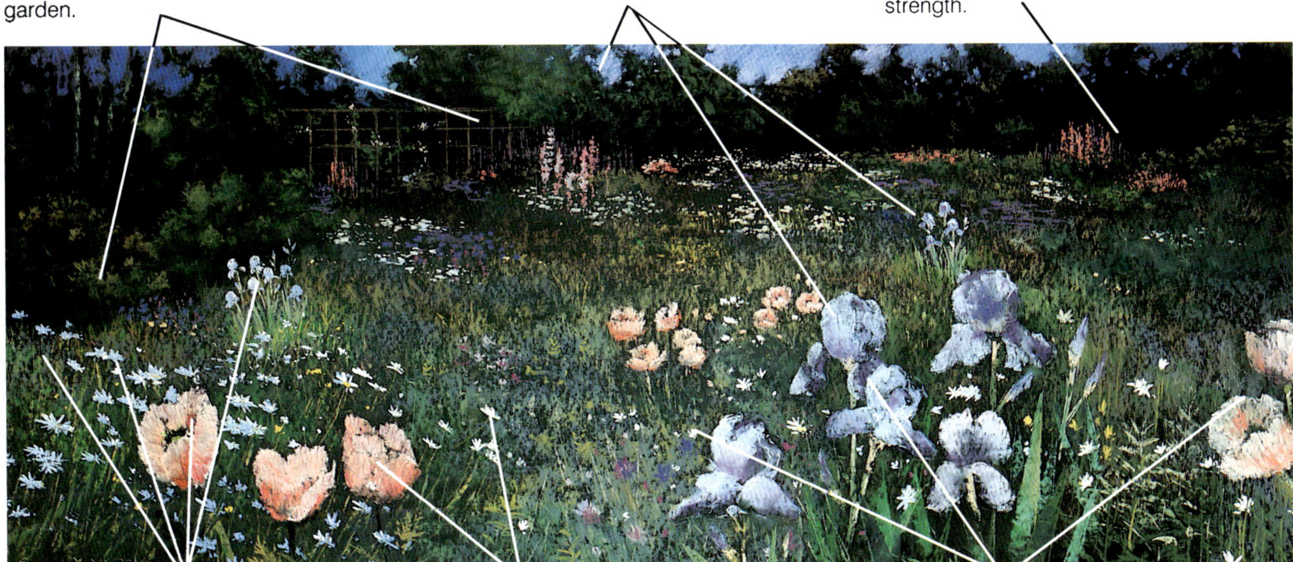

A limited palette of blue, pink, white and green was used with only a tiny bit of yellow for accent.

Variation in the size of the shapes.

Clarity of the shapes keeps the painting from becoming weak and unfocused.

UNTENDED GARDEN, SPRINGTIME
Pastel on sanded board
20" × 49"

This large painting leans toward a romantic interpretation of a garden, but the contrast between the dark background and the simple palette used for the flowers gives the subject strength.

from horizontal to vertical to square as you look, until you decide which is most suitable.

Choosing a format for the subject matter you have selected means that you determine, with the help of the movable viewfinder, the shape of the picture you intend to paint based on where the center of interest will be situated within that shape, and how much of the scene to include or exclude.

If you must work from a photograph, you can move the L-shaped pieces over the photograph until you find the area that interests you most and then use only that for your subject matter.

The size of your painting surface can be altered by scissors or saw, or simply by taping off the portion you will use, in which case you can remove the unused portion before framing.

Always base format decisions on what will enhance your interpretation of the subject matter. Filling up space on standard-sized surfaces just because they are readily available in convenient packages is often counterproductive when you consider the end result.

MAINTAINING STRENGTH IN A ROMANTIC INTERPRETATION

Springtime beauty is everywhere. You may be captivated by the apple blossoms, the swaying daffodils, the blooming hawthorn and the budding maples, but if you become distracted by these accents or try to put them all in one painting based on "if a little of a good thing works, then more will be even better," your painting might be unfocused from the start and you may never know what went wrong. Because

one dessert topping would be delightful, will ten be better? Think about this in your paintings. If you decide to use a type of flower in the foreground of your pastel to complement your center of interest, will several varieties improve it even more? Probably not.

Romantic interpretation of a landscape based on emotion must be accompanied by full awareness of your intentions, and then tempered by a reserved subtlety. In this way, you use emotional input from the senses to add to your work rather than control it, which is what has frequently happened when paintings become weak and saccharine.

THE SPRING PALETTE

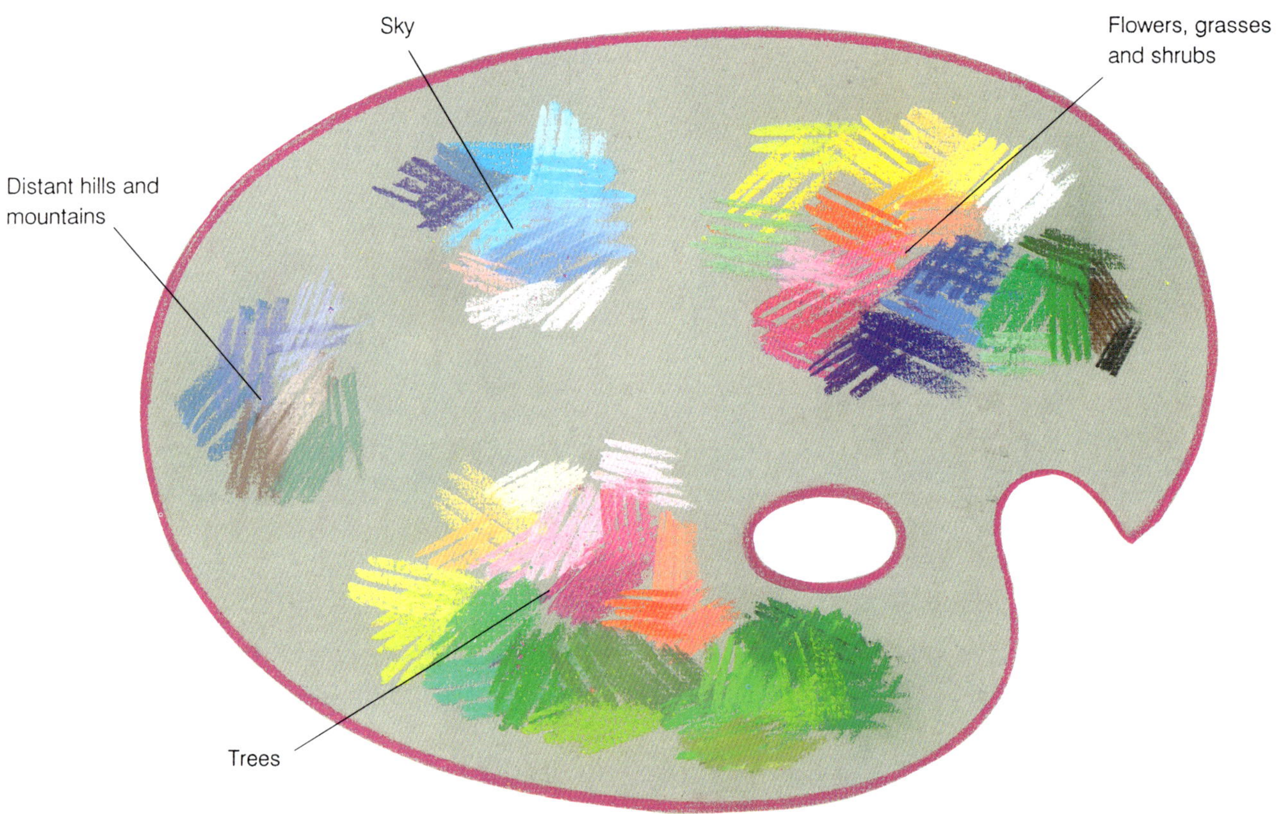

Spring's explosion of color can be overwhelming. Nature's superiority is evident in riotous combinations that defy all complement. But remember, the whole world is nature's canvas. Even with color wheels and intensity charts, human beings fall short when attempting to put springtime's full panorama of color onto a small, two-dimensional surface.

Bits of color surprise show up wherever we look . . . the red-winged blackbird, the cheery crocus and, later, the speckled egg in a nest and the butterflies. Running water is picking up color from the new, young greens in the grasses and the warming blue in the sky. Blossoming trees lace the hillsides and orchards with white and pink.

Despite the return of color into the landscape, spring is a time of less obvious contrasts than other seasons. Just after the leaf buds open, there exists a short period of time that is best noticed, appreciated and then, in my opinion, dismissed as a source of subject matter. Although the qualities of balance that make a painting strong are present, they are difficult to find. For example, the predominant colors are pale and warm; pinks, cream, yellows and yellow-greens. The soft edges of new growth create a temporary fuzziness. Large, solid shapes disappear under delicate foliage. Unless you are aware of these problematic spring conditions and then take compositional steps to resolve the unbalance, lack of contrasts in color, temperature, value and edges may result in work that appears insubstantial, or even, in a pejorative sense, too pretty.

THE ORCHARD
Pastel on sanded board
9" × 14"
Collection of Phyllis McCabe

*Light colors and indistinct shapes can
weaken spring paintings. Here, the large
tree shadow helps. Compare with* Lenny
Bee's Old Wagon, Woodstock.

LENNY BEE'S OLD WAGON,
WOODSTOCK
Pastel on sanded paper
8" × 14"

*This small painting shows how the young,
high-value colors we associate with spring,
as well as the general fuzziness of the season, can be grounded by the contrast of
deeper value and color. Here, the rich, dark
colors and sharp edges of the old wagon
add solidity to the painting.*

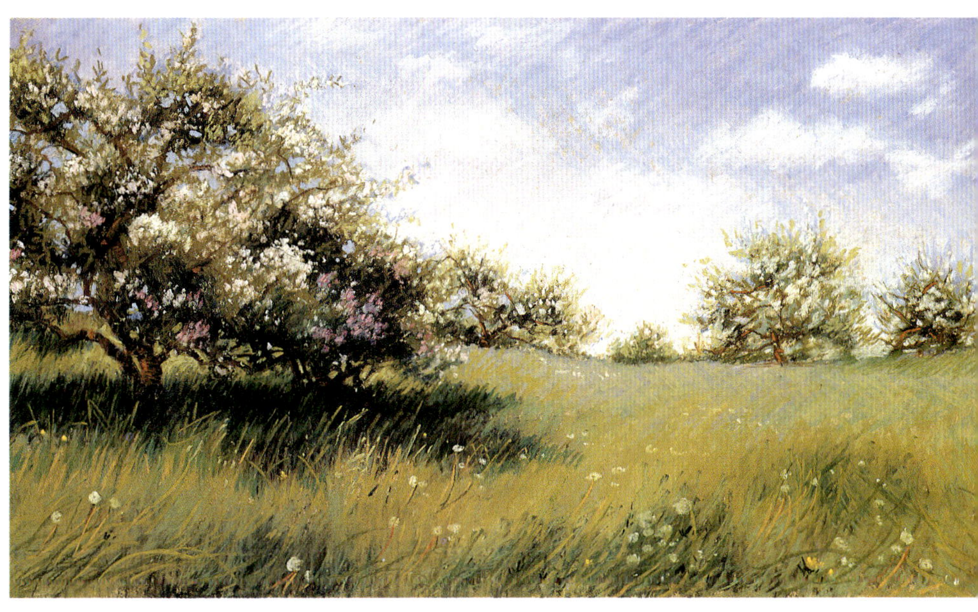

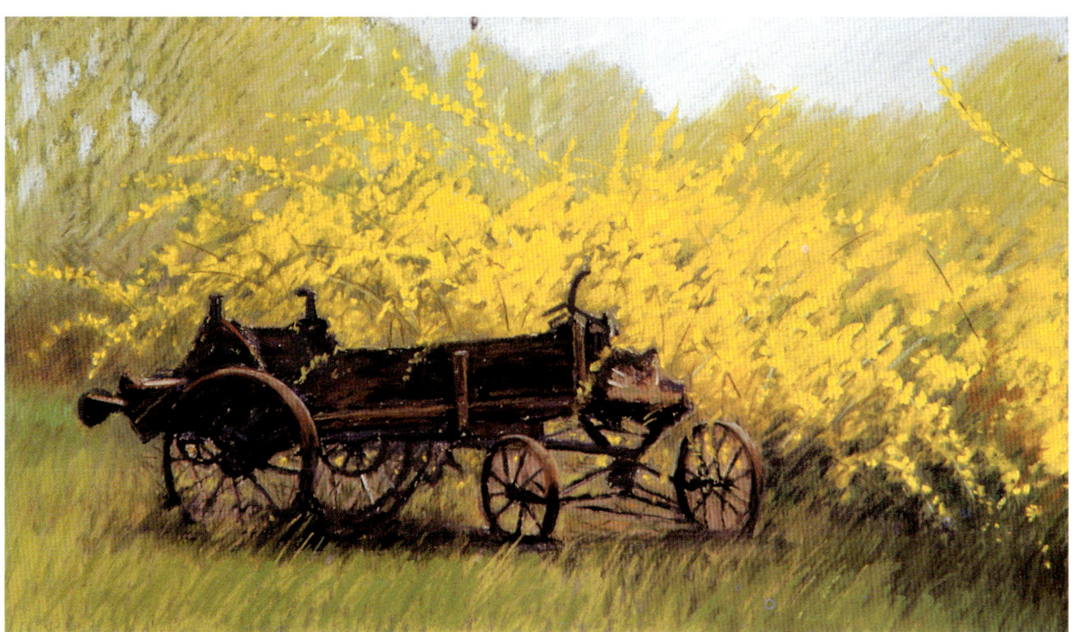

*The painting above began as a pastel
drawing of the wagon on a clean surface,
done at the site. Later, in the studio, I
brushed in some color around it with Turpenoid and a polyfoam brush for a beginning unity on which to lay the bright, spring
colors of the trees and bushes.*

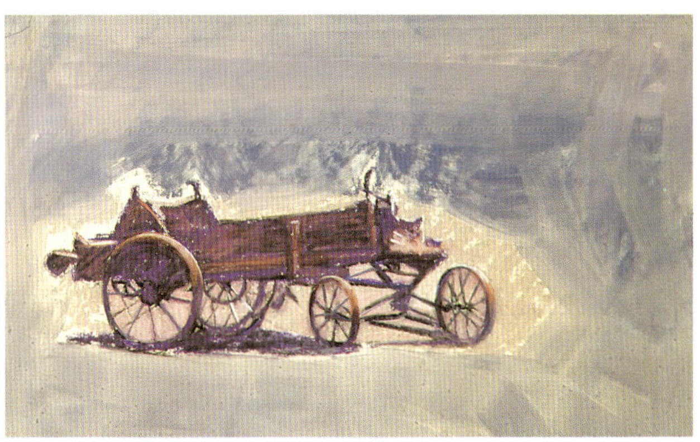

ACHIEVING HARMONY WITHIN THE SPRING PALETTE

This is a season to be in awe of color and to use it with thoughtful respect. As we are confronted with pink, orange, yellow, scarlet and fuschia, each showy and weighty, we realize that together, on a limited painting surface, they can be oppressive. Several approaches to handling spring color include (1) choosing one strong color to dominate, and subordinating the others by using them sparingly, as accents, and (2) exploring fewer colors in greater depth by varying temperature and value. The possibilities of color expression without repetition are incredible with pastel, and you will have many opportunities to use the colors you purposely choose to pass by today.

Less distant (more green)

More distant (gray-green and gray-blue)

Most distant (blue)

You can put movement into a sky by sweeping side strokes of one color over another color that has been blended with closed strokes. Once you begin a sweeping stroke, don't hesitate.

Get distance with cooler, blue or gray color.

Low horizon gives space and emphasis to the typical sky movement following a spring shower.

No detail is needed in the distant water.

STORM KING AFTER THE STORM
Pastel on sanded board
19″ × 24″

With rain, the marshlands in the foreground freshen with new young color.

The impact of the sky would be compromised by use of a more extensive palette in this painting. Here, foreground colors are limited to fresh, spring greens.

AFTER THE ICE, THE RUNNING WATER

When spring rains add to melted ice and snow, small streams tumble down even the slightest slope and often overflow their banks. As the season continues, you will find that you can visit the same painting site week after week and the shapes of the moving, falling water will be different all the time, depending upon the increases and decreases in water level by as little as a half inch. For instance, when the level of water decreases even slightly, what may have been one solid fall of white water will now be divided into two narrower falls by a rock that wasn't visible a week ago. Multiply this by fifteen other rocks that now appear because of the lower water level,

and you see a completely different painting than you worked on previously.

When painting a scene that includes rocks and running or falling water, you will save all areas of white water for a few pristine passes of pastel at the very end. This means that when you first lay value shapes into your painting, you will not have the light value of the falling water for reference. This does not have to be a problem. With pastel, you are constantly making adjustments in color and value as you work, and after you do add the white water, you will evaluate again before making final adjustments.

On a gradual slope, water gurgles and waltzes gently over the

rocks, whereas when the incline is greater, it will crash and splash into a livelier dance. Yet later in summer, the very same stream may be completely dry. In painting a streambed, the rocks over which the water flows have to make sense, just as the figure beneath the drapery has to make sense. The position of the rocks determines the water's course and, therefore, the way you will paint it. Whether water parts around a high rock, trickles over a flat one, or crashes down a pile of rocks depends upon the height of the rocks, the depth of the streambed and the water level on the day you are painting it.

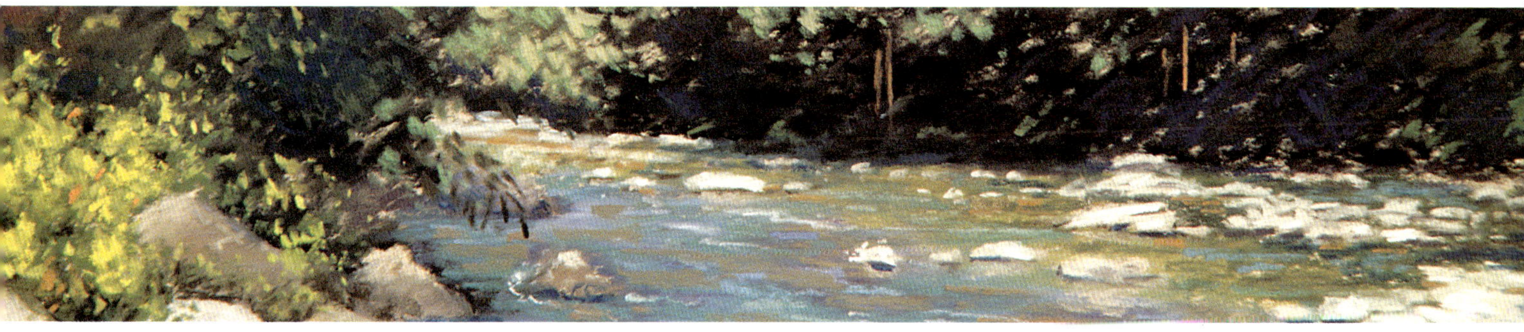

VERMONT STREAM
Pastel on sanded board
3½" × 15"
Collection of Annie and Randy Ross

This small, on-site study gives an idea of what kind of information to record when you are outdoors. See how the streambed gets warmer at the far edge of the water and at the right corner, where the water is shallow. Visible rocks and pebbles will frequently tell you where those areas are.

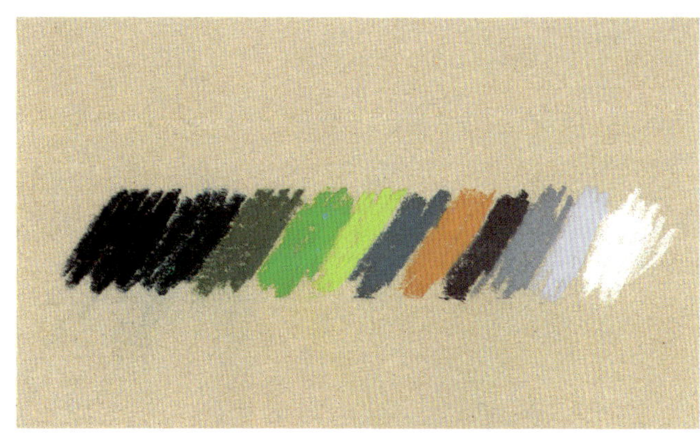

Although you do not need many pastels for a small study such as Vermont Stream, you can see that a full value range was used.

PAINTING RUNNING WATER IN A STREAM

Painting running water in pastel is not difficult if you first use a viewfinder to find and limit the scope of your painting to that which interests you most. Once you decide on the format, make sure to give the center of interest enough size and space to make it important. Then begin blocking in the large landscape shapes. Squinting will help you to eliminate some detail at first, but be careful about this when you block in the rocks, because it is easy to "get lost" as you look out to your subject and then back to your painting surface.

Get down as many large shapes and planes as you can find. You may choose to combine some shapes, but refrain from "making up" the rock shapes. "Made-up" rocks lack the important planes that give them weight and solidity.

It is essential to establish a streambed over which the flow of the water will appear natural. Where the white water occurs, except for merely suggesting the dark rocks underneath if your surface is light, leave the area untouched until late in the painting. Often, palest blue or pink or green tints are more effective than white for painting running water, and can function as subtle repetitions of the colors you use in the sky of your painting.

Use the lightest touch possible for the rushing water, letting the texture of your surface impart freshness and sparkle. Evaluate after each stroke, and perhaps add a few splash dots, but sparingly. Finally, add desired detail if it helps your painting, but pass it by if it does not.

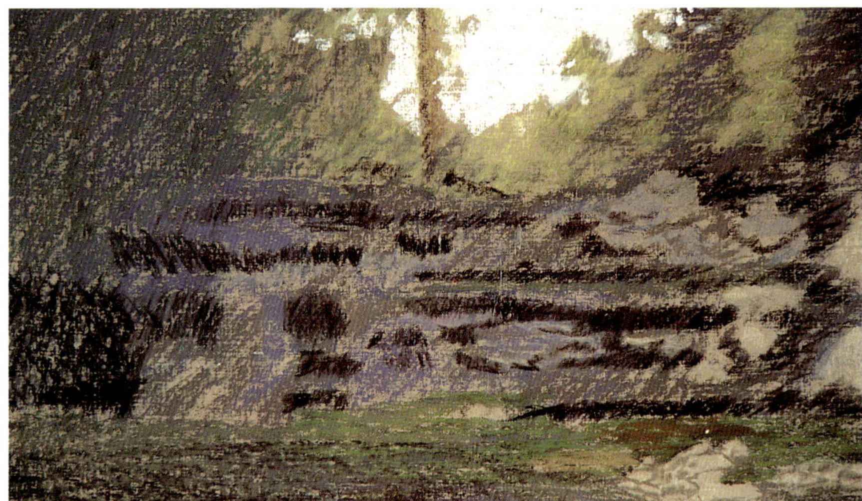

Step 1 Getting the Large Shapes Down
After finding the view that interests you most, block in the major shapes with a first layer of soft pastel on a medium to dark pastel surface. Where running water will occur, barely touch the area with dark color, such as deep violet or dark green, to suggest the rocks underneath. No water yet!

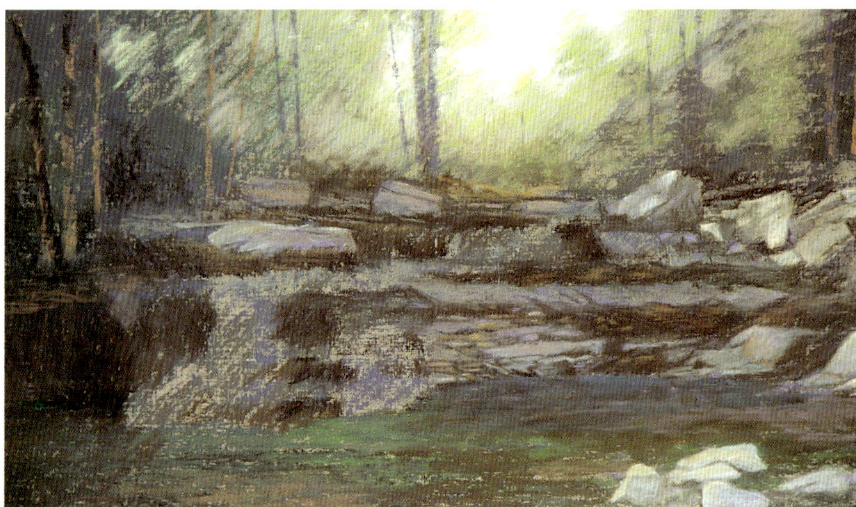

Step 2 Setting the Scene
Blend the sky with closed strokes. Shape the foliage and indicate the major tree trunks. Then spend some time pulling out some of the rock shapes. You are preparing the streambed for the water here. Don't be concerned that your surface is unevenly covered with pastel.

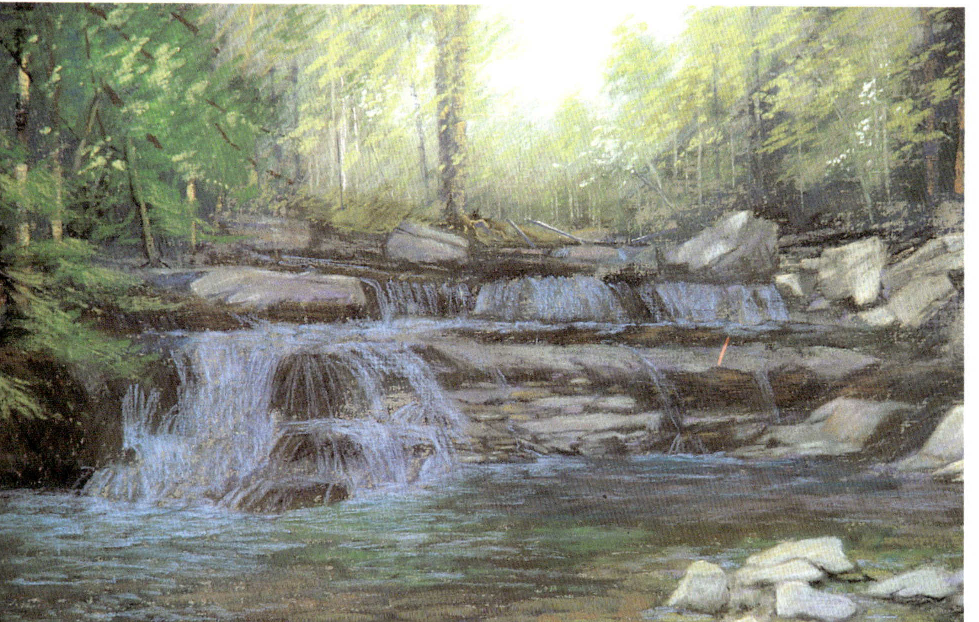

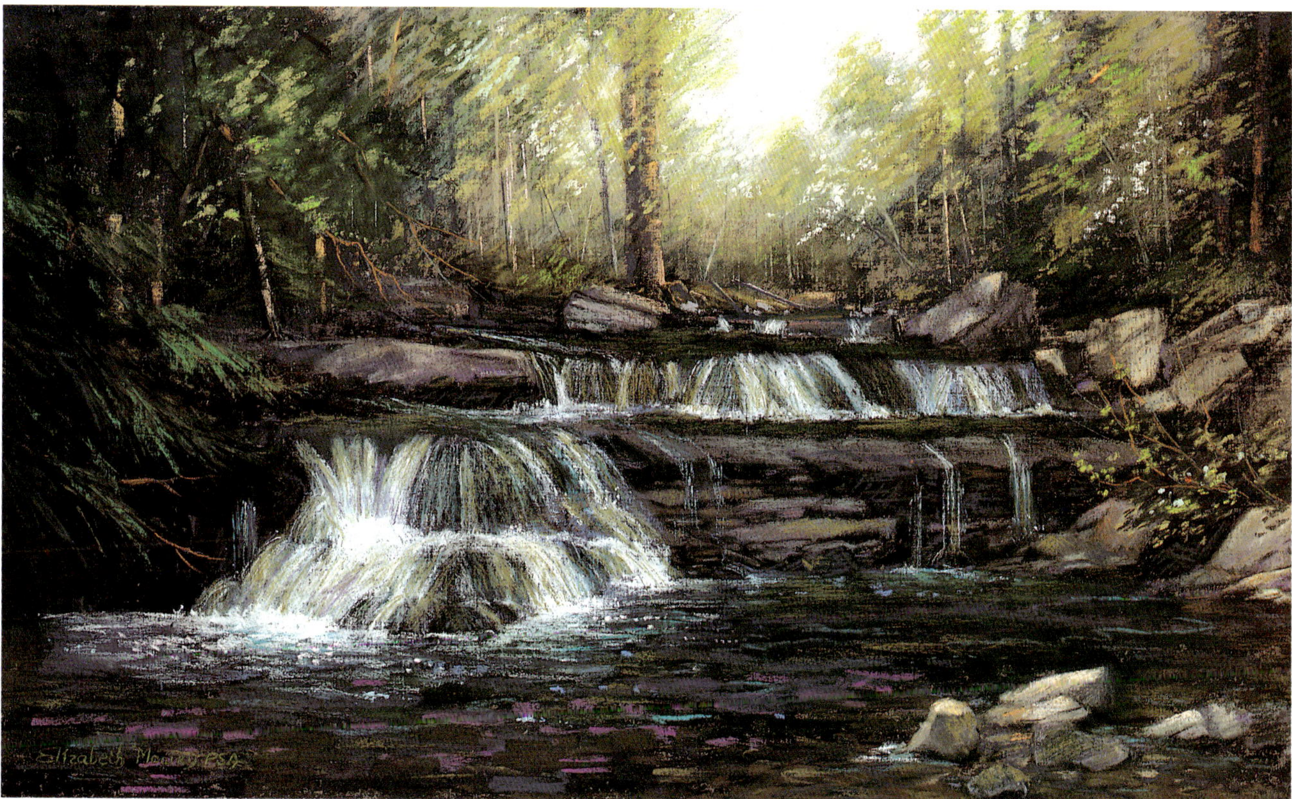

Step 4 Letting the Water Flow
Use a high-value color tint as well as traces of olive green and blue-green to run the water over the rocks with carefully placed, delicate strokes. Evaluate after each stroke. Then, based on the completion of your value range, make final adjustments. For example, add some color into any dead areas without changing value. Put directional movement strokes into the water. Highlight a few of the rocks with warm sunlight using rosy ochres, and add secondary foliage detail and branches.

WOODLAND MUSIC
Pastel on sanded paper
12″ × 20″

ZEROING IN ON SPRING

If working in pastel is a new experience, you may find it beneficial to do some studies of single landscape components. A painting of a single flower will reinforce skills having to do with placement on the surface, varying strokes for effect, use of color and value for balance, and background treatment that resists overpowering or competing with the focal point. Honing these skills in manageable, single-component studies can only enhance your work as you enlarge the scope of your paintings. The investment of time and materials for studies is less burdensome than for full-scale work. Because studies are less precious, you will be more inclined to take the risks necessary to try new techniques. If your study fails, you can dis-miss it, knowing that time spent learning is never wasted, and the small surface you worked on is dispensable. And sometimes . . . sometimes you will surprise yourself with a remarkably satisfying study that merits a place among your best works!

USING CLOSE-UP STUDIES TO SOLVE PAINTING PROBLEMS

Zero in if you are having difficulty capturing the essence of some component in nature. For instance, if the rocks in your streambeds all look alike, then zero in on rocks. Get up close. Take time with the planes and shadows on each. Do small group portraits of rocks. You will find that after just a few studies directed at that small portion of nature, you will paint rocks in your full-scale paintings with much more understanding and, consequently, with more skill.

Suppose the flowers in your pastels always seem to have a lollipop look. Then zero in on flowers. Study a type of flower close up. Are the stems stiff or graceful? And check the width. (A common problem is making the stems too wide and disproportionate to the flower.) Look for repeated angles and shapes in the blossoms and buds. Then use those shape and angle repetitions to capture the essence of the flower you are painting. (See Painting Flowers Where They Grow, on pages 69-72.)

You don't need an instructor for this kind of learning. All you need to do is use your time to quietly and carefully put down what you see. No more is required.

TIME IN THE GARDEN
Pastel on sanded paper
8½″ × 7″

Sometimes you will find that the feeling for place can be conveyed more poignantly by portraying a small portion of the subject than by trying to show it in its entirety. In this case, a painted corner of my garden conveys the density, color and sense of proportion that exists even more than if I had backed away to fit the entire garden onto an even larger surface.

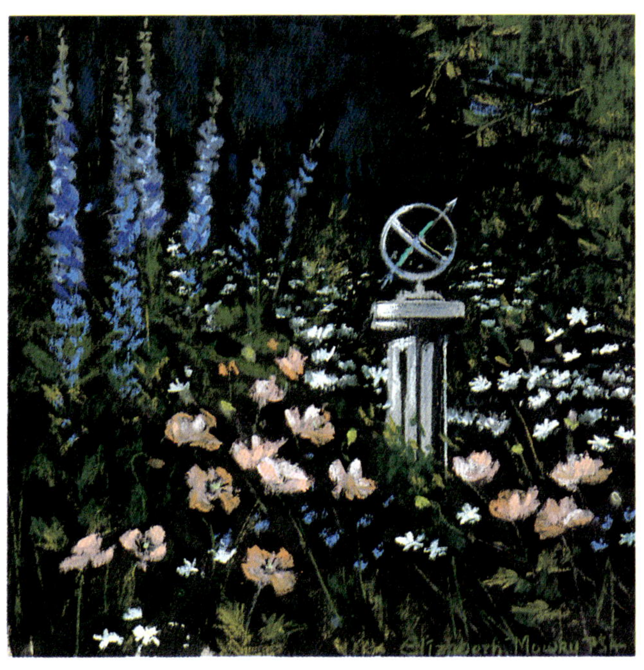

FOCUSING ON A SINGLE FLOWER

During a summer workshop, I did this drawing sketch of a white peony by narrowing my concentration to one flower. I wanted to learn for myself how to help students paint white flowers that would no longer resemble oversized cotton balls. Putting your undivided attention on a small area, such as a single flower, gently prods you into deeper levels of perception. In this case, I found that slightly exaggerating the shadow areas within the petals helped to form the distinctive appearance of the peony.

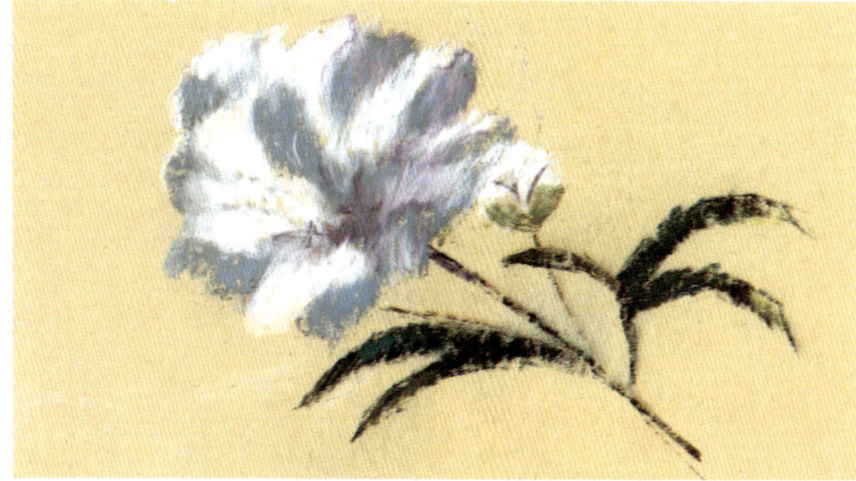

White flowers are sometimes difficult to express. Once you find the darker areas within the white whole, exaggerate them slightly to pull out the planes that are distinctive to the particular flower you are painting.

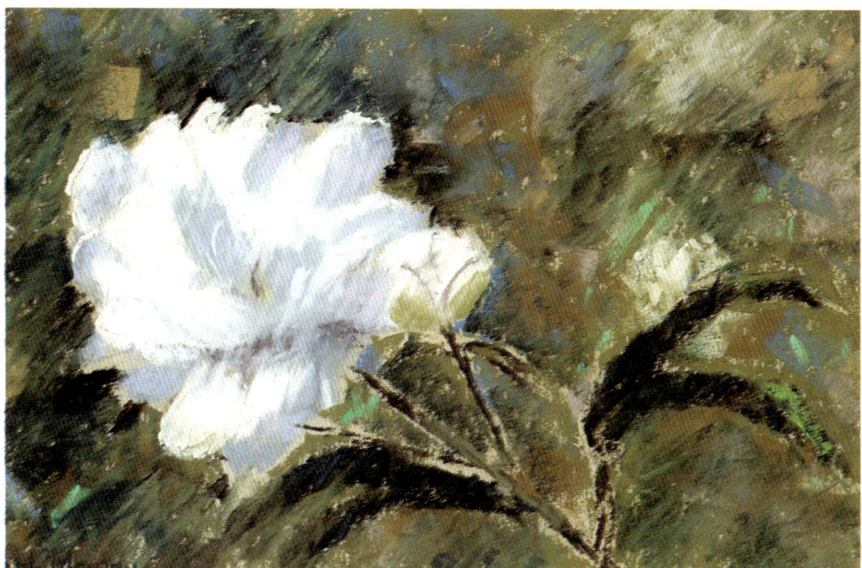

By using side strokes of same-value colors around the flower with just a few darks and lights to vaguely suggest leaves and buds, you can transform a drawing into a painting. The color changes are subtle, and they add rather than detract from the focal point. Notice how the slightly deeper background makes the flower appear whiter. Notice, also, how the background moves in to define the flower edges and give the flower dimension. See how subtleties in a background can coexist with definition at the center of interest.

THE PEONY
Pastel on sanded paper
5″ × 9½″

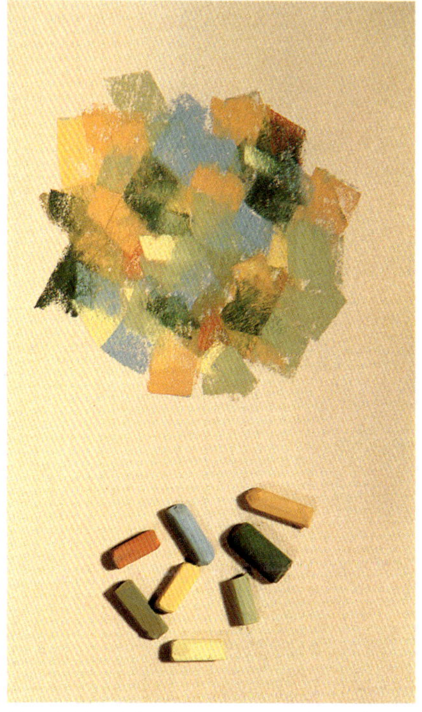

Here's the side-stroke treatment used for the background in The Peony. *Don't hesitate to break your pastels into pieces to get the effect you want. The strokes, made with half-inch pieces of soft and hard pastels, stay fresh and distinctive because there is no blending.*

PAINTING THE LUSH GROWTH OF SPRING

By late spring, the landscape becomes a proliferation of color, activity, sound and scent. The well-defined shapes of winter have disappeared. Bare tree branches that opened views over great distances have been transformed. Now foliage interferes with the view, and underbrush shapes merge together in confusion. If you attempt to portray nature exactly as it exists, you may even begin to find that too much reality can be a disappointment.

THE IMPORTANCE OF FOCUS

Spring, at least for me, requires an aesthetic and intelligent simplification. Ask yourself, as I do, "What is the main idea I am conveying here? How much of this subject is essential for the idea, mood or sense of place to be conveyed?" Next, make the distinction between the center of interest and all that is secondary. This becomes critical to a good landscape, especially during this season's multiplicity of growth and detail. For example, while it is true that you will see and paint more detail in a foreground than in a background, even within foregrounds, much detail can be merely suggested, and your painting will be stronger because of it. Just because we can see leaf formations clearly close up, do we have to painstakingly paint twenty of them on a foreground flower stem that has twenty leaves? Of course not. Your pastel will be far more painterly if you detail one or two, then detail a few parts of several others, and only hint at the rest with appropriately shaped strokes that do not detain the eye. When the abundant shapes of spring's foliage, grasses and flowers seem overwhelming, squinting may help you to combine some of them into larger shapes.

Remember, when attempting to establish a focus in your springtime pastels, (1) clarify your idea, (2) eliminate whatever does not add strength to your pastel and (3) use selective detail. Simplifying takes practice, but it does lead to stronger pastel paintings.

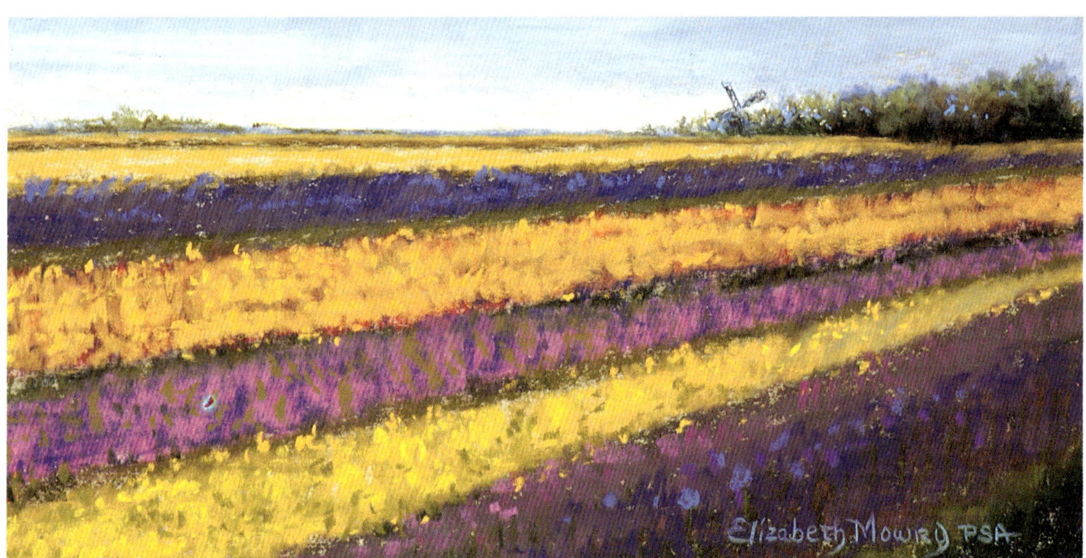

The Windmill *shows ultrasimplified color masses taking the shape of diagonal layers across its surface. The small size of the windmill and the converging layers give an illusion of depth. Time limitations while you travel may force you to simplify your work as in this pastel, which was done outside of Amsterdam where rows of purple hyacinths divide fields of daffodils each spring. Although I wished for more time then, I believe that any added detail would have weakened the painting.*

THE WINDMILL
Pastel on sanded
paper
6" × 11"

SIMPLIFYING SPRINGTIME'S ABUNDANCE

Give some thought to your painting before you begin working. It will always save you time. Work out some approximation of light and dark areas in your mind or in a value sketch if you need one. You can think of this as your map. You probably would not build a house without a plan, or drive into a big city without a guide map, and it helps to have an idea of where you want to go. Keep the sketch on your surface minimal and quickly put in the large approximate shapes. Do not fuss in any one area or get caught up in any detail. The pace of your painting should be fast at first, as your pastels feel their way around your surface. Later, the pace of your work will slow down as you begin to pull out shapes and refine others, carefully referring to your subject. Toward the finish of your painting, you will be looking more and more while your pastel strokes become fewer and fewer. Observation is a big part of an artist's life, and an important part of the painting process as well.

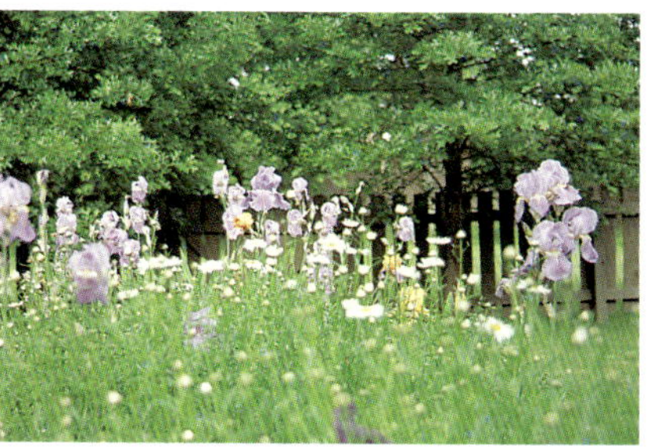

The reality of this scene is much more than I wanted to portray. Here, I used reality to formulate the idea for my pastel and then later as a source of reference for the specific details of the iris.

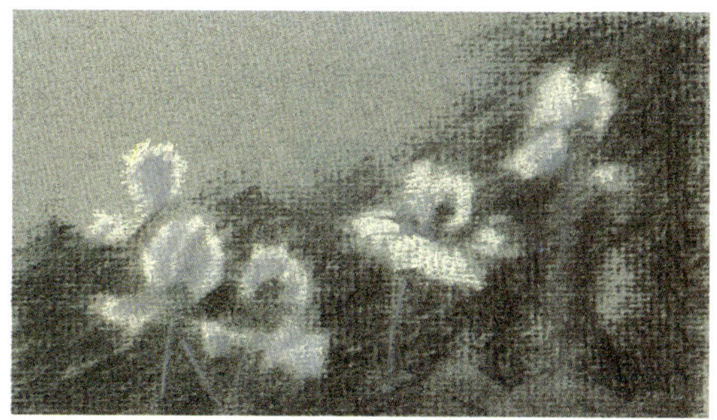

First, I worked out the pattern of lights and darks in a 1½" × 3" sketch, placing five dominant flower configurations on a horizontal format.

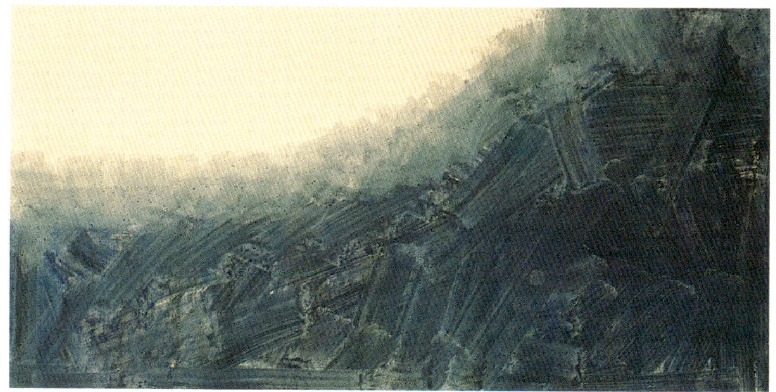

Step 1

With a polyfoam brush, I applied a wash of Turpenoid over dark green and indigo pastel on part of the surface of a buff sanded paper that was taped to a drawing board, and allowed it to dry thoroughly. This gave me a dark surface without using any tooth of the paper. Flowers that go over this dark area will stay clean.

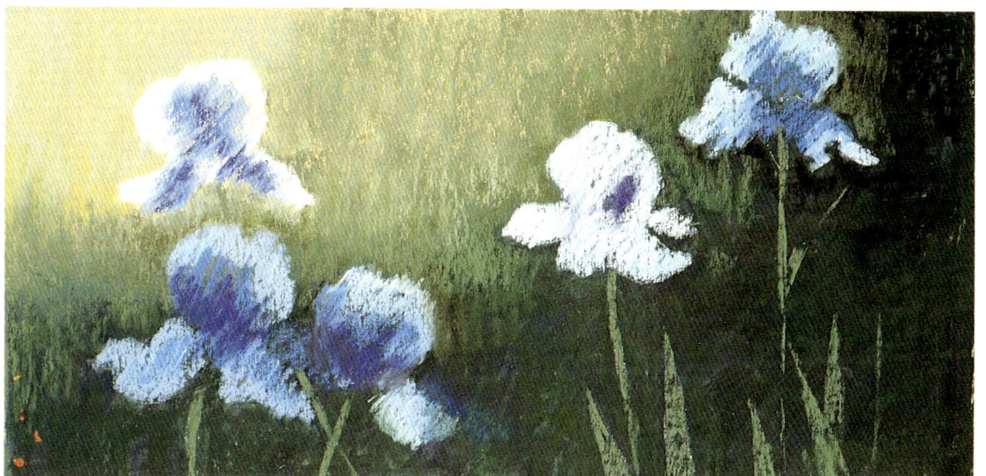

Step 2

I blocked in the major flower shapes with approximate color and then covered the background with soft pastel, aiming for a gradual value transition from top to bottom and from left to right.

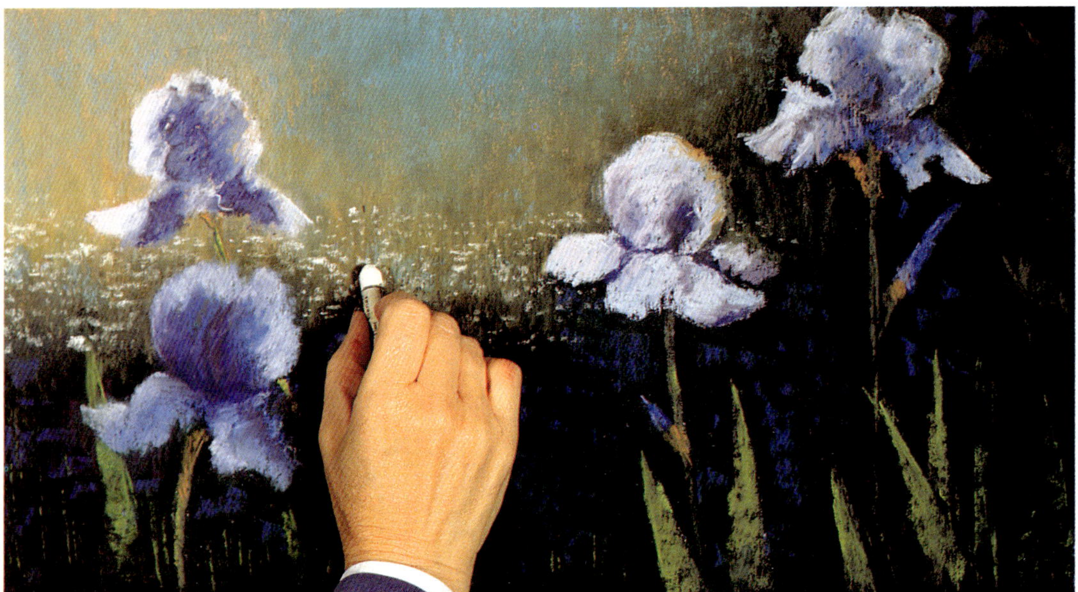

Background, though simple, has interesting contrasts, which show gradation from light and warm on the left to dark and cool on the right.

The vague, simplified background does not detract from the flower shapes.

Background colors merely hint at the sky and growth of the season.

Emphasis goes on the iris through attention to form and detail.

In the dense areas, where many dark shapes exist, it is necessary to pull out just a selected few.

Tips of a few iris-leaf shapes are clear; others are merely suggested.

IRIS AND DAISIES
Pastel on sanded board
11″ × 21″

Nearer massed daisy configurations are larger and more detailed but are kept in reserve by the shadow of the iris.

Middle ground strokes hint at a profusion of far-off daisies.

Step 4

I completed the flowers outdoors with the subject matter before me for direct reference. Finally, back in the studio once again, and after several weeks of casual evaluation, I made color and shape adjustments throughout.

STYLE AS A MEANS OF SIMPLIFYING REALITY

Simplifying subject matter can mean many different things to as many different pastelists. It has much to do with degree. How much you simplify your subject matter by changing, combining or eliminating, ultimately depends upon your own preference. Faithfulness to that preference, whether it is based on an art philosophy, your experiences, abilities, or an underlying idea, will result in your style. Style is personal. It may develop quickly, or over a very long period of time, and it may change after a while or frequently.

No one can teach you your own style. They can only teach you theirs. You can learn much from many instructors, but their style belongs to them. As you assimilate all the instruction you receive, and after a time of taking risks and learning from your own work, you will begin to hear that someone recognized a piece of your work, and you will know that the elusive quality called style is evolving in your pastels.

Below are three different approaches to simplifying that represent distinct differences in painting styles.

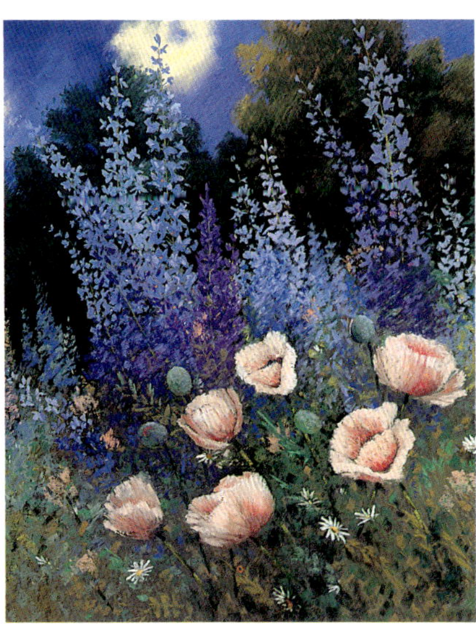

DELPHINIUM SKY
Pastel on sanded board
28″ × 22″

This painting of poppies and delphinium is the most literal of the three examples of simplification. There is selective detail in the poppies' crinkley petals, but stems and leaves are lost and found again without the viewer's losing sight of what they are.

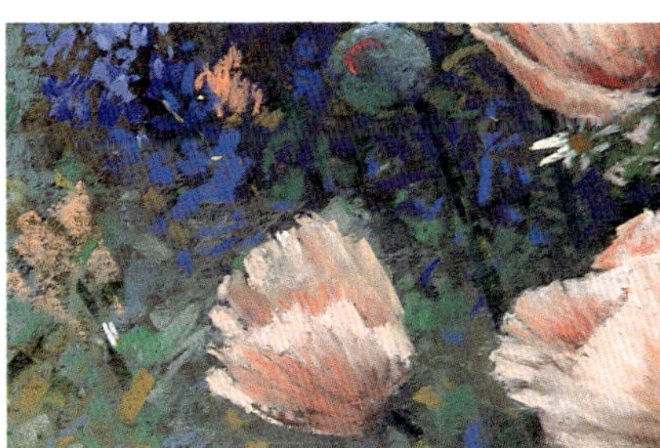

In this detail of Delphinium Sky, *small, suggestive strokes are left for the eye to blend.*

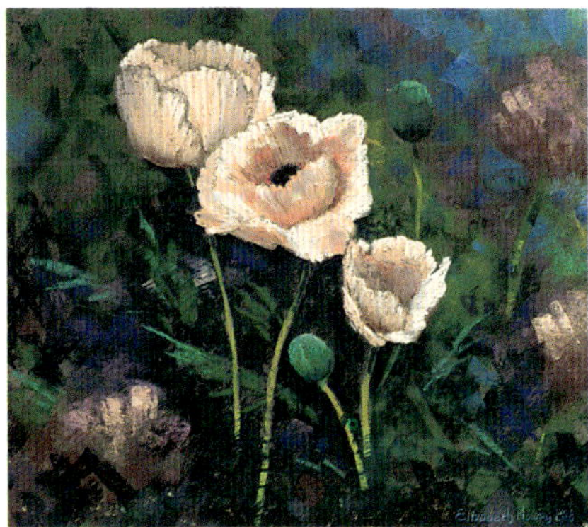

POPPY TRIO
Pastel on sanded paper
16″ × 17″

In this painting, the poppies are emphasized more when everything else is simplified. Dense growth is evident, but the poppies dominate because of size, color and minimal background treatment.

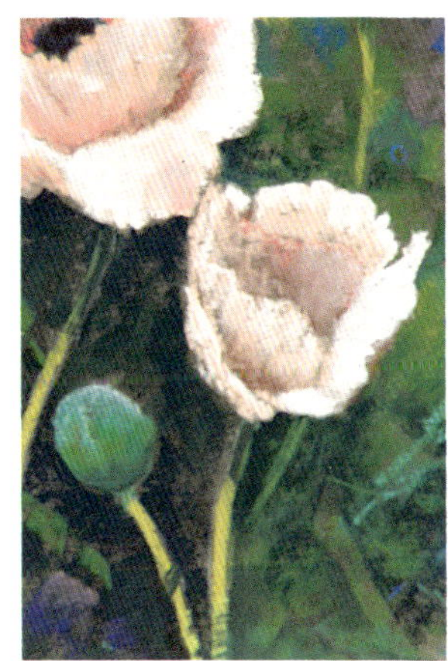

This detail of Poppy Trio *shows the large, bold strokes, as well as a background that appears to fade away.*

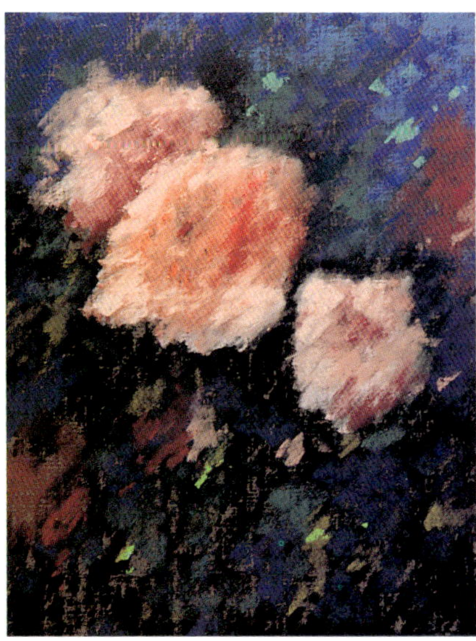

POPPY CONFIGURATION
Pastel on La Carte Pastel
9″ × 7″

This study of shapes and color, quickly executed and without detail, is the least literal example of style as a means of simplification.

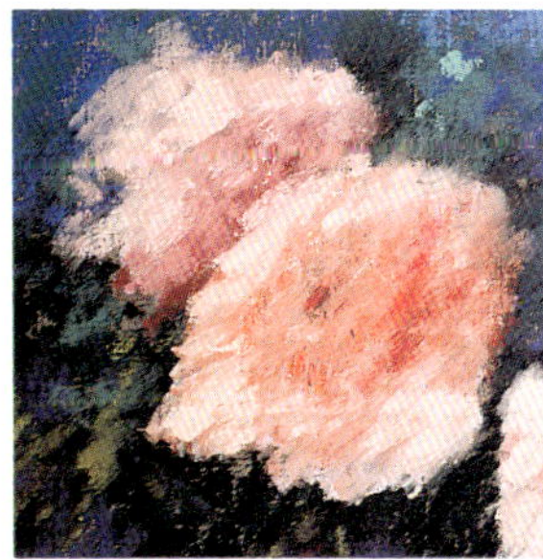

This detail of Poppy Configuration *shows loose strokes, unrefined shapes and lots of surface showing through.*

FIVE EASY STEPS TO PAINTING A FLOWER

Perhaps after all of those pastels showing poppies, you are thinking, "Yes, but still, how do I go about *painting* a poppy?" Well, here's how:

Anytime you wish to make a study of a flower or plant, or to place a specific flower in your painting, it is necessary to refer to it constantly while you look for the distinguishing shapes and the patterns of light and dark within it. Resist the temptation to paint from memory. Instead, scan the flower frequently for distinctive characteristics. Check out the tilt of the flower head, the bend of the stem, the formation of the bud or seed pod, the configuration of the leaf and its pattern of departure from the stem. Make size comparisons, check negative spaces and, above all, put your full attention on the flower. As you do this, more and more of the information you are looking at will register. If you are not interested in your subject, or if your attention is elsewhere, it is very possible to look at a flower (or anything else) without seeing it at all.

You may want to put a few lines on your surface to indicate placement and size of your flowers, but it is not necessary to draw in the entire flower. In fact, your flowers will be more painterly if you avoid the coloring-book approach, and go for shapes instead. Sometimes beginners feel more secure with a detailed drawing on their painting surface. Naturally, this takes time, and therefore it becomes very precious. They do not want to lose the drawing by covering it with large value shapes, and it isn't possible to have both. Details at the beginning of any pastel result in "tight" work. Working around the small shapes tends to make the pastel worse. Throughout this book, I encourage you to lay in large shapes quickly, then spend time refining, and save details for last.

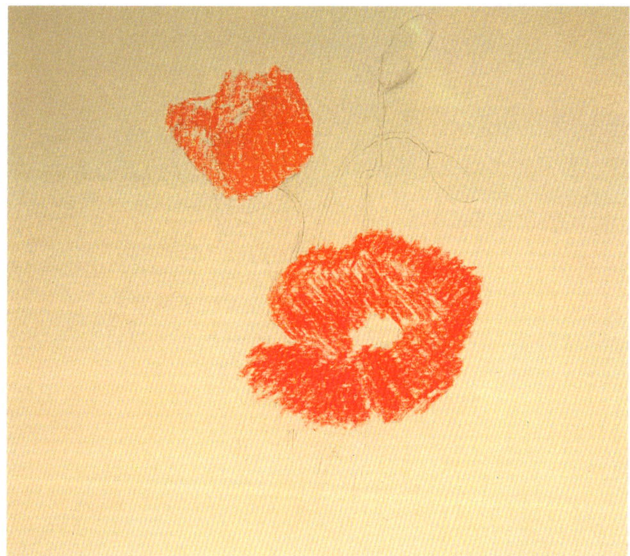

Step 1
First of all, put middle tones into the flower shapes. (Here, for the poppy, we use cadmium orange.)

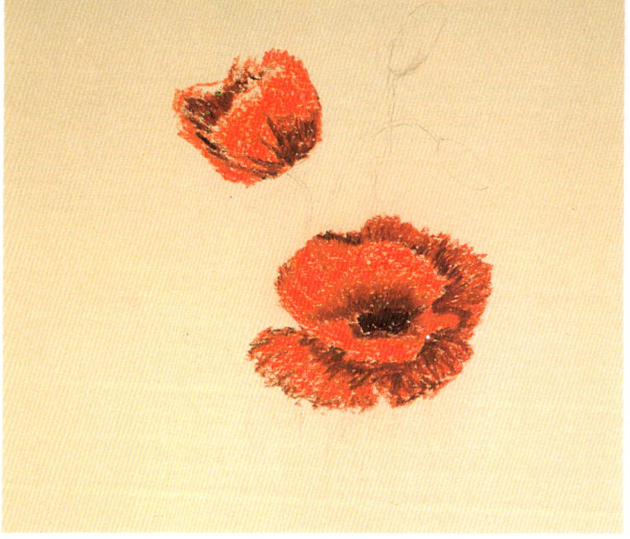

Step 2
Now find the darks by squinting at the real flower, and then put them into your pastel. (Here, we apply shades of burnt sienna and dark green.)

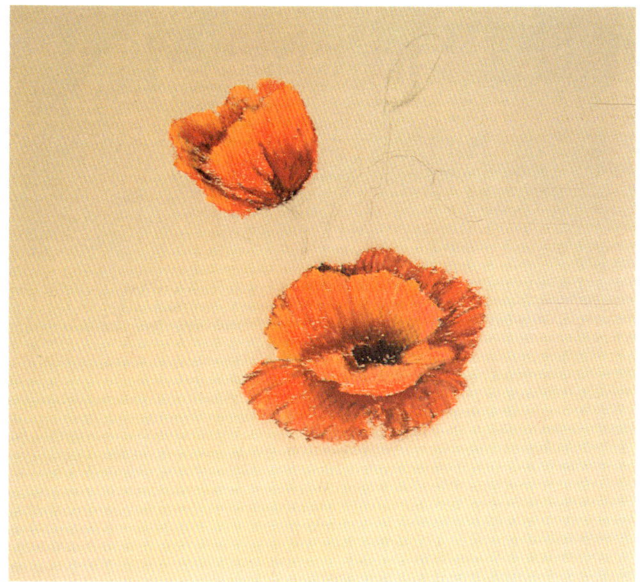

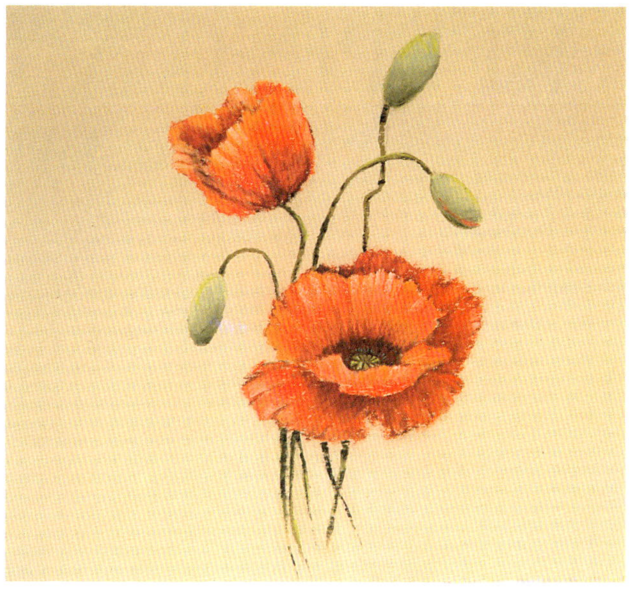

Step 3

Now look for the lights and highlights, and stroke them in lightly with soft pastels. (In this case, we use two lighter tints of orange.)

Step 4

Finally, we make adjustments in color and shape. Now is also the time for stems, buds and more highlights. These are added last so that clean, objective placement can be based on what already exists and what is needed to make the sketch better.

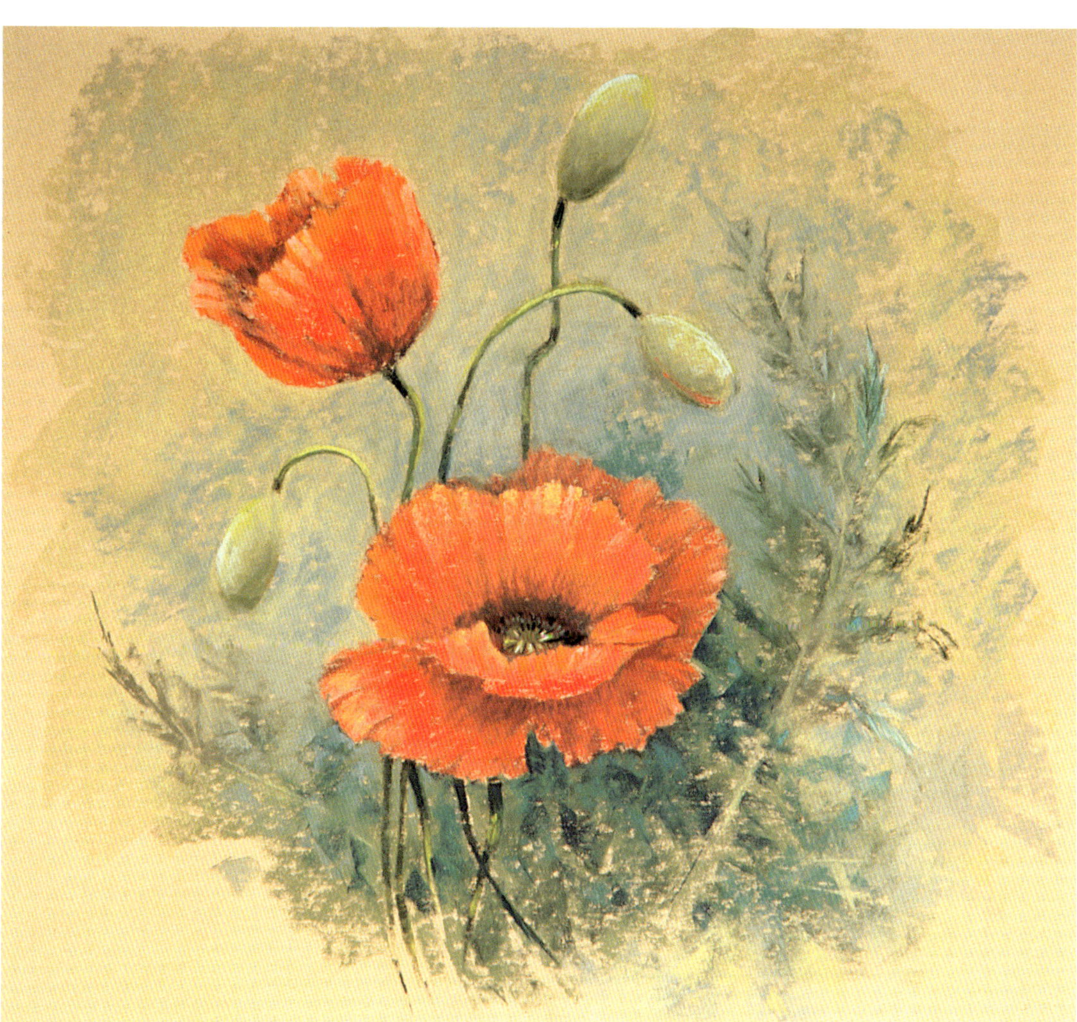

POPPY ESSENCE
Pastel on sanded
paper
13″ × 14″

Step 5

Use the background to shape the outside edges of the flowers. Side-stroke is an easy background to tuck around a sketch to transform it into a painting.

KEEPING MOUNTAINS IN THE DISTANCE

The ability to put distance into your pastels is necessary for landscape painting in all seasons, and it is very easy to do.

Whenever you wish to distance some part or parts of your pastel landscape, reduce the size where applicable, use a grayer, bluer, lighter and cooler value of color and, finally, soften or lose some of the edges. For instance, distant hills often appear purple or blue. So if the mountains in your pastel appear too close, and you want them to appear farther away, simply tone or crosshatch them with gray or blue, and then soften any hard edges and lines.

This view of the Hudson River from Garrison, New York, shows great distance between the far-off Catskill Mountains and the Highlands of the Hudson just north of West Point. Comparing and adjusting values throughout your painting will help you to achieve the illusion of distance in your work.

Distant trees and growth are soft-edged and indistinct.

No detail is necessary when portraying distant water.

Intermediate mountains show gradual changes in value.

Light value keeps this far mountain distant.

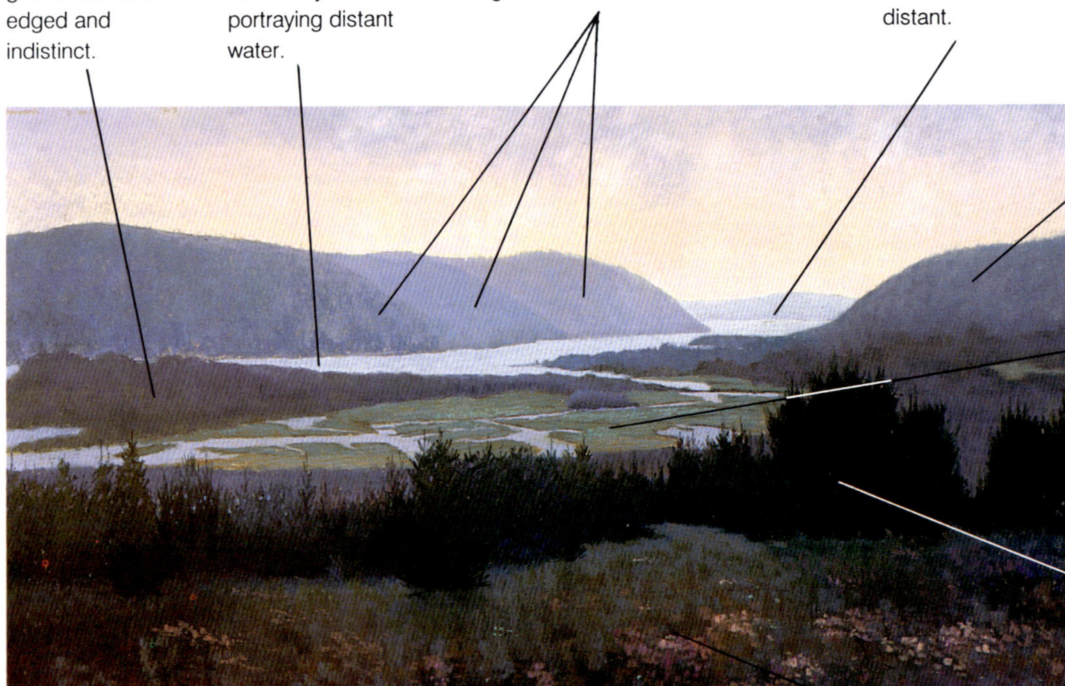

Nearest mountain is darkest in value.

Marshlands begin to green in spring as nature's cycle starts again. Still no detail was used here because of distance.

Ridge of evergreens is put in with dark value green and indigo pastel. Lots of vertical strokes are evident here.

In some landscapes, such as this one, you do not want the eye to get stuck in the foreground, or any one place, but rather to take in the totality of the scene. So even the rule about saving detail for the foreground — as well as any other rule — should be tempered by what effect is desired, and by what is right for the painting.

HUDSON HIGHLANDS, SPRINGTIME
Pastel on sanded paper
26″ × 49″
Private collection
Photo by John Kleinhans

Very little detail goes into the foreground. Even the spring flowers are merely suggested so as not to detain the eye.

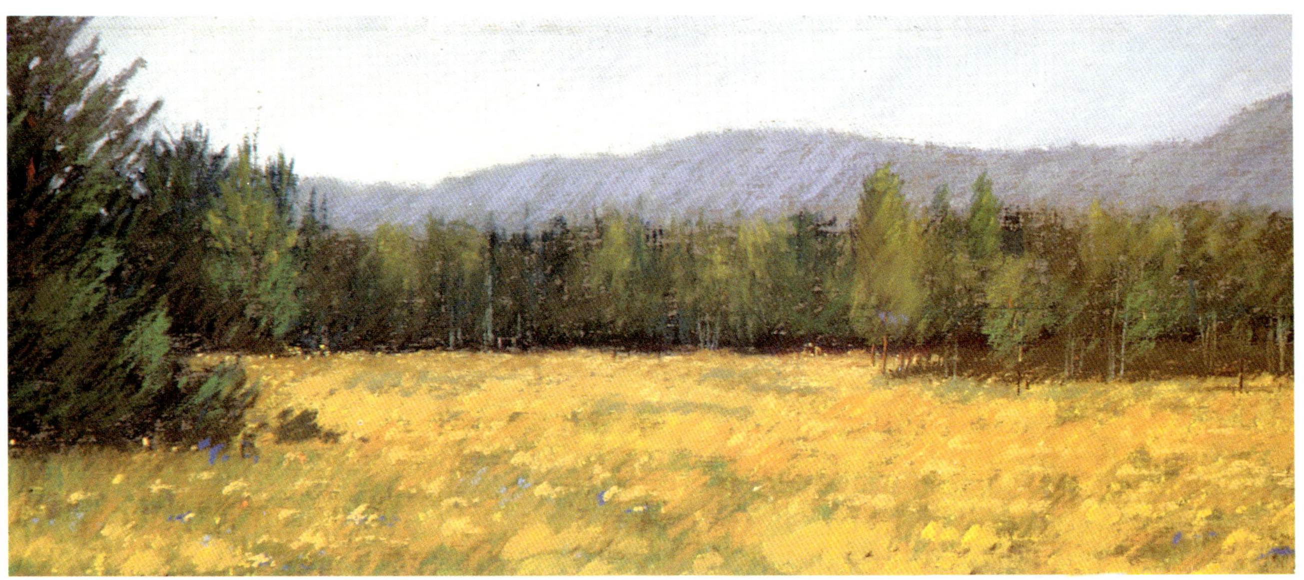

In this pastel, the mountain is nearby, and the grayish blue color effectively achieves the slight distance that is required.

THE MUSTARD FIELD, WOODSTOCK
Pastel on sanded paper
10″ × 18″
Collection of Rebecca and Paul Huebner

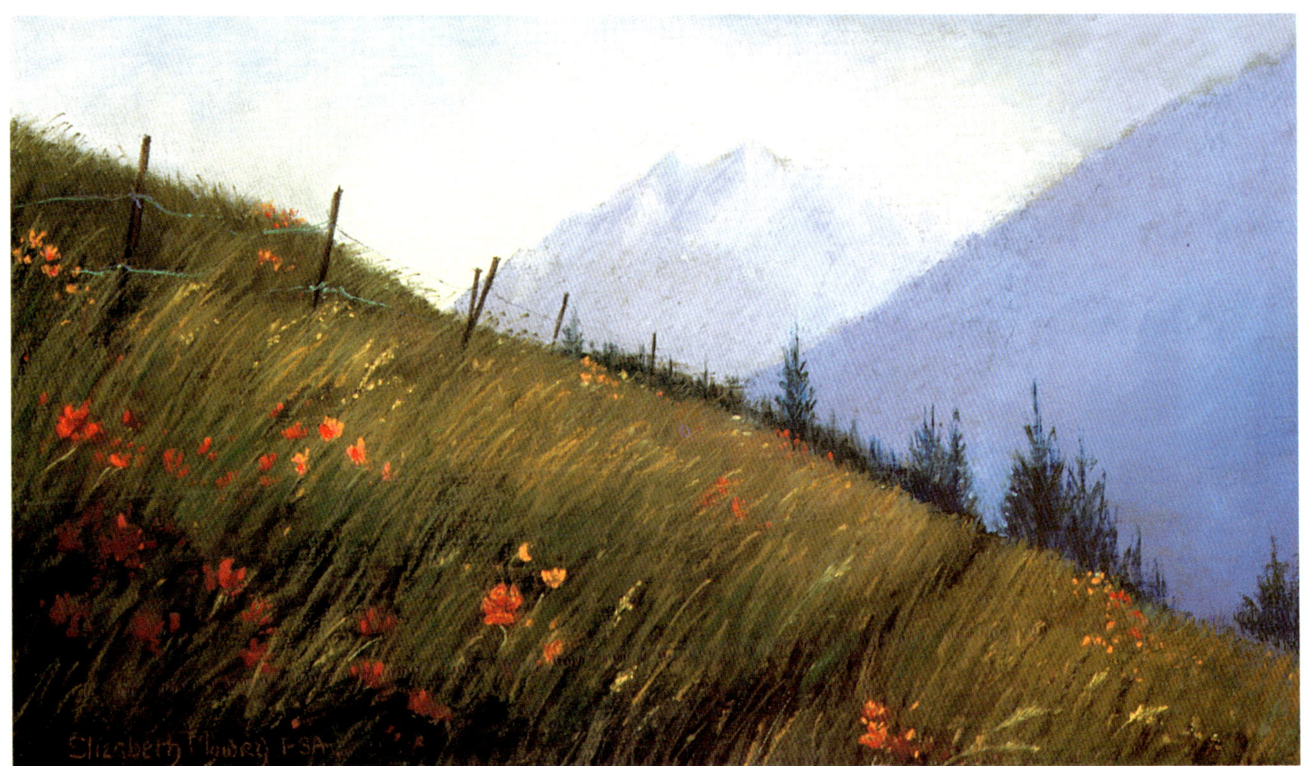

The composition of this painting clearly shows how distancing can be achieved. Detail exists only in the nearest mountain. The many miles between the nearest and the middle mountain are shown by a complete color change to blue as well as by absence of detail. Distance between the middle and the far mountain is shown by still lighter value and by some lost edges.

SWISS PASTURE
Pastel on sanded board
12″ × 20″

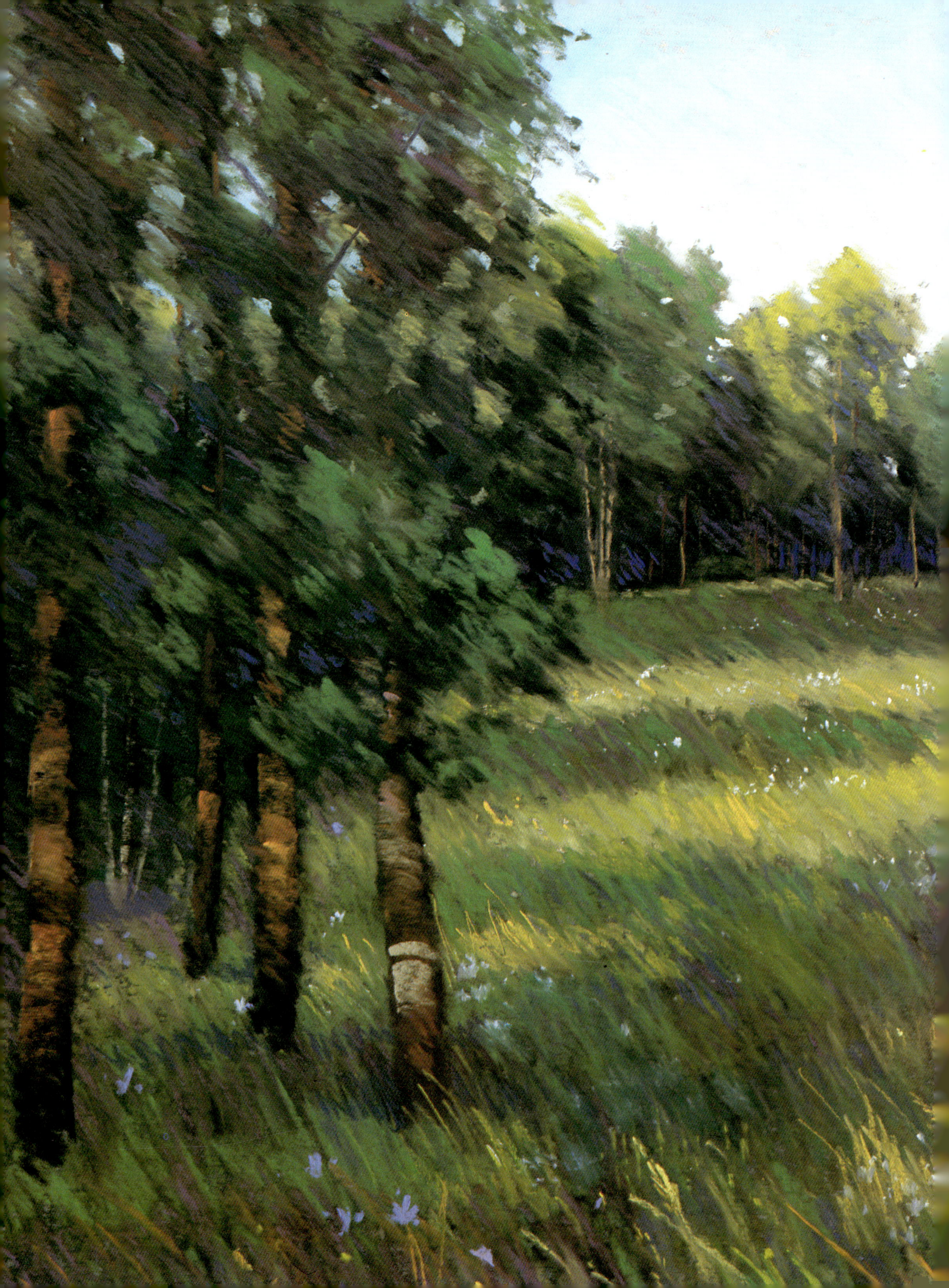

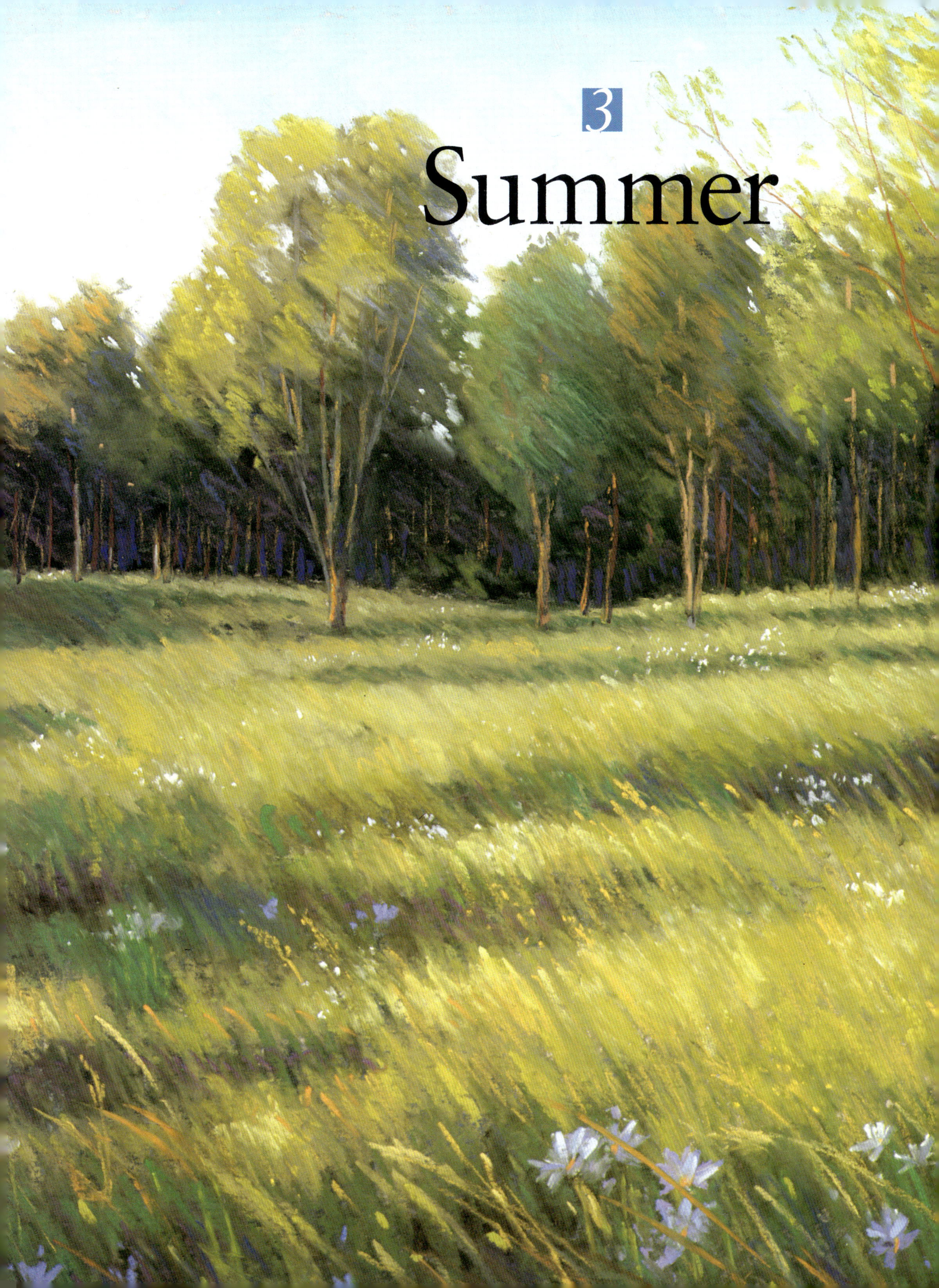
3
Summer

A RESPONSE TO SUMMER

At the height of full summer, the landscape is often quieter than in young spring or vibrant autumn. Growth reaches its apex, and wild grasses are ready to throw seed. Notice the softened edges of the meadows as the tallest flowers bend and sway. The fields offer up their gifts for the artist; black-eyed Susans begin to appear; blue wildflowers such as lupine, baby-blue bonnets and chicory repeat in foregrounds the cobalt skies. Orange lilies lend quiet elegance to lowly ditches and roadside banks, and blueberries smell sweet at the edge of the woods where animals feed in early morning and late afternoon.

Foregrounds are rich with mature color and definition, whereas backgrounds frequently recede into hazy, unfocused blueness. On hot summer mornings, you will hear crows call noisily across mown fields, where the pungent smell of seeds and hay hangs suspended in the dry air. Cows huddle together in the shade, tails switching. Near the garden, baskets of ripened tomatoes, rich in their redness, wait to be canned, and the scent of herbs is unmistakable. Even when no breeze moves the leaves on the trees, the faint rumble of distant thunder can often be heard. Later in the day, you can watch the shadows stretch and linger over the landscape contours and then make patterns on fences and tree trunks before crossing and re-crossing the curving roads. By being mindful of the changes each summer day presents, and including them in your compositions, you use your keen perception as a vehicle for personal expression.

The grace that enriches all maturity is evident now in summer. Grasses bend low. Flower stems, once straight and young, yield under summer showers, while rounded cumulus clouds float overhead and giant sunflowers bow under a brilliant sun. The boughs of fruit trees arch to the ground with the weight of maturing fruit. Everywhere, stiffness gives way to curve. You can use these graceful lines in your pastel paintings and drawings to design compositions of superb form. Each season has its own glory. Even now, as we paint the seed pods that have replaced springtime's buds, we know that they are tiny assurances of nature's continuance.

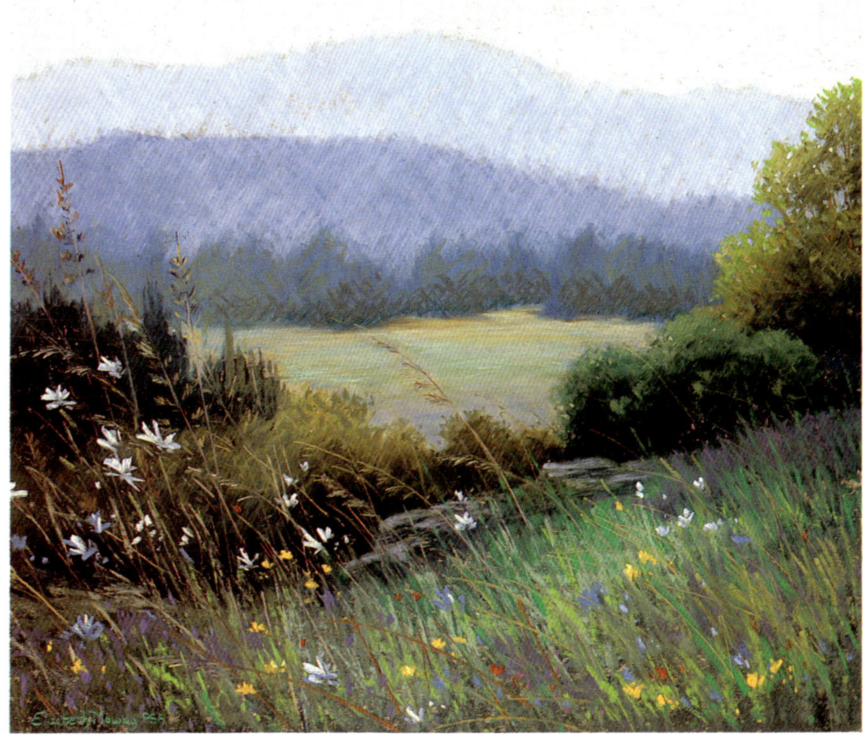

PICNIC PLACE
Pastel on sanded board
14″ × 16″
Private collection

To achieve the lightly hazed background, I introduced blue pastel into everything beyond the near trees. A few summer wildflowers mingle with tall grasses to establish a strong sense of foreground.

HINTS FOR BETTER SUMMER PAINTINGS

In summer, foliage consists of millions of leaves that move and catch the light, making it difficult to sort out the large, massed shapes of trees and shrubs. But painting the leaves will not result in a painted tree. First, study the trees you intend to paint until you can find some of those large foliage groups. Squinting may help to eliminate smaller distracting shapes and details. Second, once you have put down the large groups of foliage in your tree with a middle to dark value, be careful not to lose them again by breaking them up with too many separated highlights.

VALUES

A keen working knowledge of values is essential to painting successful trees, shrubs or anything else. Particularly as pastelists having hundreds of lush colors at our fingertips, we might remind ourselves that in spite of using many sticks of pastel during the course of a painting, an adequate range of values may still be lacking.

I once overheard an artist say, "I don't concern myself about value. If I have the color correct, the value will be correct." Although this holds true if your perception of color is faultless, and only if you are slavishly trying to copy nature, I believe that value relationships are paramount in my approach to painting. I've become more concerned with personal interpretation, creating a mood and using color as a means of expression.

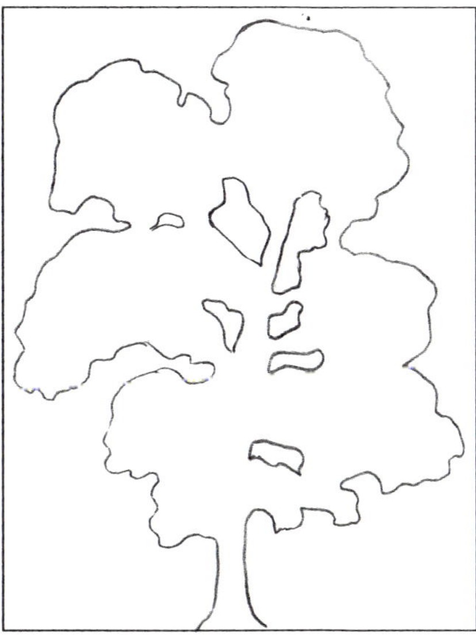

This outline of a catalpa tree helps me to find large foliage groups.

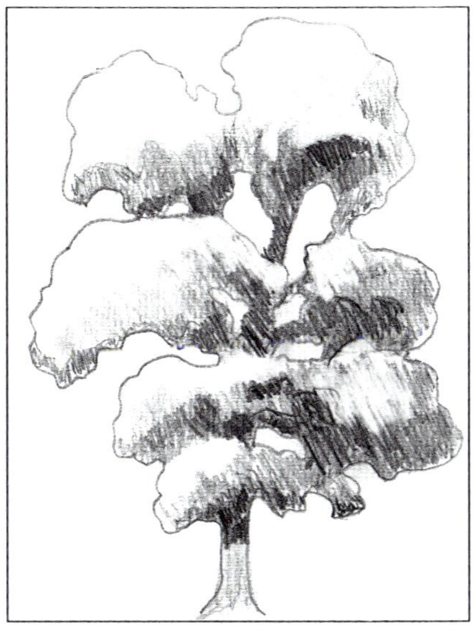

Close observation and some modeling makes major shapes even clearer.

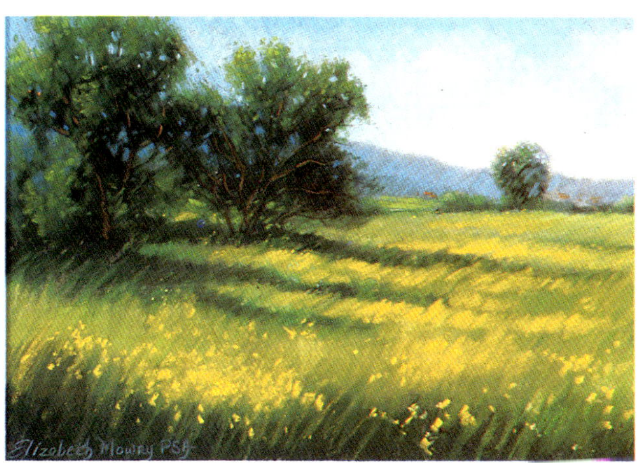

BUTTERCUP FIELD
Pastel on Sennelier La Carte
8″ × 11″

In this small painting on green pastel surface, my subject is simple and I have not used many colors, but the value range is wide enough to make the painting work. At right, a black-and-white photograph of Buttercup Field *clearly shows the range of values.*

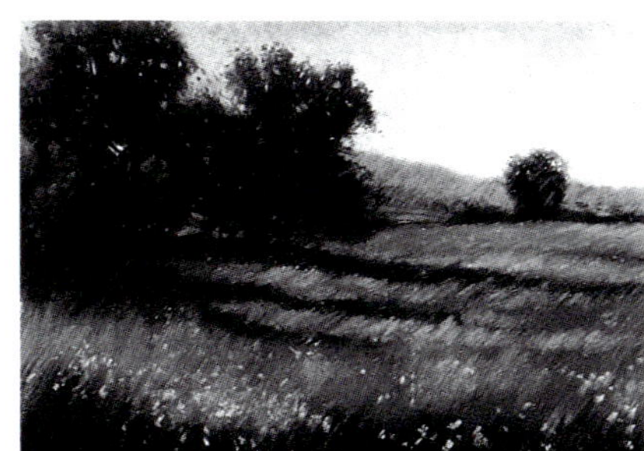

Values, simply put, are the lights and darks in your subject matter or in your painting. Relate them to one another. To do this, think not only whether an object appears light or dark, but how light or how dark compared with other elements in the scene. Ask yourself, "How dark are the shadows in the tree compared with the darkest part of the sky?" or "How light are the highlights on the tree compared with the lightest part of the water?" There are infinite degrees of light and dark. Trying to see in black and white makes it easier to see value. At first, try to find just three values: light, medium and dark. When you can successfully do that, work with five values, and if necessary, add more later. Until you see values in nature, you cannot expect to use them effectively in your pastels.

THE VALUE SCALE

If you feel that your understanding of values is scanty, make yourself a nine-value scale like the one pictured at top. First, draw nine squares vertically. Put white or near-white into square 9 at the top, and put black or near black into square 1. Then put a medium gray into the middle square, number 5. Proceed as follows: Number 3 should be a shade midway between numbers 1 and 5. Number 7 should be a tint midway between 5 and 9. Fill the remaining squares 2, 4, 6 and 8 so that there is an even, gradual progression from 9 to 1. You may have to mix grays to get the gradation, depending upon the number of pastels you have. Then, if you choose, you can fix this scale and tape it between two strips of hard, clear plastic, or laminate it, and keep it as a handy reminder with your pastels.

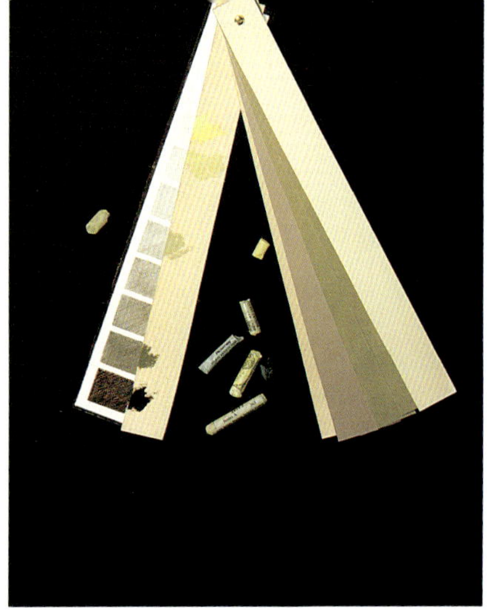

Here, some trial patches of green pastel are matched up to high, medium and low gray-scale values to ensure sufficient contrast between sunlit areas and shadow areas in tree foliage. To do this, stroke a pastel onto a sample strip of pastel paper that is the same color as the surface you're using in your painting. Place the strip next to the gray scale. If the pastel patch blends into the gray on the scale, you have found the value of that color.

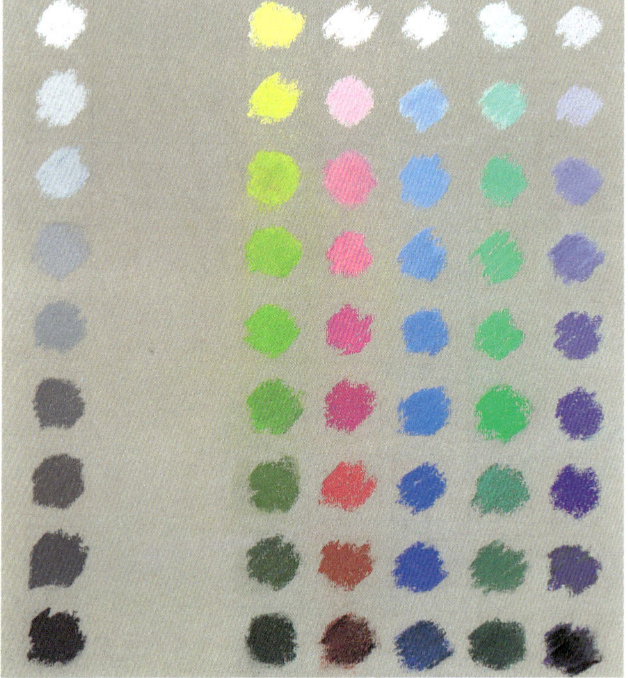

Some summer colors matched up to the value scale make us aware of the wide range of value within each color.

MATCH COLORS TO VALUES

All colors have the same values as your simplified value scale, and many more. When you put a color next to a gray on your scale and squint at it, it will blend with the gray if it is the same value.

Using the value scale is easy. To return to the problematic tree foliage discussed earlier, if you have the medium-green value foliage groups stroked in on your painted tree, you may want to match up another green to a darker value on your scale and use it for the deep, shadowy recesses in the tree. Next, you could match up more greens to a lighter value for the highlighted areas. Later, when you become accustomed to seeing colors as values in your subject matter, you can skip this entire exercise. Seeing and using value relationships, once understood, becomes second nature. Remember, first get a clear idea of the values you are looking at, then enjoy using any palette you wish.

THE SUMMER PALETTE

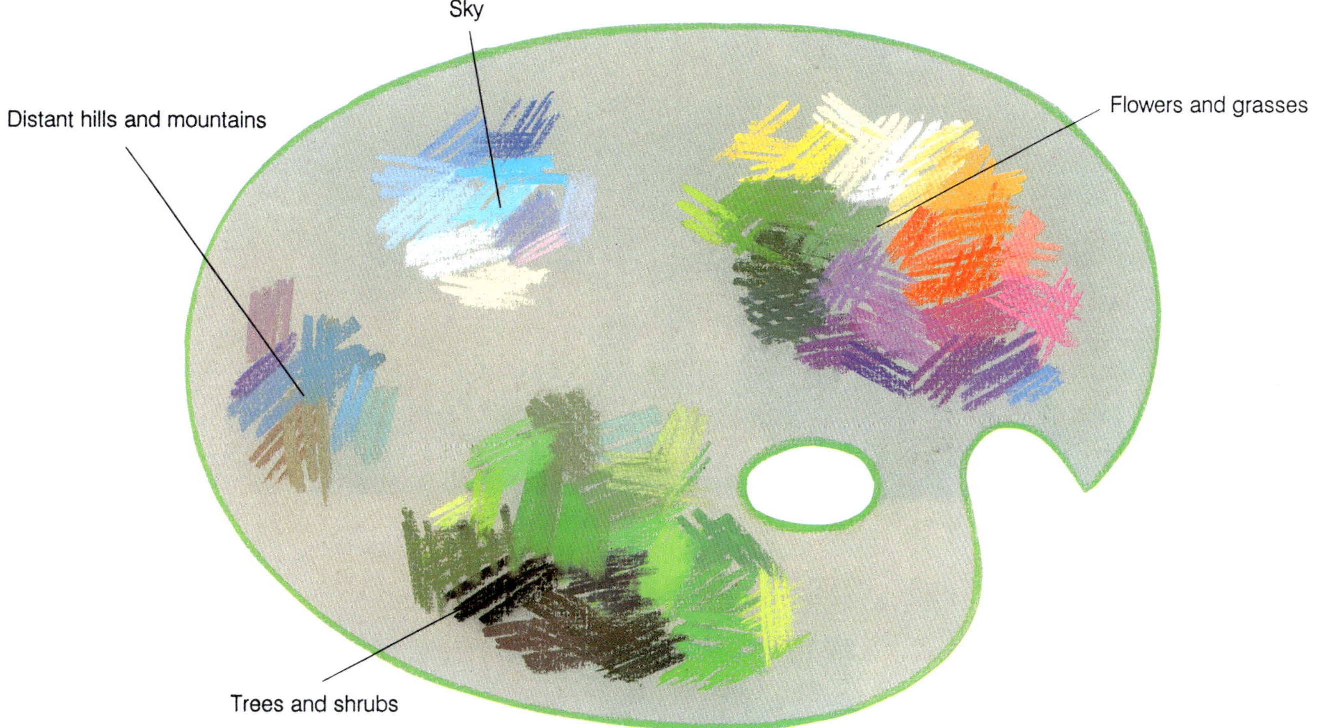

At the height of summer, the hills of the western part of the country have long been transformed to straw-colored contours that show off the dark green sprawling oaks. Deserts and canyons make their own kaleidoscopic magic under the bluest of skies. In the northeast where I live, however, after the blossoms disappear from the trees and the shrubs, and just as summer workshops begin and pastelists show up with hundreds of luscious new colors in tow, green is everywhere, dominating the landscape.

MAKING GREENS WORK FOR YOU

When variation in color hue decreases, it is a good time to explore other properties of color such as value, temperature and chroma. By juxtaposing cool and warm greens or high- and low-value greens, or intense and dull greens, you can bring shapes back into your paintings where summer's dense foliage and growth have confused them.

It also makes sense when you are painting summer landscapes outdoors to include lots of different greens in your supplies. Having the supplies you need is essential. Single sticks of pastel are readily available from many suppliers. When adding greens to those you already have, go for variety in value first, because having an adequate range will multiply the effects you can achieve in your paintings.

Whenever you are attracted by subject matter that you, nonetheless, retreat from (for example, the greenness of a summer landscape), it is frequently because you are reluctant to put your full attention on it. When you do begin to sort out the complications of greenness, your explorations will catapult you over the obstacle. To start, try adding some purple or indigo crosshatching into the deepest green areas. Within lighter green masses, crosshatch some blue or ochre, or even sienna.

After you become comfortable using other colors within your greens, you will even begin to see minute traces of those colors when you stare at the green landscape. Overstate those traces of color just enough to make your painting more interesting but still believable so that the viewer can relate to it. Sometimes you may choose to overdo for special effect. Be clearly aware of your intentions as you move from reality into fantasy. Being right at the edge is an exciting place to be.

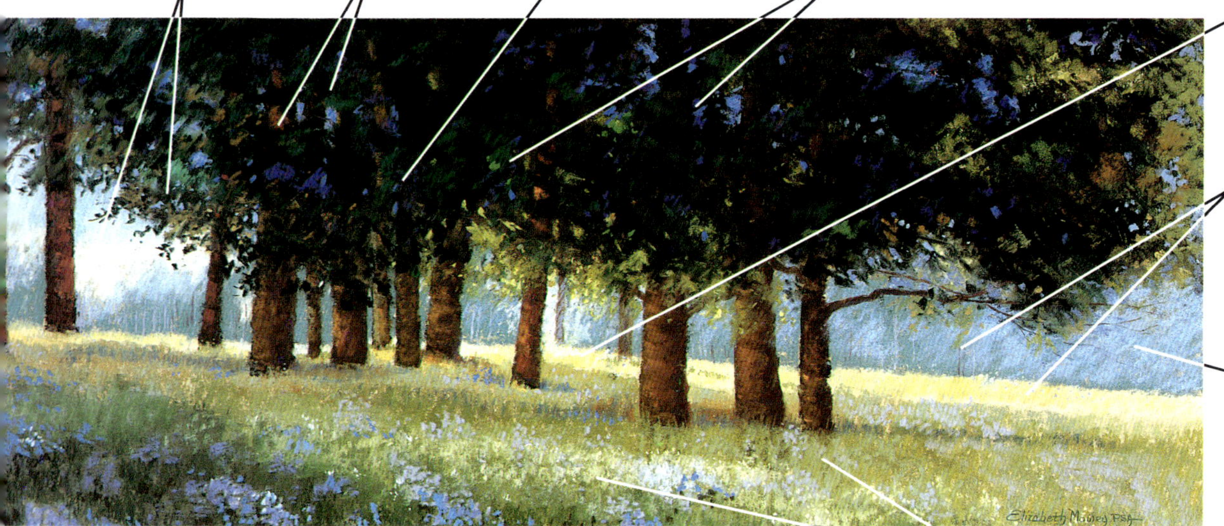

A green landscape can become poetic with the creative introduction of other colors within the greens.

LENOX AFTERNOON
Pastel on sanded board
14″ × 32″

Minimized detail in the foreground does not detain the eye.

EXPRESSING THE WARMTH OF SUMMER

Summer is synonymous with *warm*. When you highlight grasses and flowers and rocks, reach for sun-dried colors that remind you of heat and dryness. Open up to input from all your senses! Allow your feelings and experiences to be the special ingredient for conveying personal expression. Since this is difficult to explain, I will share a personal example:

When I painted the strawberries at right I did not paint without rec-ollecting images of picking them as a child . . . the squashed berries, the stained pockets, the taste of jam spread thick on a slice of home-made bread. I did not paint without recalling the joy of discovering the first glimpse of red peek out from beneath the familiar trio of leaves at the beginning of each summer. When we are moved by even the simplest of life experiences, chances are greater that we will move others with our work.

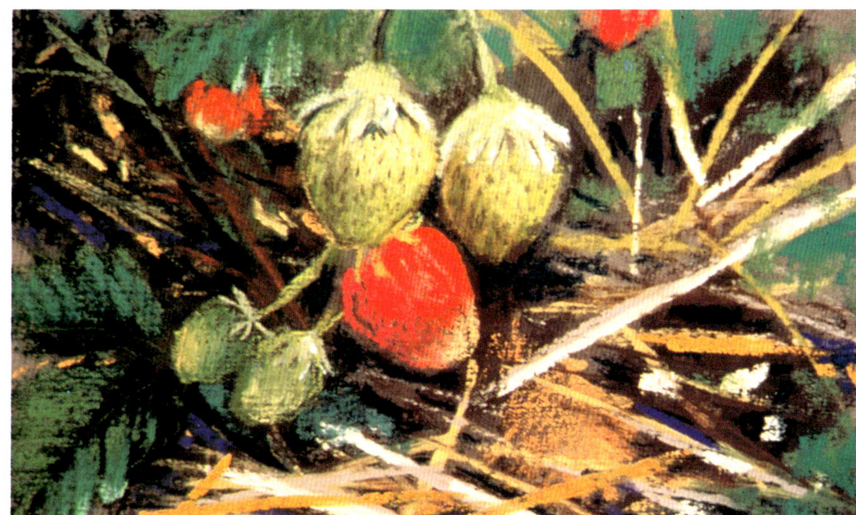

STRAWBERRIES
Pastel on sanded paper
5″ × 7½″

The scent of sun-warmed berries mingles with the pungent smell of the straw that is put down to keep them from touching the dirt. All of the senses play a role in your choice of subject matter and the outcome of your paintings. This small study is successful because there are lots of contrasts: light and dark values, rounded and angular shapes, warm and cool colors, hard and soft edges, and color complements (red and green).

PAINTING WATER IN PASTEL

During the long, warm summer days when much of our time is spent outdoors, the associations we have with water make it an attractive subject. So it follows that the places we like to be, such as near ponds and streams, lakes and rivers, will find their way into our pastel paintings.

Heightened perception is the key to acquiring skill in painting water in pastel. The portrayal of water involves many considerations such as whether the water is near or distant, moving or still; the effect of light on the water; and the influence of weather and atmosphere. Added to that, we must determine where the water

is getting its color from; why reflections are sometimes mirror-like and, moments later, broken lines of color; and how to simplify so that we can capture the essence of the water's movement without tediously attempting to paint the entire reality. Using a camera to strengthen your observation of water can be a useful aid, but you will not want to use photographs as a substitute for the opportunity to paint water directly at the scene.

While you develop your skills at painting water, you can use your pastels as either a sketching medium or a painting medium, depending on your preference and intent.

When you use pastels for sketching water, try a quality pastel paper, such as the beautifully toned Ingres by Daler-Rowney. Whereas surfaces with deep tooth or grit invite thick layers of pastel, papers, especially toned or colored papers, encourage you to sketch. Since you will be leaving much of the paper exposed when you sketch, you will have more of a tendency to go immediately to the important part of the subject matter. With backgrounds that are minimal, the pastel can be kept back from the edges of the paper, and focus will remain intact. Sometimes you will use your sketch as a personal resource for future paintings, but whether you

EDGE OF THE STREAM
Pastel on Daler-Rowney Ingres paper
9″ × 12″

When sketching with pastels, you can focus directly on the center of interest without the distraction of trying to get a background to work.

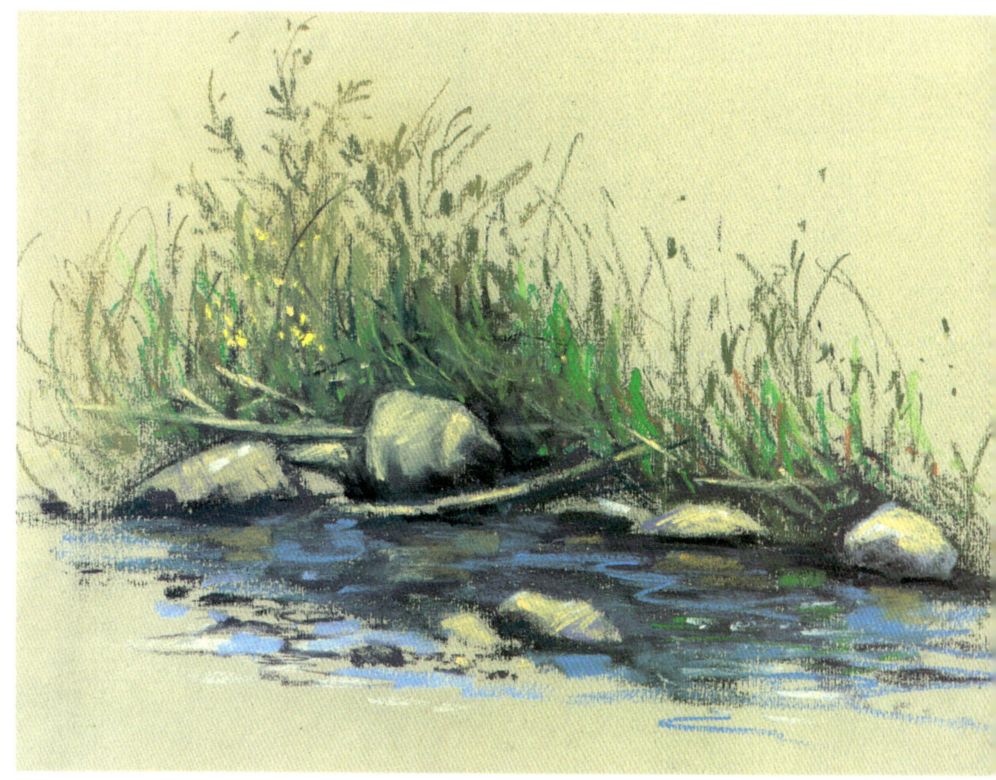

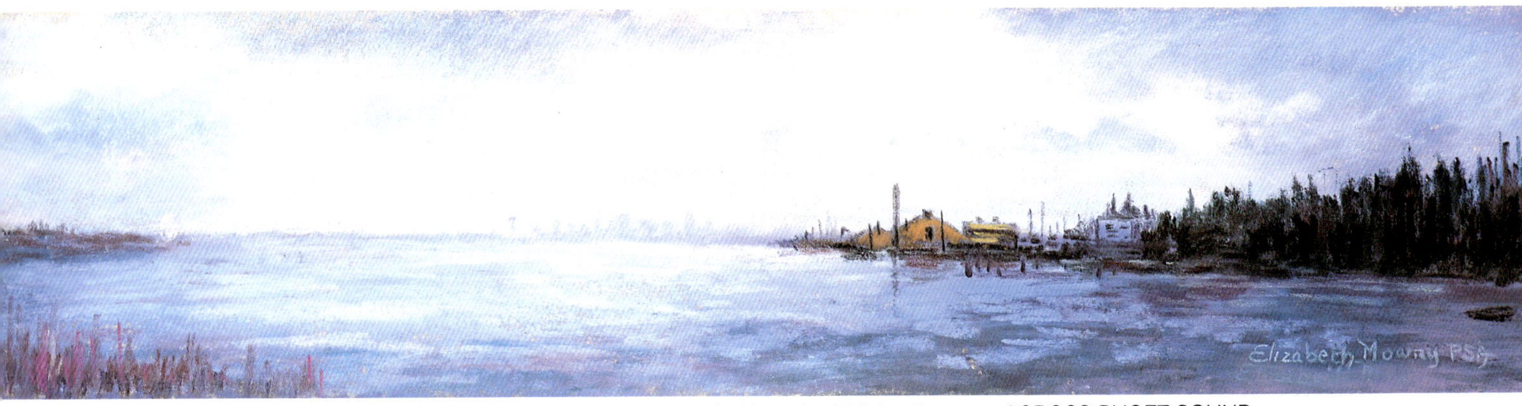

Here, several layers of pastel cover the entire surface of a sanded board, which has been cut to size with this painting in mind. Although the painting process was spontaneous, the idea for it was well-conceived beforehand.

ACROSS PUGET SOUND
Pastel on sanded board
3½" × 15"

do or not, you can get a lot of information down quickly in a sketch.

When you completely cover the surface of the ground you work on, you are painting with your pastels. Even though pastel is very direct, you will become involved in building up layers of pastel on the textured or abrasive surface. It is helpful when painting with pastel to have a clear idea of the scope of your work and of how to go about attaining the effects you want.

SHALLOW WATER

In summer, streams become shallow, leaving islands of flat rock and interesting little water pools. The dry conditions provide an opportunity to reach the previously inaccessible, far banks of streams, whose swollen waters raged assertively over the same areas in spring. We can cross and recross the stream as we decide on the views we wish to sketch and paint.

You will find that foreground water is usually more transparent as you look down into it. For example, where water is relatively shallow and clear, you will see the warm color and shapes of the stones and pebbles on the bottom.

When you paint shallow, foreground water, put in the earth and rock colors first. Then lightly pull a blue pastel pencil over the rocks and pebbles to blur some of the shapes directly below you. As the water recedes into the distance, it will pick up more light from the sky on its surface.

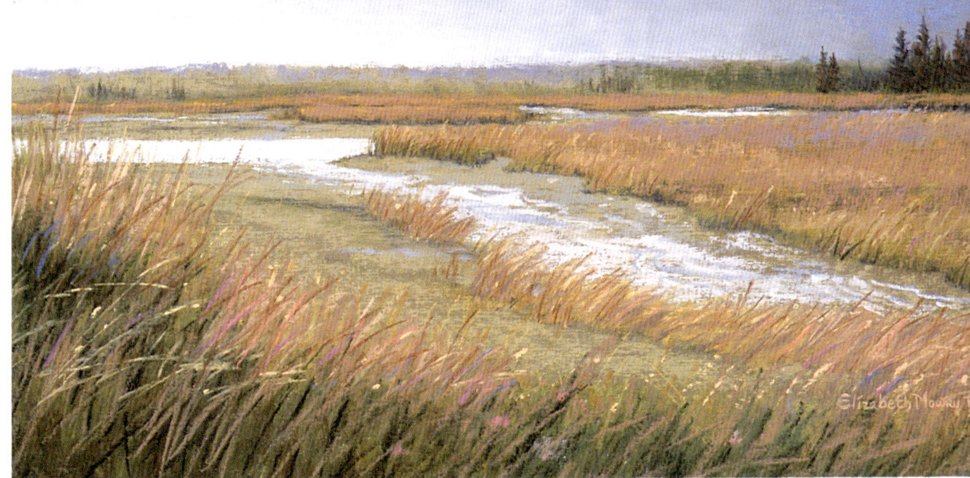

See how the water takes on the reflected light from the sky. As the water gets closer to the foreground, some directional strokes give it movement.

MARSHLANDS, MAINE
Pastel on sanded paper
8" × 18"

In that case, you will paint the streambed first and then pull a blue or gray pastel pencil near in value over it to lightly indicate the presence of the water over the stones. If you prefer to use soft pastels instead of the pencil to do this, you may want to use a tortillion to remove some of the texture of the stroke in order to maintain the sense of transparency.

As the water recedes into the distance, the angle at which you view it changes, and more and more of the reflected light from the sky will be seen on the water's surface. In the far distance, the reflected light strokes in your painting will eventually close up and blend. (See *View of the Seine* and *Sailing on the Hudson* on pages 64 and 67.)

When you consider the color of water in your painting, remember that it reflects the sky. Generally, you can create a sense of unity in your painting when you paint water a slightly deeper tone of the sky color.

You will also find that you can use directional strokes with a sky-related pastel color to give movement to your water.

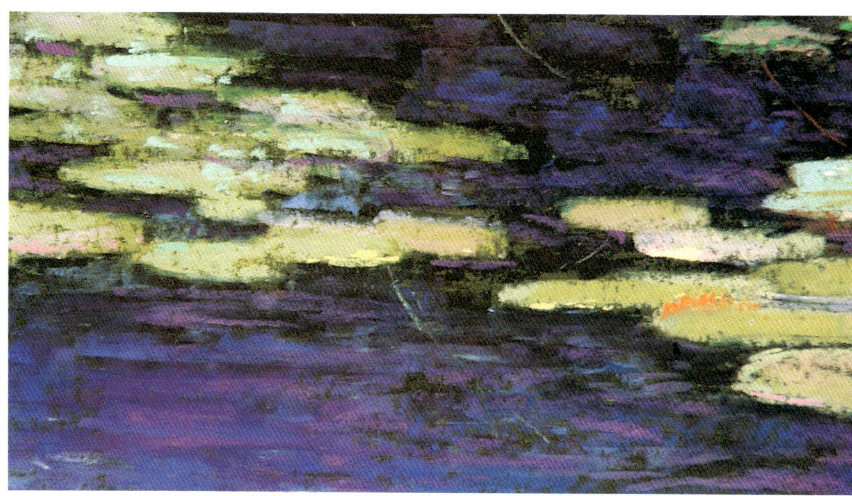

Use similar values of different colors, such as purples, blues and greens, to lay in foreground water.

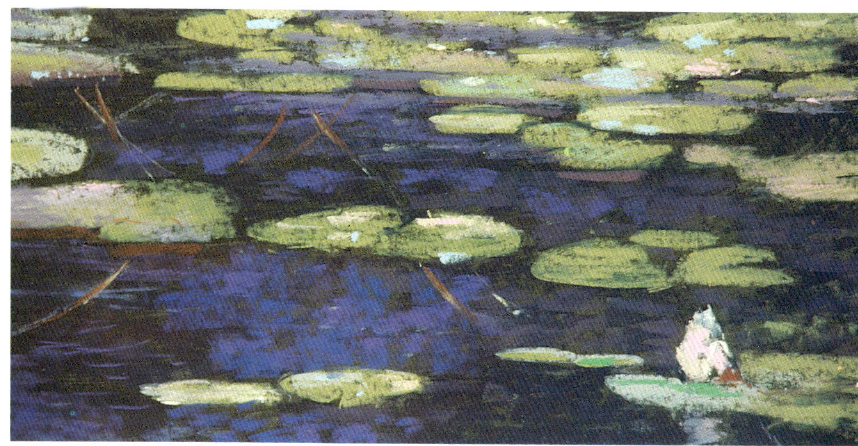

Using soft pastels gives water depth and liquidity because they fill the tooth of the paper and then visually blend together. Water that appears black in reality can be painted with dark green, purple or indigo pastel.

DEEPER WATER

Isolated ponds and lakes are a favorite summer subject for painting. Still, except for insect ripples on their surface, and silent except for the occasional single bass note of an unseen frog, they seem to typify the laziness of summer . . . nature's lag between the blossom and the fruit . . . the lull before the energy of harvest. Paired with haze-wrapped backgrounds, water speaks to us of summer.

Rather than laying in color with a single tone when you paint water in the near foreground of your painting, use a few different colors of the same, or close to the same, value. Diminish the size of your stroke with distance. When you apply several colors next to one another in broken strokes that visually blend together, the water you paint will be much more interesting. Using this technique in water foregrounds invites the viewer in for a closer look. A word of caution, though, about overdoing it: Whenever the technique becomes more important than the subject as a whole, you have probably crossed over into the "overdone" category, in which case your water will look contrived. (This sometimes happens when students first learn that horizontal lines of a different value across water can be used to indicate the calm of the water's surface. Overdone, this very technique has the reverse effect because too many horizontal lines are distracting, and they destroy a sense of quiet in the water.)

While some of these instructions seem to be very calculated, painting water does not have to be a dreaded technical feat. The key is to gradually and patiently develop your perception so that you know what you are looking for: shapes, movement and colors as values. Although painting water is challenging, once you learn to sort through what you see, and use only what is most important, it can become quite easy.

REFLECTIONS

Reflections indicate the quality of the surface of the water. Perfectly still water will have a mirror-like quality. Rippling water causes reflections to break up into wavy patterns. Reflections in choppy water often bear no resemblance to the objects being reflected at all but capture the viewer's attention with their intricately colored designs. When your intent is to use those designs in your paintings, you may need the aid of a photograph to freeze the patterns for you.

Much of how you approach such painting situations depends upon what you want to emphasize in each of your paintings of water. At times, you may want to compose your painting so that the reflections in the water are reflecting landscape that is not in your painting. In this way, you use the reflections to tell the story about what is surrounding the water.

It is easy to get caught up in the painting of reflections to the point that they overpower your painting. Being aware of this beforehand will help you to keep reflections in the water of your paintings harmonious with the painting as a whole. You do this by keeping the reflections less sharp and less bright than the reality. Always work toward unity in your paintings.

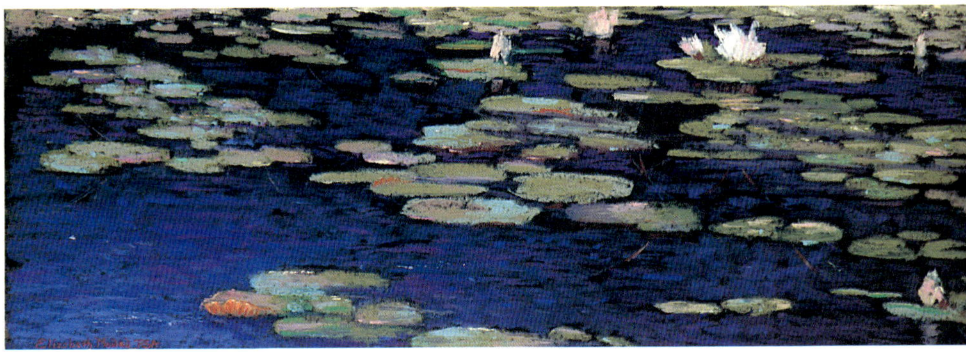

WATER LILIES, PART I
Pastel on sanded board
12″ × 36″

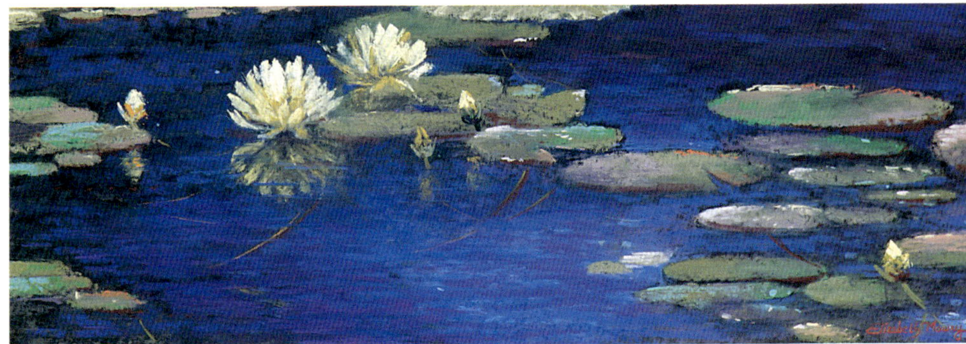

WATER LILIES, PART II
Pastel on sanded board
12″ × 36″

In the above pair of water lily paintings, I used purple, green and blue soft pastels to paint the water. Keeping each color close in value to the one next to it eliminates the need to blend.

DARK WATER

You will notice that in summer, water frequently appears to be black, in which case it can be painted a dark-value green or indigo. Sometimes you will see lighter, warm, yellow-green vegetation stretch finger-like across the dark water, punctuated only by varieties of the wild waterlily. Keep the vegetation in your painting flat in the background and middle ground, painting waterlily pads, for example, rounder only as they come nearer. If you look closely, you will see traces of sienna, orange and bright blue-green within the floating green masses. Take advantage of the opportunity to play up the striking contrast between the dark water and the warm, light-colored vegetation by overstating the colors a bit.

PAINTING REFLECTIONS ON WATER

In this demonstration, I wanted to portray the impression of the gentle Seine as it flows through the French countryside. I used a horizontal format that allowed the river to "flow" across my painting as well. The small figure sets the scale.

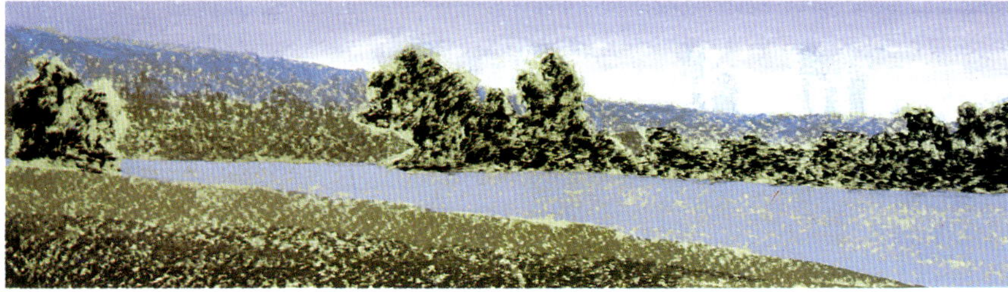

Step 1 The First Layer of Color
The first layer of color can be applied quickly with broad side-strokes, using all soft pastels. The key to flexibility is to apply the pastel lightly. In this step, the composition is blocked in with approximate color values in the large shapes. Don't be in a hurry to fill in the ground at this point.

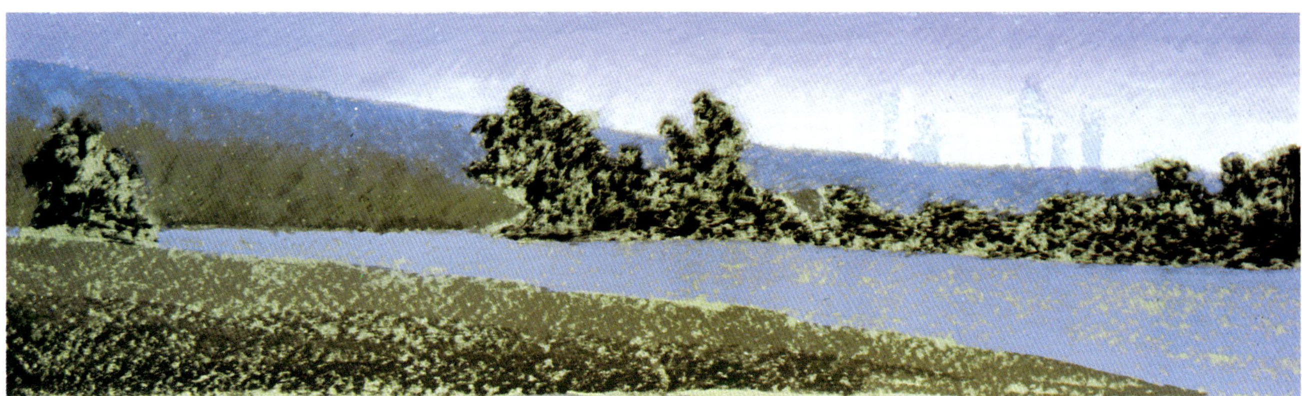

Step 2 Setting the Mood With the Background
More pastel goes into the sky area, pulling one color into another and closing the stroke. I then applied additional pastel to the distant hill and harmonized it with the sky using diagonal strokes of a blue pastel pencil. I frequently use the sky and distant hills to set the mood for my landscapes.

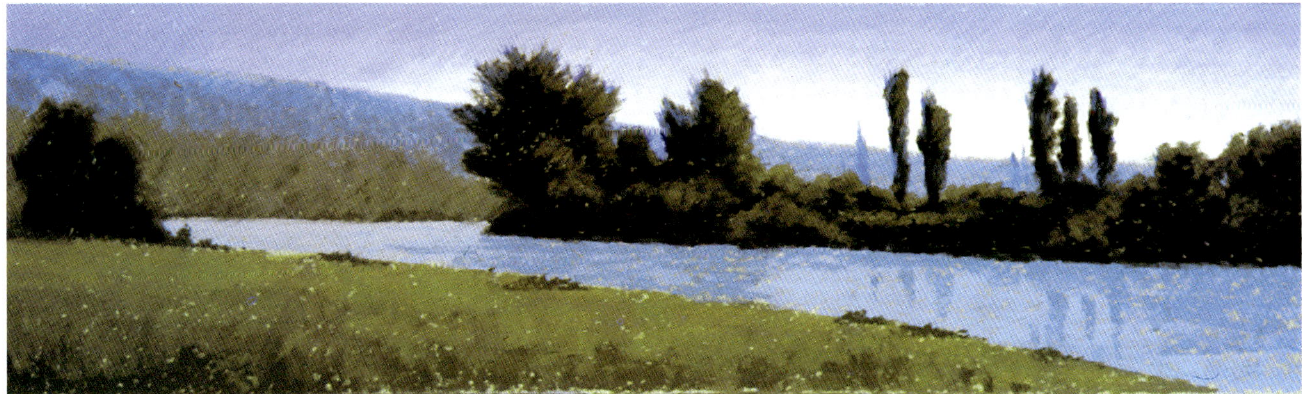

Step 3 Refining All Foreground and Middle Ground Areas
I shaped the trees with lights and darks, using blue at the edges where they meet the sky. Next, I liquefied the water with horizontal strokes of several soft blue pastels. I warmed the foreground with ochre and warm green, and inserted sky holes in the trees sparingly.

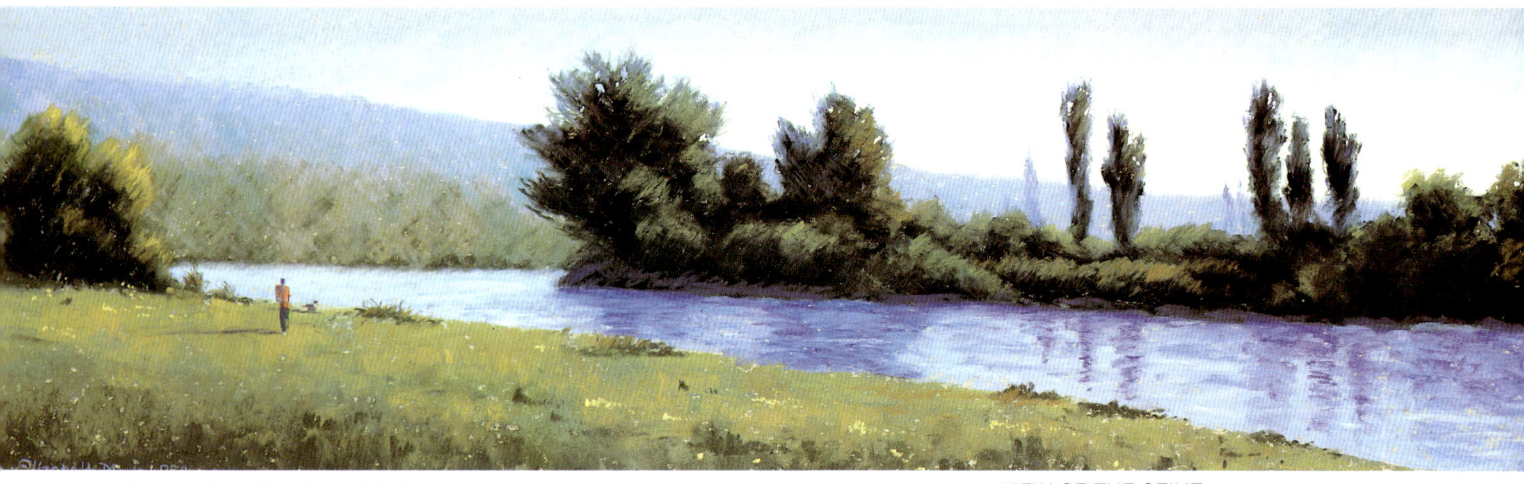

Step 4 Final Details and Adjustments
To finish, I intensified the reflections in the water with purples; drew in the figure and the dog with pastel pencils; and detailed the grasses and brush at the edge of the water. After a more critical look several weeks later, I made small adjustments, softening some edges and unifying color.

VIEW OF THE SEINE
Pastel on sanded board
13″ × 31″
Collection of Frank E. Davis, Jr.

Near mountain takes on rich, blue color because of the density of the coniferous trees that grow there.

Evergreens lose detail as they recede.

Inactive sky treatment does not compete with snow patterns on the mountain.

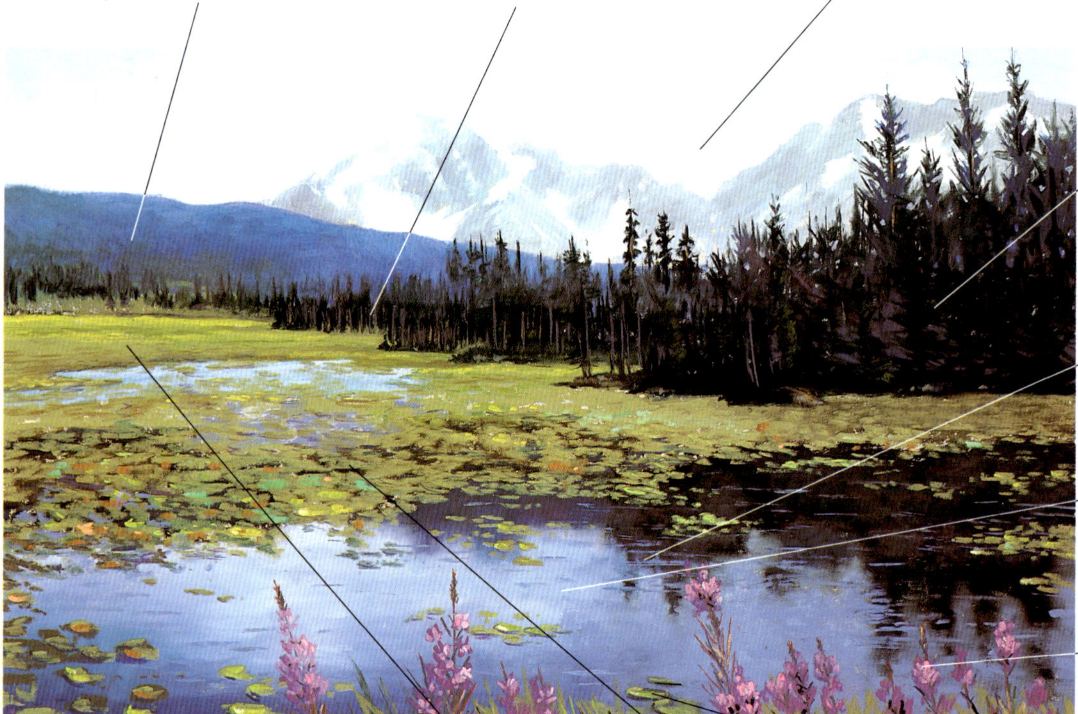

Low value of the dark evergreens provides contrast and balance for the light sky and vegetation.

A few horizontal strokes through the reflections indicate water.

The water is painted a deeper tone of the sky color.

Magenta fireweed in the foreground complements the yellow-green water vegetation.

QUIET HARMONY
Pastel on sanded board
14″ × 22″
Collection of Jennifer Marie Novak

This Alaskan scene shows some of the summer vegetation that covers many lakes and ponds. The vegetation is painted with horizontal, short strokes.

Distant water vegetation is painted with closed strokes.

Middle ground vegetation begins to open up but is still flat.

Foreground vegetation shapes are rounder because of the angle of perspective.

ADDING DESIGN INTEREST WITH WATER VEGETATION

Clumps of grasses at the water's edge can send abstract designs across the water. Cattails, as they stretch skyward, can provide a break in a long, horizontal edge of a pond because they grow inside and away from the water's edge. Without getting overly complex in the scope of your painting, you can use some of these seasonal components to design enduring summer images with your pastels.

The lily pond in this demonstration is one of my favorite places. The idea of doing a painting of it had been simmering in my mind for a long time. Then one fair summer day, I hiked up to the scene and did just that, leaving only the refinements of the final step for the studio.

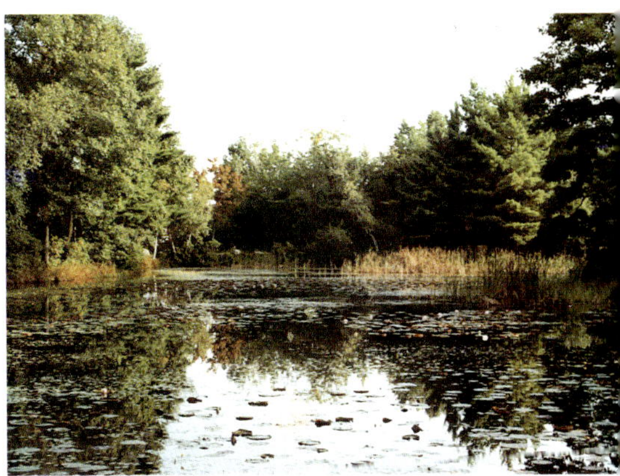

This is a photograph of the view of the Mohonk Reservoir that I painted.

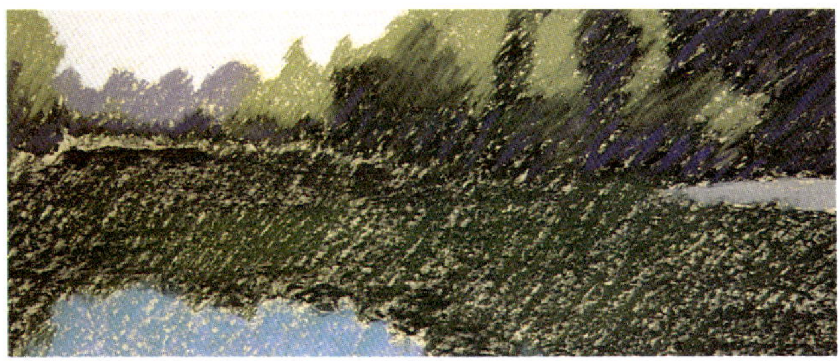

Step 1 The Large Shapes
On sanded paper taped to a board, I put down a first layer of purples, greens and blues, quickly blocking in the large shapes. I know that I will want more color in the sky and the water than reality provides.

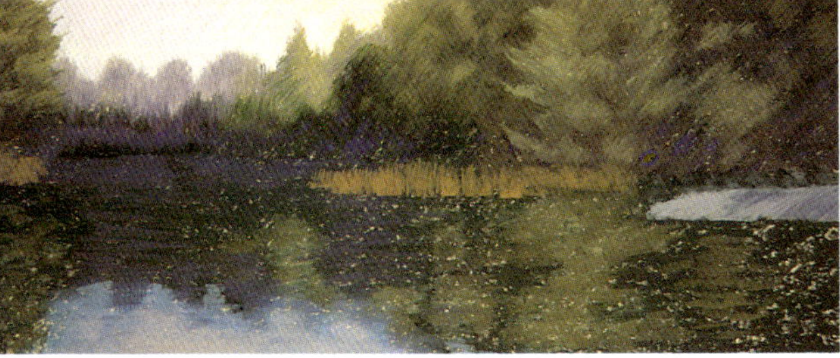

Step 2 Using Different Strokes
I put more pastel in the sky and shape the background trees with additional purples and greens. Keeping my surface flat, I begin to paint the water with more soft pastel in horizontal closed and open strokes using deep greens, cool blues and purples.

For a blended stroke in the sky, I pull one color into another.

Crosshatching in the trees is done with gray-blue and purple.

Vertical strokes shape the background trees.

Cattails are side stroked in with a ''place-and-lift'' upward movement of a squared Grumbacher pastel.

The water is put in with horizontal side strokes.

Detail *This enlargement of the upper-left portion of* Mohonk Reservoir *shows many different strokes at this stage in the painting.*

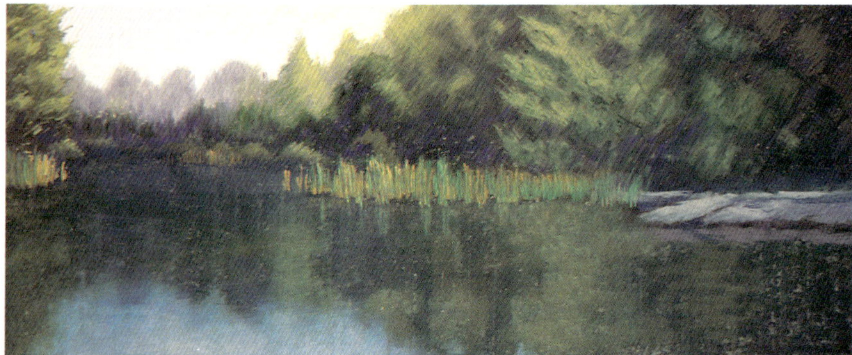

Step 3 Bringing in the Sun and the Quiet
Here, I put sunlight on the trees, bushes, cattails and rocks with lighter value pastels. I quieted the water by lightly pulling a dry polyfoam brush vertically through the water. You can also use a tortillion to achieve this effect.

Step 4 Working Toward Unity
I begin the water lily pattern across the surface of the water, relying more on my sense of what is needed than on reality. I put on some tree trunks and adjust some shapes and values, working toward a harmonious unity.

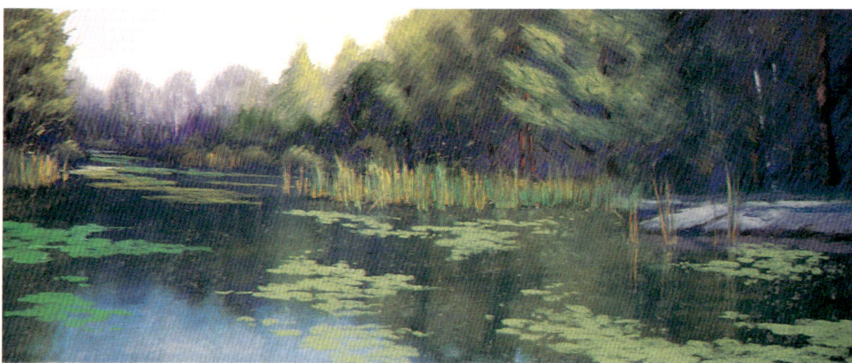

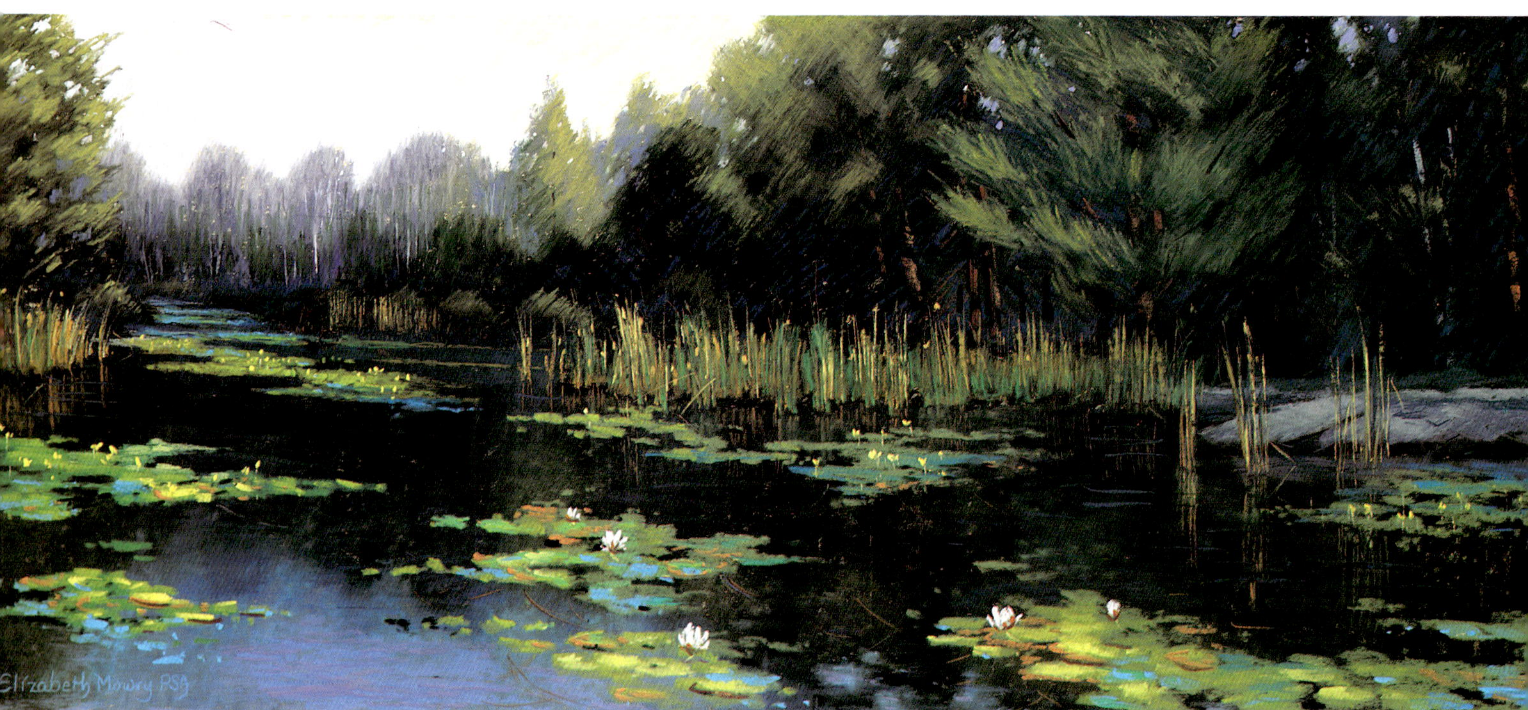

Step 5 Final Details
Back in the studio several days later, I put in the water lily details and the sky holes, and make final, small adjustments.

MOHONK RESERVOIR
Pastel on sanded paper
13″ × 31″

CHOPPY WATER

When water is active, moving or choppy in the foreground, you will be required to study the foreground water for the pattern of movement. Repetition in the movement of waves is similar, but each wave is different. You will need at least three values of color. Notice that the flattest parts of the rolling water reflect the color of the sky. Deeper color shows up under the wave's crest. In reality, the water will keep rolling; a photograph will stop the movement for a split second and show you what to look for.

Most important of all, try to simplify when you paint choppy water by painting some of the close-up waves with detail, and then use less and less detail as the water recedes into the distance. Too much repetition will get boring for you and for the viewer. By implementing suggestion through expressive strokes, you can use personal interpretation to share what you perceive according to what you feel about the subject.

Dependence on pat formulas or rules is not always helpful. Ocean waves are different from river waves or those in stormy seas. Learn as much as you can about your subject, and with the information you gather, trust yourself to formulate some rules of your own.

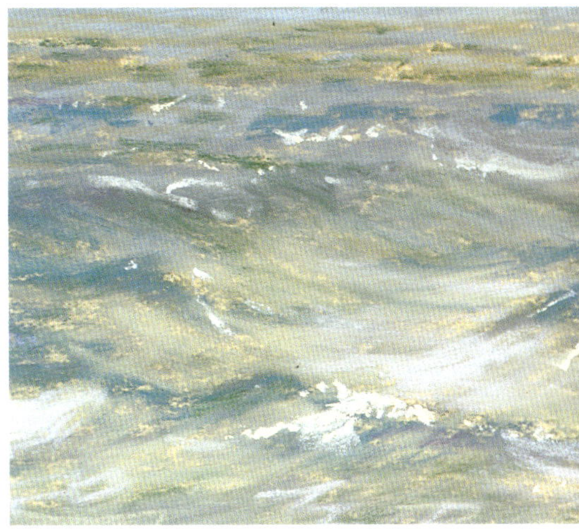

When you paint waves, gradually reduce the detail as the water becomes distant. The far side of the water can be put in with an unbroken band of color that reflects the sky.

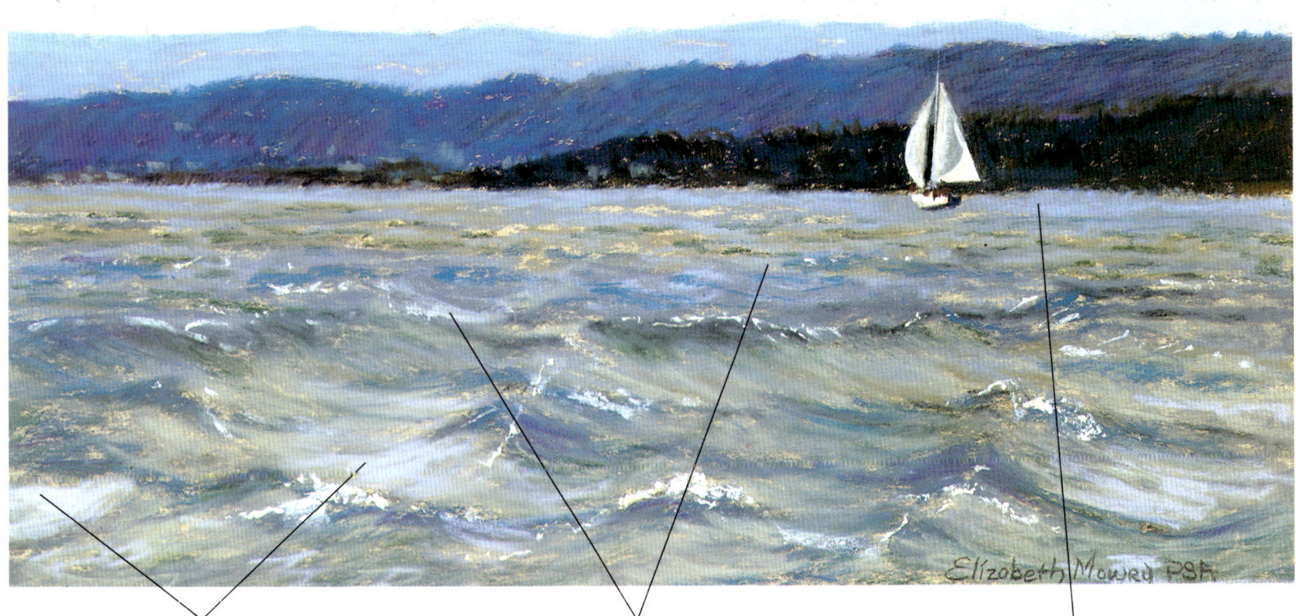

The flattest parts of rolling water reflect the sky.

Use less detail as water recedes into the distance.

Distant water reflects more of the sky color because of the angle at which you view it.

SAILING ON THE HUDSON
Pastel on sanded paper
6½" × 11"
Collection of Albert Joseph Novak

Sweeping, closed strokes that curve upward give the choppy roll to the purple, indigo and warm gray water in the foreground. The hint of foam at the top of the waves is done by rolling the tip of a light-tinted pastel onto the surface. Short, horizontal strokes take the water to the far shore. I did this small painting at the time I took sailing lessons. Personal meaning gives the focus to my work again and again.

DISTANT WATER

Distant rivers are the easiest of all water to paint. They appear in the landscape as thin ribbons of color, usually a tone darker than the sky. Probably the only way a distant river can be responsible for a failed landscape painting is if its configuration is inaccurate. *Towards Peekskill From the Highlands* at right is an example of a distant river painted in pastel.

Many times, a lake or other large body of water in your landscape is too far away for any detailed, broken stroke to be necessary. Instead, it will appear to be an even tone of one or several values, deepening in color where it is closest to you. You will probably see a few long, horizontal streaks where the light catches a pattern on the surface caused by a shift in current or depth.

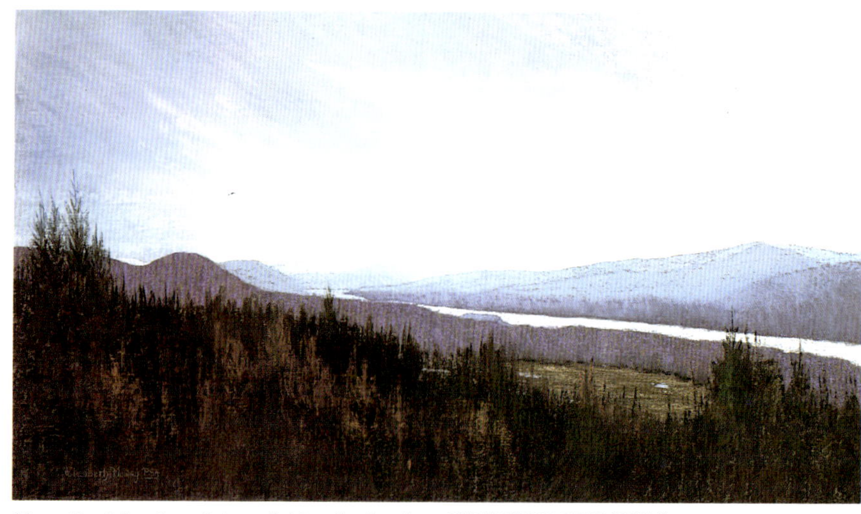

Here, the thin slice of river divides the landscape horizontally. Pay close attention to the shape of the water. Paint it similar to the sky color or slightly darker.

TOWARDS PEEKSKILL
FROM THE HIGHLANDS
Pastel on sanded board
20″ × 36″

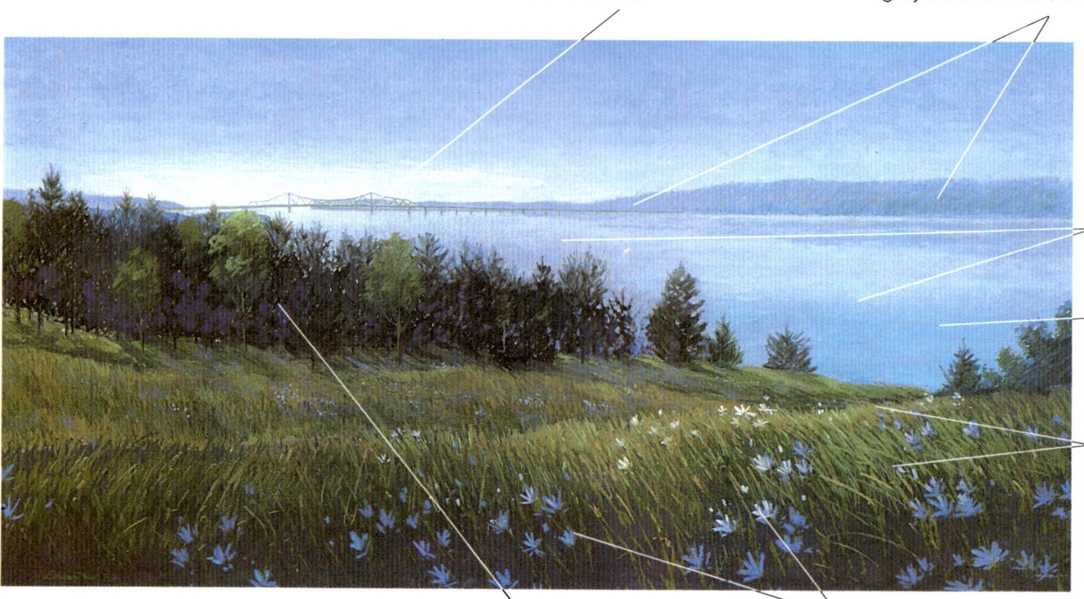

The bridge is minimized through size and distant blue color, but it still draws the viewer into the scene.

Distance at the far side of the river is attained by making these shapes small, gray-blue in color, and a light value.

Because the river is far away, it was painted with closed strokes of soft pastels.

The river reflects the color of the sky.

The graceful bend of the high, summer grasses leads into the landscape.

THE TAPPAN ZEE FROM TARRYTOWN
Pastel on sanded board
25″ × 48″
Collection of David Adler
Photo by John Kleinhans

This view of the Hudson River shows how wide the river becomes as it travels toward New York City. Because the bridge is a familiar landmark, it is an important part of the painting even though its size is small.

The dark, low-value tree line is put in loosely, dividing the background and foreground naturally.

The low value of the shadowed foreground flowers does not keep the eye from the river.

PAINTING FLOWERS WHERE THEY GROW

Flowers complete the summer landscape. Dwarfed by lofty skies and leafed-out trees, they take their unassuming places along the roadsides, in shady glens and in spacious fields. Growing flowers, as opposed to cut flowers in a vase, thrive in their unpampered freedom. In nature, flowers are always in harmony with their setting, balancing and complementing summer's greens and blues. In gardens, this is not always so.

When you want flowers to dominate your painting, give them the space they need. Use a large enough surface for leaves to sprawl and untidy stems to linger into unsymmetrical composition. Above all, paint the flowers large enough to assume their rightful place as center of interest. When deciding whether to include more or less in your painting, choose less and emphasize it more. Use a combination of detail and suggestion, lights and darks, soft and hard edges, small and large shapes, warm and cool colors.

My favorite way to paint flowers is as a harmonious, integrated part of the landscape. No longer large in size, flowers in their natural habitat can still lead the eye through a landscape with their color.

More than the details of a single flower, now you will be studying how the flowers group themselves in a field or wooded glen. Each variety has its definitive grouping characteristics.

Before long, you will know which flowers in your area are likely to be found in shade, which thrive in the sun, and those that prefer marshy wetlands.

Background consists of minimal side strokes.

Definition and suggestion are balanced.

Both large and small shapes are used.

The stained paper keeps strokes clean and definitive because the liquid stain does not interfere with the tooth of the paper.

Color complements (warm yellow/cool purple) lend added color contrasts.

Simplification is attained by painting only some of the flowers and leaves.

The stems and edges of the petals are done with the corner edge of a squared pastel.

Use of both straight and curved lines gives compositional strength.

Strong contrasts between lights and darks lend drama to a simple subject.

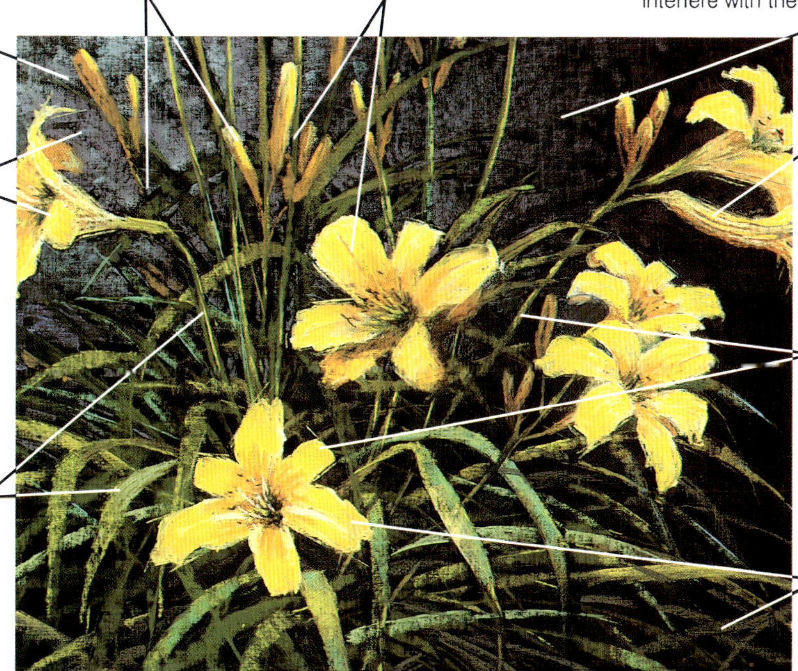

SUMMER LILIES
Pastel on sanded paper
18″ × 21″

The dark-stained paper provides a dramatic background for the yellow lilies. To avoid undue complexity, I limited the scope of the painting to only a portion of the lily plant, allowing the stems, the leaves and some of the flowers to run off the edge of the paper.

FOREGROUNDS AND BACKGROUNDS

At the same time that you haze over the backgrounds in your summer landscapes, you can stroke in sun-ripened, lively foregrounds with expressive grasses and a few selected details that lead into the painting.

Far off in the distance, flowers are painted as massed specks, or, in larger numbers, as a layer of color bluer or grayer than the foreground flowers. To capture the essence of a flower you wish to paint, carefully study its shape; for example: lupine (spike), poppy (cup), daisy (circular, narrow petals). It is the simplified shape of that flower that you will use to suggest its presence as it moves from background to foreground where it can finally be seen in detail.

One of the most important hints to remember when painting flowers in their natural setting is that they grow wherever seeds fall, not lined up and evenly spaced as in a garden. See how some hide behind others, making them only partially visible. Notice how groups of flowers crowd together within the wild grasses. Look for the shadows they throw across one another. It is this discontinuity and abandon that give flowers their elusive charm.

THE FOREGROUND
The foreground treatment of black-eyed Susans consists of yellow petals circled around dark centers, always showing the variety that is determined by the direction each flower is facing.

THE BACKGROUND
Black-eyed Susans in the background get reduced to a few grouped, dark specks with shorter petals stroked off to the sides or downward.

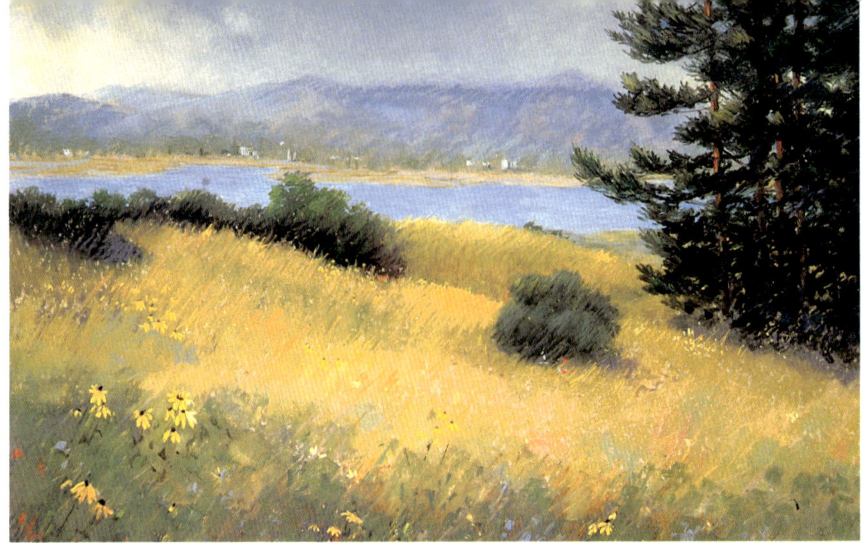

ALONG THE HUDSON
Pastel on sanded board
22″ × 28″

This painting includes many components: clouds, hazy mountains, river, trees and drying fields, but they all share a recognizable consistency with summer. Only a few flowers are detailed, but the viewer knows they are growing throughout the field.

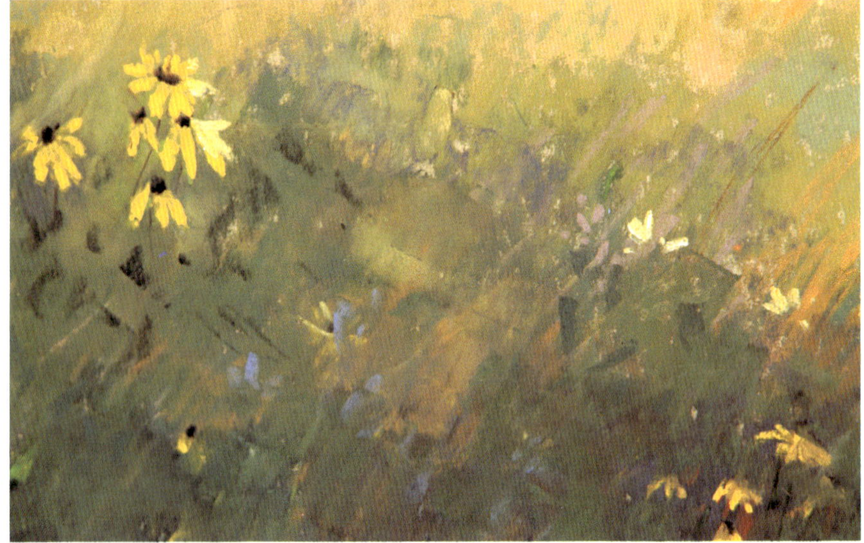

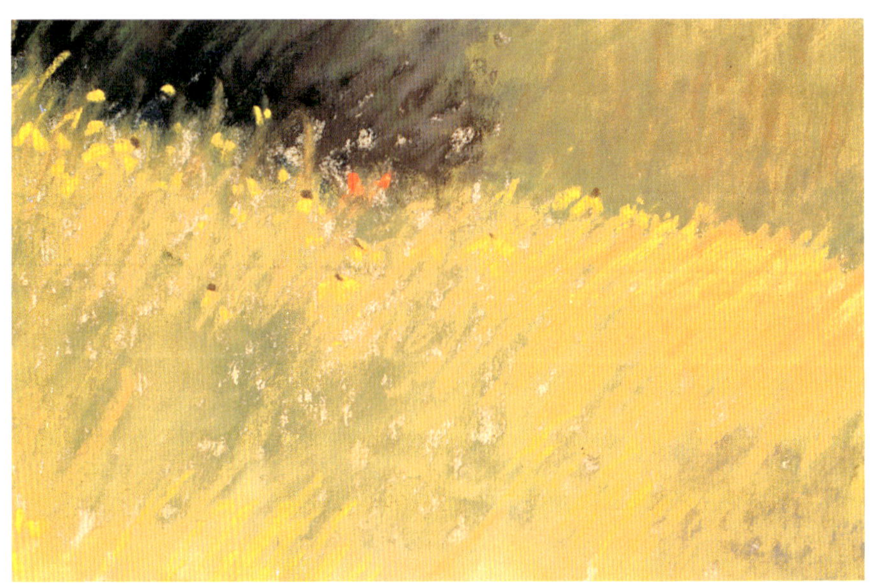

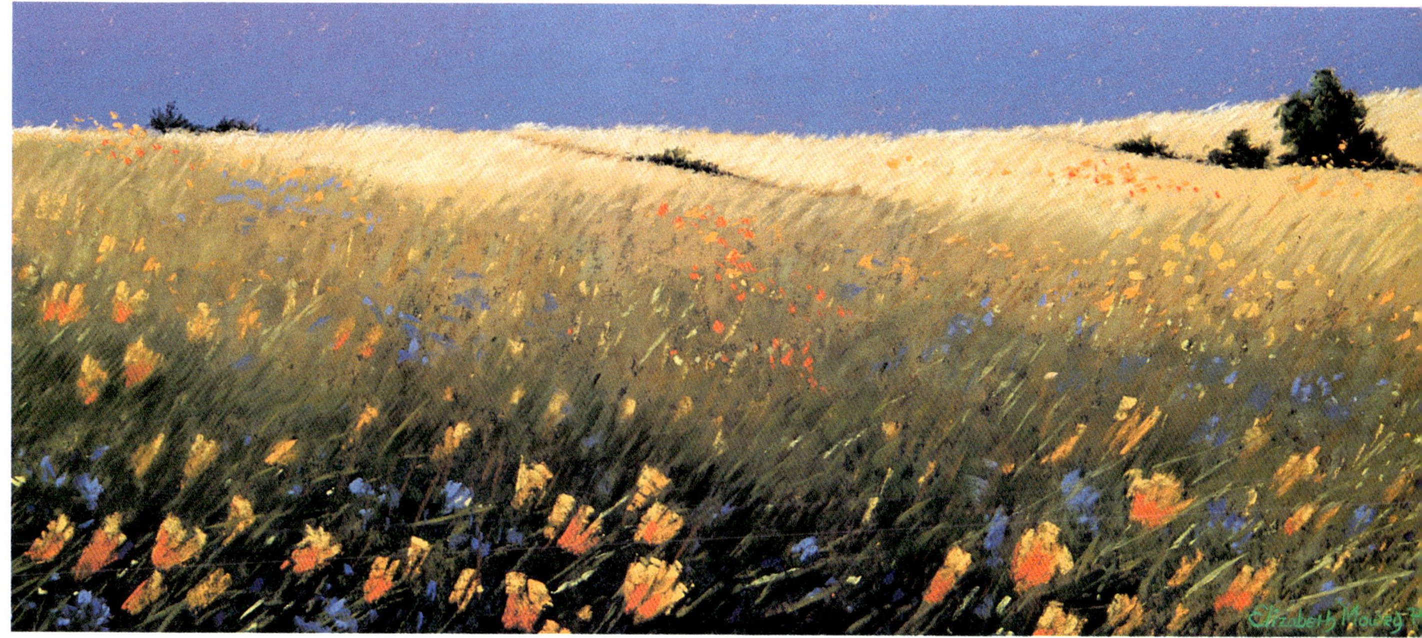

CALIFORNIA POPPIES
Pastel on sanded board
9″ × 22″
Collection of Dr. and Mrs. J. Peter Roberts

Sun-drenched fields rest under a western sky in this simply composed landscape. Use of color complements gives strength to the painting.

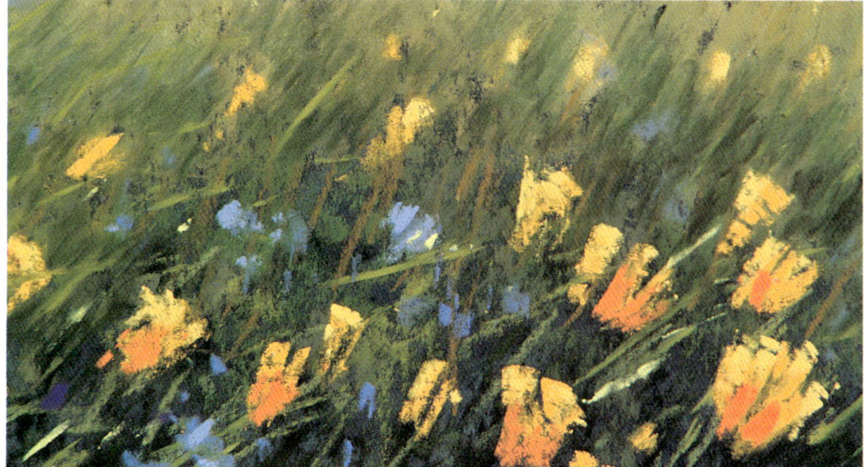

THE FOREGROUND
The foreground treatment of the California poppy takes its shape with a twisting stroke of the edge of a short, broken pastel. No more than two or three clean strokes make each poppy.

THE BACKGROUND
Background flowers are reduced to carefully grouped specks that get lost in the dried grasses. Natural grouping is the key here.

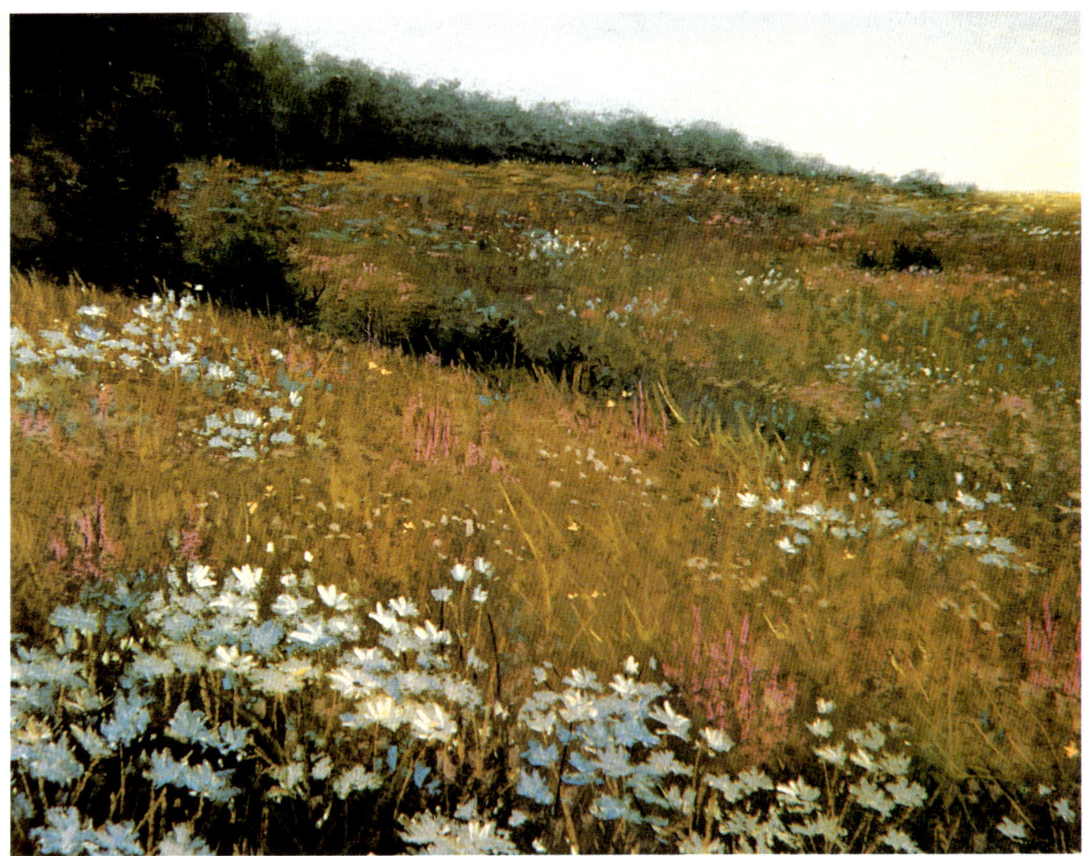

SWISS WILDFLOWERS
Pastel on sanded cloth
22″ × 28″
Collection of Bonnie Grasso

This painting was done from a quick sketch and some color notes. The scene was a common one as I hiked through the Rhône Valley some years ago. It is a simple, uncluttered composition that works because the natural wildflower groupings lead up the hills toward the light at the horizon.

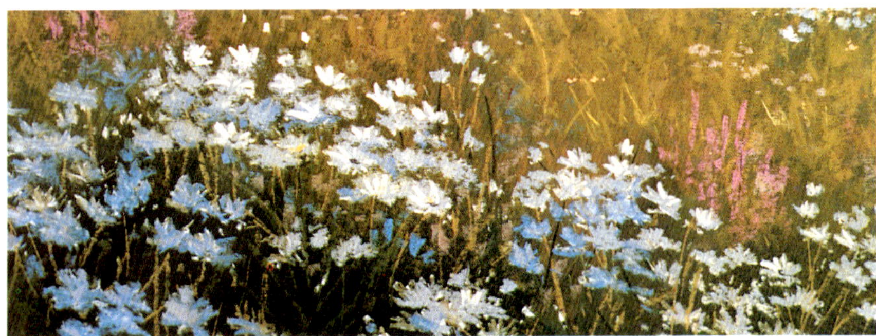

THE FOREGROUND
The charming confusion of the common daisy is familiar everywhere. Here, even the foreground flowers are not crisply detailed, but their size is captivating.

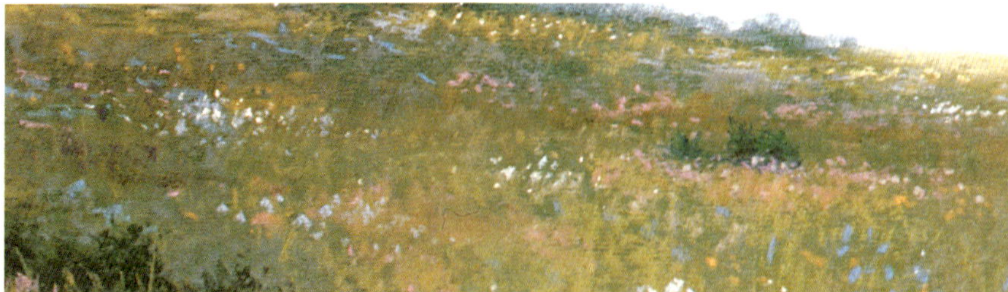

THE BACKGROUND
In the background, all the wildflowers are reduced to the minimum by the use of small specks of dotted, unblended color, which are always unevenly grouped.

SUNLIGHT ON THE LANDSCAPE

Sun dominates the summer landscape. Whether it lights up the entire side of a tin barn roof or just a few petals of a flower, the effects of the sun as it dries and warms the earth are obviously important to any artist. Keeping a close watch on how the landscape changes with the presence—or just as important, the absence—of the sun is the key to solid summer compositions.

When the sun is overhead, trees, now fully foliated, magnify their presence by laying cool shadows over the ground nearby.

As the afternoon hours pass, the imposing shadows will claim more and more of the landscape. Capitalize on those shapes as a way to enhance your work. (See *Lenox Afternoon* on page 58.)

The same sunlight that will sometimes bleach out the landscape at noon, much like an overexposed photograph, will throw enticing shafts of light into the woodlands and across meadows earlier or later in the day. These patterns create the contrasts necessary for transforming an ordinary scene into a well-balanced landscape. At dawn or at dusk, they become dramatic.

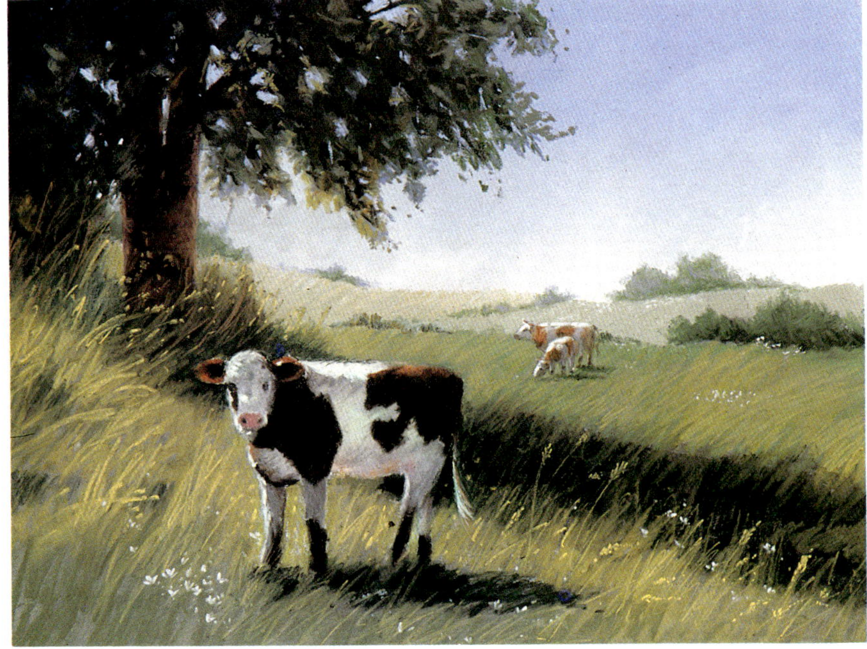

THE FRIENDLY ONE
Pastel on Windberg pastel panel
12" × 16"

Although this painting differs in context from my usual subject matter, it does show how summer sunlight causes shadows that can add interesting shapes to your composition. This curious little fellow was an excellent model, by the way.

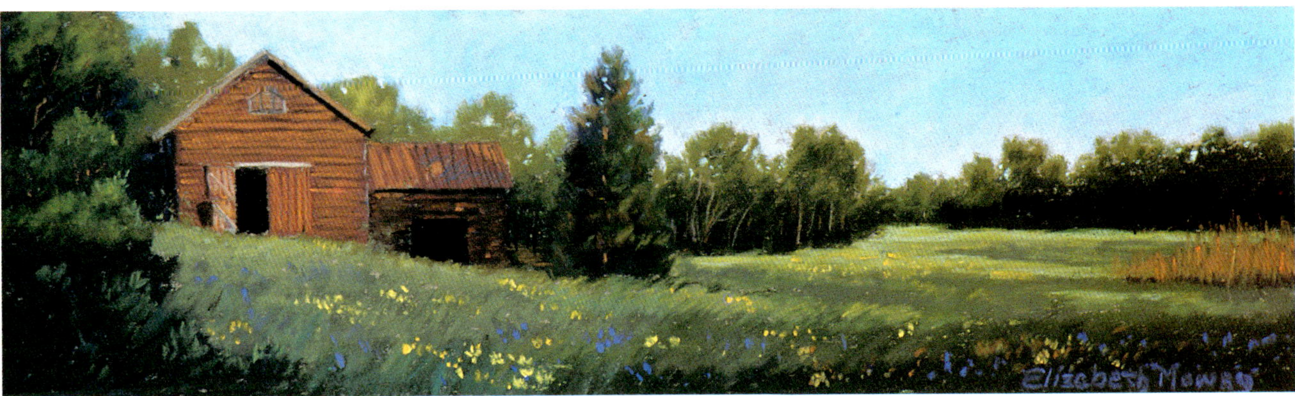

RHINEBECK BARN
Pastel on sanded board
3½" × 12"
Private collection

Patches of sunlight escape the long shadows and barely touch the fields. You will find this subtle effect of the light on the landscape in the late afternoons.

PAINTING THE GREENS OF SUMMER

This demonstration shows how to approach the green landscape common in summer. It was my intention to convey the inviting expanse of an open meadow through a pleasing distribution of sunlight and shadow using a primarily green palette.

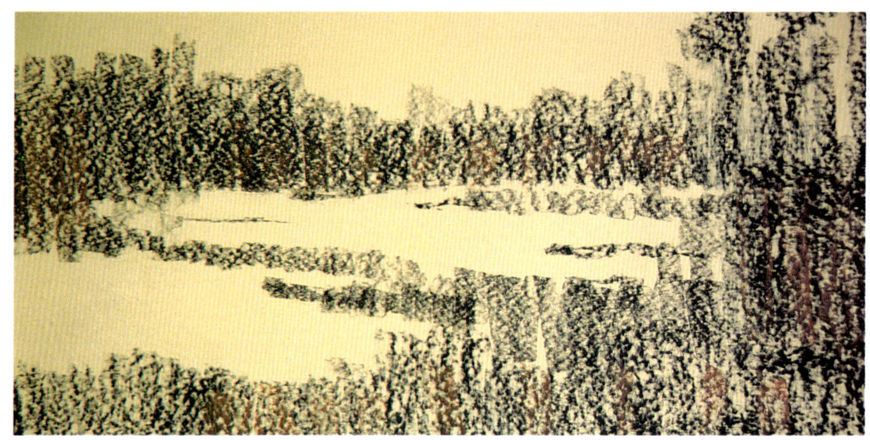

Step 1 Preparation
This scene is available to me daily, so I felt no urgency to sketch first. In this respect, familiarity (painting what we know) can be an advantage. With hard Nupastels in indigo blue and blue-violet, which would not fill the tooth of the paper, I used broad side strokes over the areas where the darkest color would be.

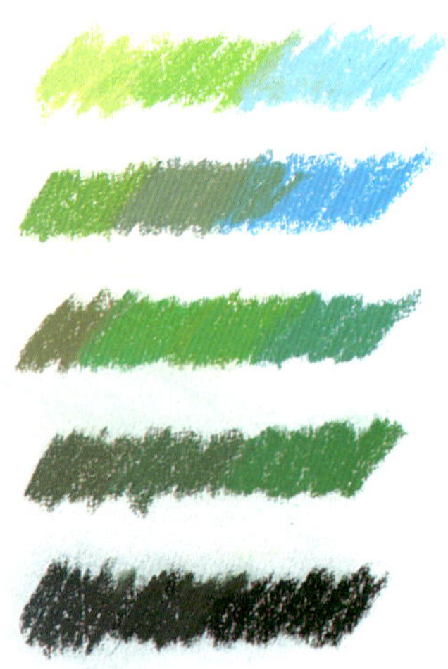

Here, you can see some of the many greens I used in this demonstration painting of Winterset Meadow. *When you want to thoroughly enjoy painting summer landscapes, expanding your supply of greens is a move in the right direction.*

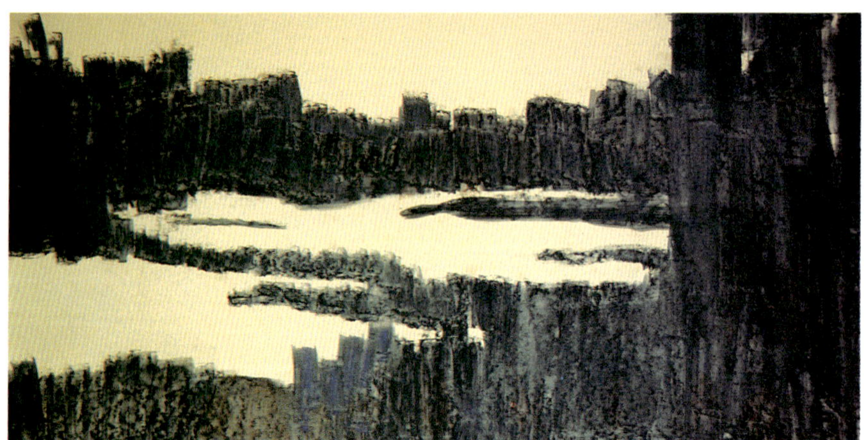

Step 2 Staining
I then brushed the Nupastel color into the surface with a polyfoam brush that had been dipped in Turpenoid.

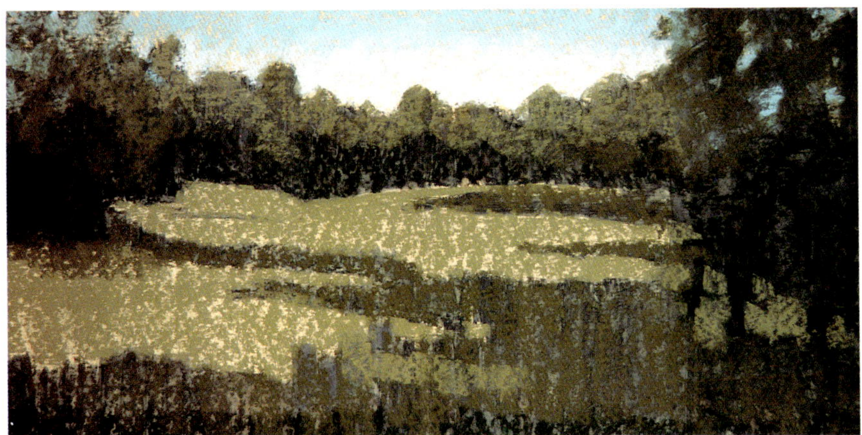

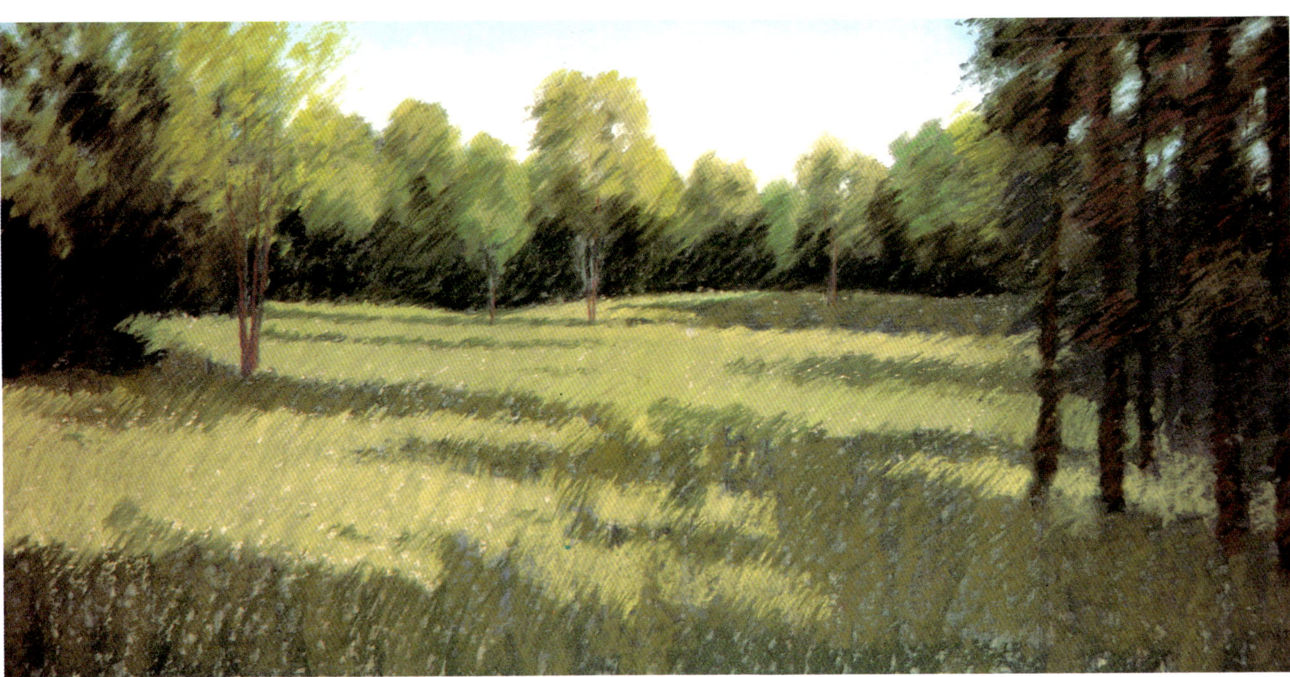

Step 4 Defining Shapes and Integrating Greens
I used short, diagonal scribble strokes over the entire painting in this step, referring constantly to the shapes of the trees and grasses in the meadow.

This is the diagonal scribble stroke in which I do not pick up the pastel off the surface. The pressure is accented on the upstroke.

Step 5 Sunlight on the Trees and Grasses
I use light, warm greens to put sunlight on the trees and grasses, and then slip purples into the shadows. Don't do this too early in your painting, because you'll have no way of judging how much you need, and the tendency is to err in the direction of too much.

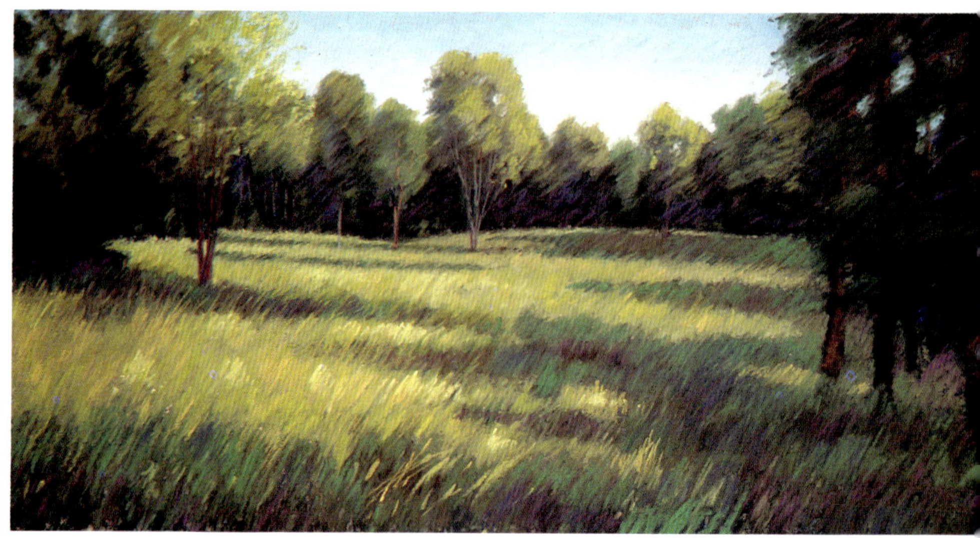

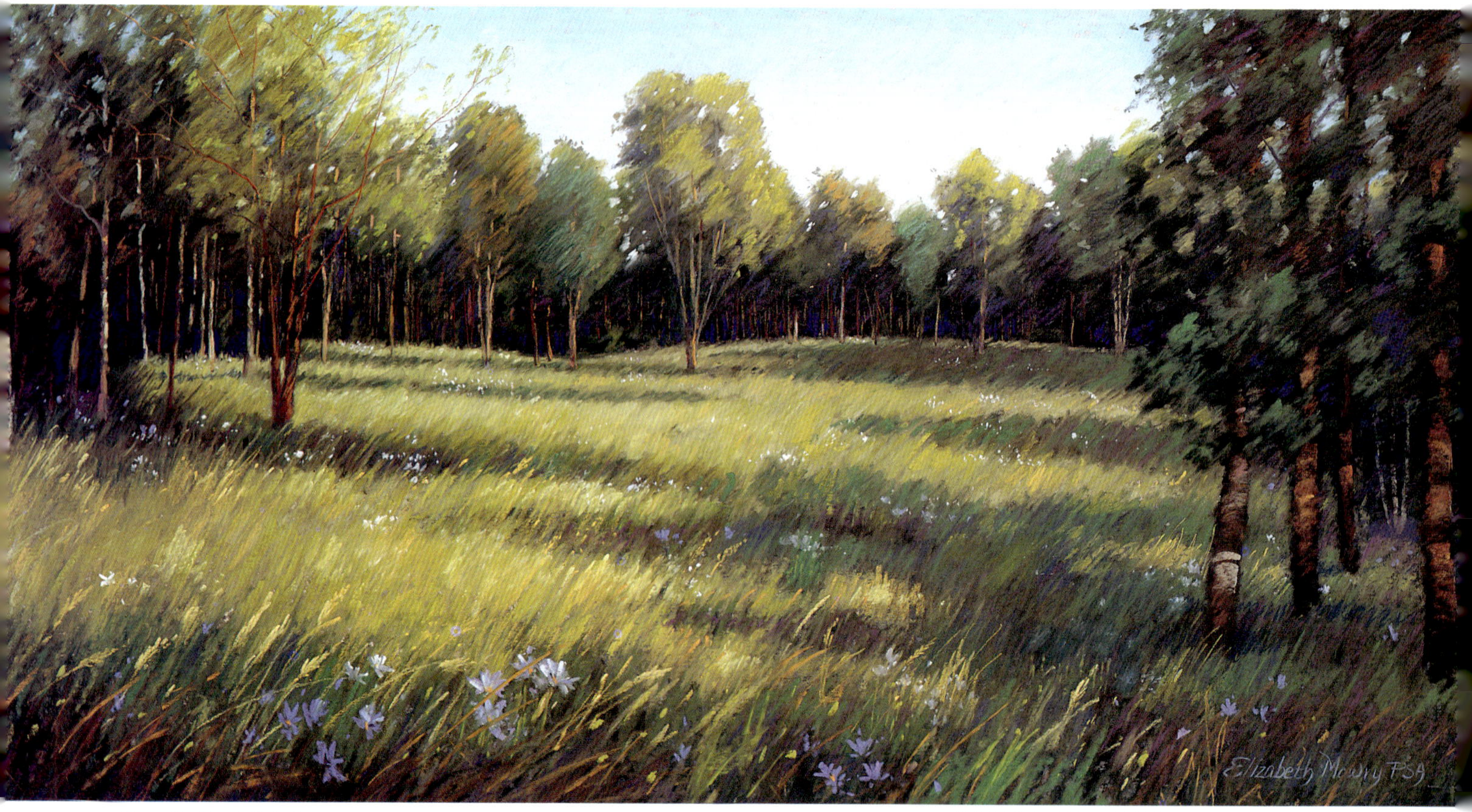

Step 6 Final Details
Finally, I put some sky holes into the trees, plant some secondary tree trunks, place some foreground detail in the grasses and scatter the wildflowers throughout the meadow. An all-green landscape is transformed by sunlight and shadow.

WINTERSET MEADOW
Pastel on sanded board
17" × 33"

SUMMER-STILLED LIFE

Still life does not have to be synonymous with *indoor studio painting*. Except for thunderstorms, summer is a season of quiet passiveness. Fruits of full growth, still on the vine, invite us for a close-up look. Flowers in the field and garden that attract the butterflies and humming birds, keep changing silently from bud to seed. So much of what summer offers as subject matter is most appealing where it is.

Consider zeroing in for a close-up view of something that interests you, and paint it outdoors.

Yes, the lighting will change, so you will need to block in the light patterns first and then adhere to them as recorded.

Paramount to outdoor still-life painting and sketching is a thoughtful decision about the size of (1) your pastel surface and (2) the objects to be painted. Choose a surface adequate in size so that your strokes will not be confined and tight. Then be sure to paint your subject large enough on the surface. Most times, this means cutting back on the scope of what you include so that your image can be large enough to make a strong impact.

For example, I have a large raspberry patch that gives me much pleasure because I enjoy making gifts of jam, cordial and tea with the berries. My associations with the patch are very positive, so it is a natural choice for subject matter. Yet were I to paint the whole raspberry patch, the berries would be too small to be visible. By zeroing in on just a few of the leaves and berries, I pay homage to a place that holds personal meaning.

The leaves exemplify a technique I call "push and lift," using small pieces of pastel on their sides. Apply pressure as you push, and then abruptly lift.

I stained all but the upper-right corner of the sanded paper with diluted, turpentine-based wood stain by Minwax.

The dark-value surface is responsible for the strong contrasts in this painting.

Blues and purples in the right corner suggest a hint of sky.

Some colors are overstated for effect.

Dark greens and purples represent the density and shadows within the raspberry bushes.

The surface is still very clean at the completion of the painting, and the strokes look crisp.

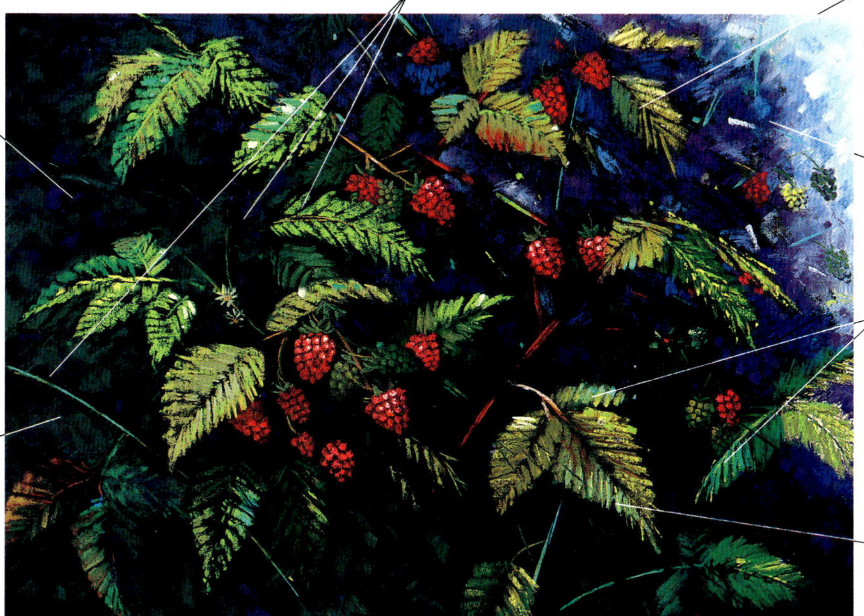

WINTERSET RASPBERRIES
Pastel on sanded paper
14″ × 19″
Collection of Dr. C.R. Webb, Jr. and Andree Webb

For this painting, I used reality as a guide only. Once I painted the first leaves and berries, I added others only where I needed them on my surface for a pleasing design.

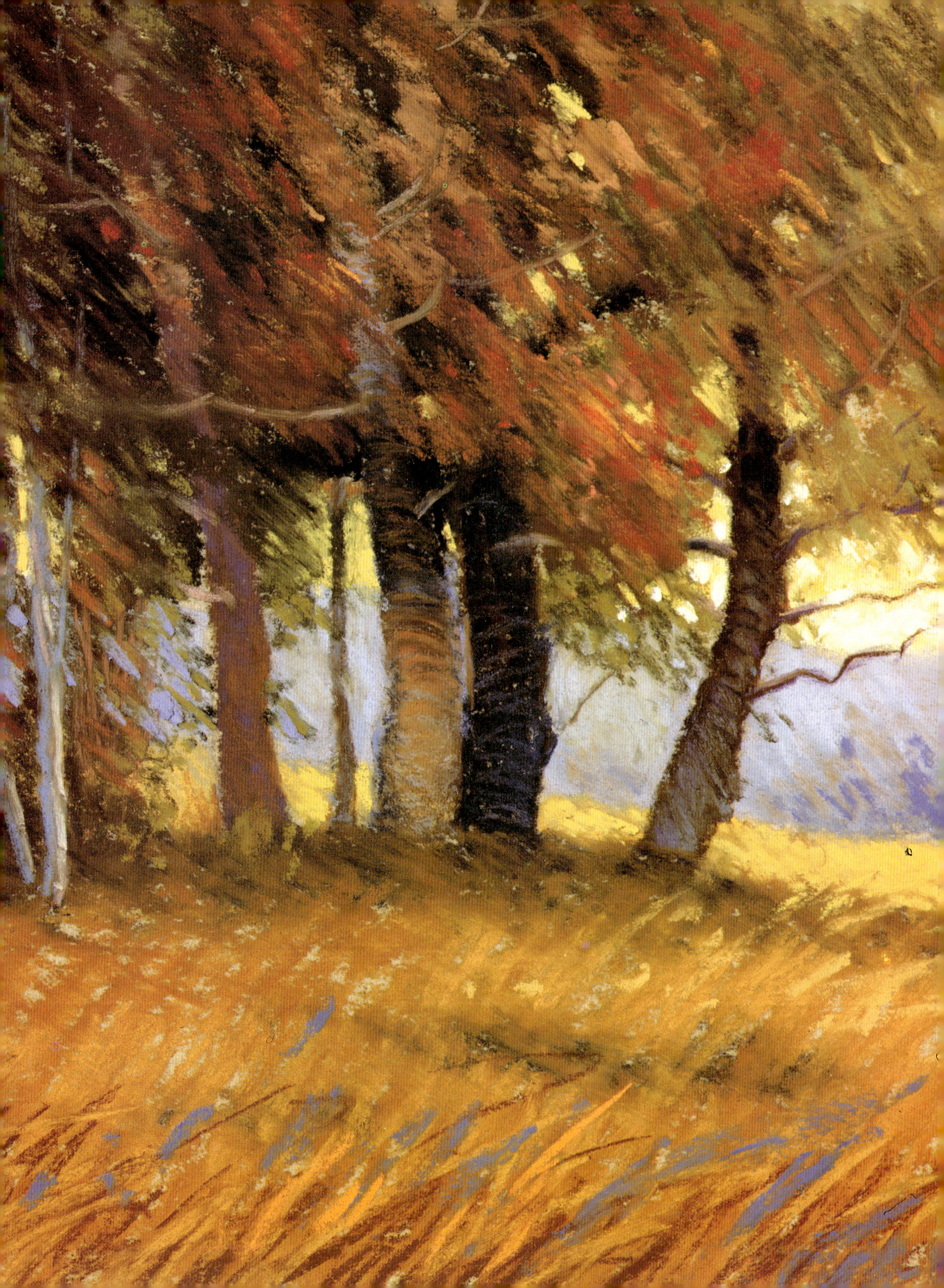

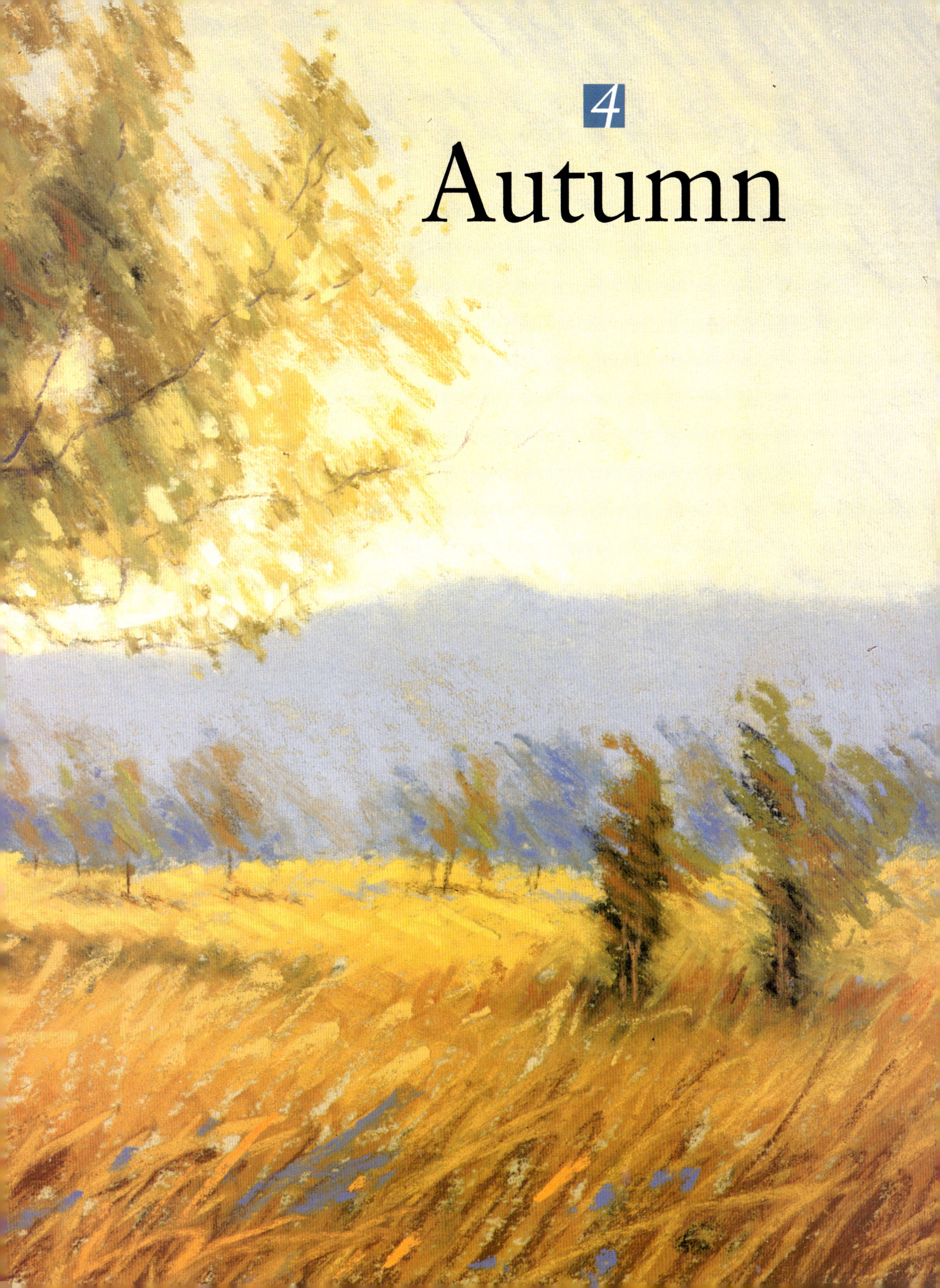

4
Autumn

A RESPONSE TO AUTUMN

The decline begins, but not before a final flourish. The transition from summer green to vibrant autumn color begins slowly. Verdant fields take on a bronze glow that gradually changes to ochre and yellow. Later, while the goldenrod fades, you can watch the roadside sumac turn scarlet, and delicately draped crimson shows how high the poison ivy has climbed into the trees. Notice how the low sun backlights some of the trees and throws their long shadows across the drying fields. Hear the crows call out to one another, as geese, in paintable formation, migrate south.

By midautumn, the spread of warm color over the landscape escalates to such a degree that even the untrained eye sees changes every day. Momentum continues until, in the woods one cloudy day, you may mistake the brilliance of yellow foliage for sunlight. Out in the fields, take note of how the tall cornstalks have been cut into rows of stubble that converge at the horizon. Look for the orange pumpkins that dot the tawny fields without arrangement. You may even see the silken milkweed seeds catch a highlight in the sun as they burst from their pointed pods and float away. And all the while, the pungent smell of fallen fruit will be mingling with the scent of burning rubble from summer's finished garden.

As the season progresses, yellow will become golden, vermilion will replace summer pinks and orange will ripen into burnt sienna. All of nature's color will mature before your eyes.

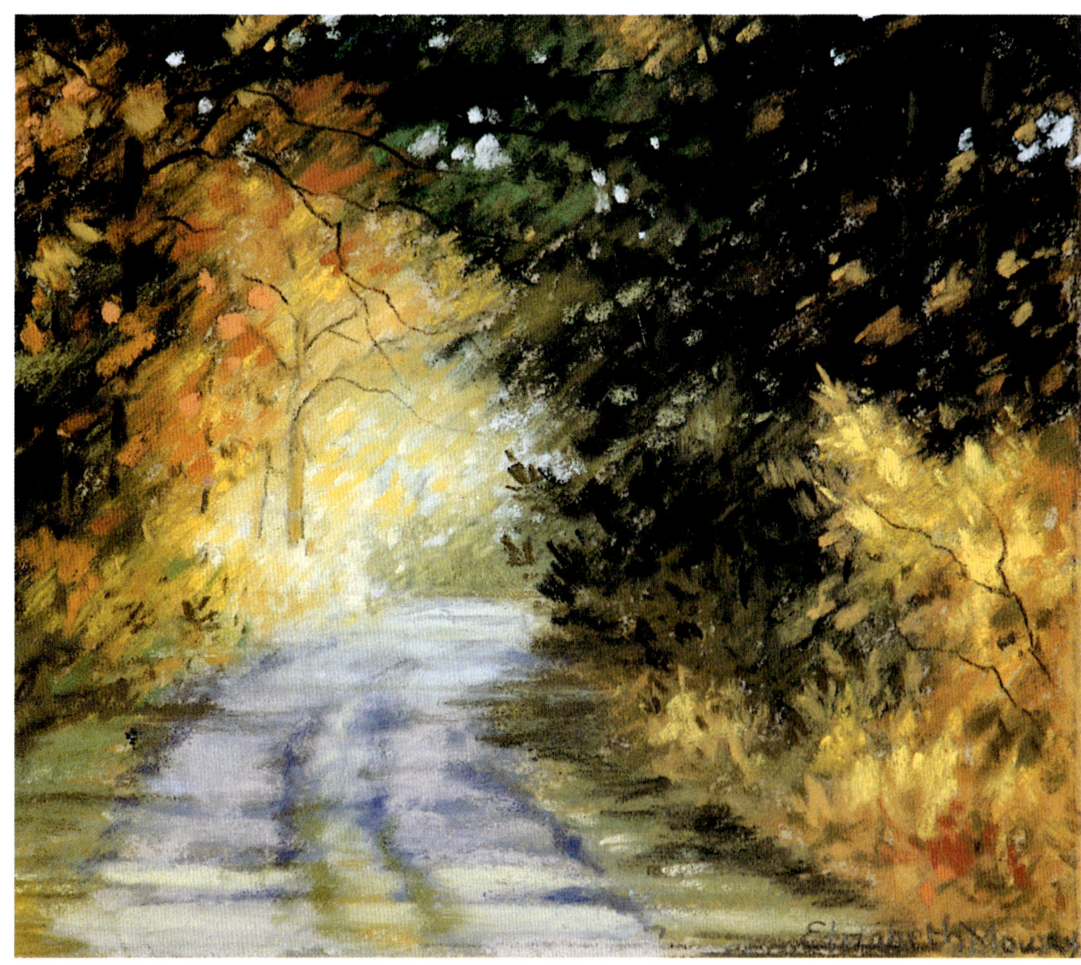

ROAD TO TIVOLI
Pastel on sanded paper
4½″ × 5½″
Collection of Frank E. Davis, Jr.

You can capture nature's maturing colors even in your small, autumn paintings. Here, warm yellows and burnt sienna are balanced by the deep, cool greens and the purple shadows that cross the road.

HINTS FOR BETTER AUTUMN PAINTINGS

Pastel is the most straightforward of all media. Despite the advantage you have of being able to render autumn color swiftly, take time to absorb the vivid impact of the season before making hurried translations into paintings. This advice may seem counter-productive as the clock keeps ticking through the short color season and the impending frost awaits. Let me explain:

I have watched beginning painters, under the alluring spell of autumn color, hurry from one place to another in quest of the brightest subject matter. Understandably so. After the green, green summer, there is a tendency to just aim yourself at color and paint, but by hastily pursuing only color, you may be compromising composition.

Some years ago, as autumn approached, I decided I would finally capture all the nuances I had missed in other years. Caught up in the excitement of the season, I traveled throughout the region doing painting after painting. After the initial rush of anxiety passed, I finished the season by casually painting some of the places I see every day. As you might guess, the early work was filled with spots of sunlight on bits of glorious color, but only the final paintings withstood the passing time and my own critical eye. In these, within the framework of a relaxed familiarity with my own area, existed the compo-

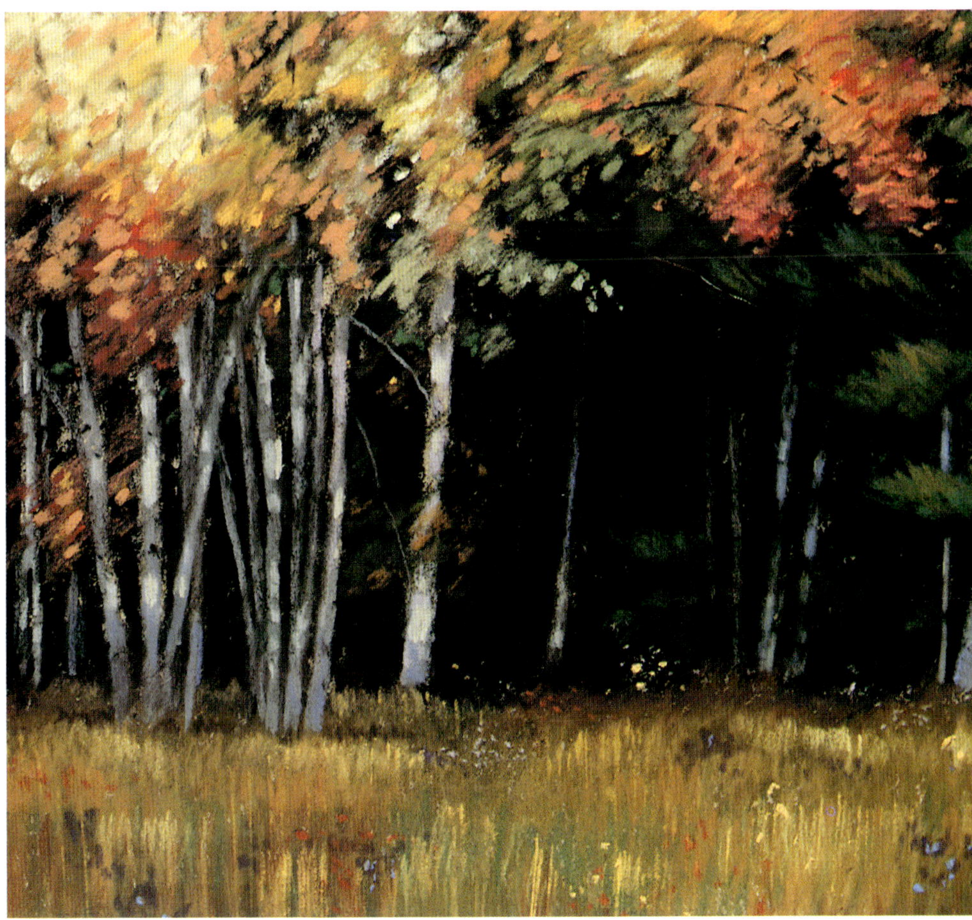

EDGE OF THE MEADOW, WINTERSET
Pastel on sanded paper
7½" × 8½"

On the left, a curve of lighter (higher-value), warmer color provides an invitation to the eye to move into the dense, cool woodlands at the center of the painting. In the upper right, red and green low-chroma complements still vibrate when placed next to one another.

sitional strength and grace that the early work sadly lacked. If this has not already happened to you, it may be that my experience will ultimately save you some time. This is an example of a subtle consideration, easily overlooked, but extremely important to the end result in your work.

THE AUTUMN PALETTE

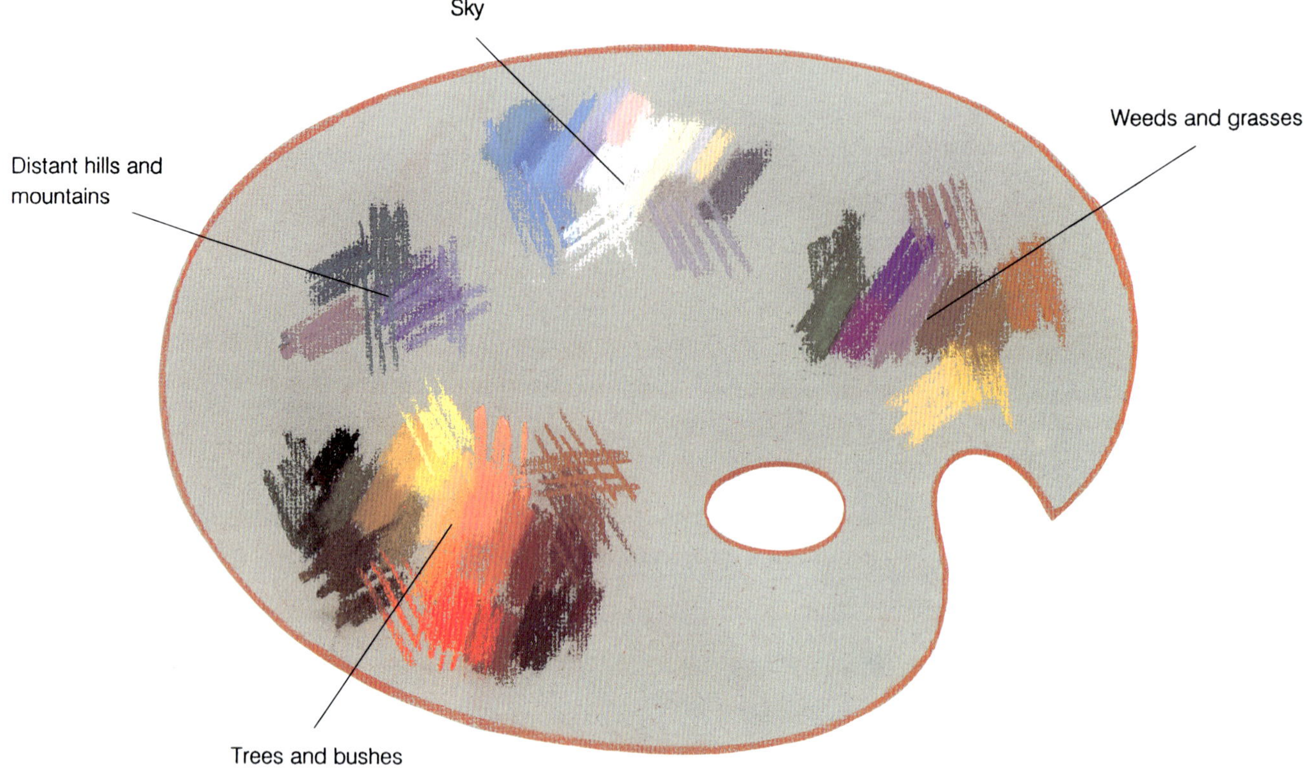

The colors we associate with autumn are warm: red, yellow, orange, ochre, sienna, etc. In fact, the palette of autumn, even with the less colorful November averaged in, is significantly hotter than any other season.

Because high color commands attention, you notice the enticing warm and bright colors first. Remember, though, that nature demonstrates exceptional balance at all times. So look again. See the violet and purples, the rich blues and browns, and the cool grays as you view the landscape, and keep this natural balancing in mind as you put the color into your paintings. For example, when you place a scarlet maple near a cool green pine, it will appear extraordinarily vibrant.

The groups of color shown are merely the beginning of many possibilities. Your personal autumn palette will depend upon your location and your purpose. For example, if you are a realistic landscape painter in Wyoming, your palette would probably include less of the orange and red reminiscent of the northeastern maples in my region, and more yellow and ochres of the aspens. Your sky colors would also reflect the intense blue and purple that dominate the large, open spaces in your landscape.

Some autumn paintings are not as effective as they could be because the colorful foliage, so breathtakingly beautiful in the vast outdoors, can be problematic within the confined area of the pastel paper or panel when it competes for attention with a center of interest. This is an elusive issue, but if it happens in your colorful autumn paintings, try composing your painting with the brightest color *at* the center of interest, and keep other color in reserve. In other words, make the color *be* the focal point. Also, abbreviate detail. Detail draws attention and scatters focus as well.

We will be looking at ways to unify bright, autumn color later in this chapter.

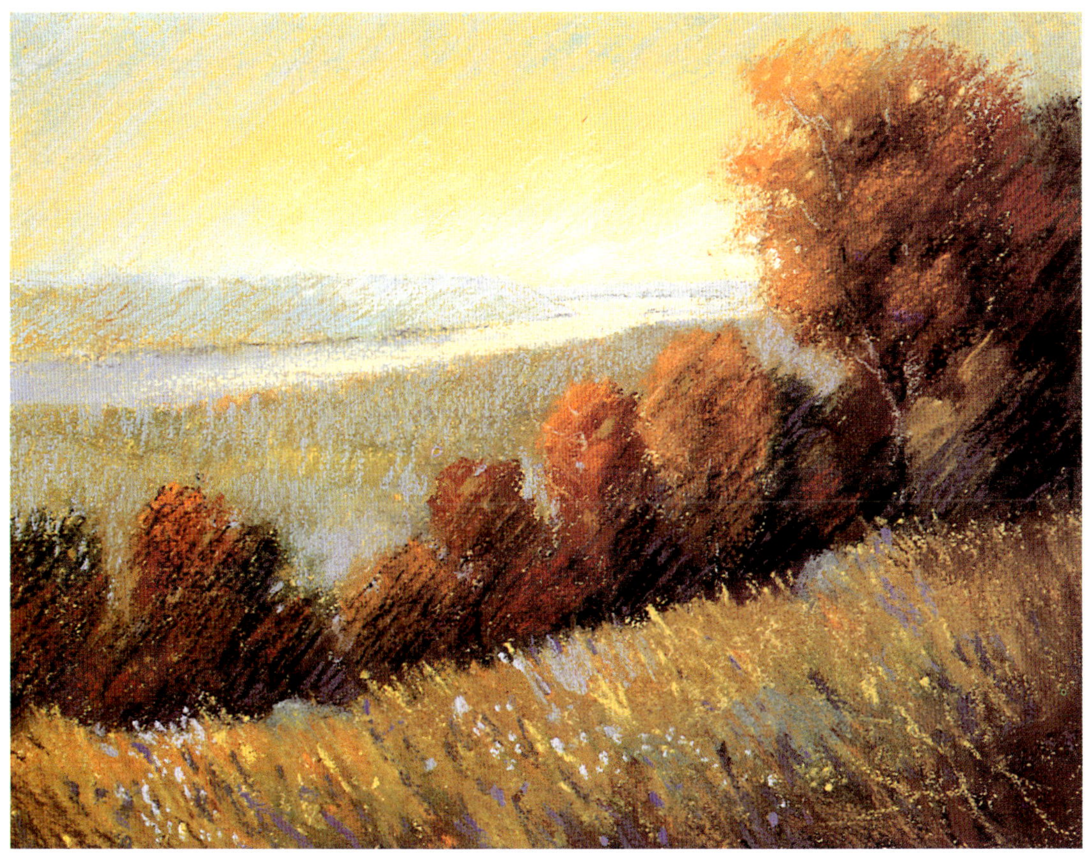

VIEW OF THE HUDSON, AUTUMN
Pastel on Larroque Bergerac paper
9″ × 12″

In this painting, the vibrant, warm, northeastern foliage is balanced by cool purples in the distance. The mustard-colored background showing through unifies all colors.

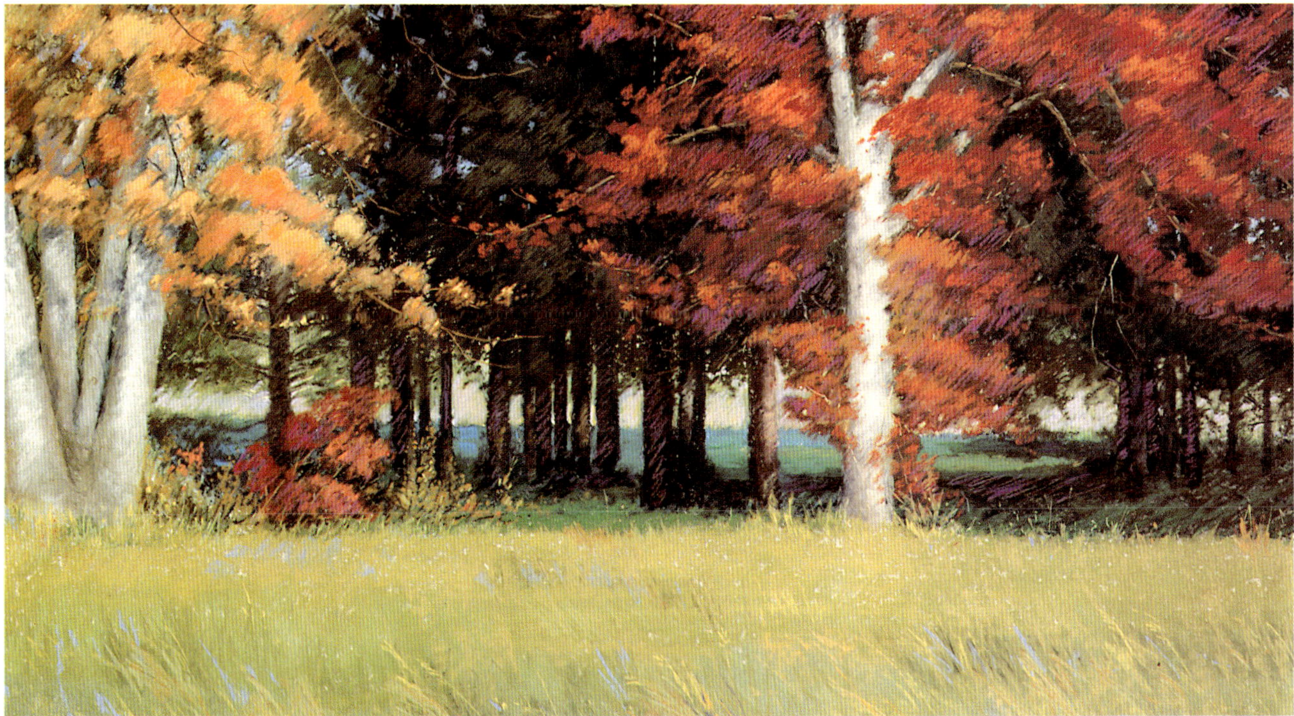

ROADSIDE, OCTOBER
Pastel on sanded paper
24″ × 41″

Use of color complements can make a powerful statement in your paintings. Here the red foliage at the center of interest appears vibrant because of support from its surrounding green complement. In fact, the palette used in this pastel is primarily red and green.

PAINTING THE AUTUMN SKY

The drama of the autumn sky is changing all the time. On a brisk, clear day, you might see a complementary cobalt sky above brightly colored foliage. The very next day the sky could be just a backdrop of gray for the passing parade of color beneath it.

Clouds are often traveling swiftly now. As temperature swings and air currents increase, they frequently slant diagonally across the sky in interesting com-positional possibilities, while low, darker clouds stretch and reach across luminous horizons.

When painting the sky and clouds in pastel, your most important considerations are the edges, and they are also a common pitfall of poorly painted ones. While the softest of edges are easily attained with pastel, you will want to be cautious about overblending. On the other hand, texture and hard edges, especially when overdone, cause the end result to resemble a collage of glued-on shapes. So step back often as you work, in order to avoid overworking in either direction.

Clouds, no matter how large or what shape, are still up in the vast sky, floating, free-moving and airy. In reality, they are not separate from the sky, but part of it. They move, change shape, appear to dissolve, and then take up form again. An impressive sky is not necessarily a heavily painted,

LATE AFTERNOON
Pastel on sanded
paper
7¼" × 13"

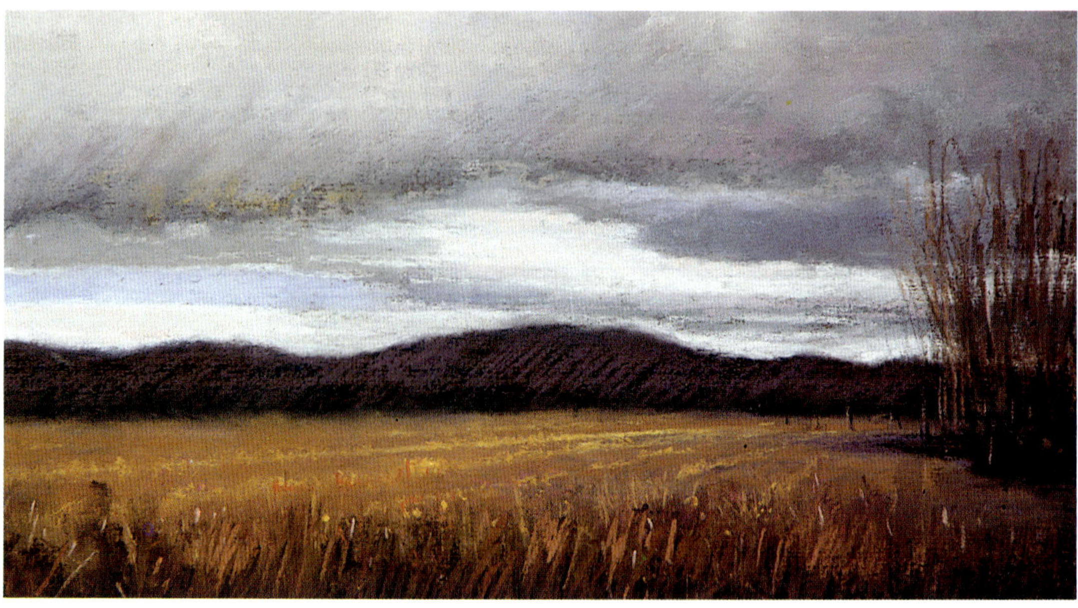

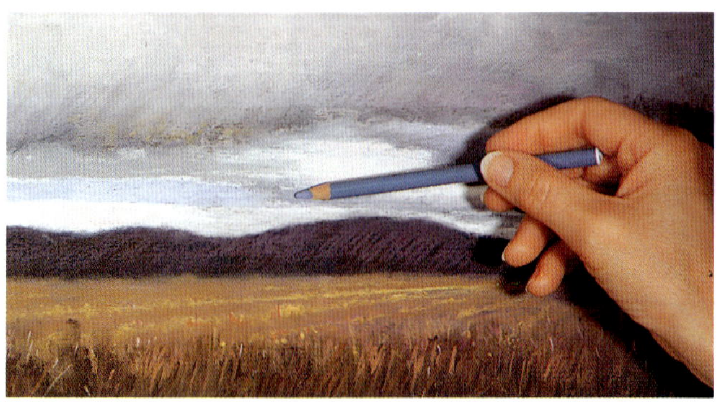

The layered sky is common in autumn and often dominates the landscape below it. I used soft edges to model the upper cumulus cloud, and then harder edges to separate and pull out the stratus layers. The clouds have darkened the mountain and the fore-ground, but some light still lingers on the cornfield.

To blend a sky with a pastel pencil, hold the pencil farther from the point than you normally do, and position it low and near the surface of the work. This will keep your stroke light.

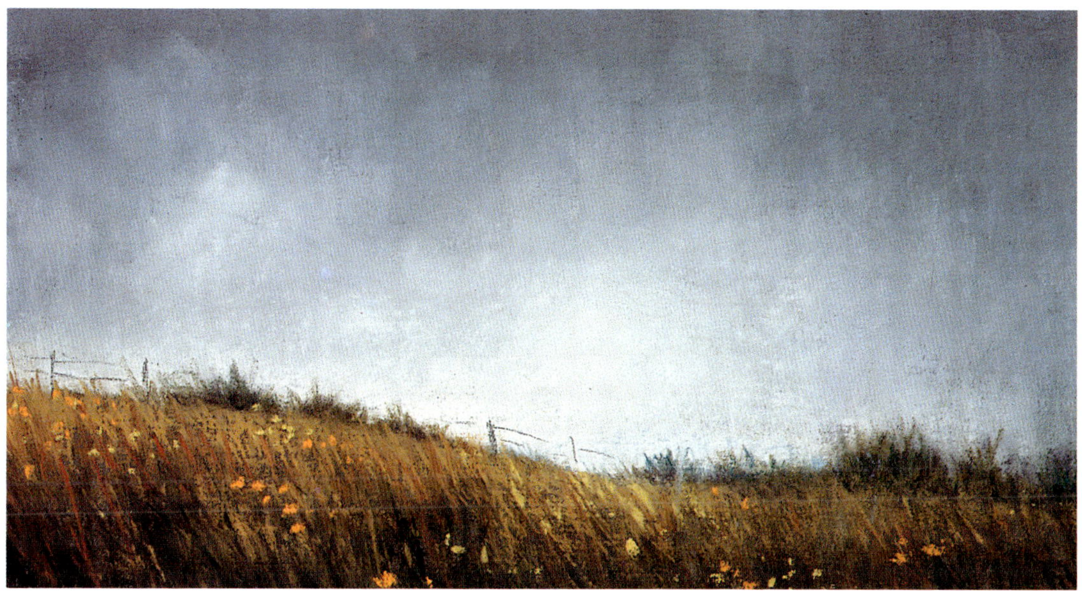

I did this small, uncomplicated landscape after an autumn rain-storm. The optimism in the clearing sky plays an important role in the painting. I used Mouse Grey (a wonderful Rembrandt pastel), gray-blue and a light tint of Naples yellow.

overtextured one. Instead, clouds need a light touch. When painting a landscape, it is helpful to think of the contrast between the lifting, airy quality of the sky and the weighty solidity of the earth.

Make a point of observing the cloud formations. Note the colors, shapes and values. When a cloud is between you and the sun, its edges will appear luminous. If the clouds are rounded, as opposed to seemingly pulled out, the edges will usually not be the lightest part of the cloud. You will also observe that the darkest clouds of late autumn will cause the earth beneath them to be even darker.

If you want more blending of the sky than you can obtain by pulling one color into another with your stroke, try using a tortillion. Sometimes I use a pastel pencil. I choose a color and value close to the color of the area I wish to blend. I hold the pencil almost parallel to the surface of the painting, and I use a very light touch.

You will find that when there is enough pastel on the surface, the pencil pushes the color around more than adding more color. This is why, when laying in a sky, I will often work on a flat surface instead of an easel. In this way, the pastel dust remains in the sky area and gets pushed around, creating soft edges where I want them. While the pencil smoothes out the texture of the soft pastel, your sky will maintain a fresh appearance that would be lost if you were to put your fingers into it. When painting a foreground, you may want lots of texture, whereas in the sky, you will want to temper that quality according to what is right for the painting.

And what *is* right for the painting? I suggest saving the final touches in the sky for the last step whenever possible. At that time, when you are evaluating your en-

tire painting, it is best to be away from the reality and back in your studio. In this way, you are able to look at your painting without comparisons to the real scene, and to make adjustments based on what needs to be done to make a good painting. Ask yourself:

- Does the sky treatment help convey the mood that first inspired you to paint the scene?
- Or does it need more blending to keep it quiet, or more fresh strokes to give life back to overblended parts?
- Could it use a slightly deeper tone on one side to add drama?
- And finally, will the painting as a whole stand on its own without explanation?

CAPTURING COLOR AND MOVEMENT

Do not be overwhelmed by a swiftly changing autumn sky. Study it briefly and set aside some of the colors you see in it, paying attention to the value range you will need and the temperature of the colors. Then compose and block in your painting. When you are ready to begin painting the sky, take another long look for generalities, and work swiftly and lightly as you distribute the color into the large shapes. Then you can zero in on one smaller area at a time for refining and blending. The sky will change as you work, but the general treatment will remain the same for awhile. Beginners may feel more secure by taking a reference photograph to use in the studio.

Familiarity with your pastels and with what you can do with them will enable you to paint skies that are exciting and fresh. Practice strokes, particularly edges, on little scraps of paper or panel to see what effects you can obtain. This will eliminate frustration out in the field. At those times when the clouds seem to race across the sky before you are able to get down what you need in your painting, you may find your file of sketches and photographs or small color studies a useful backup.

Sky Patches

I taught myself the techniques for sky treatment by doing little "sky patches," as I call them, and I still enjoy doing these simple, horizontal-and-diagonal layerings of color in which I pull one color into another. Use the softest pastels you have. The direction of your stroke will determine the movement. Notice what the cloud edges are doing. When you can get the edges and the movement, you're on your way. These sketches can be done quickly and spontaneously.

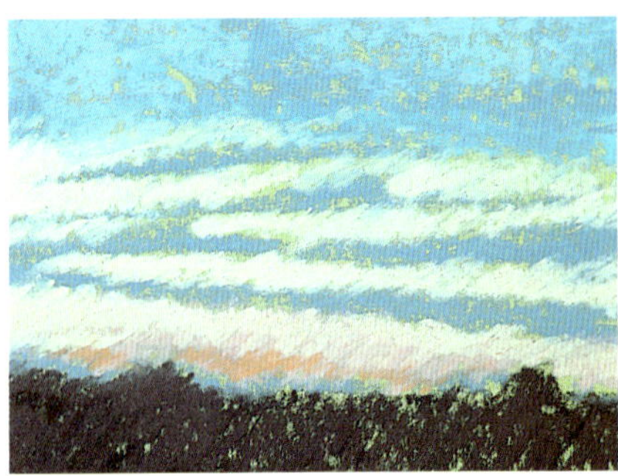

Step 1
I did these three sky-patch studies on consecutive autumn days. Each shows an interesting sky treatment on a small 6″ × 7½″ sanded paper surface that was taped to a board. Working on a flat surface, I put an initial layer of color down lightly and with a broad stroke. I used some Sennelier iridescent colors as well as regular soft pastels. It is best to try to get both value and the movement of the sky in this first step.

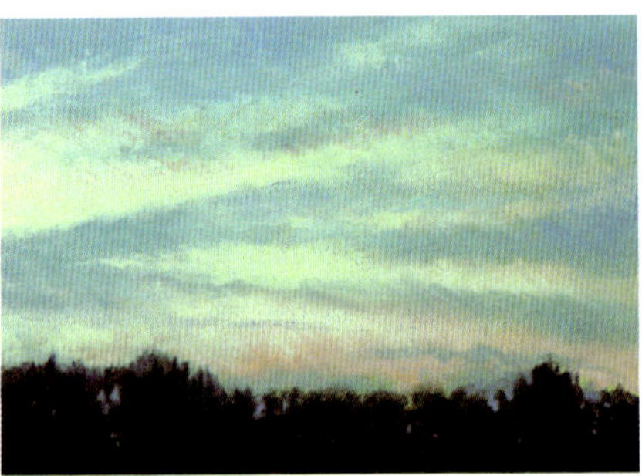

Step 2
Having recorded the value and movement of the sky, I apply additional variations of color with more soft pastel. After pulling some of the color together by working one color into another (no need for fingers on sanded paper), I finish with a few carefully placed fresh strokes to extend the movement.

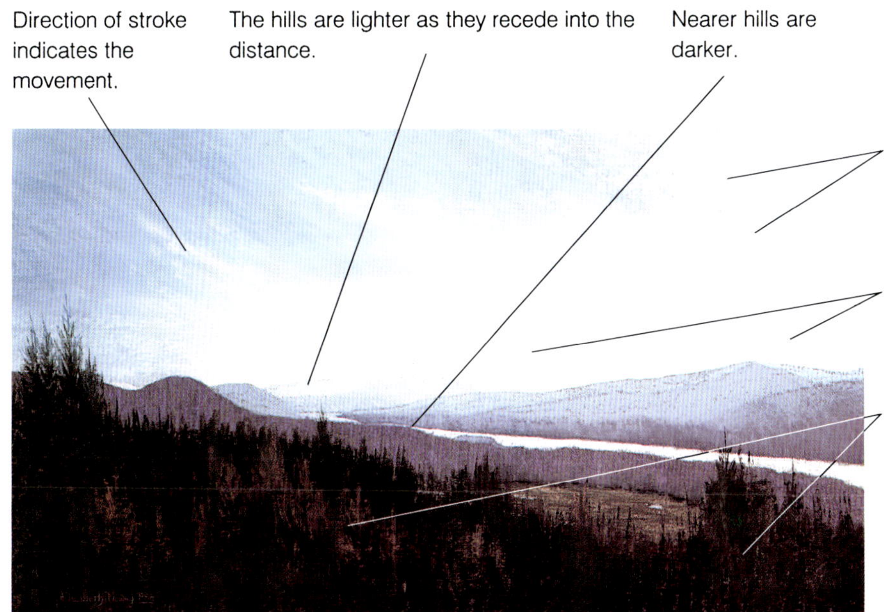

TOWARDS PEEKSKILL FROM THE HIGHLANDS
Pastel on sanded board
20″ × 36″

I attained the subtle movement of the sky, which dominates this landscape, by loose, sweeping side strokes of pink pastel over the blue sky. The absence of detail in the dark, foreground pines allows the viewer's eye to move to the river and the rolling mountains bathed in the light from the sky.

USING THE SKY TO SET THE MOOD IN YOUR PAINTING

When the sky in your painting is filled with clouds and movement, you are suggesting an active mood. If the other parts of your painting are likewise filled with lots of color and detail, you will create tension. Handled well, moderate tension can be interesting and provocative. But overdone tension will leave your work unfocused, so balance is essential.

The sky is often a key indicator of the mood that permeates the landscape. A painting that succeeds in portraying this link will be more successful than another equally well executed one that does not.

Graduated color, either vertical or horizontal, will suggest a quiet, restful mood in your painted sky. Making some color sketches of the sky will help you to build awareness of how the sky can indicate vastly different moods, even within the same day.

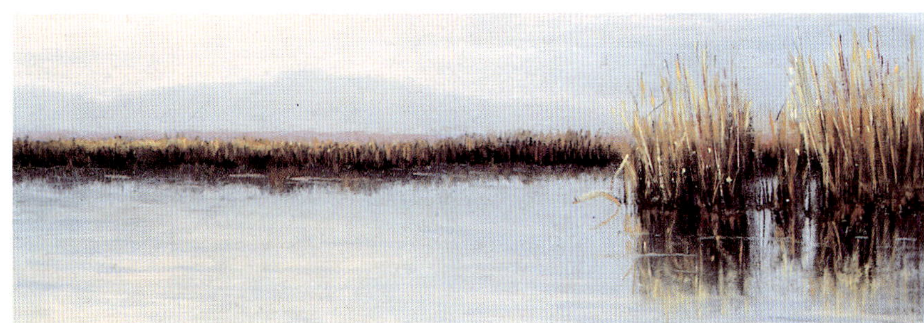

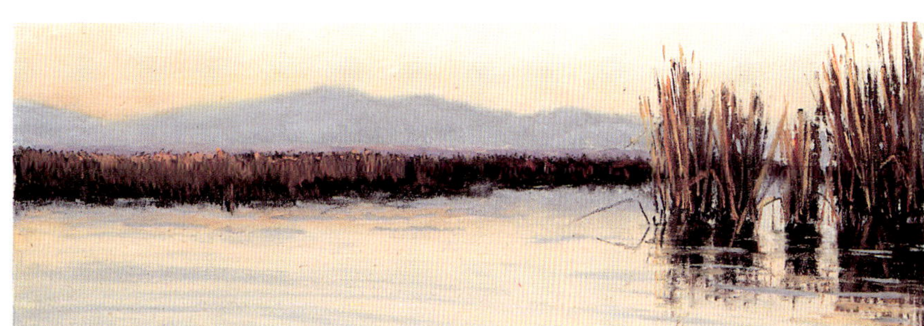

THE CATSKILLS FROM TIVOLI
MARSHES I and II
Pastel on sanded panel
3½″ × 10″
Collection of Mathew Warnecke

In these two studies, I explored the changing drama of an autumn sky. The time elapsed between the two was less than one hour. These modest examples make it clear that the sky, because of its effect on everything else, is an integral rather than an isolated landscape component.

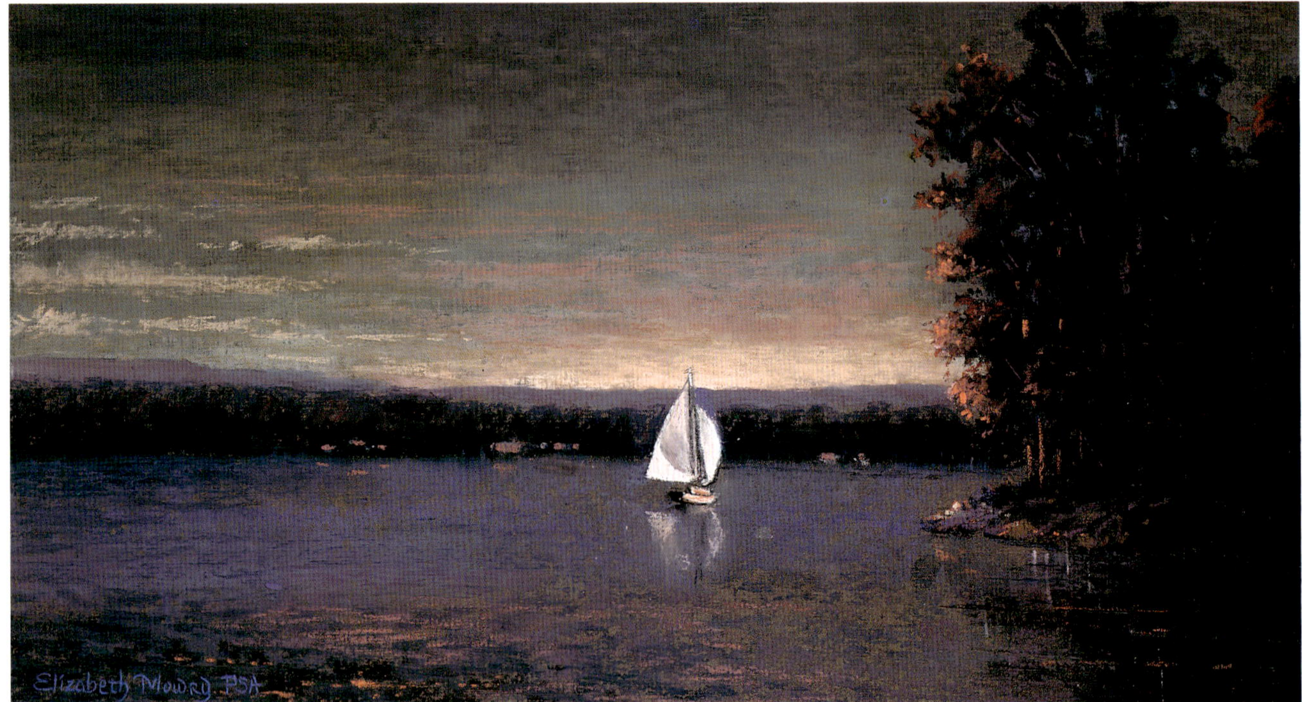

SUNSET ON THE HUDSON
Pastel on sanded board
20″ × 36″
Collection of Key Bank

Most of the sky in this pastel is low in value and chroma, and the subtle highlights on the trees and river are minimal. These qualities create a dramatic mood for what may be one of the last sailing excursions of the year.

Once you have determined the sky color and value in your painting, thinking about that color while you work will help you establish the mood you desire in your painting. Consider, for instance, the reflective qualities of that color in lakes, rivers, and even puddles. Notice again the way the warm or cool light in the sky affects everything beneath it. Relate the temperature of the highlighted parts in your painting to the color in the sky you have painted.

In shadowed areas that are due to objects in the path of the light in the sky, you can create the drama of a narrowed focus by refraining from highlights. Keeping some of these things in mind as you work will help you to create mood in your pastels.

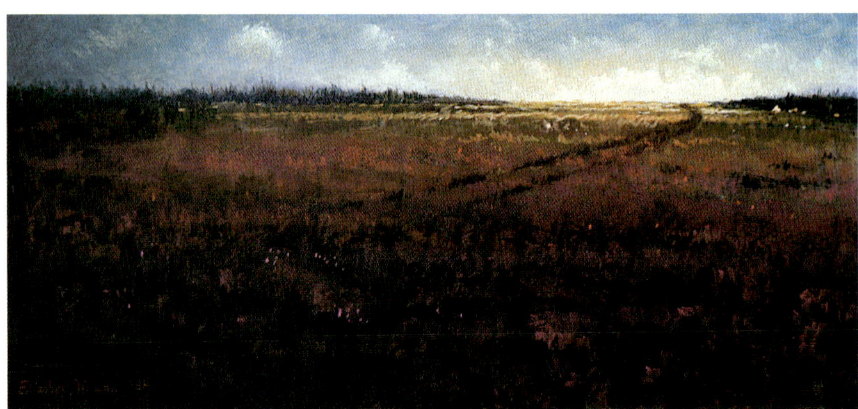

BLUEBERRY BARRENS, MAINE
Pastel on sanded board
12″ × 25½″
Collection of Ted and Lois Buley

Placed indiscreetly, detail can cause the eye to bounce all over your painting as opposed to seeing the work as a whole. In this painting, the near absence of detail in the vast, rich-colored blueberry barrens keeps the eye moving across the fields to the light at the horizon.

UNIFYING AUTUMN COLOR

You can unify the autumn color in your pastel paintings by (1) using a colored surface, (2) preselecting your palette or (3) cross-toning.

COLORED SURFACES

One of the most common ways to integrate color is to work on a colored surface, allowing the color of the paper or ground to become an integral part of the work by slightly, or even blatantly, showing through in many areas. The color of the surface you work on harmonizes the colors applied to it. If you have been working in pastel, the idea of using surface color to unify your work is elementary, and many fine surfaces in color have become available over the past few years. (See *View of the Hudson, Autumn* on page 83.)

Anytime you use a colored surface to work on, the ultimate unity exists at the beginning of the painting, and you control how much or how little of that surface color you want to keep as your painting progresses.

PRESELECTED PALETTE

Another way to keep color unified is to limit it by preselecting your palette. Since an abundance of immediate color is the hallmark of pastel, you may find the word *limit* disagreeable. But what I refer to here as limiting color actually extends the range of what each of the fewer chosen colors will accomplish.

No matter what palette you select, with an adequate value range, you can create intriguing pastels with a color-limited palette. I recommend using a practice sheet for color exploration. Try sticks of color beside, over and under one another in a variety of strokes to get a good idea of what will work best for your subject matter. The more you work with the concept of preselected color, the more you will surprise yourself as to just how few colors are sometimes necessary for a pastel to be highly successful.

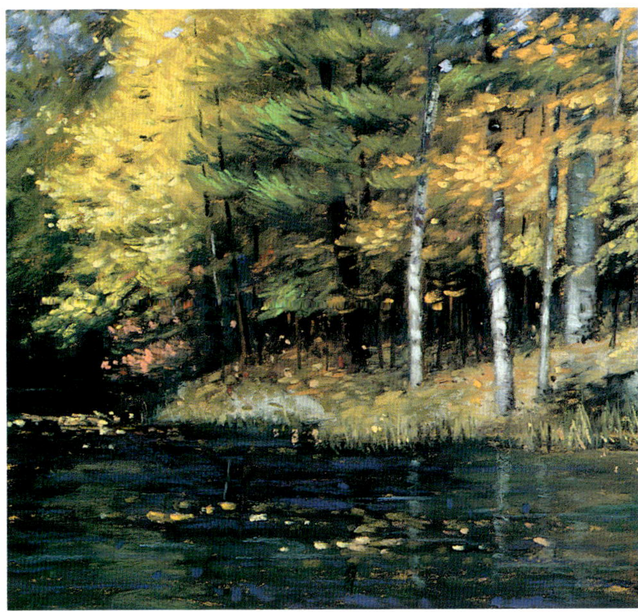

DUG HILL POND
Pastel on sanded panel
7½" × 8"

Much of the orange-toned surface shown in the illustration above shows through in this small, autumn painting.

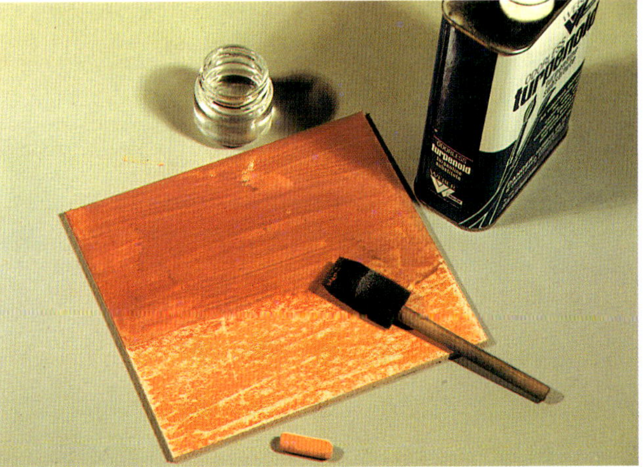

I side-stroked orange pastel over this sanded panel and then brushed it in with odorless turpentine. when the panel was completely dry, a unity was evident from the start.

PRESELECTING YOUR PALETTE FOR
A SLIGHT VARIATION ON REALITY

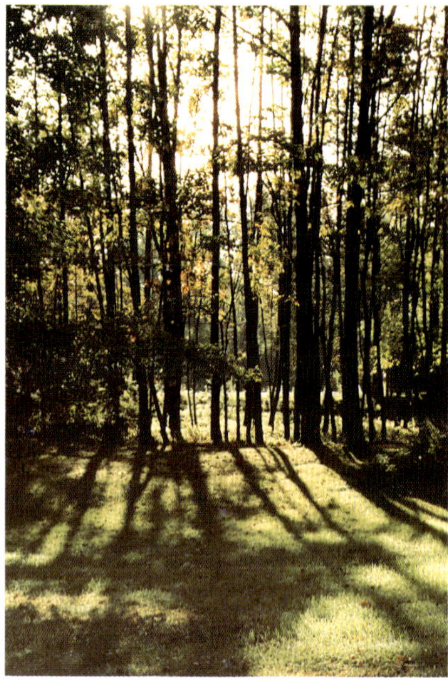

THE SCENE
One morning in early autumn, I happened upon these splendid shadows spilling out across the meadow grasses behind my home. Although unable to paint the scene on sight, I was happy that I had my camera along.

If you tend to rely on copying the colors in a photograph more than you wish, preselecting your palette will help you to keep form and color separate, and can ensure the color unity you need to convey a mood.

For example, in this demonstration I based the composition, or form, on the tree and shadow shapes shown in part of a photograph that was taken at the very beginning of autumn. My preselected palette of primarily warm colors ensured that the outcome of my painting would convey a mature, rather than a young, season, which is what I wanted to do.

A harmonious palette selected beforehand helps maintain unity throughout the painting. And since much of my work revolves around mood, I use this method to convey a sense of quiet to many of the paintings I do.

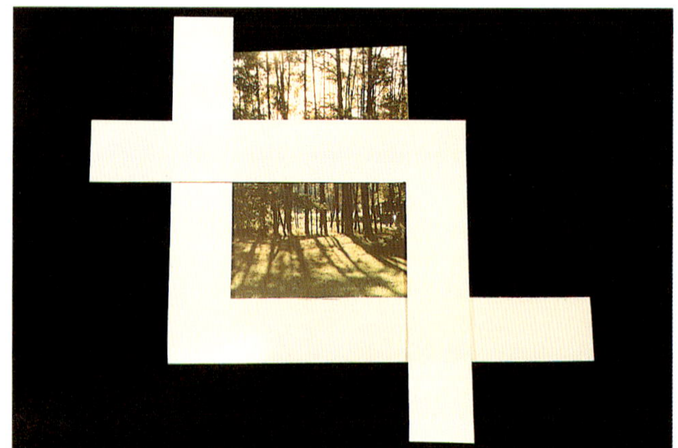

THE COMPOSITION
Later into the season, I moved my L-shaped viewfinder around on the photograph until I had cropped all but the image I wanted.

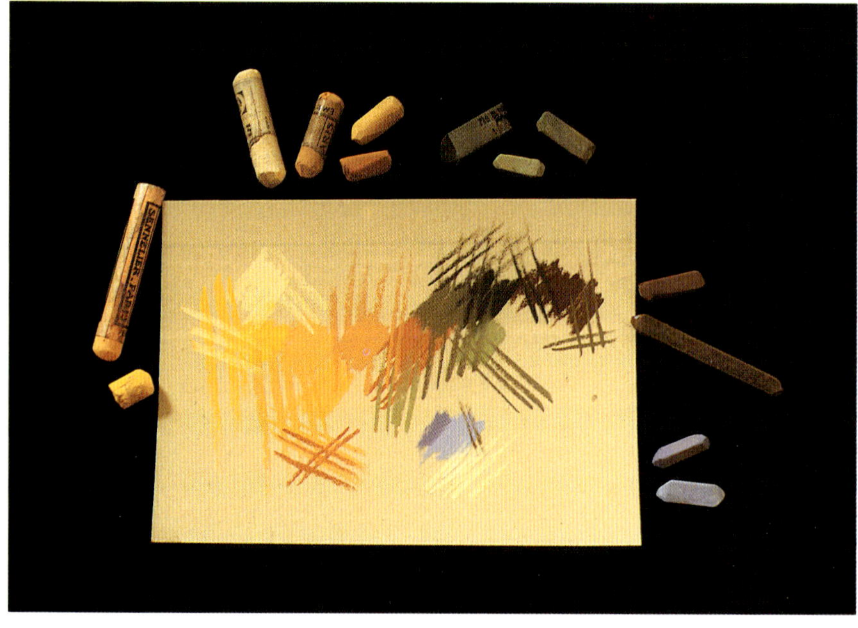

THE PRESELECTED PALETTE
To convey a matured autumn mood in my painting, I chose a primarily warm palette of Naples yellow, ochres, raw sienna, low-chroma greens, red-browns, and for complement, two tints of blue-purple for the minimal background.

I wanted the painting to look warmer than the photograph. So, one at a time, I chose the colors, trying each one with the others already selected. When my value range was covered and I was pleased with the way the colors combined, I stopped.

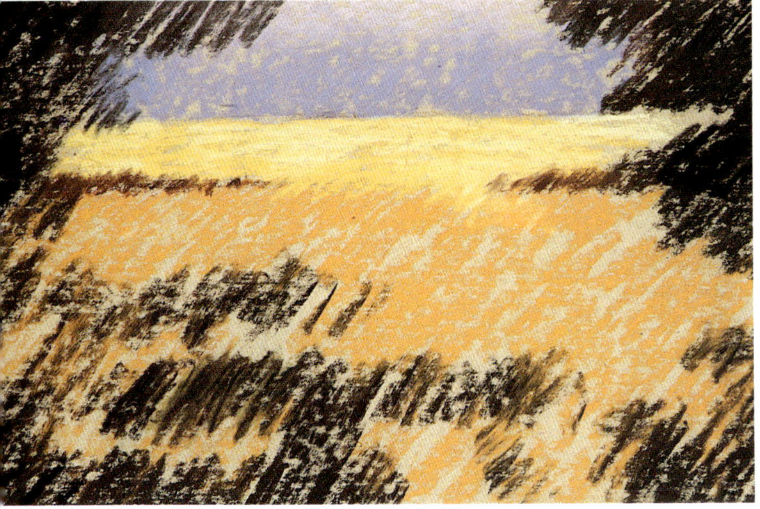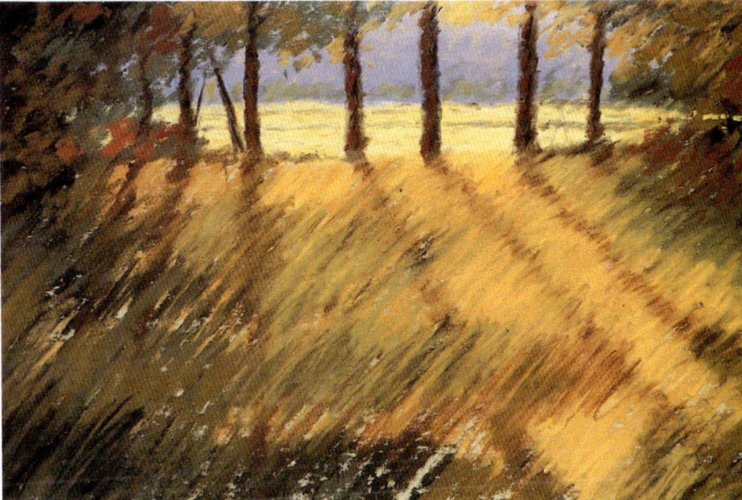

Step 1 The Large Shapes
I used soft pastels chosen from the preselected palette with loose, broad strokes to establish the large, high- and low-value areas in the painting. Since the palette had already been selected, I was no longer encumbered in the process of painting by color decisions and possibilities that would dilute my focus and the mood of the painting.

Step 2 Refining Shapes
Next, I chose colors from the middle-value range of my preselected palette to soften, darken or lighten areas. I also placed the tree trunks and shadows across the painting and used a slightly harder pastel to integrate some of the colors.

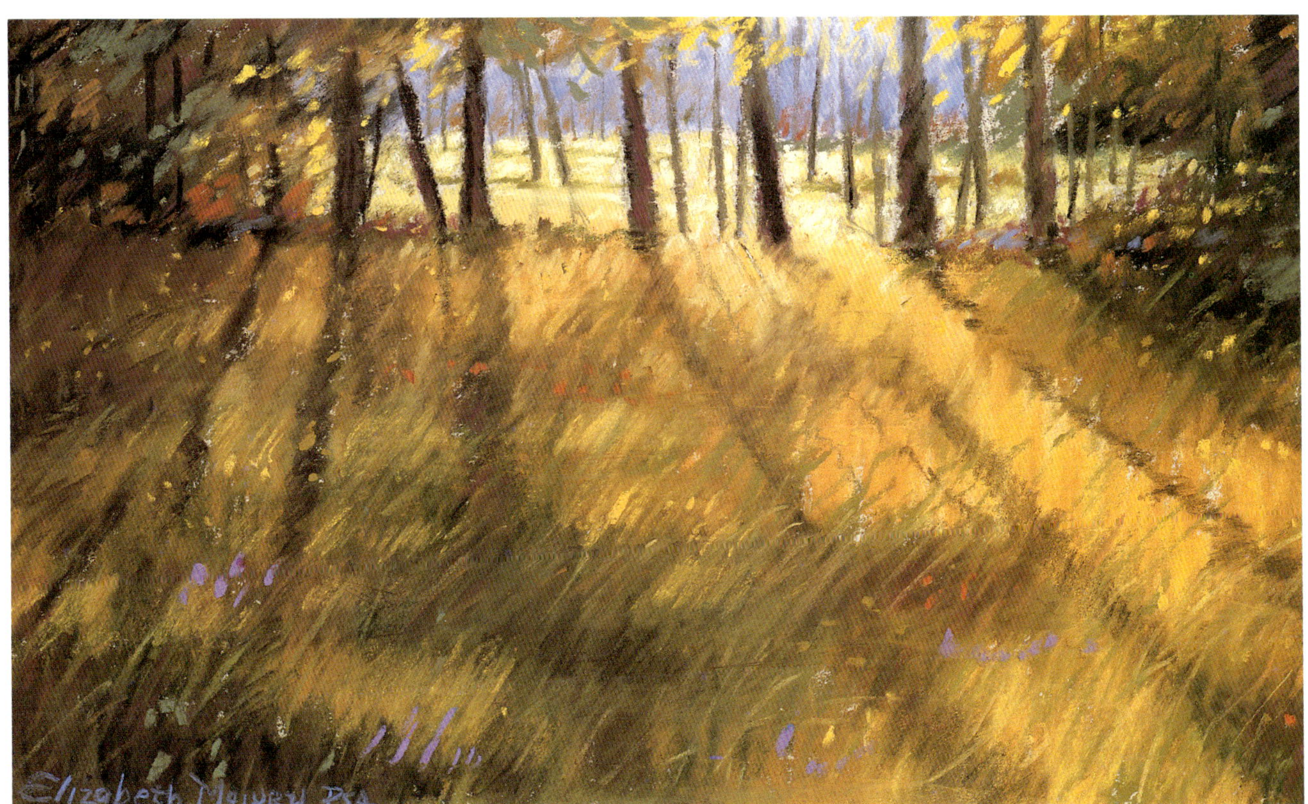

Step 3 Final Details
I made the final color and value adjustments, added the secondary tree trunks and highlighted the trees. Here, I have used a meager thirteen pastels to effectively paint a scene that would have lost impact if I had used a full palette.

OCTOBER MORNING SUN
Pastel on sanded paper
6" × 10"

VARIATIONS IN PALETTE SELECTION

Once you select your subject matter, choose the colors for painting it based on either those you actually see before you or those you visualize the subject matter as having. The choices are many and include a primarily warm palette, a primarily cool palette, a monochromatic palette, or a complementary, analogous, or low-chroma one.

In a *monochromatic*, or single-color, palette, only the values change.

An *analogous* palette consists of related colors, such as violet, red-violet and blue-violet. An analogous palette with a *complement* might be orange, red-orange and burnt sienna with a touch of blue complement.

A *complementary* palette would consist of any two opposite colors on the color wheel, and all variations would result from some combination of the two.

A *low-key*, or low-chroma, palette consists of colors that have been softened and made less intense with the use of complements, or other colors.

A *high-key* palette is made up of bright, unaltered color.

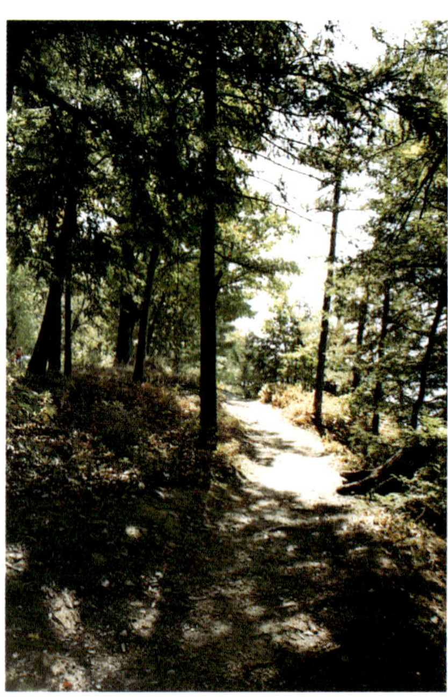

One rainy, autumn day I came across this photograph and recalled the summer beauty of the place where I had taken it. I decided to do a small painting using the composition but dramatically changing the color to that of the present season.

When preselecting my palette, I selected by sight some analogous pastels, tried them together on a practice sheet of ground, and then added a few more to cover the range of values I would need. A total of eleven pastels was selected — analogous colors with a touch of complement.

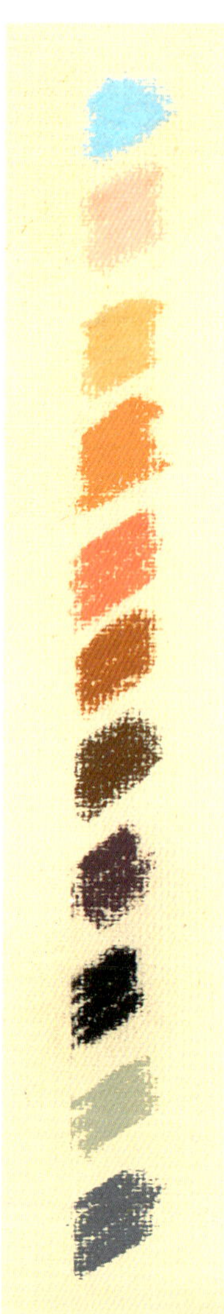

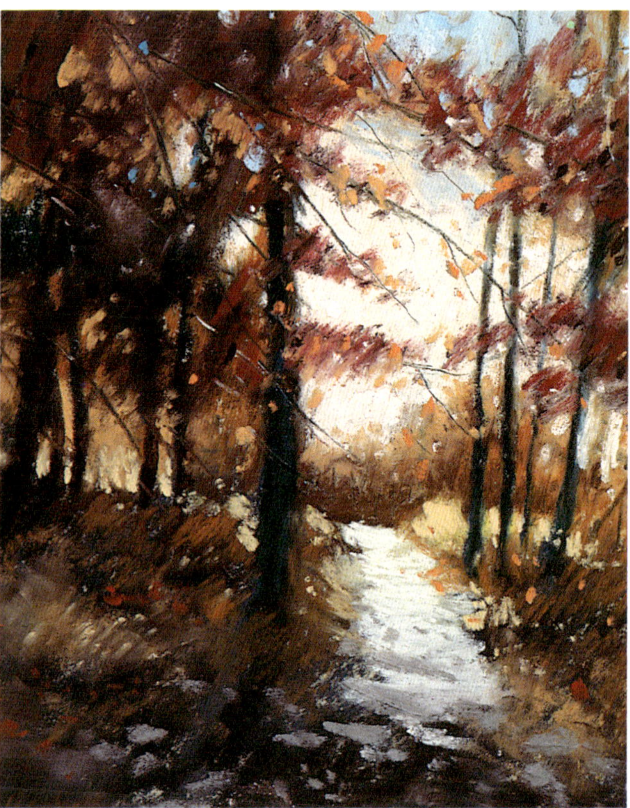

NEAR BARD ROCK
Pastel on sanded panel
6½″ × 5½″

The composition of this painting was based on a summer photograph that I had taken earlier in the year. Because I wanted to capture the feeling of solitude that I originally experienced in the place, and the fact that this would be a small painting, I felt that too much bright color would not be right. I kept this in mind as I selected my palette.

CROSS-TONING FOR UNITY

Cross-toning a pastel is similar to glazing an oil painting. In this procedure, all of the colors already in a painting or within a sizable portion of the painting are toned by another color or several analogous colors for a specific effect. Therefore, it is done at or near the completion of a work. Although cross-toning can help to blend color, its primary purpose is to unify color.

To cross-tone an area, apply light, open strokes with either pastel or pastel pencil into the existing colors in a direction different from the one already used—thus, cross-toning. Vary the pressure according to how much additional color you want to leave behind. Most often, only a hint of the cross-toning color is enough. Edges may soften, but existing shapes will not be changed.

Some of the most effective colors in cross-toning for a warm effect are ochre, sienna and sometimes magenta, and you will find others. Blue, purple and gray work well for a cool or distancing result. Experiment on a practice strip of surface to determine what color and pressure will give you the desired outcome.

Use the cross-toning technique with discretion. It will not correct a poorly composed painting, nor will it mask incompetent drawing skills. Overdone, it will destroy the freshness of clean work. However, used wisely, cross-toning is an effective technique for putting distance into background hills and mountains, or harmonizing a foreground that calls too much attention to itself. Cross-toning strokes can be used to add interest to an otherwise flat mass in a painting as well. For special effect, cross-toning can either warm or cool an entire painting.

In all of the solutions mentioned here for unifying color, you are in control. The degree of control depends on the effect you want in your finished pastel. Keep in mind that more than one solution may work successfully. Using small color studies will give you the opportunity to try more than one approach.

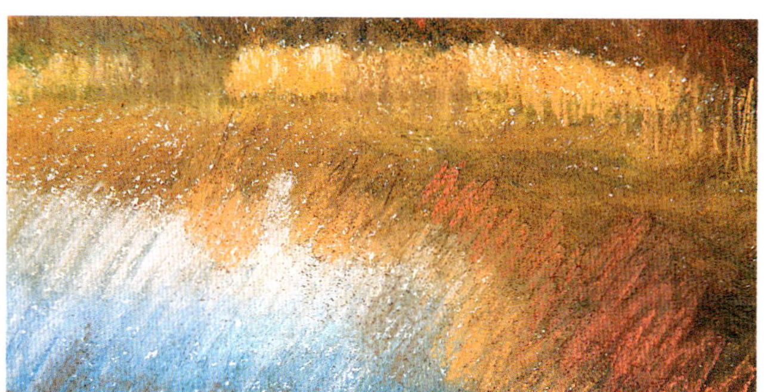

Suppose that in your painting you have some bright autumn reflections in water . . .

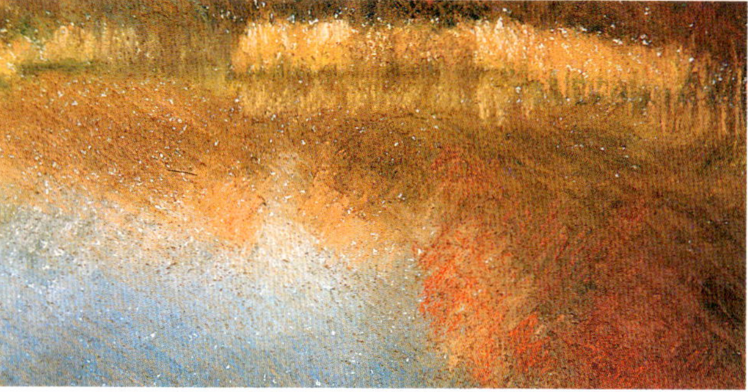

Light cross-toning, done here with a middle-value burnt sienna, will unify the colors slightly.

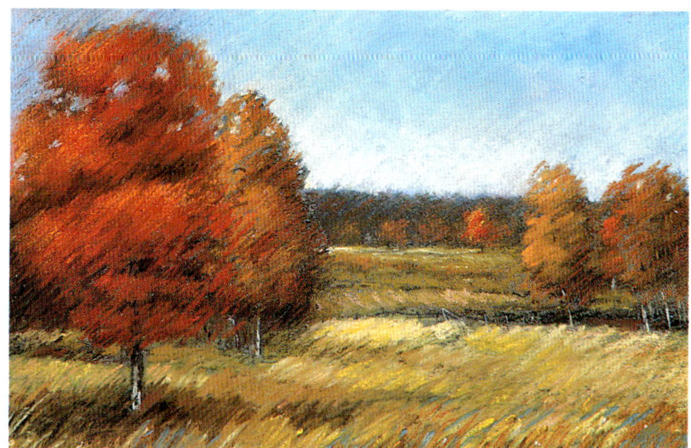

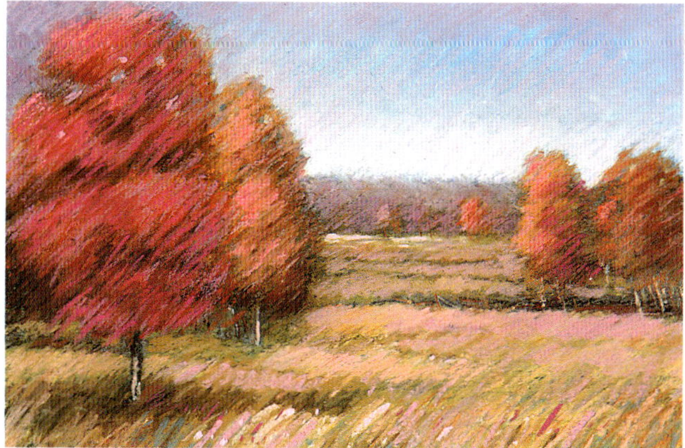

Heavier cross-toning, as in the example at right, using two values of red-violet soft pastel, can change a painting considerably.

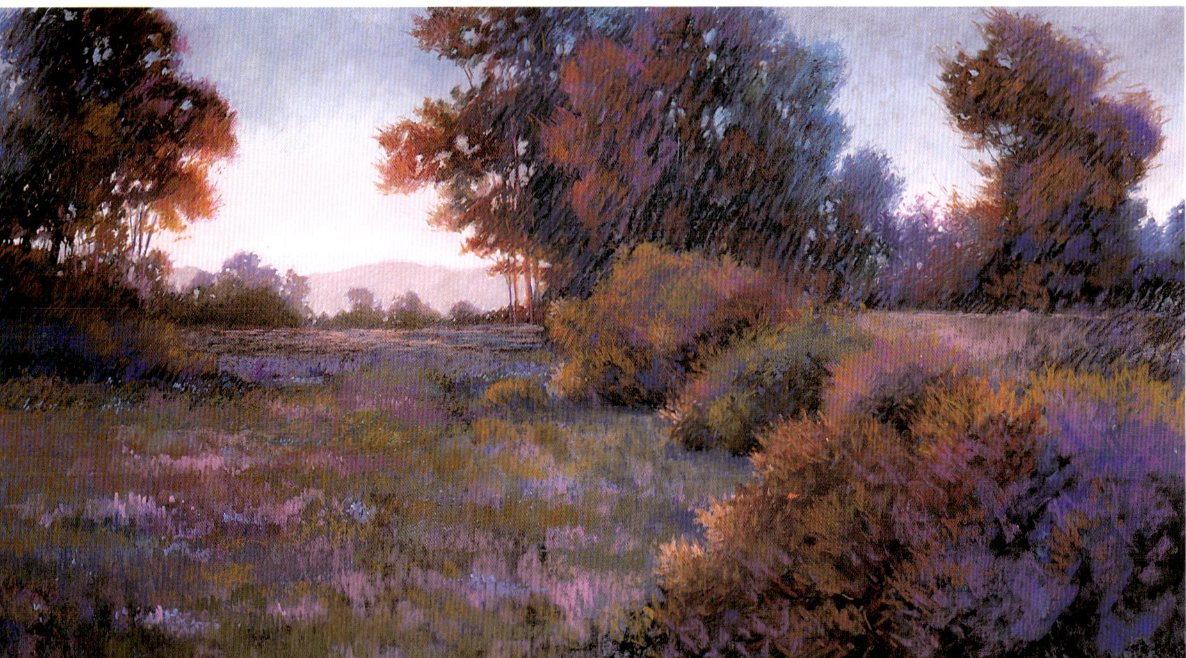

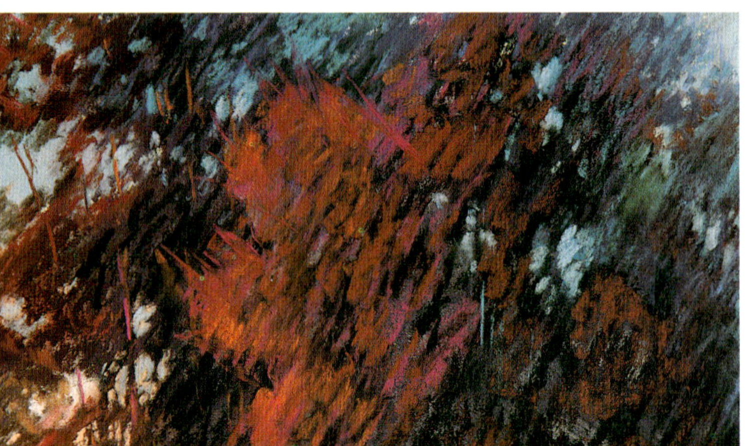

In this painting, I used several methods to unify color. First, I selected the palette to convey the harmonious mood I wanted to create. Then I brushed Turpenoid over the first layer of color in the lower portion of the painting for additional unity on the surface. Finally, some areas needed cross-toning to quiet the color. Unified color can transform the character of a pastel landscape from one with skillfully scattered color excitement to a statement of peace and composure.

This close-up detail of September (left) shows some diagonal cross-toning strokes of analogous colors (low-chroma red, burnt sienna and deep ochre) placed over initial layers of color to achieve a serene unity in the painting.

NEAR WALLKILL
Pastel on handmade surface
8″ × 12″

The feeling of autumn is realized in this landscape by the warm temperature of the palette. I did some selective cross-toning of the yellow sky and the background hill using purple-gray to complement the foliage color. Then I introduced burnt sienna into most of the trees to unify the color and to keep the tone of the painting quiet.

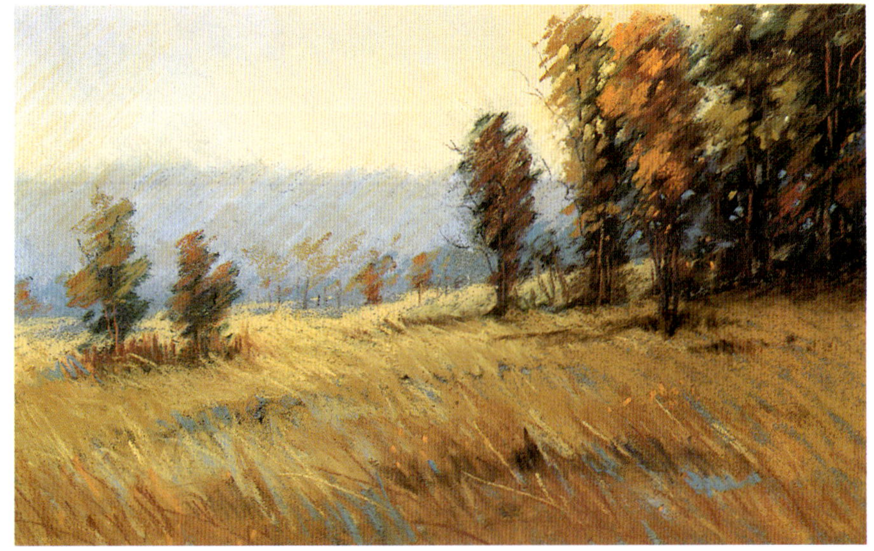

LATE AUTUMN'S TRANSITIONAL PALETTE

The final phase of autumn arrives overnight with the first substantial frost. The colored foliage falls, sometimes within a few days, and the change is dramatic. Between the leafless shapes of trees that begin to appear, you will be able to see far into the woods. Mountains, hidden in summer, will become visible again. Rock walls are more interesting now than at any other time of the year. Notice how the low November sun accentuates the soft and hard edges of the gray stone shapes that are entwined here and there by frost-ripened bittersweet.

Nature's limited palette of remaining color is often overlooked because of the excitement that has just passed, but there is restful harmony in what lingers. Subdued grays and browns and blues predominate now, but again, these are delicately balanced by warm purples and ochre. Clouds, their edges luminous, stretch across rosy sunsets. Open meadows still show the greatest variety, depending on what grew there earlier in summer. Purple fields, once majestic in their glory, are now a surprising, rich sienna. Berry patches and woody-stemmed brush take on a deep, magenta glow. Warm earth colors wash up against the cool gray of trees and sky.

I really enjoy painting the landscape in this last part of the season. I exchange the multitude of colors in my painting box for a meager pocketful of pastels and do quick color studies outdoors. Value becomes more important than color in composition now. Nature simplifies itself, and the uncomplicated landscape leaves room for the feelings of the artist to become part of the work.

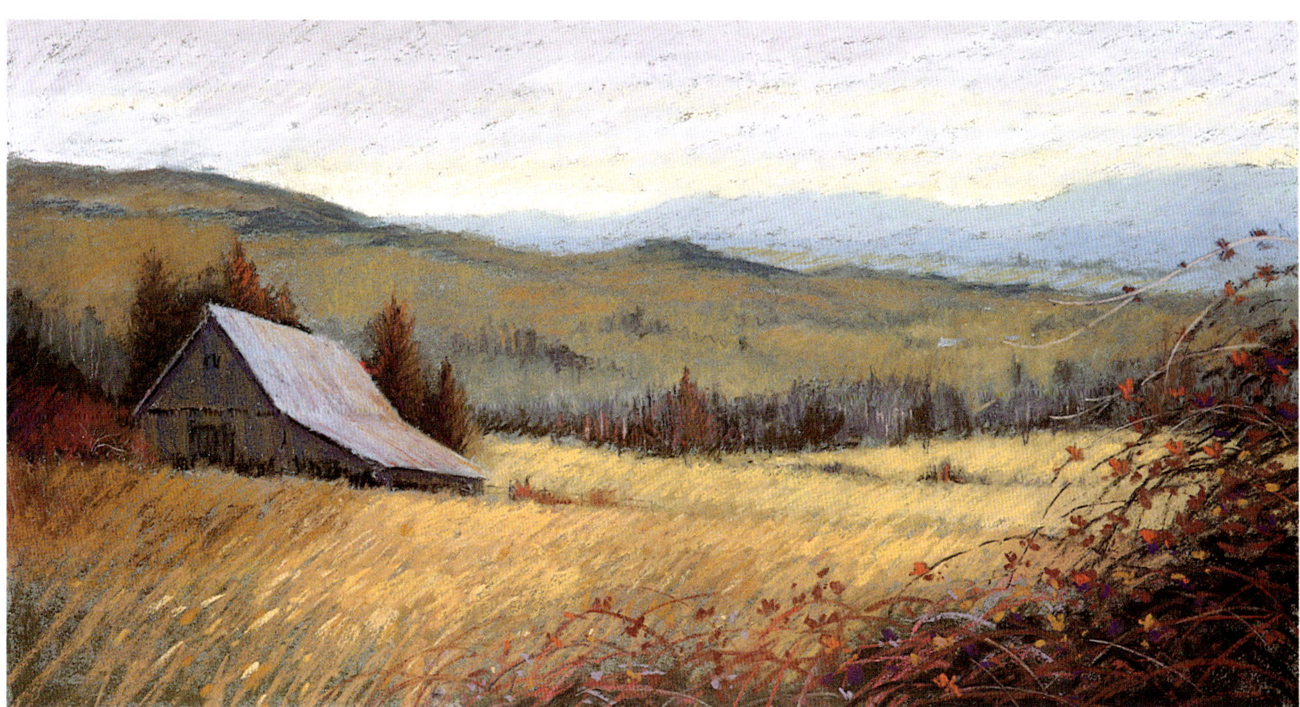

IDAHO BARN, AUTUMN
Pastel on handmade surface
10" × 18"

Within the quiet, low-chroma palette of late autumn, contrasts in value and color temperature can be used to create a pleasing composition. Here cool blues and grays in the mountains and barn roof are balanced by warm ochre grasses and the cedars and tangle of foreground briar bushes that are painted with sienna and violet. This is an example of how color can convey mood . . . in this painting, the barren isolation of oncoming winter.

THE TRANSITIONAL PALETTE OF LATE AUTUMN

This is a view of the Catskill Mountains near my home. It is a simple, layered landscape. Nonetheless, it changes in character as the seasons unfold. Here, in late November, it is cold but sunny. The leaves that fell in October have all blown across the fields into their own hiding places. The mountains have probably already had their first snow, but in the valley, brittle grasses still catch the afternoon light.

In a painting such as this, in which the palette is subtle and the composition appears deceptively simple, it is essential to construct a value structure with effective contrast, or the painting will be lifeless. Here, sufficient contrast at the area where the grasses meet the woodland was especially important.

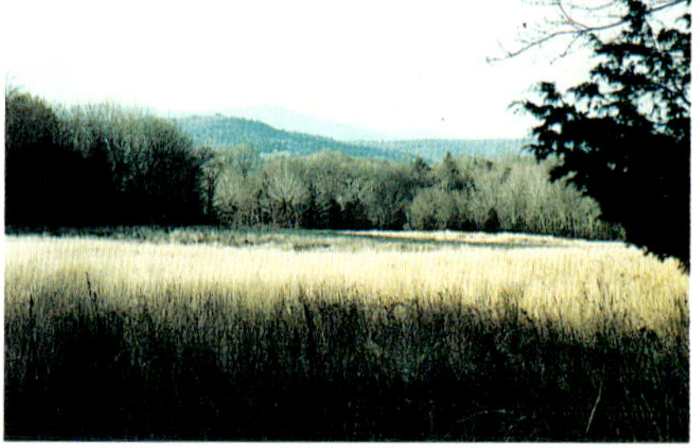

Photograph of the site from where I painted November Afternoon.

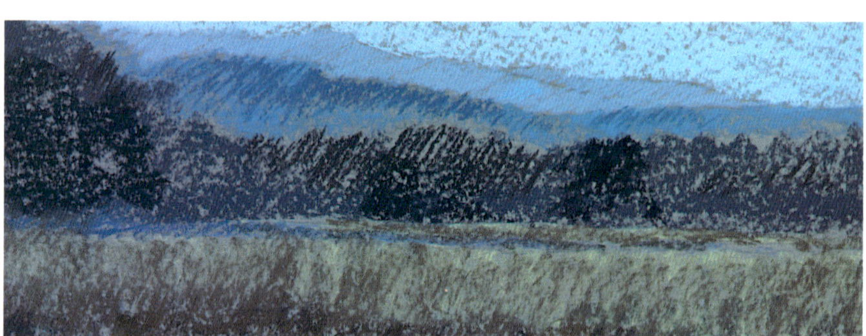

Step 1 The Shapes
Here on location, I apply the first pass of soft pastel. This establishes the basic shapes that compose the landscape, which are, in this case, layers of subtle color. The deep ochre you see in the foreground will show through the light grasses later.

Step 2 The Values
Now I refine the values with another layer of pastel. The value differences between the sky and the far mountains are minimal, giving the appearance of distance. I introduce darks into the tree line, leaving the darkest mass of suggested evergreens on the left; this dark value gives some compositional weight to the left and breaks the symmetry. I put in the grassy field with light-value diagonal strokes.

Step 3 Cross-toning
Back in the studio, I cross-tone the mountain layers with gray and blue pastel pencils to unify the color slightly.

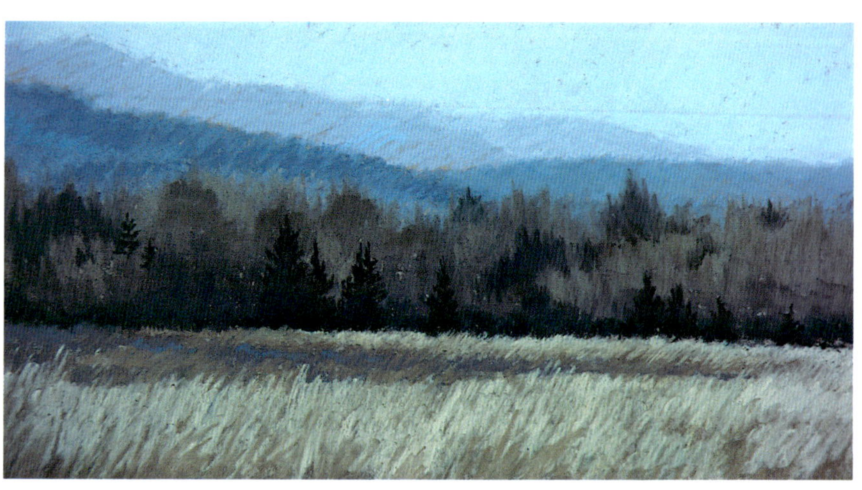

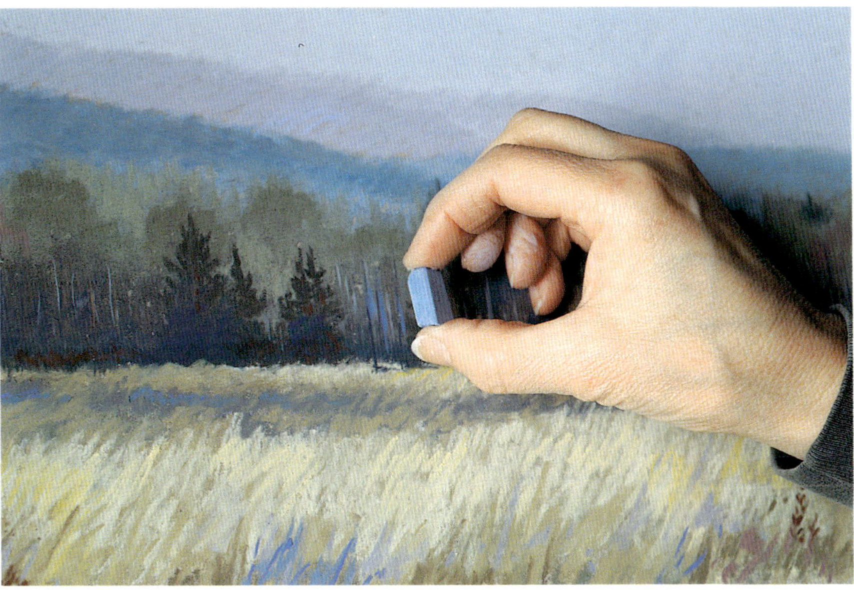

Step 4 Vertical Strokes
By using the edges of squared pastels in vertical strokes, I suggest the direction of the dark and light tree trunks within the wooded area.

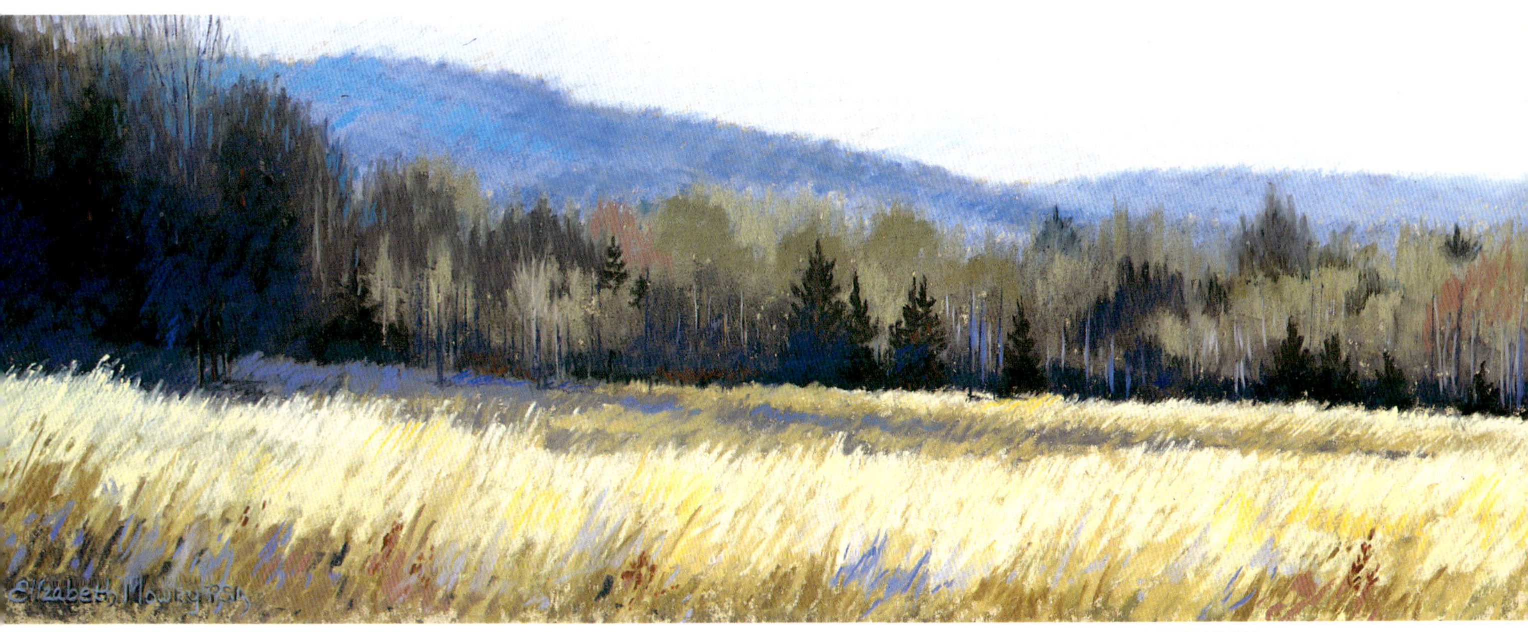

Step 5 Final Adjustments
Bits of warm sienna, as well as a small amount of blue for color repetition, go into the tree line and the foreground grasses. I cross-tone some deep purple into the darkest mass at the left. Then, with a wiggly stroke of light yellow ochre, I indicate the edge of the field against the trees on the right. The surface of the painting is still fresh and clean because all the strokes have been lightly applied.

NOVEMBER AFTERNOON
Pastel on sanded board
9″ × 23″
Collection of Judith and John Missell

ZEROING IN ON THE HARVEST

Autumn is traditionally a time of harvest, when man and beast prepare for winter by storing and preserving the fruits of summer's growth. There is a sense of urgency as the daylight hours shorten and a chill permeates the air. As an artist whose subject matter is nature, you may recognize the tendency to hold on to what is passing by taking what remains of the season inside to paint.

As you become more and more in tune with nature's recurring cycles in your own region, you will be alert to signs that can expand the scope of your work immeasurably and lengthen your autumn painting season.

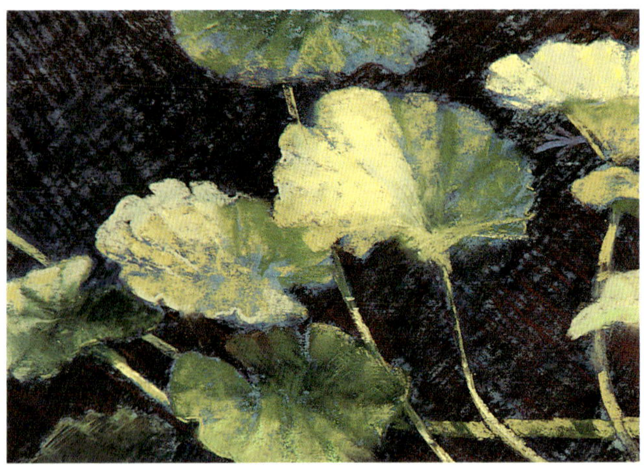

This detail of Winterset Pumpkin *shows the clean, turped-in ground showing through.*

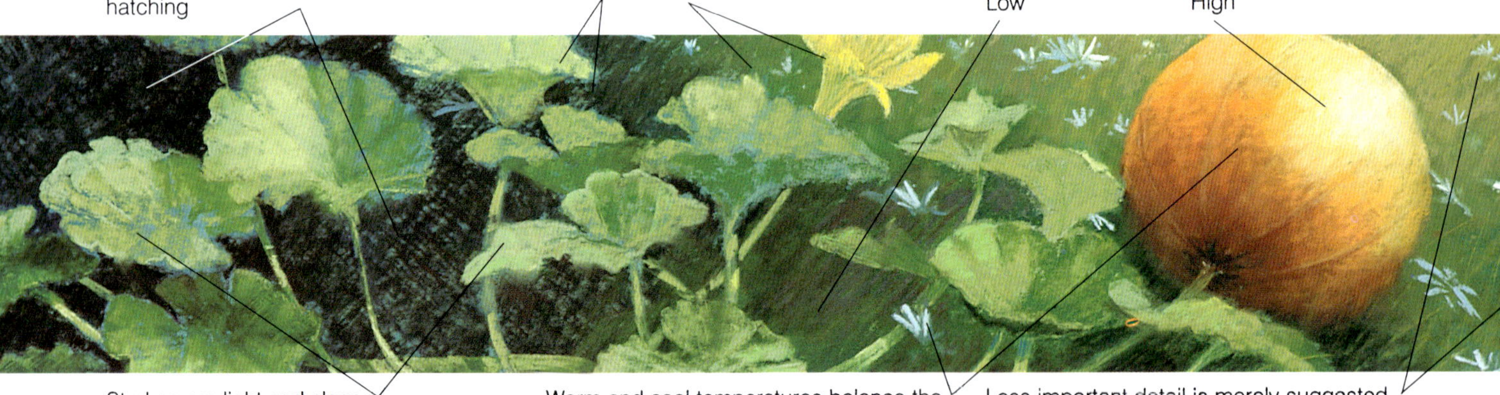

In late September, this pumpkin was still young, but the patterns of the leaves and vine called to be painted. I intentionally chose the horizontal format because it allows the vine to "grow" across the painting.

First, I darkened the ground by brushing Turpenoid over a layer of indigo Nupastel and letting it dry. Because this liquid layer of color sinks into the ground, it does not interfere with the grit's full capacity to accept color, which was essential for the crisp treatment of the leaves.

The suggestion of a few lingering daisies provides a delicate shape contrast to the larger, highlighted pumpkin.

WINTERSET PUMPKIN
Pastel on sanded paper
8″ × 30″

OUTDOOR STILL LIFE

During the final pleasant days of autumn, consider the idea of painting at least one outdoor still life. Before harvesting, take advantage of the abundance of painting compositions already in place. For example, zero in on the pears or apples on the trees, or the exact spot where they fall. You might be surprised at how often nature's arrangement surpasses our own.

This phase of outdoor still life is short, limited as it is by the unpredictability of weather, but by developing a familiarity with "what happens when" in nature, through observation, notes and sketches, you will discover an expanded offering of evocative subject matter that might otherwise be overlooked.

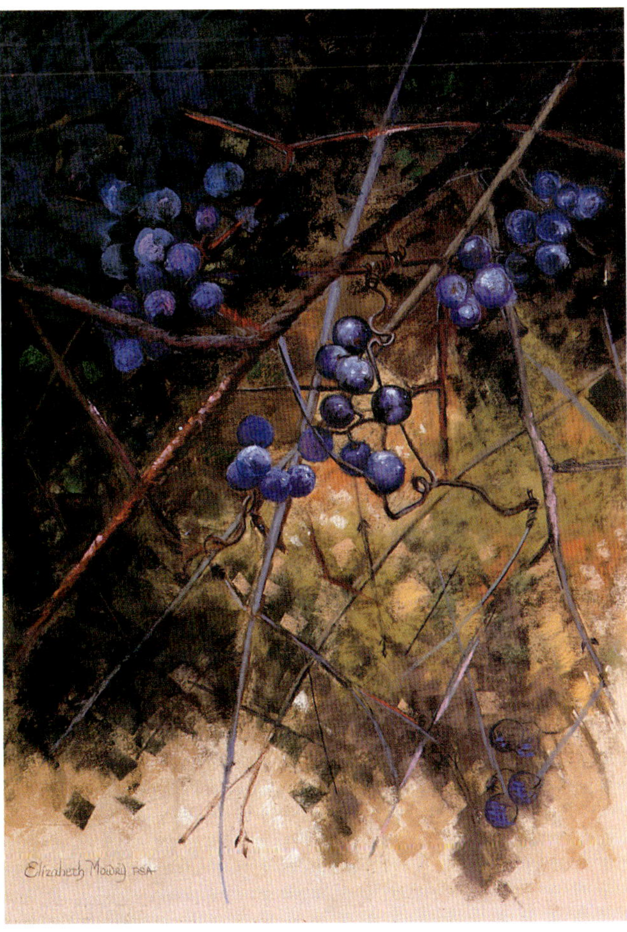

SEPTEMBER PATTERNS
Pastel on sanded paper
17″ × 13″

This is a study of grapevine patterns and shapes as they exist in their own environment. Each season is filled with expanded painting possibilities when natural settings are given consideration. Just remember to get up close to your subject matter. Limit the scope of what you paint, and work at almost life size. Don't be afraid of filling your painting surface.

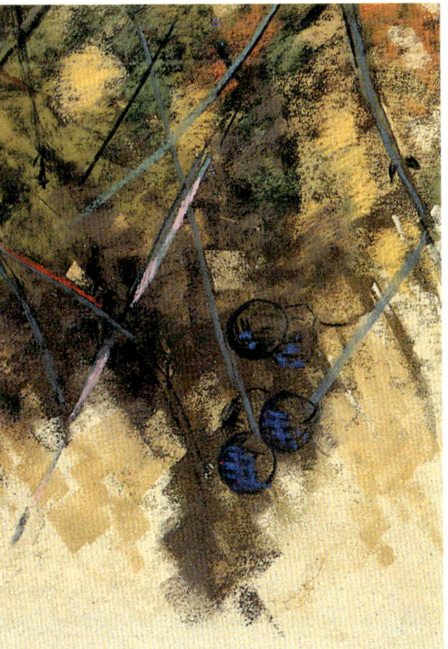

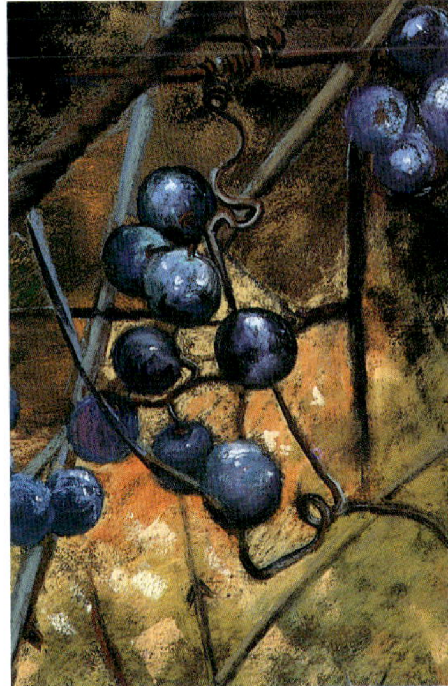

The detail above left shows some of the drawing strokes in September Patterns. Simple lines suggest the grapevine stems, and outline strokes define grapes outside the center of interest. Above right, some bold, clean painting strokes model the shapes of the grapes, and then broad, short, sidestrokes paint the background and push against the shapes to give definition.

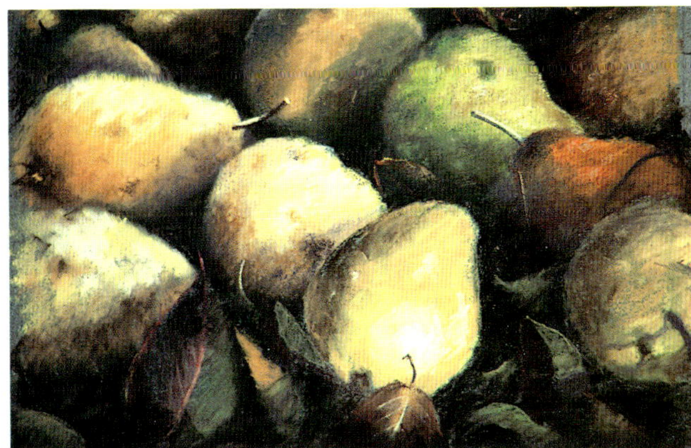

After putting in the darkest areas with soft pastels, I added some of the brighter colors to the life-size pears, then carefully modeled the shapes with subtle color.

PEARS
Pastel on sanded board
8″ × 12″

BRINGING NATURE INSIDE

Eventually, it is time to gather our turnips and apples, the cones and pods, and the dried flowers and grasses. As we bring our varied harvest from outdoors to inside, filling jars and crocks and baskets, the action itself becomes a statement in our work: Nature rearranged in humankind's environment.

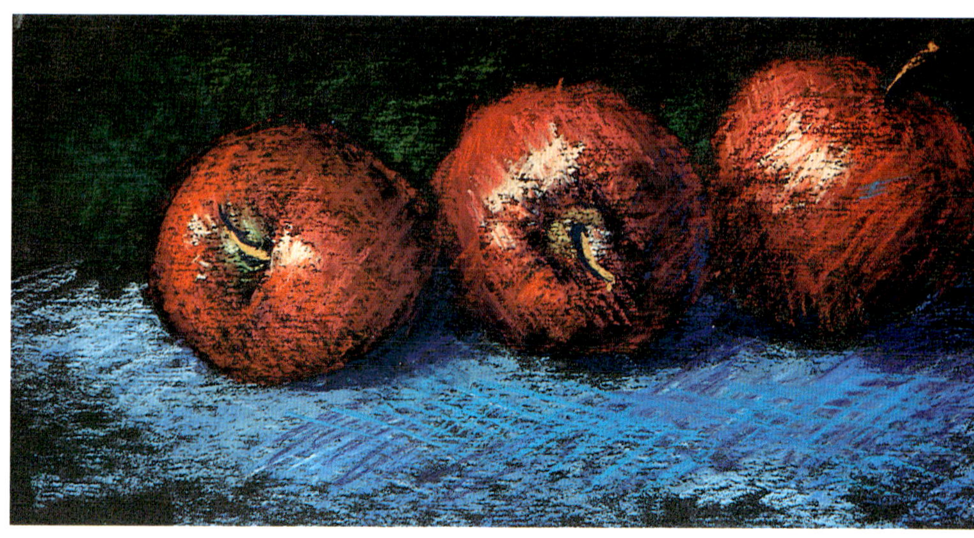

THREE APPLES
Pastel on sanded paper
6½″ × 12″

I painted these apples with soft pastels on a dark-toned ground, much of which I left untouched. The loose, broken strokes give shape and highlight to the apples. Light crosshatching suggests the blue table covering. Shadows are soft and indistinct.

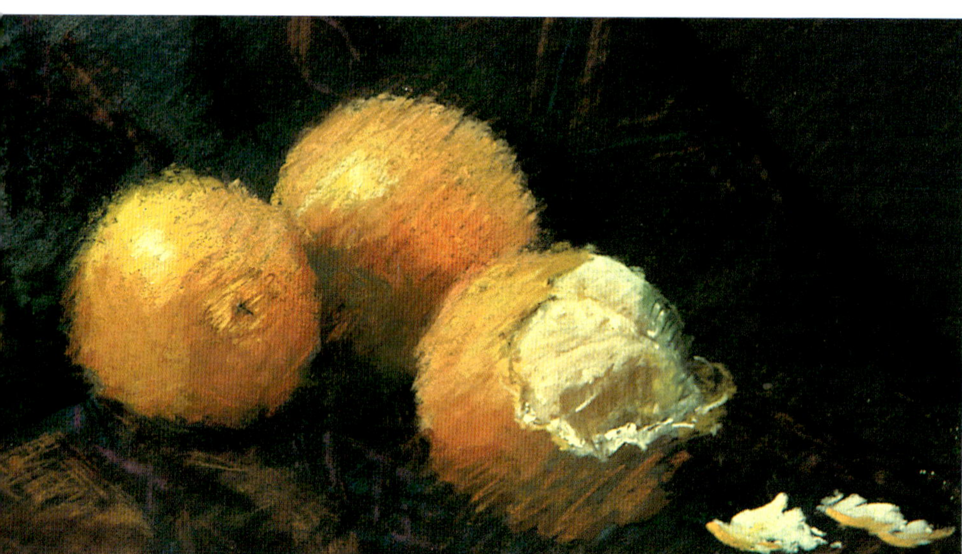

ORANGES
Pastel on sanded paper
7″ × 11½″

Here, I've built up three shapes on dark paper in open strokes, beginning with low-value burnt sienna on up to the pale highlights. The Oriental rug is merely suggested by the low-chroma, low-value, crosshatched color.

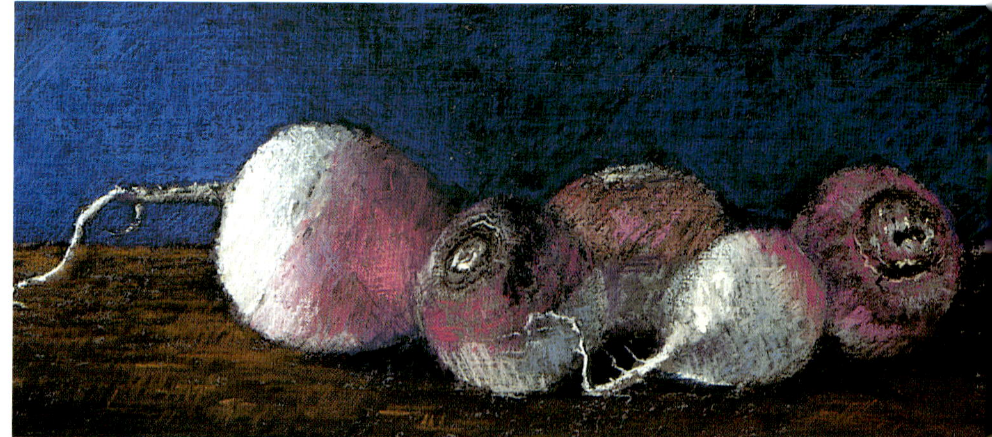

TURNIPS
Pastel on sanded
paper
6½″ × 13″

The dark-toned ground shows through the lightly applied, soft pastels. As in this case, fewer than ten pastel sticks can be used to make a pleasing painting. Complicated still-life setups are generally an exercise in technique. The simple subject, on the other hand, leaves room for the viewer to respond to what is presented.

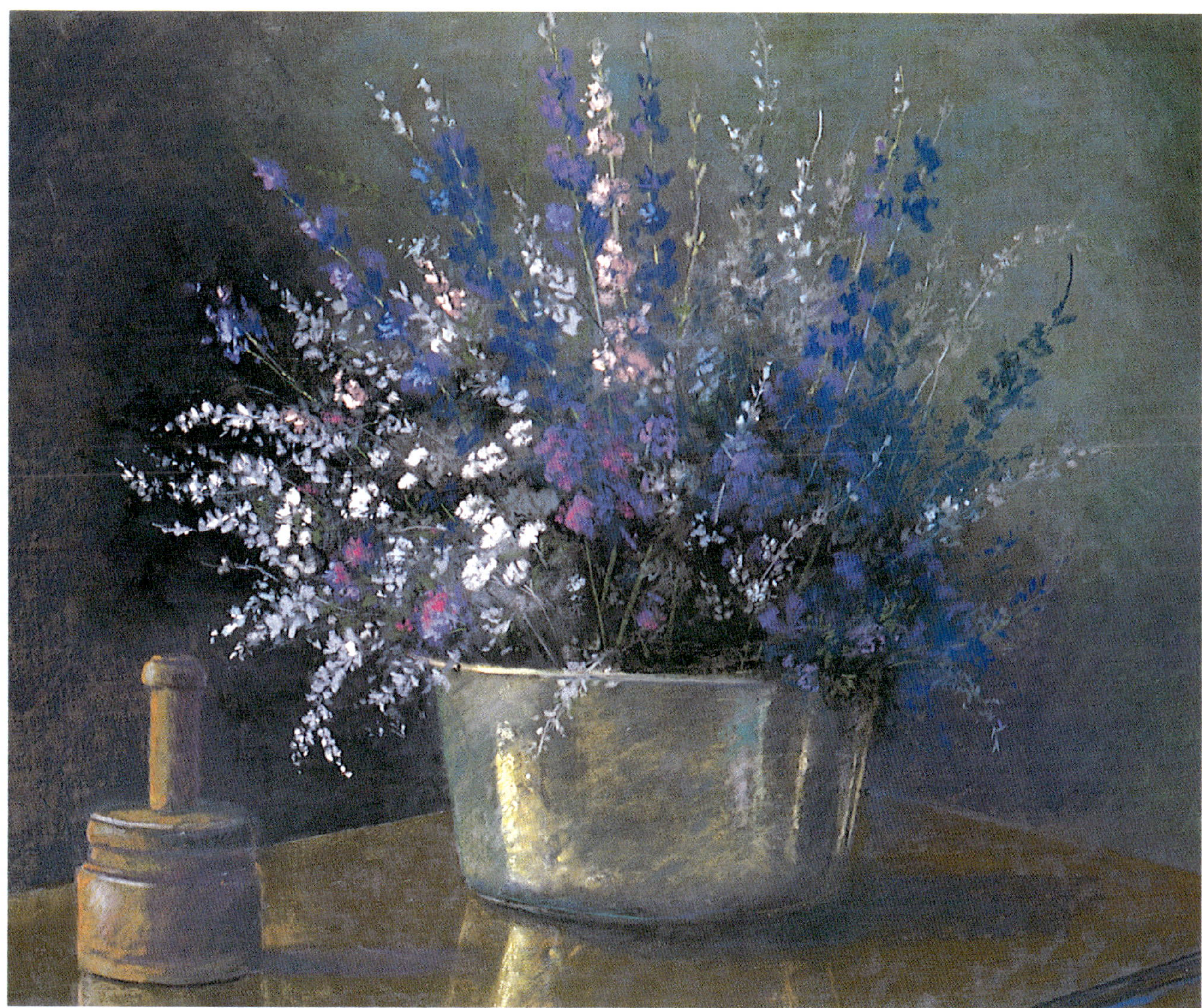

DRIED FLOWERS AND THE
BUTTERMOLD
Pastel on sanded panel
22″ × 28″
Private collection

*Finally, at the end of the season, the flowers have been dried and arranged. Painted on
a dark-toned panel, this low-key still life keeps color and value in reserve. Edges lost in
the shadows make this painting more interesting than if they were visible.*

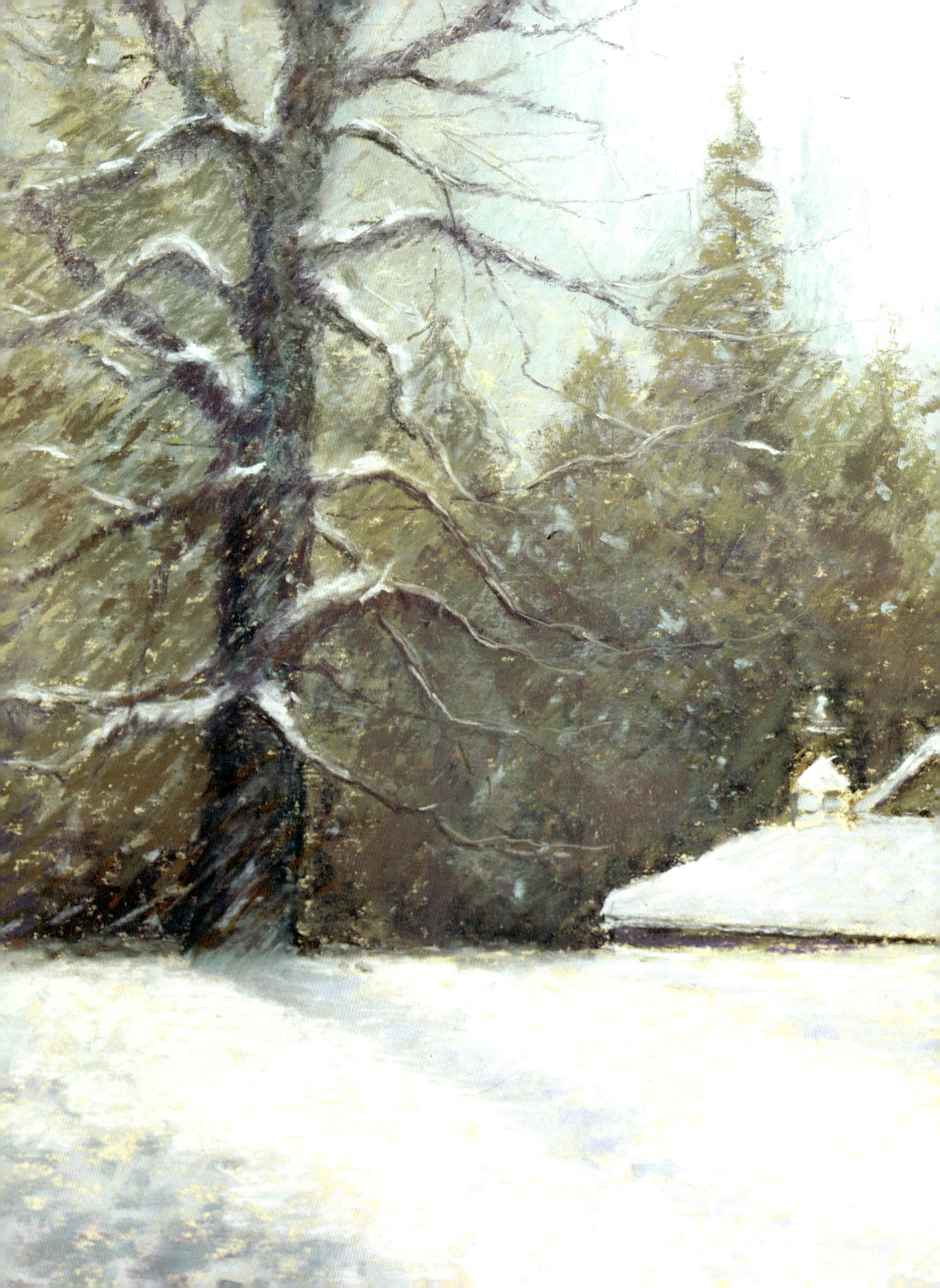

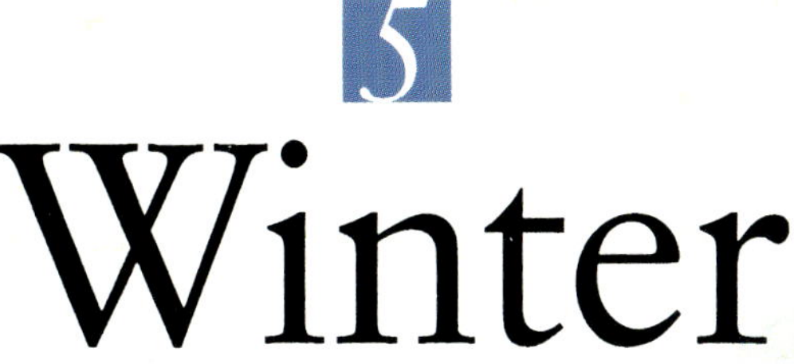

5
Winter

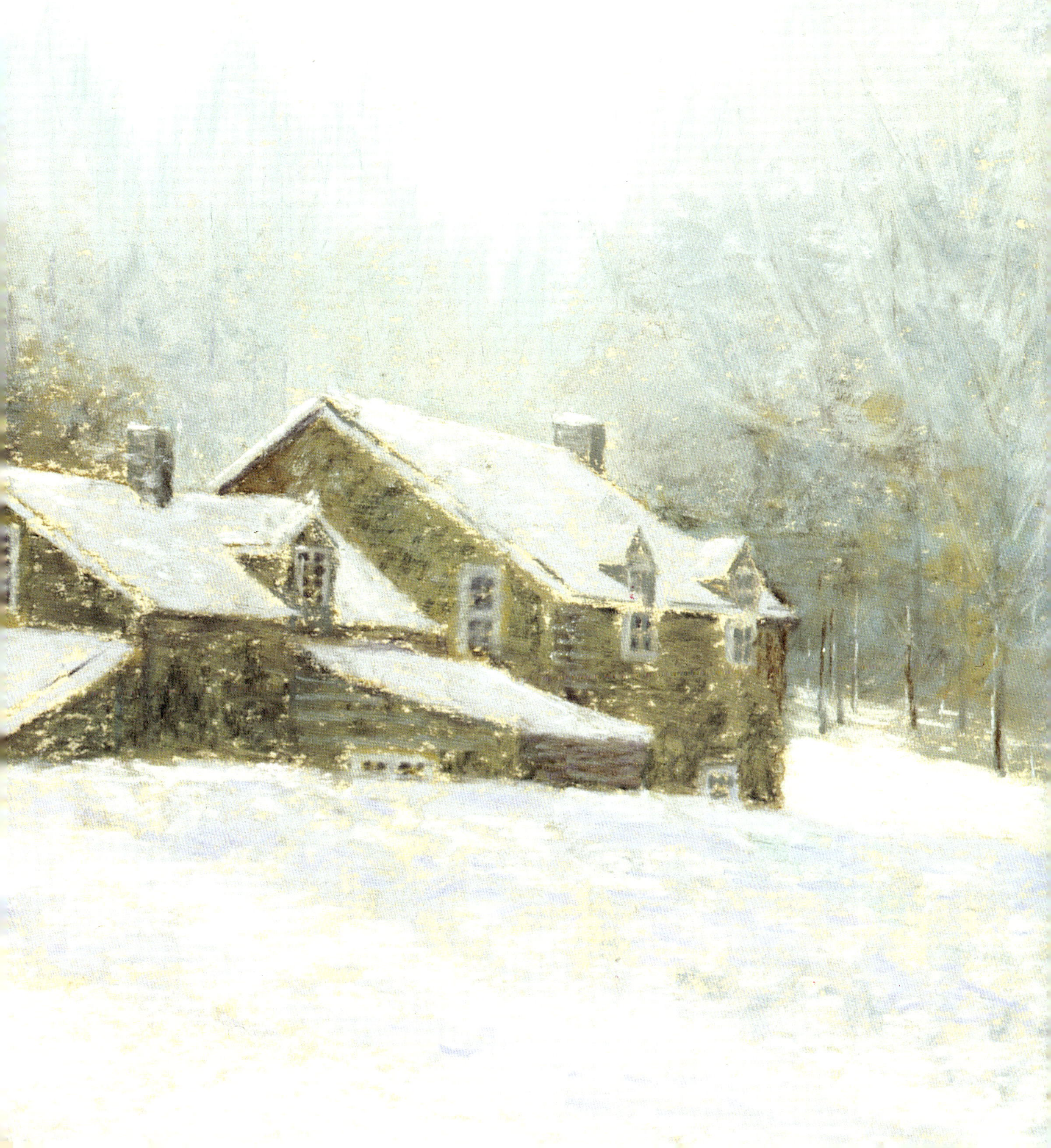

A RESPONSE TO WINTER

Winter embraces all the remnants of color from the weary year and then sometimes drops a fresh, white color over them all. With the addition of snow over the landscape comes the potential for both exciting, and beautifully quiet, paintings.

As you look for subject matter in the fields and in the woodlands under the dry tree branches that crackle in the wind, you will see that a clear sky in winter appears more intense in color than at other times of the year. There is also a great variety in cloud formations. Dark storm clouds hang very low in the sky, and as they hover near the horizon, they tend to stretch out like pulled taffy. Be mindful, too, of the stark beauty of barns and outbuilding shapes against leaden skies.

Be sure not to allow the winter sunsets to go unnoticed; they can be as spectacular as those of other seasons. They happen quickly and early, and the conditions for watching outdoors are not leisurely. Nevertheless, on your way home from a walk, as you hurry toward the warmth that awaits inside, take a moment to watch an early-setting winter sun color the sky with rich violet, magenta and orange just above the darkened horizon. For a few brief seconds, the light will swiftly change, and change, and change before it almost explodes and is gone.

On moonlit winter nights, witness yet another drama in the sky. Patterns of clouds, as they open and part over and around the moon, are hypnotic in their beauty and can provide endless material for skyscapes.

I happen to love the winter landscape under any conditions, but I find it particularly exciting to allow the light in the sky to assume a dominant role over a minimally painted end-of-day snow scene. The end of the year, together with the end of the day, conveys a beautifully poignant intensity that I often try to portray simply because I am deeply affected myself.

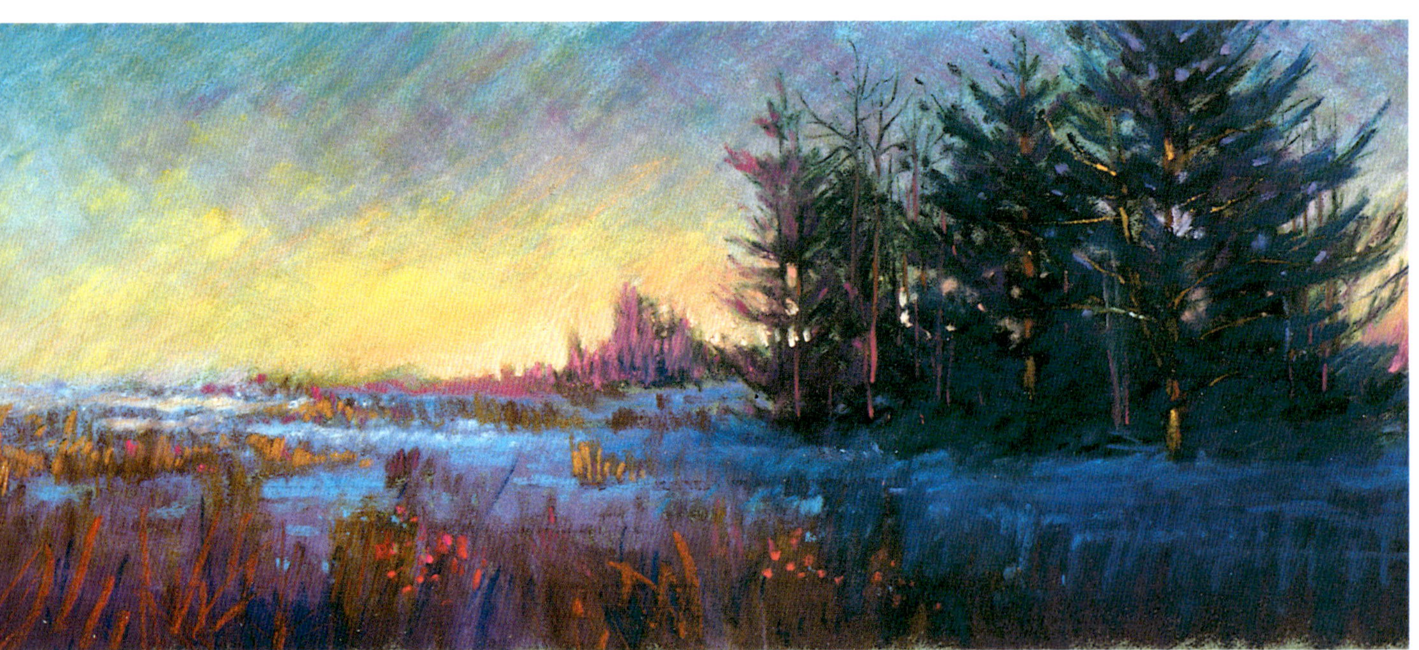

A dramatic winter sunset intensifies the light at the edges of trees and grasses in the darkening landscape. Sky colors are cadmium red light, Naples yellow, violet and blue, all of which are absorbed momentarily by the snow. In this end-of-day, end-of-year scene, the diminishing light in the sky conveys the emotional essence of the painting.

YEAR'S END
Pastel on Sennelier La Carte
5½" × 13"

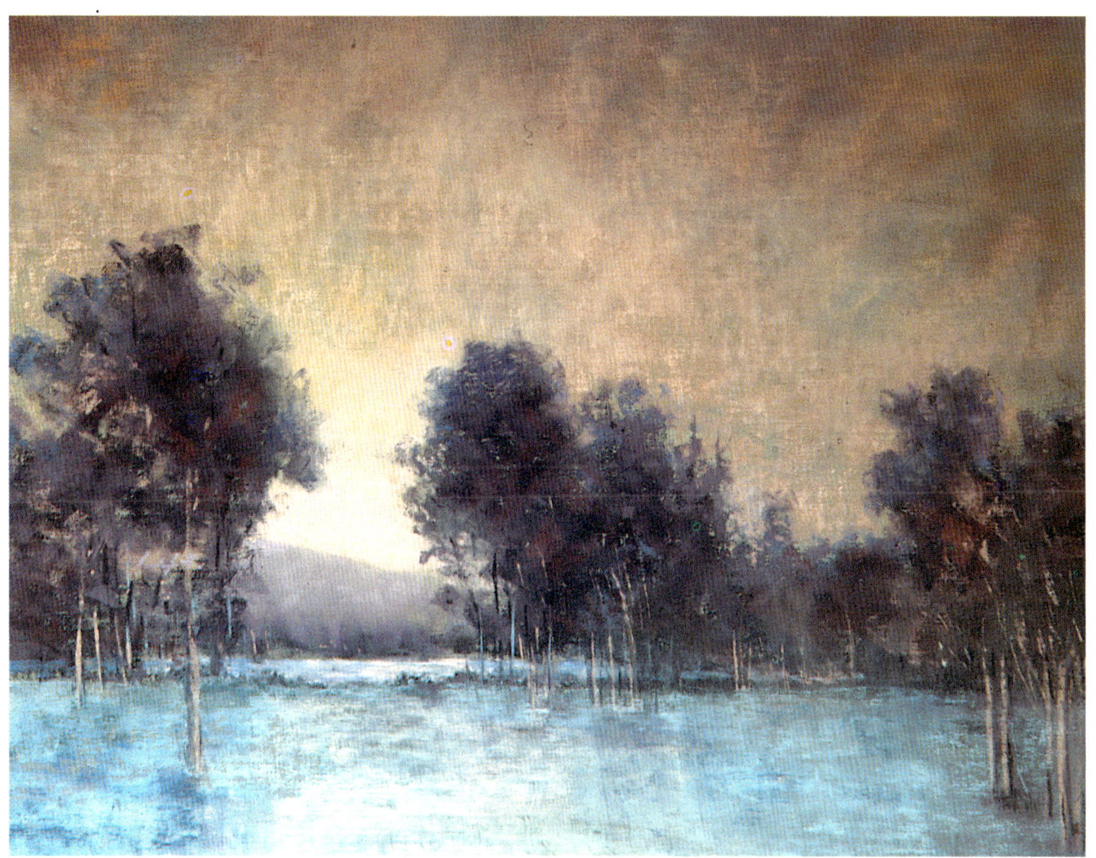

WINTER ALLEGORY
Pastel on sanded board
15″ × 18″

*Cadmium red tint and brown madder sky colors warm this winter
painting. The snow, being a horizontal plane, absorbs the warm
light from the dominant sky, whereas the trees with their vertical
orientation, are cooler, darker purple-gray.*

*The dark cloud formations that frame the center of interest on this
Daler-Rowney Ingres paper are two values of gray-blue. You can
obtain a blended look in your pastel sky studies — without the use
of your fingers — through a generous application of soft pastels
using closed strokes, repeating the layers if necessary.*

HINTS FOR BETTER WINTER PAINTINGS

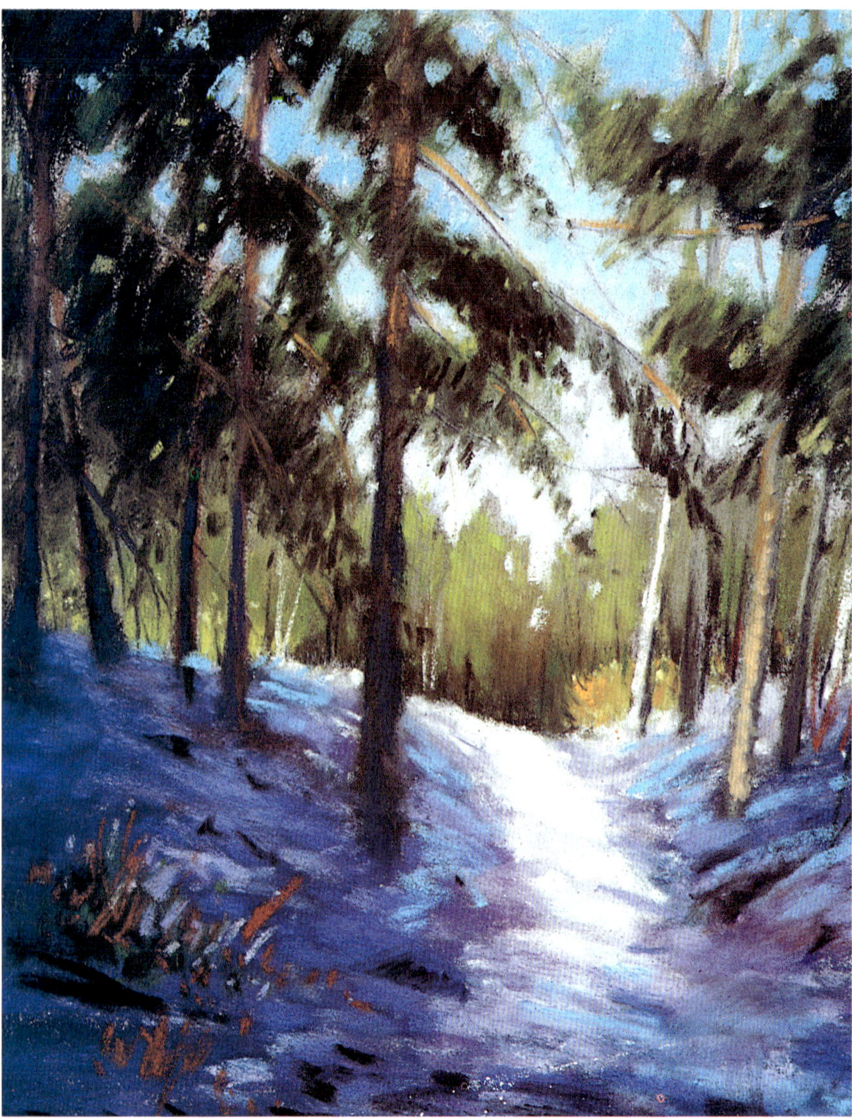

BARD ROCK PATH IN WINTER
Pastel on La Carte Pastel
9" × 7"

The small area of sunlit snow represents the highest value in this modest winter painting. The deep green coniferous trees and their blue-and-purple shadows are the lowest value. Compare this painting to Near Bard Rock *on page 92 in "Autumn." The striking difference is due to the change in color temperature.*

In winter, the landscape is reduced to the essentials. Structure, much of which is hidden during other seasons by foliage, becomes prominent. How convenient that nature simplifies itself for us in winter; fragmented summer foregrounds now appear as one large area under a covering of snow. For example, the autumn field of colorful weeds and different varieties of brush is transformed overnight into a mass of white, divided perhaps by only a narrow, ice-edged stream. These large shapes are the strength of this austere season. They can become the strength in your paintings as well.

Examine color closely as you look at your winter landscape. In the distance, a jagged tree line might appear purple under skies that range from clearest blue to overcast. The dark blue mountains that rest behind the trees will soften to palest lavender as they recede. The rich greens of the coniferous trees may frequently be the deepest (or lowest) value in your winter landscapes. When snow occurs, of course, it will replace the sky as the highest value in your paintings.

On a sunny day, because of the high value of snow, there will be lots of contrast, even in shadow. Observe the snowcapped rocks rising from the black-green streambed. See the swirling indigo water at the bottom of a partly frozen waterfall. Study the low, graceful hemlock branches

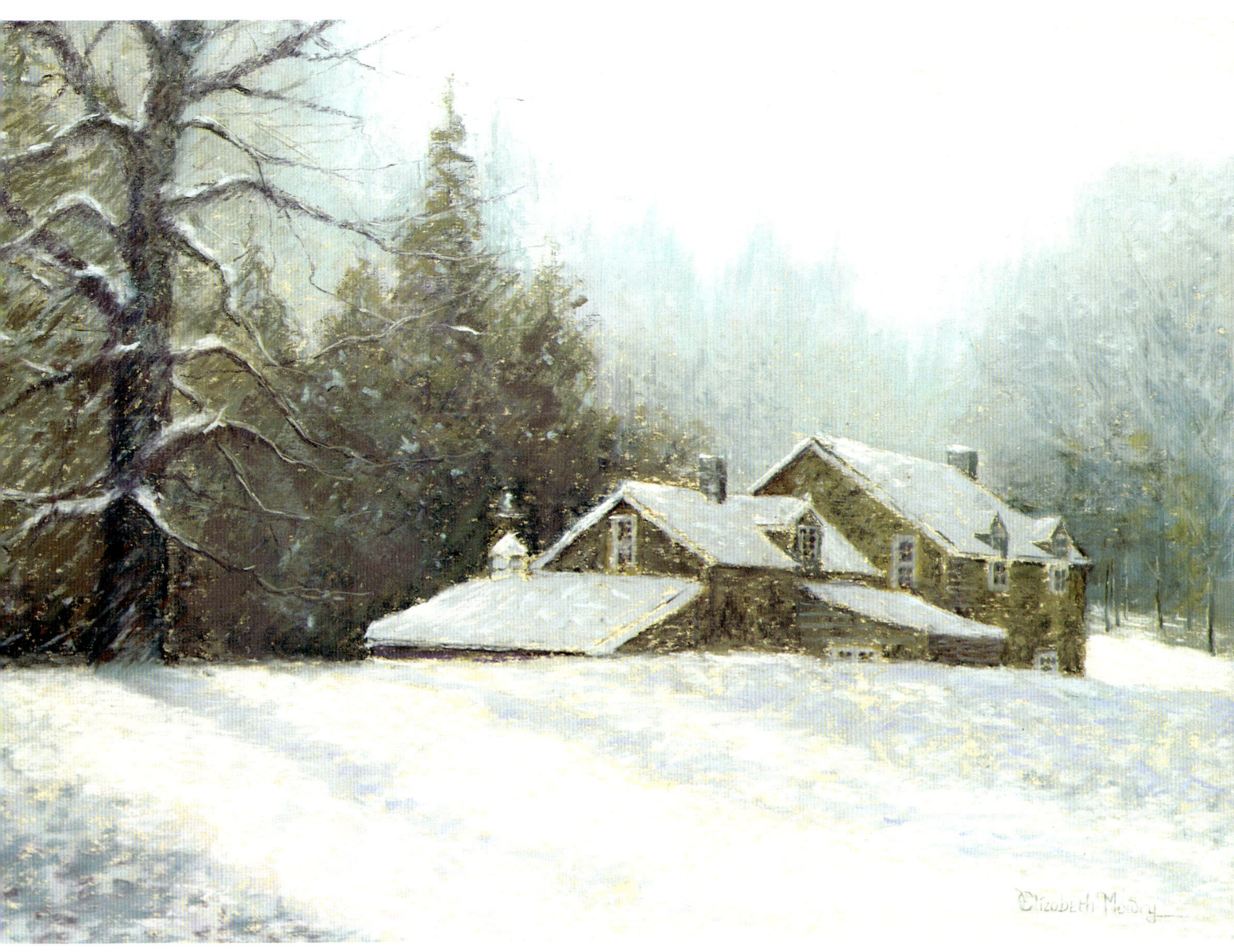

above a sunlit, brilliant snowbank. Areas of high contrast can
be assimilated into strong landscape compositions that are uncomplicated by the high color of
seasons past. (See *Minnewaska
Stream*, on page 129.)

Conversely, you will notice
that on an overcast, winter day,
the range of lights and darks, or
values, narrows considerably; it
narrows even more on a snowy
day. Some of the most beautiful,
emotion-evoking masterpieces,
such as Monet's *Ice Floes*, are
painted within an incredibly limited middle-value range. Explor-

ing the narrowed range of values
within a painting is a challenge
because whenever you purposely
hold back contrast, you risk a
washed out, indecisive appearance in your painting. Here the
painting process balances on the
tenuous edge of what will work
and what will not. Every step has
to be evaluated in those terms.
One thing is sure, though: As you
try to meet the challenge, you will
be enthralled by weather conditions that your nonartistic neigh-
bors find immensely disagreeable.

WINTERSET
Pastel on sanded board
14″ × 23″
Collection of Andrew Joseph Novak

*On a sunny day, this scene would have
been painted with much more contrast;
here, on the morning after a snowfall, the
light in the sky was still weak, and the range
of values is narrower.*

THE WINTER PALETTE

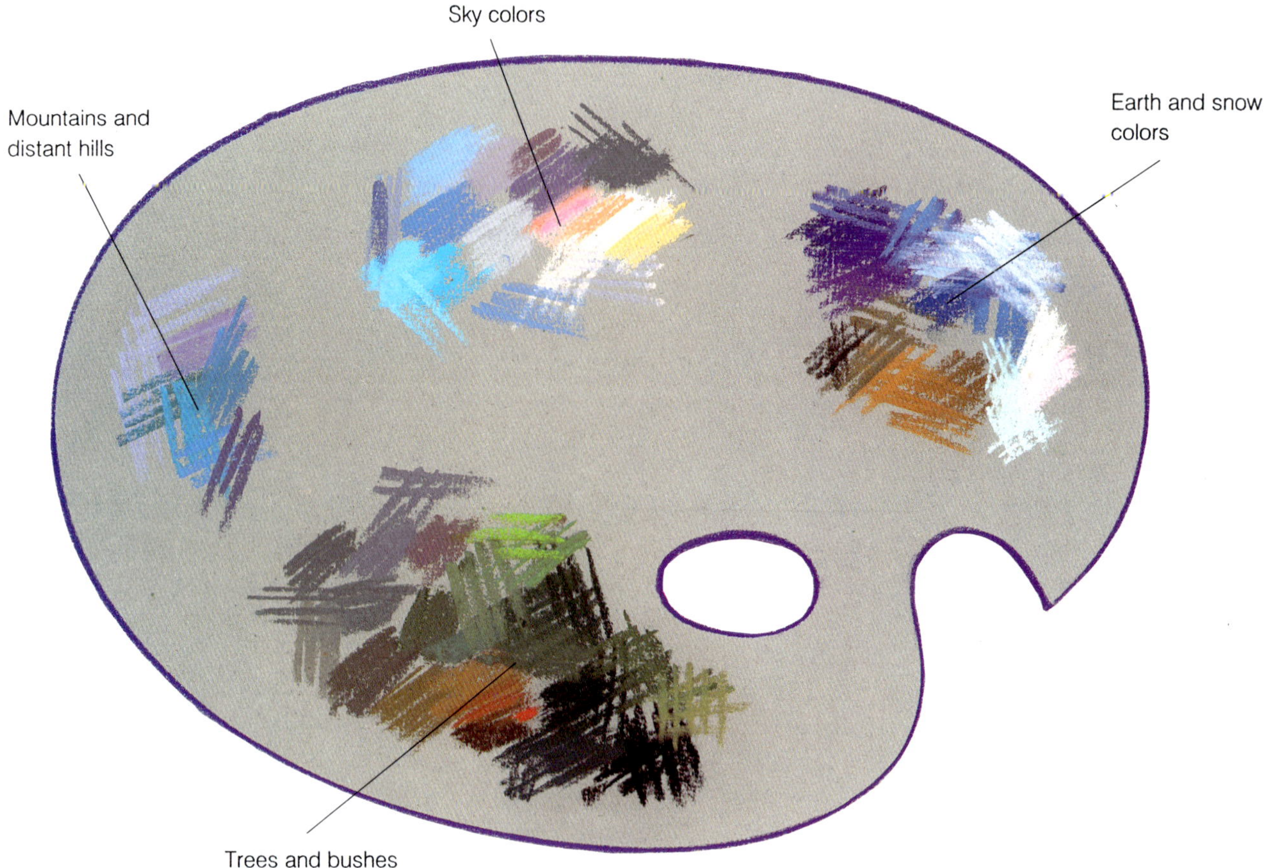

Nature's winter colors are somber but elegant in their quietness. The warm, pure hues of autumn have faded; now, subtle grays and blues dominate a cooler palette.

Compared with earlier seasons, winter may appear lacking in color, but those colors that remain are worth exploring closely. Just glance toward a large mass of leafless trees and you will realize that at no other time of the year can we distinguish so many variations of gray and brown, each one distinct in its own temperature and subtlety.

Now might be the time to add a few sticks of muted color to your supply of soft pastels. Look for names such as red-gray, Van Dyck brown, reddish purple, olive-brown, burnt madder, Van Dyck violet, Indian red, black-green, purple-gray, to name but a few. As you hold four or five of these nonbasic colors together in your hand, you will immediately understand the quiet beauty of muted color that's such an important part of the winter landscape.

If you are not ready to purchase additional sticks of convenient color, with a little bit of time and practice on scraps of sanded paper, you can produce beautifully subtle, neutral tones by using complementary colors together, either blended or left in broken strokes on your surface for the eye to blend.

As you construct the winter palette of color for your region, look for the minute traces of warmth that will complement the cool purples and blues and grays. They can be found in scarlet winter berries, the lingering sienna oak leaves, or the tall ochre grasses that edge an icy stream. By introducing small amounts of these complements, you will intensify the other colors in your winter pastel paintings.

During the winter, it is quite often enough that I get myself to a painting location and stay warm

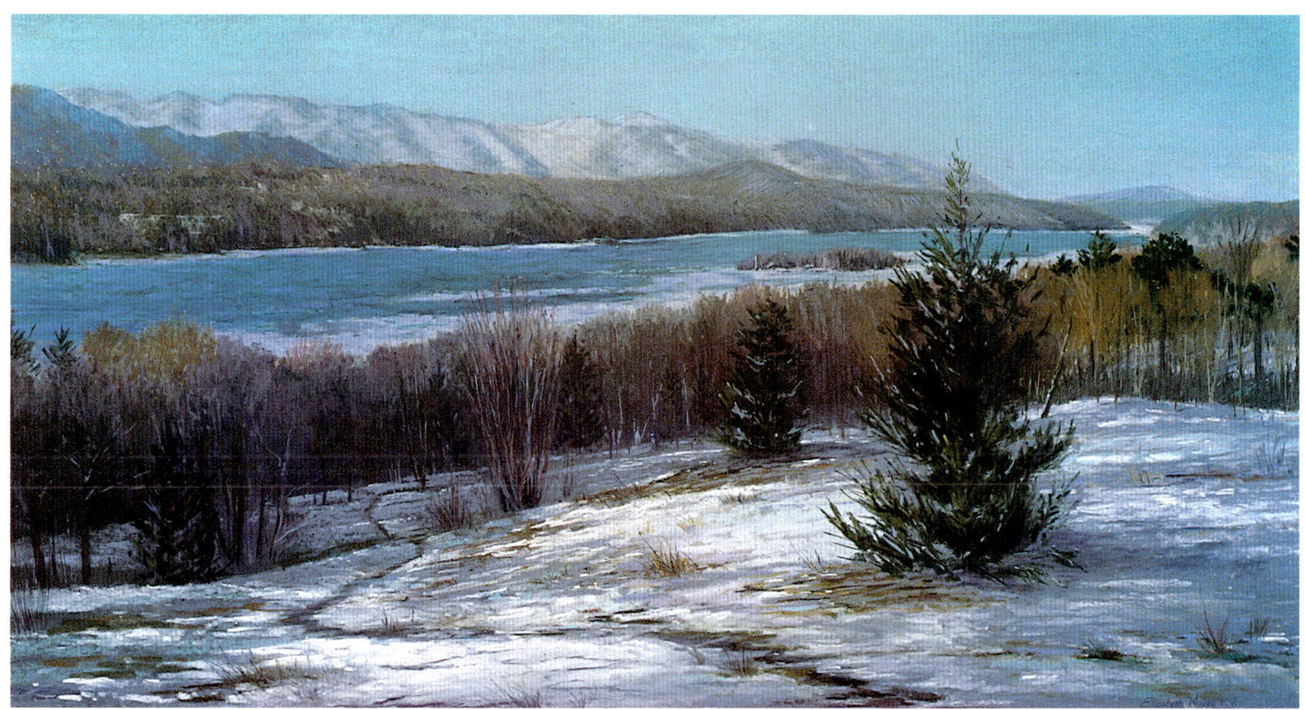

THE HUDSON FROM
VANDERBILT'S ESTATE
Pastel on sanded board
26″ × 47″
Collection of David Adler

The use of browns, grays and ochres in the tree line warms and balances this large, winter landscape. Single sticks of muted colors such as gray-violet, red-brown and deep ochre will add variety to your somber winter palette and quiet harmony to your pastels. When color hue is limited in nature, direct your attention to contrasts in value and temperature.

for the time it takes to get down the information I need. I really don't want to be carrying a lot of supplies while trudging through snow or through mud and ice. So for color sketching and studies, I have put together a list of twenty pastel pencils that will give most of the color range you will find outdoors in winter (see the chart below). Together with a small sharpener, they fit easily into a pencil case and are conveniently transportable that way.

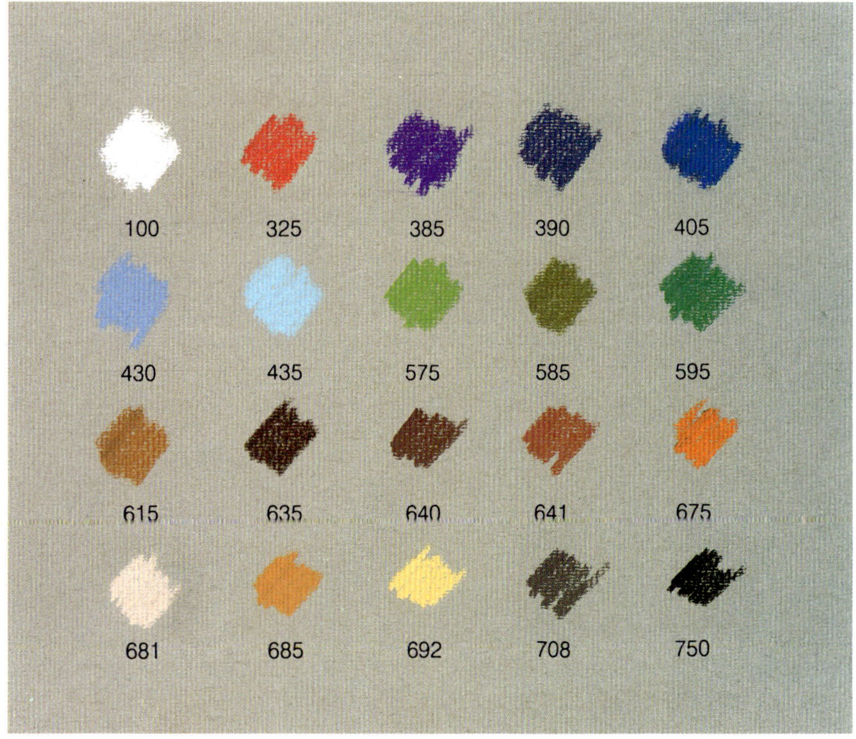

Here are twenty pastel pencil colors for on-the-scene color studies in winter (Schwan Stabilo Carb Othello 1400 Series).

Row one: 100 Titanium white, 325 Carmine red deep, 385 Violet deep, 390 Prussian blue, 405 Ultramarine blue.

Row two: 430 Ultramarine blue middle, 435 Ultramarine blue light, 575 Leaf green, 585 Olive green, 595 Leaf green deep.

Row three: 615 Dark ochre, 635 Bistre, 640 Caput mortuum violet, 641 Caput mortuum middle, 675 French red ochre.

Row four: 681 Light flesh tint, 685 Sienna, 692 Golden ochre light, 708 Grey 5, 750 Black.

TREES: AFTER THE LEAVES, THE STRUCTURE

Winter is an excellent time to study tree structure. Trees have form, mass and volume in addition to color, height and width. Learning all you can about the anatomy of a specific tree helps you to capture the expression of that kind of tree during the other seasons of the year. Just as the knowledge of human anatomy is essential to drawing or painting the figure with excellence, so is an understanding of a tree's organizational framework in order to paint it with expression. And just as clothing does not usually mask a poorly constructed figure, neither does foliage conceal careless tree structure.

Trees are the largest and oldest living things on earth. If we are to be painters of nature, it makes sense to learn something about them. I have set the modest goal for myself of making the acquaintance of one kind of tree each year, and I watch its changing details throughout the year so that I can recognize it in all seasons. There is no need to be overwhelmed by the fact that there are over a thousand different species native to North America alone. In fact, for the purposes of sketching or painting, you don't have to know the name or the kind of tree you are looking at. Personally, I happen to like knowing, and I have found that there are many guides to field and forest that provide a wealth of information about trees.

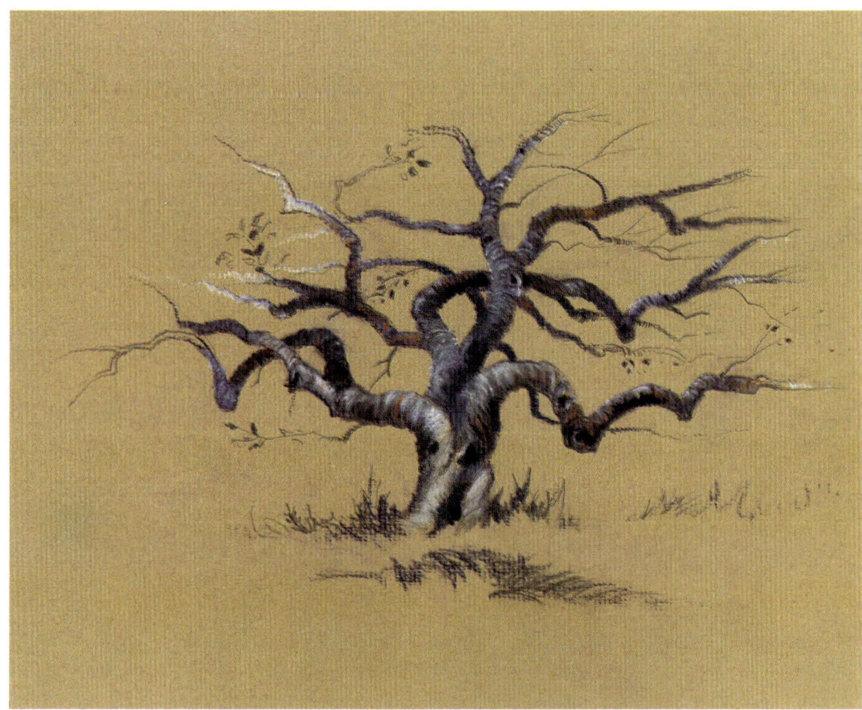

The most interesting characteristics of the apple tree exist as a result of pruning in which vertical growth is discouraged. Therefore, the branches often come to an abrupt stop and then twist toward another direction, attaining a contorted appearance.

When I go to the woods to sketch, I usually have a sketchbook, a kneaded eraser, some sharpened pencils and charcoal. I may do several sketches but of only one kind of tree on each outing.

On a pleasant, winter day, take yourself out into the woods and choose a tree that interests you. Look at the trunk and notice the color and texture of the bark. Study the network of branches in relation to the tapering trunk. Scan the height as compared to the width. Look for consistencies in the shape and stretch of the branches and the angle at which they depart from the tree trunk.

First you will see generalities and then specifics. For example, the hickory tree branches will have a different pattern of departure from the trunk than those of the apple tree. The graceful bearing and classic shape of the elm has little resemblance to that of the swarthy oak. Poplars, willow and birches all have distinctive, picturesque qualities for you to use in your landscapes.

Soon you will begin to recognize on sight the characteristics of a particular tree species. As your familiarity grows, your drawings and pastel sketches will move from the literal to the more expressive without compromising

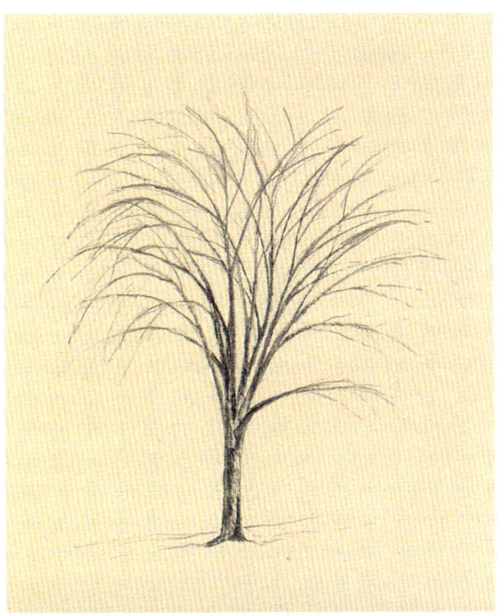

The classic elm shape is that of a graceful fan.

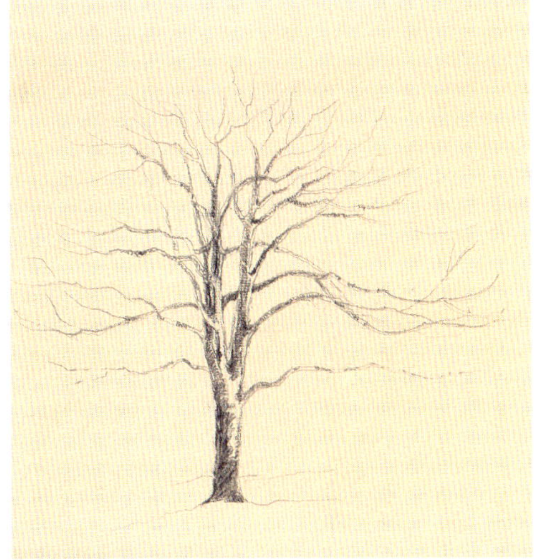

The branch structure of the brawny white oak is irregular.

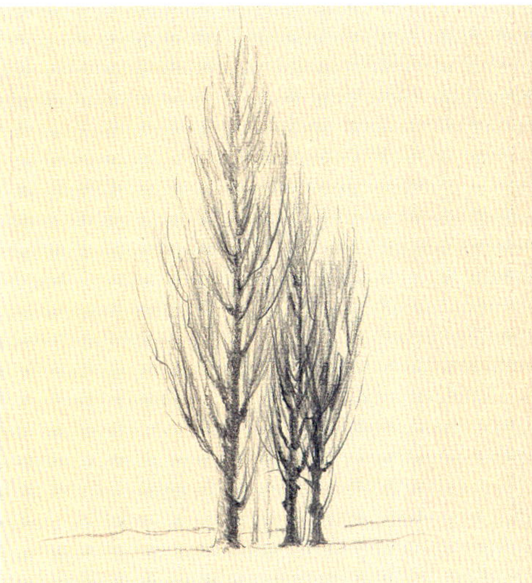

The tall poplar grows in a narrow, upright fashion.

quality. This progression is gradual, but all of the stages of learning can be rewarding and well worth the time and effort you invest.

As you begin to acquire an intimate acquaintance with trees in the winter landscape, you will recognize that what they lack in bright color is compensated for by form and grace. This is often overlooked by those who insist on bemoaning the fallen leaves and who drearily anticipate the length of winter. Nature offers us the thrilling phenomenon of constant change. It is in our best interest to take advantage of this exhibition. With each passing year, I see more deeply, and I frequently feel unable to fully absorb all of the changes that I find so interesting. However, another magnificent quality of nature is its continuance. Again and again, winter will return. What I am not able to capture in my work in one winter, I will have the opportunity to try again to capture in another.

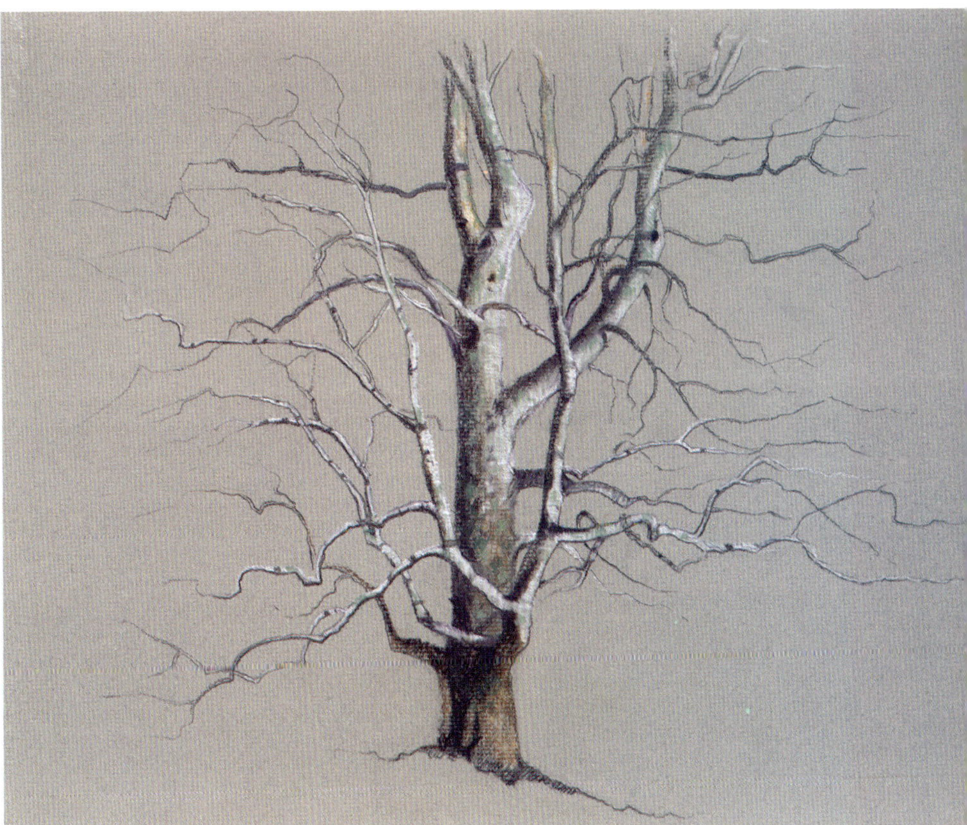

THE SYCAMORE
Pastel pencil on Ingres paper

In the study of trees, you have an excellent opportunity to use pastel pencils as drawing tools. The five pencils used here were white, leaf green, dark ochre, gray and black.

PAINTING TREE TRUNKS FROM A STRUCTURE SKETCH

Right from the start, I was taken by the winter sunlight filtering through to these tall evergreen trunks. My little pencil sketch provided the incentive to go for strong contrasts in my painting. Sometimes it is helpful to remind ourselves what it is we want to accomplish in a work, and then resist shifting from what that is. Here, I wanted to show the overall beauty and grace of the trees by focusing only on the sunlit trunks. Simplicity in overall design was what I was striving for when I began this painting. Had I allowed myself to get carried away by the delight of applying more color and detail into the dark portions of the painting, it would have lost its focus. In some areas of the painting, the darkened surface has no pastel on it at all, and in most places, there are no more than two layers. I treated this painting as a large sketch, getting down what I wanted and then stopping. I was pleased with the dramatic, almost abstracted result.

Sometimes you will find that painting a portion of a tree can be just as effective as painting the entire tree. This is true if your interest centers more on an in-depth study. If you have already painted a type of tree many times and have used its complete shape in your work, you may be ready for a closer look.

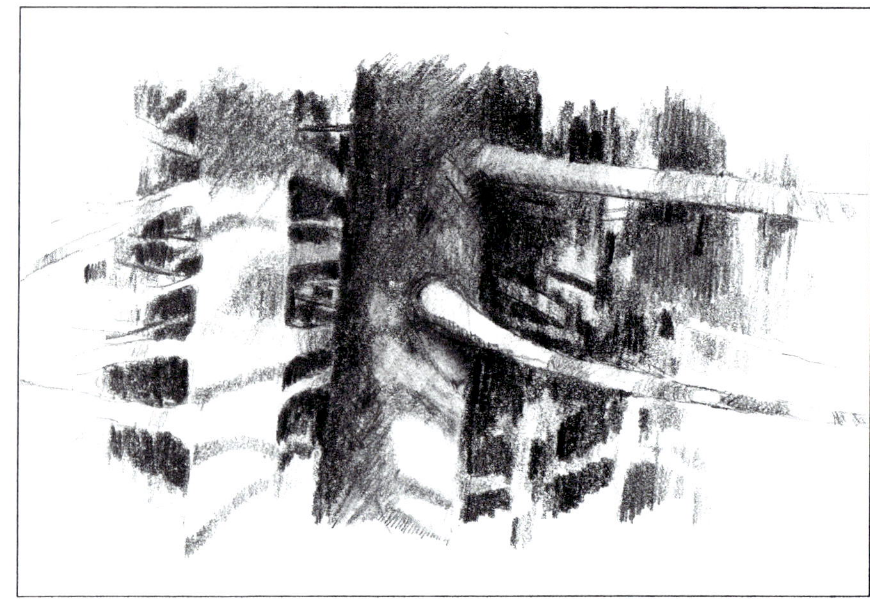

Pencil sketch from the author's notebook.

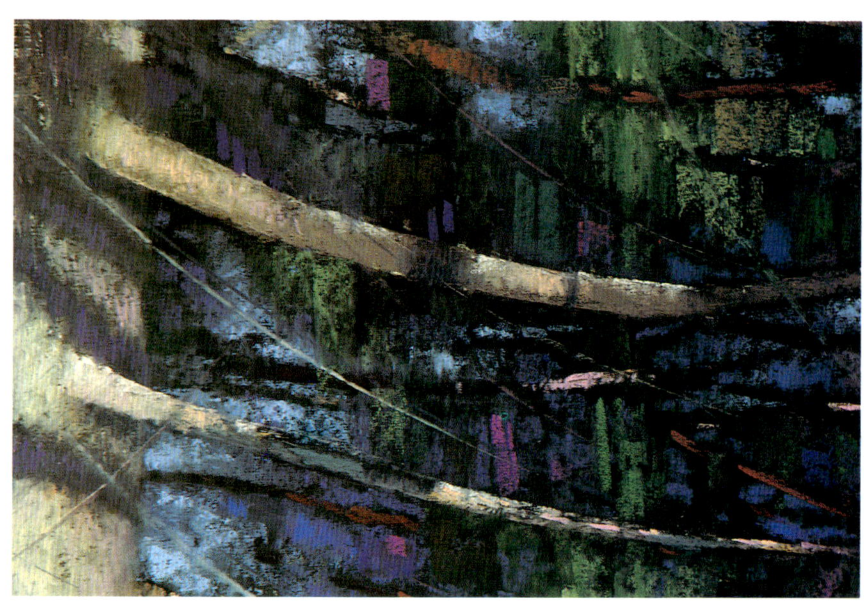

This detail from Sunlight on Norway Spruce shows that the full-textured appearance of this painting is not due to a heavy application of pastel, but rather to fresh, rich color side stroked onto the very dark background. With minimal layering (which is where stained sanded ground is at its best), the lightly dragged side strokes of soft pastel leave a gritty pattern on the surface that would not occur if several layers of pastel had already begun to fill the tooth.

A few spontaneous
swing strokes give
movement. No
hesitations here!

Cast shadows,
painted deep
purple, and blue
sky spaces
become part of
the design.

Focal point is
the area of warm
sunlight on the
tree trunks.

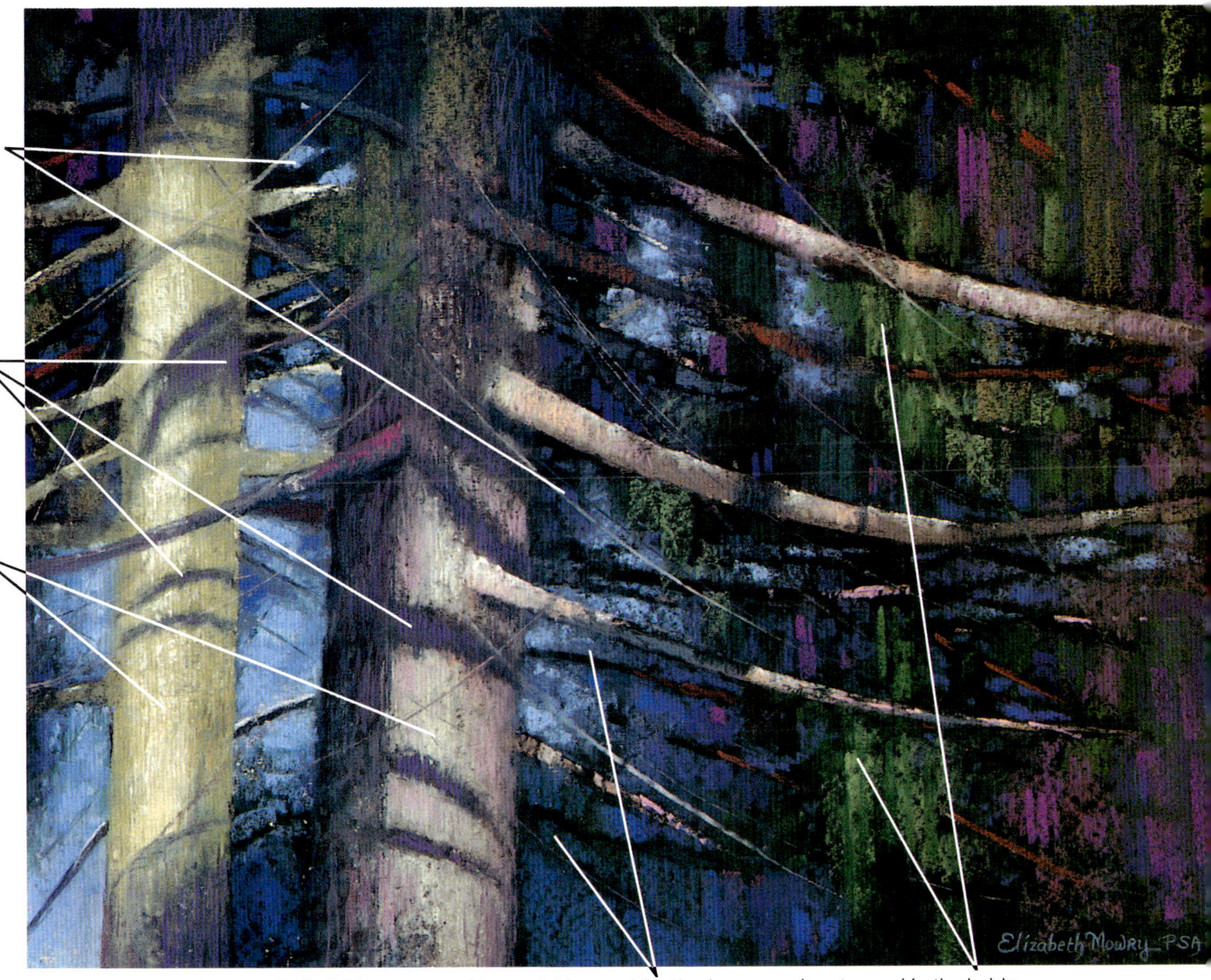

SUNLIGHT ON NORWAY SPRUCE
Pastel on sanded paper
22″ × 28″

*I stained a buff-colored sheet of sanded
paper with diluted Jacobean wood stain in
the areas where I would want the deepest
values. In that way, I could be certain that I
wouldn't have to overload the surface with
pastel in an attempt to get rich, dark values.
I lightly sketched the trunks and main
branches on my dark surface with gray
pastel pencil. Then I stroked in low-value
purples and greens, and a lighter value of
blue for the sky, using soft pastels on their
sides. Next, I worked into the bark of the
trunks with ochre, deep purple and several
values of pink and red violet. Cast shadows
are cool purple.*

No pastel is used for the less prominent
branches. Instead, other colors were
abruptly lifted off the stained ground where
I wanted to indicate a branch, and then put
back down immediately afterward.

Vertical side
strokes are used to
merely suggest the
drooping, green
boughs.

PAINTING SNOW WITH COLOR

During winter in many parts of the world, snow accumulates to become a temporary addition to the earth's surface. Like other horizontal surfaces, it is directly affected by the light in the sky above it. Fine-tuning your perception, and learning to convey the qualities of absorbed light will give you the key to painting mood into your work.

Depending upon the time of the day and the color of the light in the sky, snow can appear blue, purple, pink, yellow, orange, blue-green or another color. Here are some small studies that illustrate how the light in the sky affects the color of the snow, and therefore, the tone of the painting. Even when no sky is visible, it is easy to guess the color in it.

CHOOSING THE MOOD

When you are working from your pencil sketch or a charcoal drawing, as is often the case in winter when weather limits the time you spend outdoors, the mood in your paintings is your choice. You will decide on the source of light, the time of day, the color of the light. Don't be overwhelmed by all the control you have. Enjoy it. At first you may say, "Where do I begin?" Simple. Starting with the sky, visualize your scene in several ways. For example, picture it on a clear day with a blue sky. Then imagine it under a warm, yellow sky, or even at dusk, with a rosy light over the darkened landscape. Then de-

cide. Most important, be faithful to your decision. Save the other possible choices for future paintings, and each one will be stronger than if you use a mix-and-match approach. Just make sure that within your chosen color theme, based upon the color of the sky, you cover the full range of values that your sketch requires. Try the colors together on a scrap of the same surface you will be working on. If you like how they interact next to, over, and under one another, chances are you will be pleased with the color harmony in your painting.

In essence, what you will be doing is simply taking the color of the sky you have chosen, and then putting some of that into the snow you are painting. That's it!

PAINTING AN OVERCAST LANDSCAPE

You may be thinking, "What about all of the overcast winter days?" On overcast winter days, the snow appears to lose all contour. The sunny-day, high-contrast changes in value are now gray and flat. Unless you have a specific reason for portraying those qualities—and in some instances, you may indeed— you will probably not want to paint all of your winter landscapes in that manner.

What I do is this: I take my time finding subject matter that I feel attracted to, and then I do a compositional sketch with pencil, getting down the information I need and some sense of the value range that

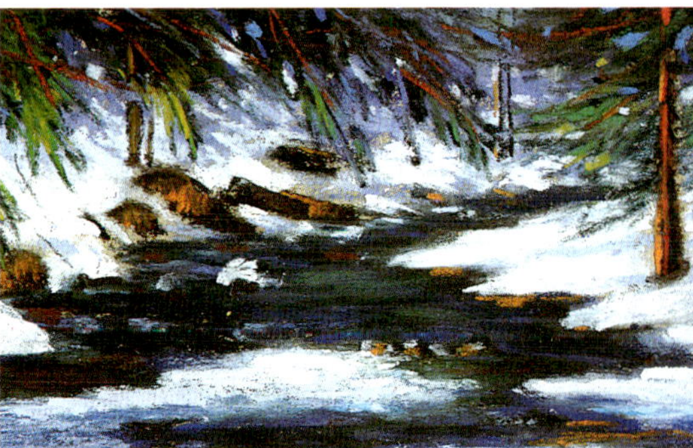

Cool snow under a blue sky.

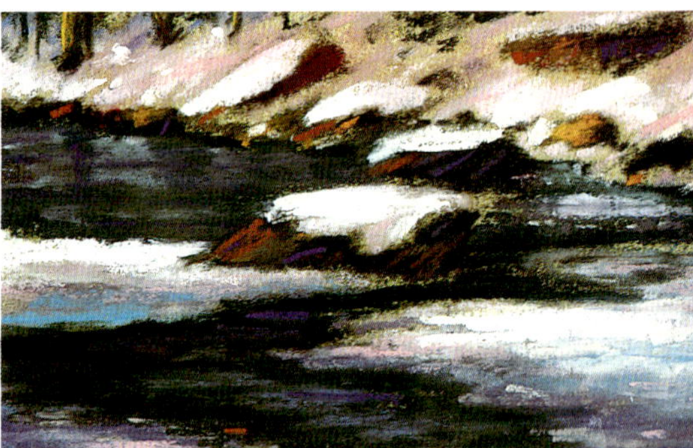

Warm snow under a rosy sky.

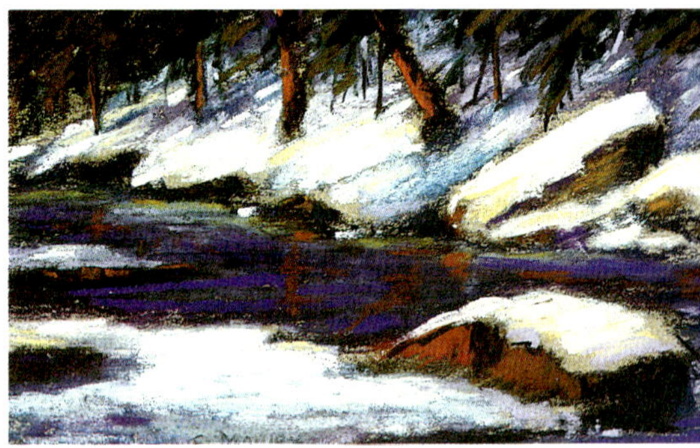

Warm snow under a yellow sky.

exists. Then I return to my studio. I find that on gray days when no strong shadows exist, reality can be a hindrance. Once I move away from the gray and lifeless scene, I feel more free to visualize color and mood into my studied sketch.

I always begin with the sky. Do I want it to be dominated by blue-green, palest saffron, or lavender? Once that decision is made, I try to imagine how the selected sky color would affect the color of the other components in my sketch. (If you have difficulty with this, think of a sky-colored transparent veil or glaze dropping over your sketch.) By this simple visualization, I have a general idea of what I will be aiming for in my pastel interpretation of the sketch.

Next I choose some colors with that unity in mind. I probably would want a trace of complement for color vibration. In essence, I will be setting the tone for the painting, knowing that I am free to add colors from my supply of them as needed. Whatever colors I choose to work with, one thing is certain: I will have several values of the chosen sky color available. In that way, with light cross-toning, I can relate any area of the painting back to the sky tone and keep my color theme intact. This is a very exciting way to work.

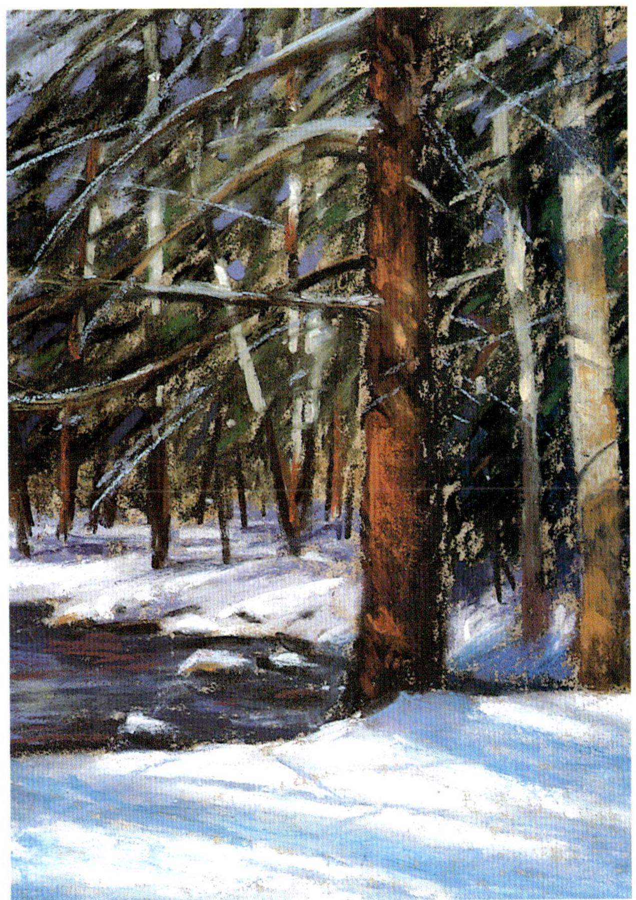

In this small, winter color study, the blue sky is repeated in the shadow areas of the snow, warming where the sunlight is stronger.

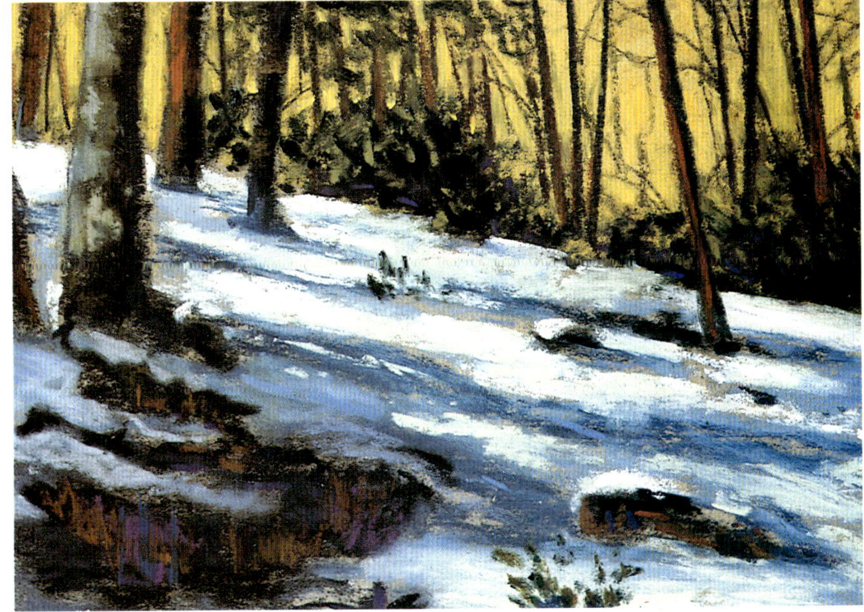

A lavender sky would cool this small study considerably.

WORKING FROM A WINTER SKETCH

Montgomery Place is a restored mansion along the Hudson River that is now open to the public. Although the house is impressive, I felt more attracted to this uninhabited cottage on the estate. Surrounded by wild vine growth and what may have once been a garden at the time of my sketch, it was a vacant structure situated in deep snow that was penetrated by obstinate weeds. Everything about the place called out to be painted, and I knew from the start that someday I would do that.

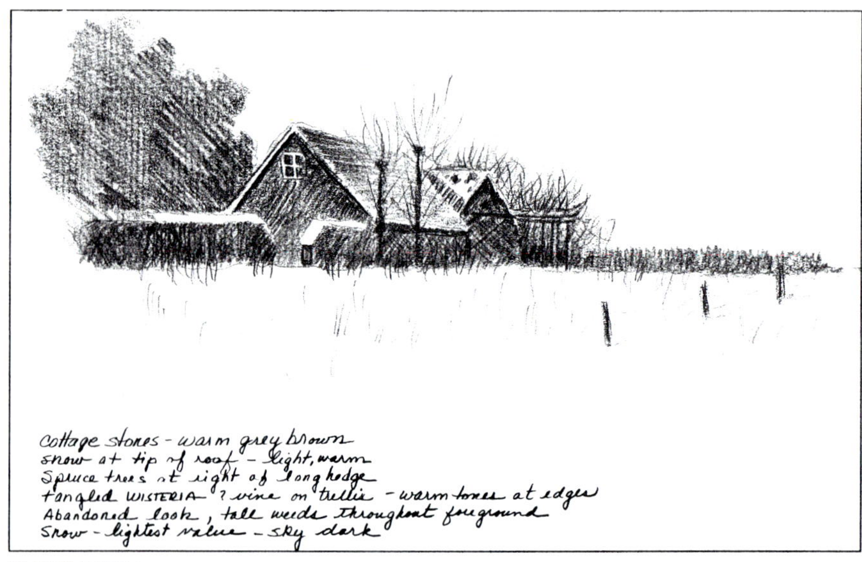

THE SKETCH

In this small pencil study done at the scene, I was concerned mainly with the lines of the structure. Later, in my painting, the mood would come from the impression that the place made upon my memory. I made a few notations about the source of light and color of the stone cottage, but I did not want to be tied too much to reality.

Step 1 Setting Up Value Differences
Some time later in the studio, I visualized this scene as cool, quiet and blue. I decided on a palette that would be simple and cold except for some light on the snow, and a bit of warm complement in the weeds. I did a minimal sketch on my surface with gray pastel pencil, and then used soft pastels on their sides for rapid, even coverage. Three light layers of color in the sky provide an adequate base of pastel before blending.

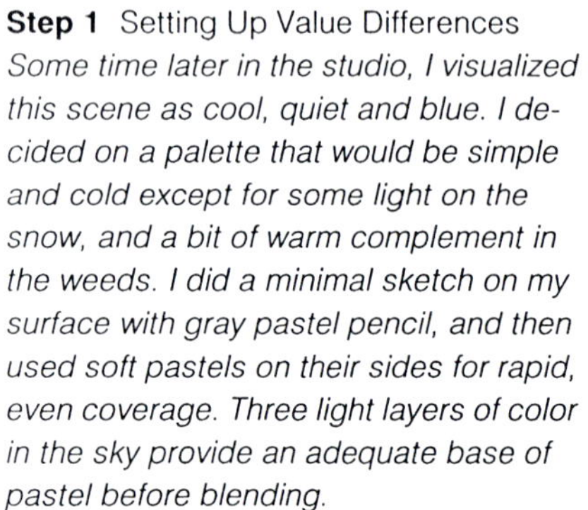

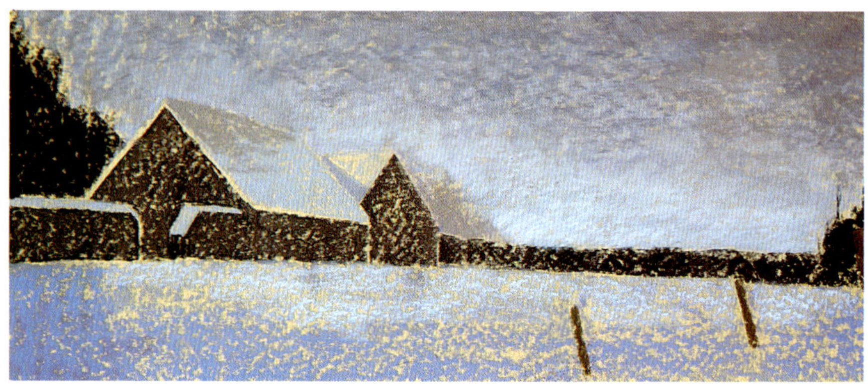

Step 2 Adding Color Definition
A gray-blue Grumbacher pastel is just the right hardness to blend the soft pastel colors in the sky into one another. I use warm, deep grays and ochre in short, broken strokes for the stones in the cottage. Next, I add some same-value colors to the trees and hedge before putting another layer of sky-related color on the snow.

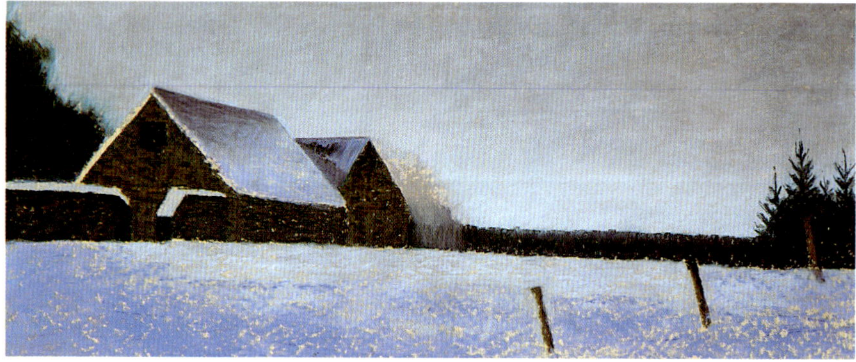

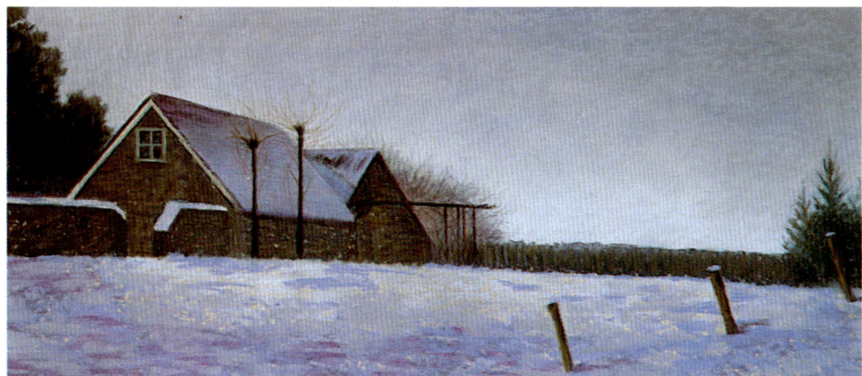

Step 3 Refining Color and Shape
I go back into the blended sky with some side strokes of gray-purple to renew the freshness. After that, I extend the ever-green edges into the completed sky. Trees and vines are drawn in. I use blue and purple soft pastels for foreground snow, drawing on my memory of the place for color selection. Being away from the reality gave me the freedom to exaggerate the snow colors for effect.

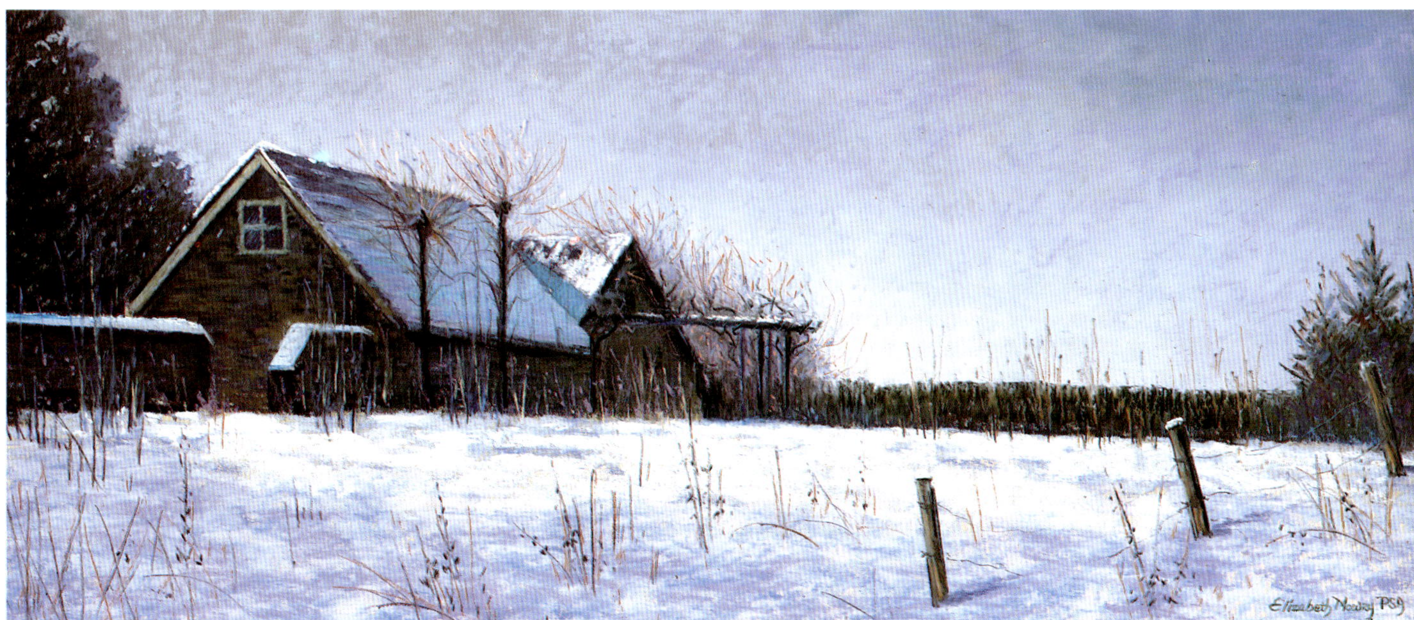

GARDEN COTTAGE AT MONTGOMERY
PLACE
Pastel on sanded board
13″ × 31″

Step 4 Final Adjustments
I use a tint of Naples yellow for the light on the snow, attach wire to the posts and break up the solid evergreen mass with a few sky holes. At this point, I refine and adjust overall color.

Nature provides us with both warm and cool color each season. Here, even with an abundance of snow on the ground, there are warm-hued grasses, weeds and vines that catch the light.

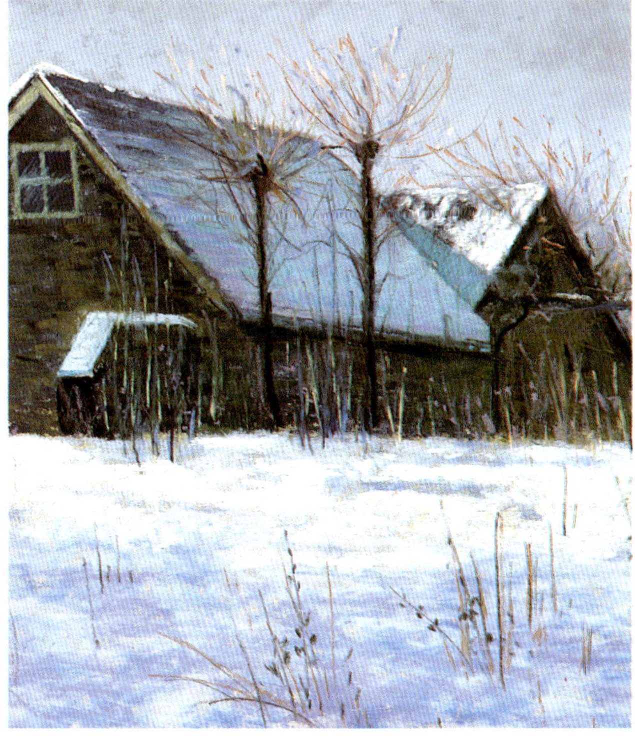

USING SHADOWS FOR INTEREST AND FORM

Snow is a covering. Unless wind interferes, it generally conforms to the contours it covers. If there is something between the sky and the earth, the snow will accumulate first on that object, and less will fall on the ground. These facts are elementary, but sometimes we forget to apply all that we know to our paintings.

When snow continues to fall on a large, open area such as a field or pasture, it will eventually cover the interesting grasses and weeds, the tractor road, and the walking paths. In short, details disappear. Now is the time to celebrate the beauty of simple form, which is more clearly evident in winter than at any other time.

A large expanse of white can be very dramatic in some paintings.

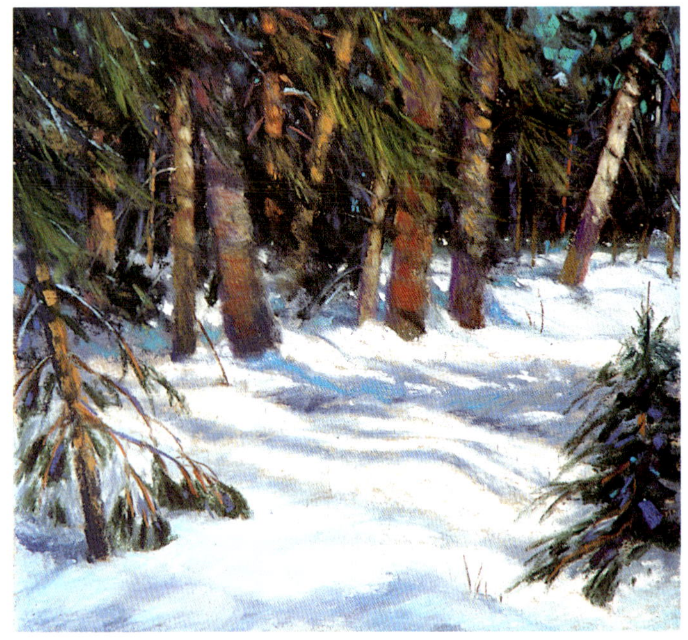

WINTER CORRIDOR
Pastel on sanded board
7½″ × 8″

Sunlight and shadow gently take the eye over the contour of the snow.

A WINTER STUDY
Pastel on sanded paper
6½″ × 10″

Cool, blue shadows across the snow add interest to this on-the-scene, woodland study in which warm browns, violet, gray and white are the only other pastels used.

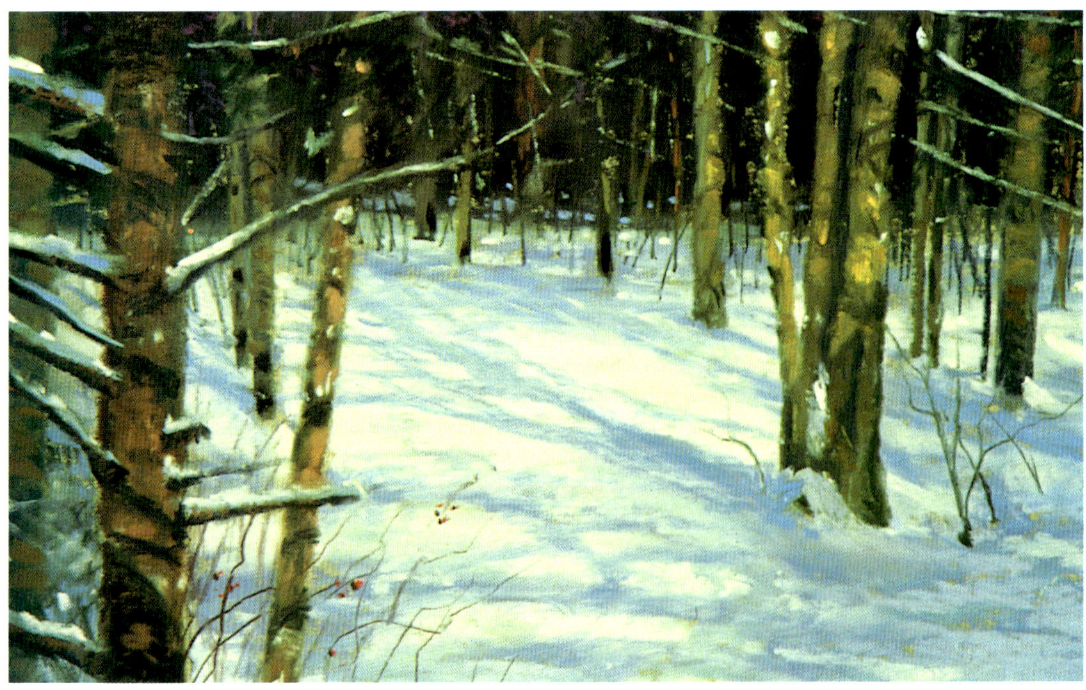

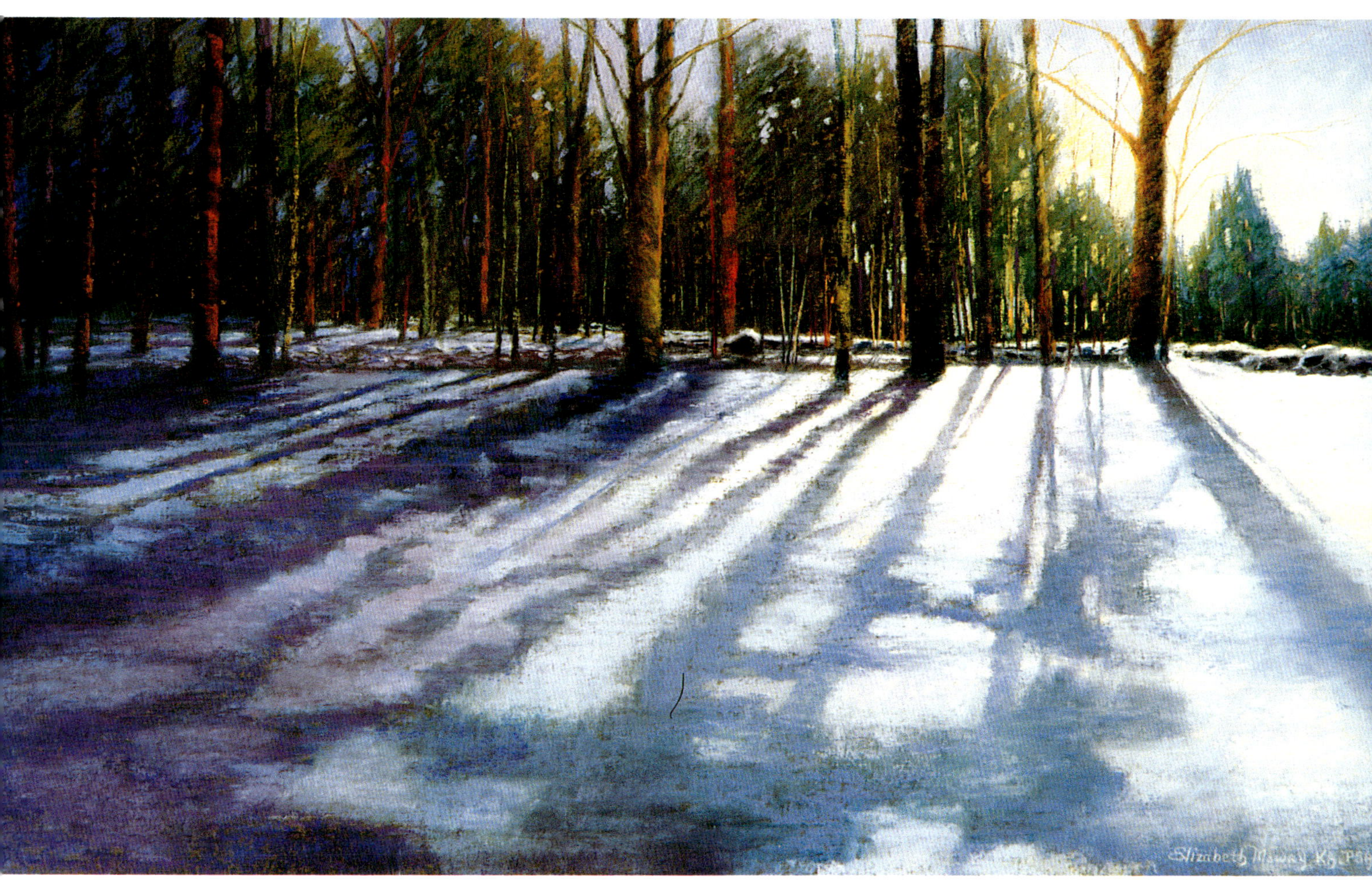

In others, the large, light area will appear more interesting if painted at a time of day when nearby objects embroider their purple-and-blue shadows across the surface and lead us over the contour of the land beneath.

Striking foregrounds in snow scenes can be created by using shadows as a prominent compositional element in your painting. You can use shadows to send the eye of the viewer wherever you want it to go.

Morning and afternoon will send shadows in opposite directions, and you may want to visit a favorite place at both times to compare what happens. And do not limit your shadow study to those that stretch *across* your landscapes. Face the sun or source of light a little more directly, and you will see the shadows reach toward you: creative angling that you control.

Shadows tell us about the roll of the land, the tractor ruts that we can no longer see and the paths that have been lost. Shadows write the story of the snow-drenched field for the artist.

MORNING LIGHT
Pastel on sanded board
20″ × 36″
Collection of Frank E. Davis, Jr.

Strong shadows spill down a slight grade toward the viewer in this landscape made up of horizontals, verticals and diagonals. Complementary tints of lavender and yellow color the winter sky, and then are absorbed by the snow with richer intensity. Evergreens in the background are low-chroma greens, complemented again by warm patches of Indian red light in the tree trunks.

ZEROING IN ON NATURE IN WINTER

When standing above a large vista that spreads itself out before us in all of its grandeur, we are very likely to feel flooded with a keen appreciation for all of nature. Many of us can relate to how we felt hiking up a mountain with friends: breathless, but conversing all the way, happy to be with kindred souls and so close to the clouds on a perfect day, and then experiencing, as we reached the top, those first few moments of blessed silence as we took in a view that any words would ruin.

Between those special times in our lives, and on another level, new appreciation is possible every day as we focus with fresh interest on some small, familiar fragment of nature.

Zeroing in on nature is easier to do in winter than in any other season, because in winter, nature has already reduced itself to what is basic. The frills of other seasons are gone. Snow may cover whole fields and woodlands, eliminating more and more detail with every inch that falls. What remains becomes more precious, and therefore more worthy of closer scrutiny. As we walk along familiar paths during winter, we no longer merely notice changes, we also begin to look for changes to notice. This turning point could very well be the beginning of a love affair with your surroundings as well as an influence in your life and in your paintings.

So check out the matted weeds that throw deep violet shadows across the snow in abstract designs. Visit the blackberry patch out of season and note the crisscross, purple arches of the fruitless bushes. Examine the brilliant color inside of the iced-over rose hips, and how about the daisy heads in the meadow, petalless and broken, but still alluring?

Get up close to the detail. Whether you choose to paint detail or to eliminate it is irrelevant. Seeing things close up enlarges our understanding of them, and understanding subject matter and its parts makes better paintings.

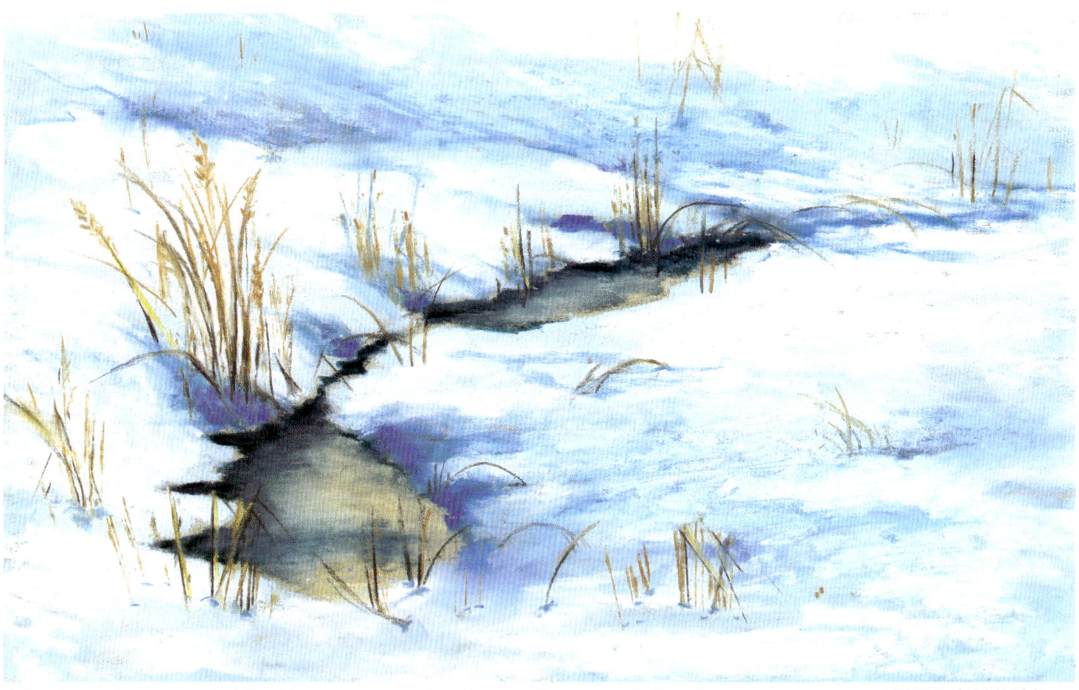

I liked the shape of this little bit of water carving its way through a field. The warm ochre used for the grassy weeds is repeated in the reflected light of the stream; it provides a complementary balance to the cool blue-purple of the snow.

LITTLE STREAM
Pastel on sanded paper
6½" × 10"

CLOSING IN ON A SIMPLE SUBJECT

Sometimes students visiting my studio are impressed by a simple study of some small part of nature, such as a few strawberries, or a tiny stream making its way through the snow. I often wondered why they would be taken by something so simple, but I have come to realize that here, it is not my technique, or my materials, or anything having to do with skill that delights them. It is *recognition*. What touches them is that I have selected so simple a subject—one they have seen as well—and that I found it worthy to paint.

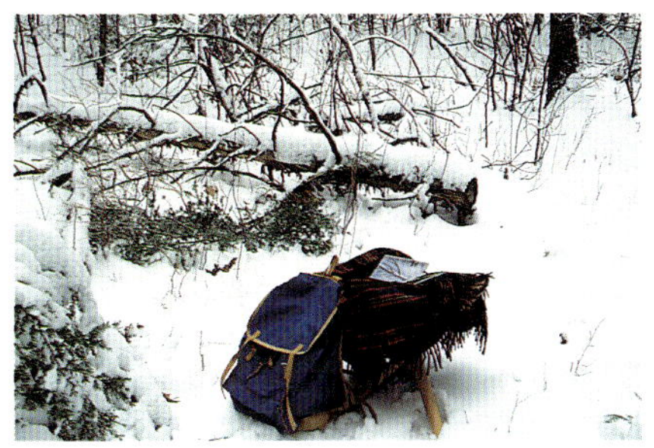

SKETCHING AT THE SCENE
On one of my winter sketching hikes in the woods, I was attracted by the gracefulness of this snow-draped tree and decided to do a small 5″ × 5″ color sketch with my pencils. In the backpack pictured, I had some small pieces of sanded panel, my twenty pastel pencils, an orange, the blanket and a folding stool.

Step 1 Beginning the Painting
Later in the studio, referring to my hasty color sketch, I lightly drew the fallen tree on 8½″ × 10″ sanded paper, being more careful of placement on the paper. Then I applied several values of soft pastel to begin what would be the snow.

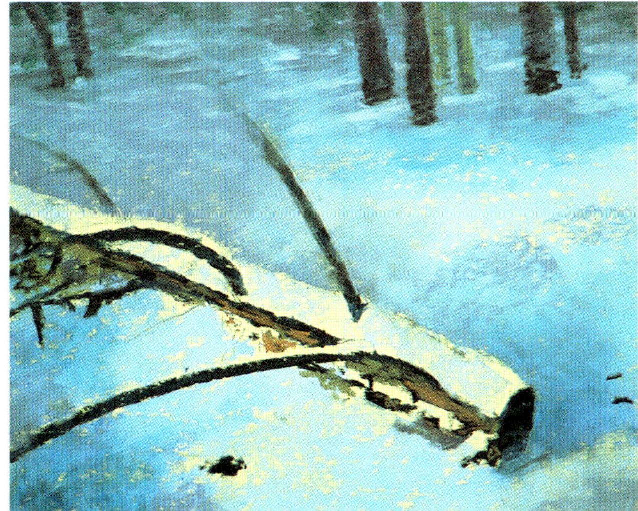

Step 2 Putting In the Dark Values
I added a deep purple to the snow purely for effect. I put the dark values on the tree trunk and only some of the branches, reserving the flexibility of leaving some out. At the top, I vaguely indicated the edge of the woods. This put a ceiling on the large light space above the tree.

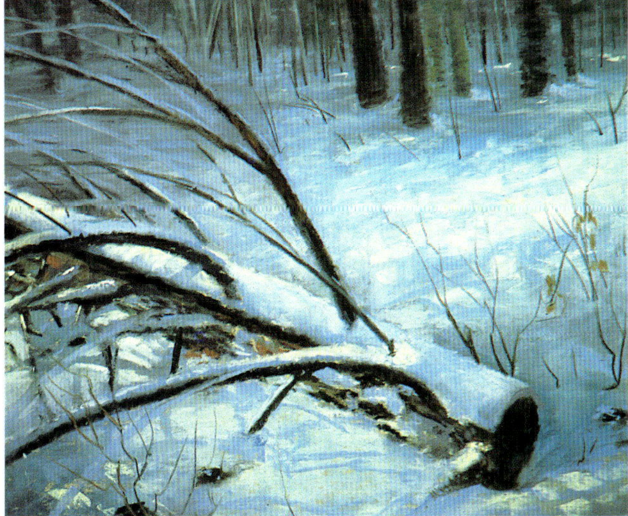

Step 3 The Finishing Details
I put additional branches on the tree and covered all with shadowed snow. I accentuated the contrast in the snow even more because I liked what was happening. The addition of some secondary growth in the woodlands and in the foreground completed the painting.

EVERGREENS IN THE WINTER LANDSCAPE

During summer or autumn, a scattering of evergreen trees and bushes in a deciduous woodland would hardly call attention to itself. In winter, however, after the leaves have fallen, those evergreens become more prominent.

Nature's complementary balance is exemplified within the evergreen itself. Above a circle of reddened, fragrant needles on the earth, green branches extend outward from bark that lights up orange in the sun.

Color variety within the types of evergreens is also more extensive than we tend to think. Of course, the hue of the blue spruce is obvious, and even a novice can plainly see the color difference between the bright green, long-needled pine and the dark mountain laurel. But it takes a keen eye to pick up the rich sienna glow at the edges of the red cedar. There are many subtle nuances among the numerous species aside from highlight and shadow that can be used to enhance both backgrounds and foregrounds in our paintings that include evergreens.

Evergreens en masse provide a striking backdrop for other compositional elements, such as a meandering stone wall, a snow-covered roof, a snowbank at the edge of a pond, or the mottled sycamore tree. Placed prudently, a stand of evergreens will tell something about the contour of a pasture, the distance of a background or the slope of a snowdrift.

In a coniferous forest, there is much to learn about form. Distinctive evergreen shapes and even branch direction can be used in the design of your compositions. The red spruce sends branches that tend to stretch upward in an even configuration, whereas those of the eastern white pine are more erratic in shape and length. The balsam fir, in addition to being the most fragrant of all evergreens, is distinctly pyramidal in shape. Hemlocks, though spindly and flat when young, mature to lofty height, with gracefully drooping limbs.

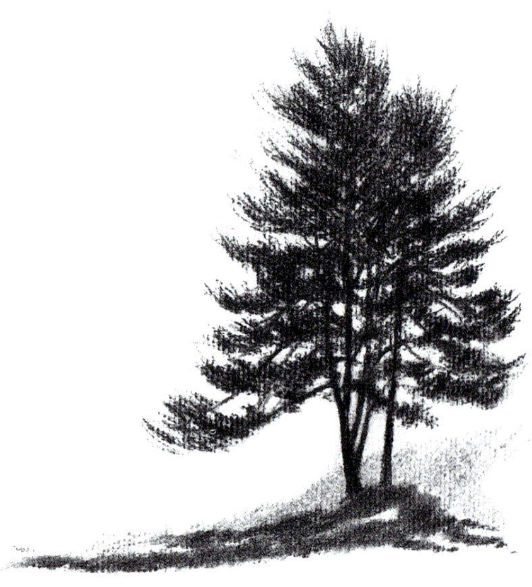

Charcoal study of a single white pine, from the author's sketchbook.

This study of cedar, pine and fir (left to right) demonstrates the color variety that can be found in evergreens. Strong sunlight would accentuate the color differences even more. This study was done with soft pastels on La Carte Pastel.

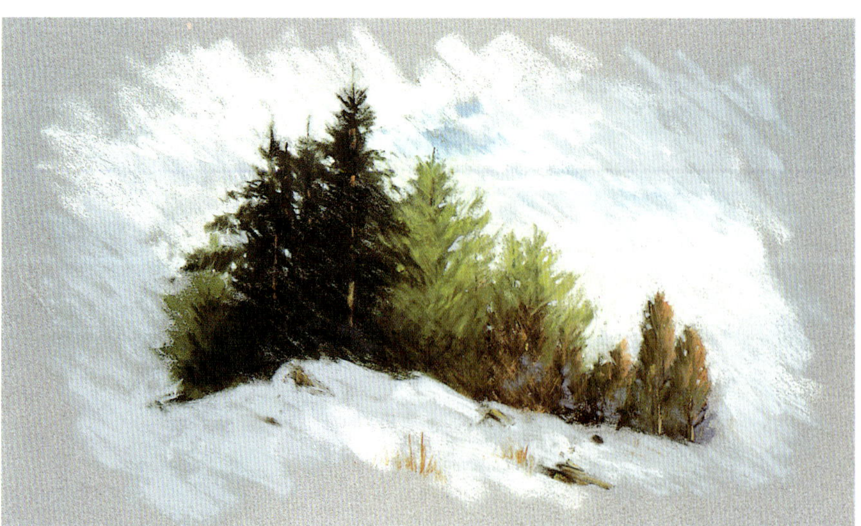

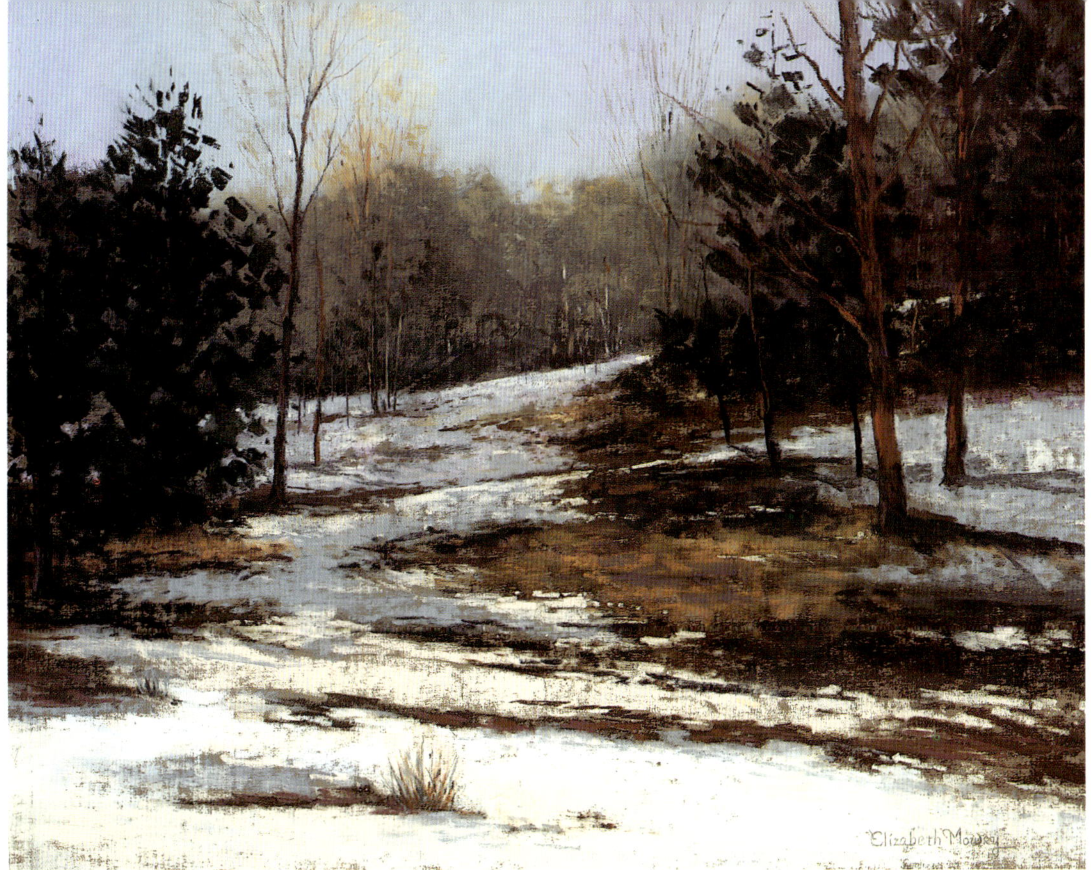

Evocative textures can add interest to winter paintings. The rich, dark evergreens are used as the deepest value in this landscape, and the sunlit, high-contrast snow provides the highest value. The foreground patterns of earth and snow were well conceived beforehand so that clean, unblended strokes were easily put into place; in this way, I avoided the futility of trying to apply light over dark or dark over light in large areas.

FEBRUARY THAW
Pastel on sanded board
18″ × 22″
Collection of Harold and Terrin Levitt

EVERGREENS IN THE BACKGROUNDS

A gray or brown band of deciduous trees in a winter landscape becomes more interesting when it is interrupted by the tips of random evergreens. The deep color of the pines and hemlock along with the lingering dry, sienna leaves of the oak that stay on till pushed off by new buds in the spring, add variety of color, value and temperature to paintings in which the leafless forest is part of the subject. You may want to accentuate this variety in some paintings and treat it with reserve in others.

You can use the squared edge of a pastel to simulate an entire distant tree line with no fussing or overworking. Try it.

The evergreens in your paintings will appear farther away when you

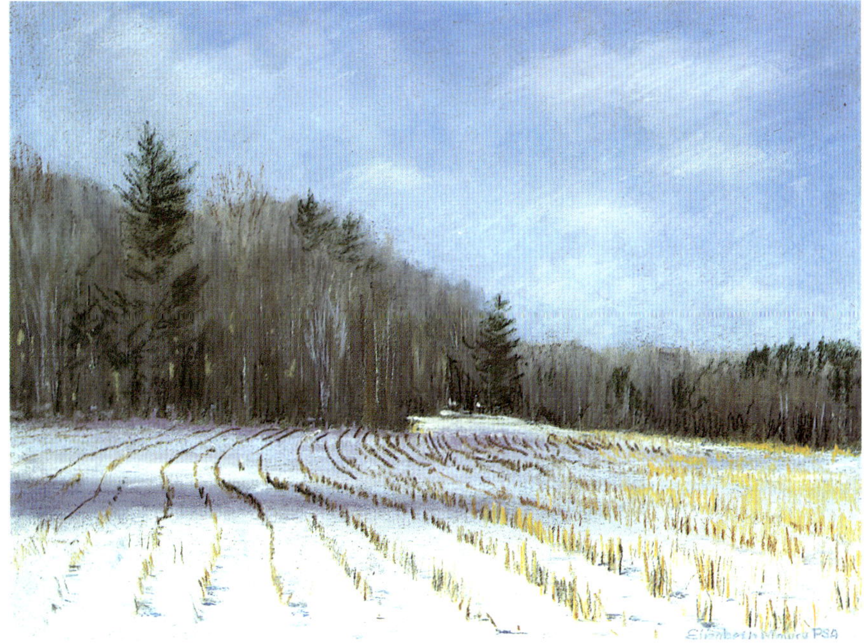

Here is an example of the subtle introduction of evergreen color and shapes into an otherwise gray-and-brown, deciduous winter tree line.

STONE RIDGE CORNFIELDS
Pastel on sanded board
9″ × 12″

use some cool blue or gray in them. You can also add more distance to background evergreens as you near completion of your painting. By cross-toning with gray-blue strokes, you can make trees recede dramatically. Just be sure their size is proportionately smaller as well, and keep the edges very soft.

Atmospheric subtleties can also be obtained by blurring edges of trees or other objects with a tortillion. Or you can try stroking the sweeping movement of a few snowflakes (avoid overdoing this, though).

CLOSE-UP EVERGREENS

When painting the needled branches of a coniferous tree, try to think of the character of the entire tree. Avoid rendering each needle; that is the surest way for something that could be sublime to become ridiculous. Instead, plan your tree. When placing its branches, strive for fluidity in your strokes, even if the branch you are drawing goes off the page. Practice so that your strokes will be free and visible. (When you have to retrace small branch strokes, your movement is likely to be hesitant, and

the double stroke may be thicker than you want, as well as awkward.)

Then, leaving some sky spaces (more than you need at first), put in some middle-value color masses at the densest parts of the tree. Now begin refining the edges of each mass. You may want to join some of the masses, or extend others with edge strokes that push in the direction toward which the branch is growing. Step back so that you do not overdo this step, because very little detail quite often tells enough.

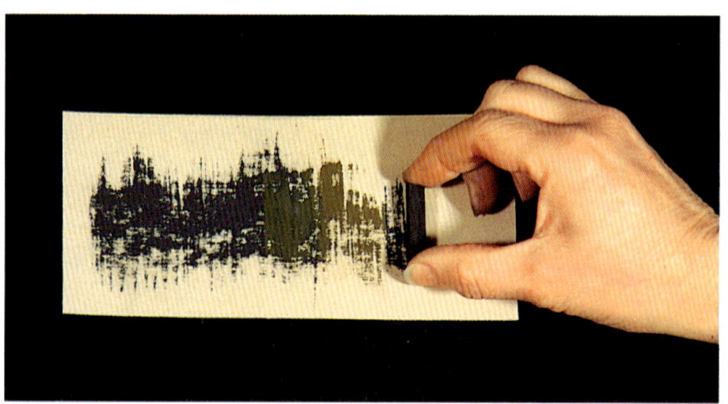

By pushing a squared pastel on edge, in short, vertical movements while slowly pulling it horizontally, you can simulate cleanly a distant tree line of evergreens. Always try to avoid overworking.

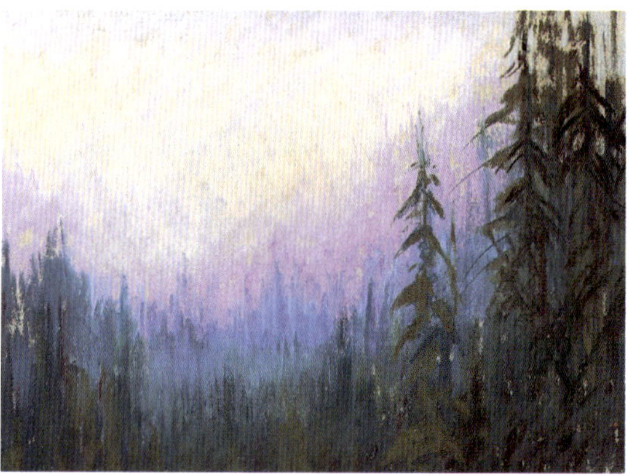

This little 5″ × 7″ shows evergreens in receding planes. With smaller proportion and lighter, cooler color, you can put a great deal of space between your foreground and background trees.

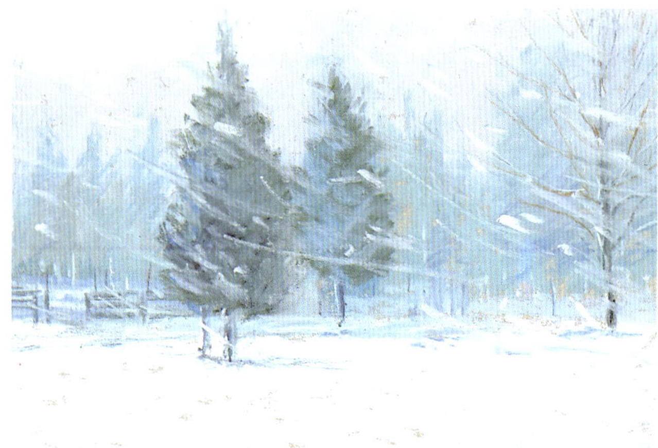

Here you can see how, under some winter atmospheric conditions, trees appear less distinct. You can do this by cutting the contrast with blue or gray pastel.

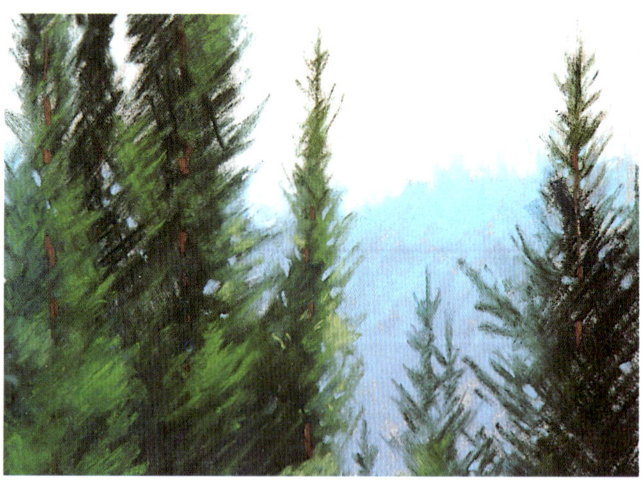

Even close-up evergreens can be painted in a loose stroke. Practice going for the overall tree shapes rather than separate parts.

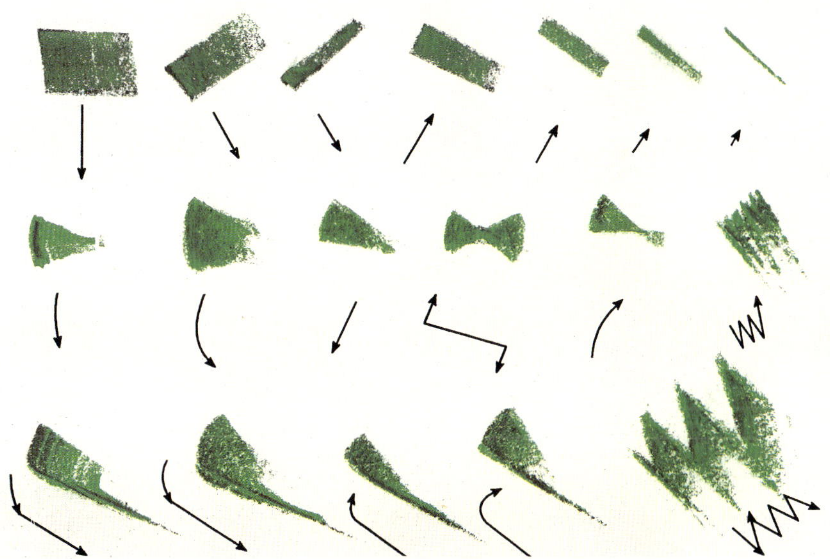

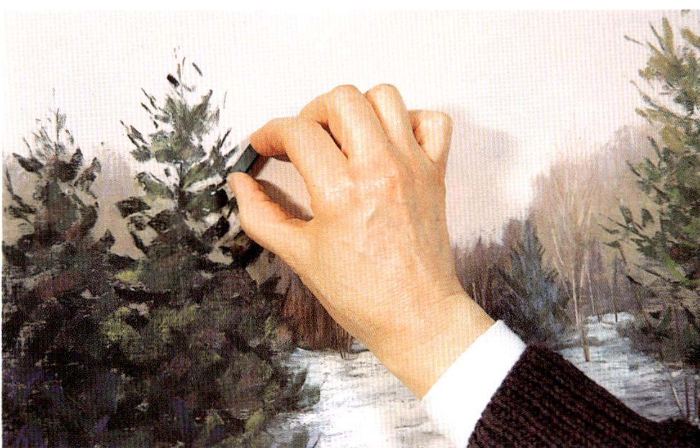

Here are the above strokes in action.

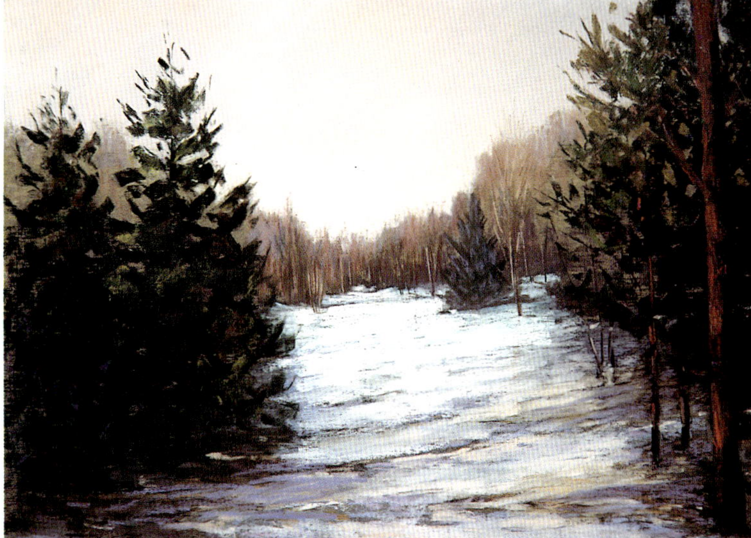

*Here, the evergreens are adequately suggested by broad, green
strokes. Definition, which is shown by smaller strokes, is reserved
for only the edges of the trees.*

REMBRANDT AND WINSLOW
Pastel on sanded paper
18″ × 24″
Collection of the artist

*When doing these spruce trees in snow, I used a very loose and
light stroke, leaving lots of the dark gray paper surface exposed.
Allow the texture of the surface to play an important role in the
painting, and exaggerate the color of the shadows as needed.*

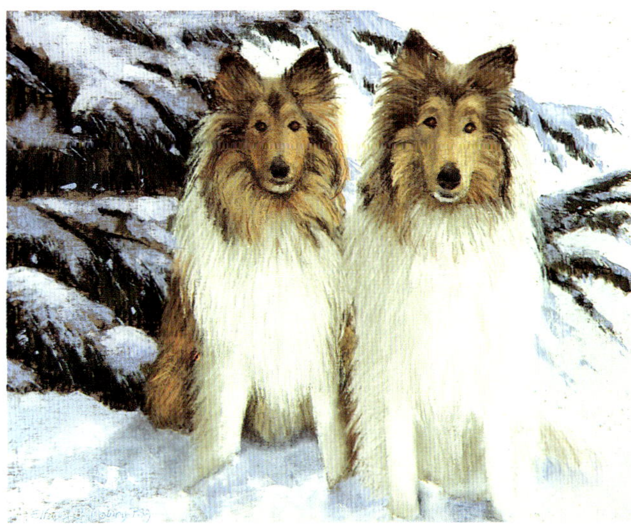

BUILDING AN EVERGREEN TREE

Before painting an evergreen, first plan it around a well-proportioned trunk and a tapering branch structure. This will help you determine where the massed shapes will appear most dense. Put those in with broad side strokes, using small pieces of pastel on their sides. Work quickly and cleanly, and above all, without detail. Instead, save definition for only the edges of the masses, which are the only places that texture is clearly noticeable.

Then gently build up the warm, highlighted portions of your tree; introduce cool darks as needed into the areas of shadow as you model your tree with careful attention to subtle gradations rather than abrupt value changes.

Once you build a few trees in this manner, you will be mindful of how, in most cases, the trunk tapers from the ground to the top. You will no longer paint trees in which portions of the trunk or branches are too thick for where they are. You will eliminate trees in your paintings whose branches have no relation to the trunk, or become mysteriously shaded by foliage, never to reappear.

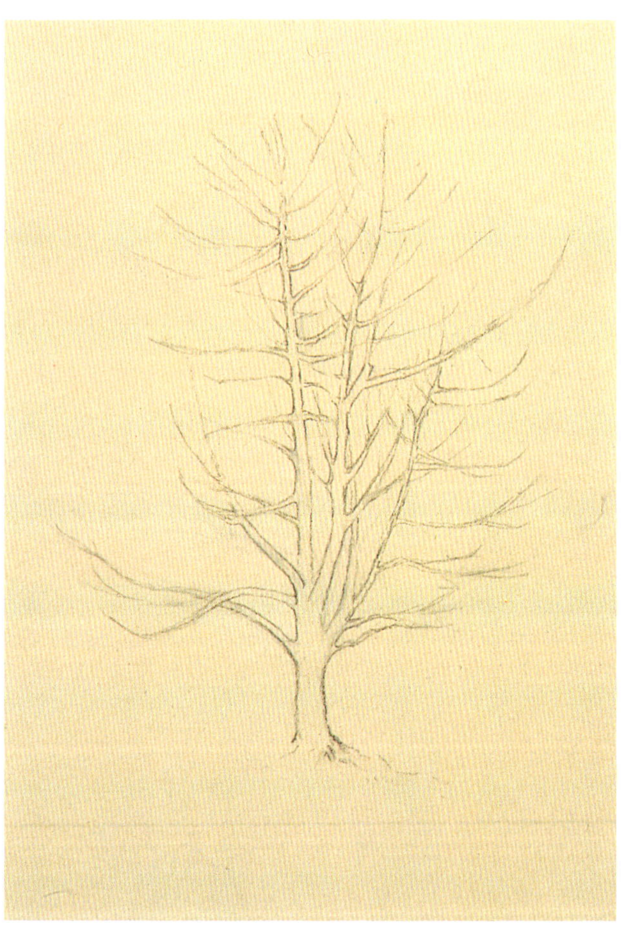

Step 1

The structure of a tree begins with the trunk and branches. Free, fluid strokes here will give your finished tree a natural rather than a stiff appearance.

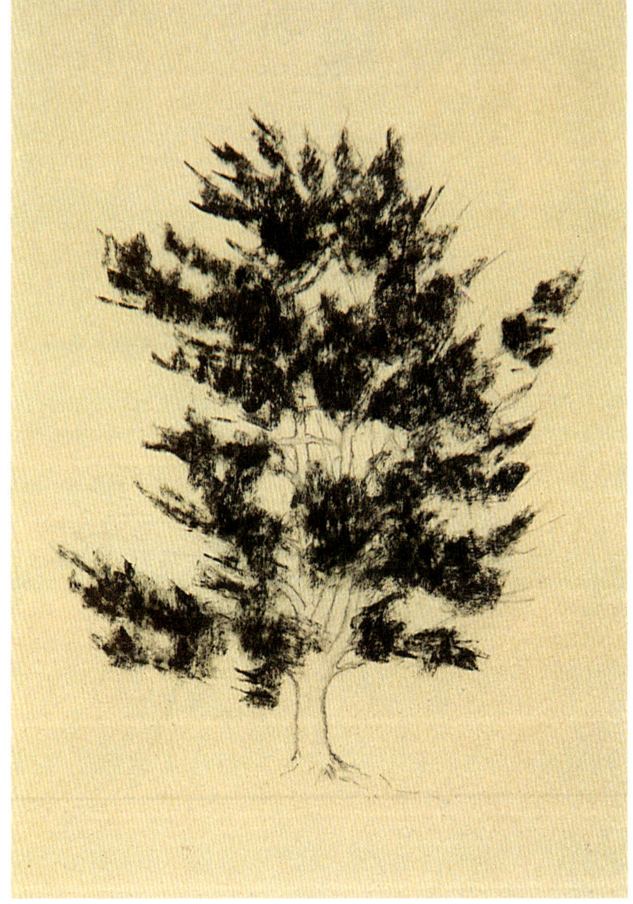

Step 2

Middle-value color masses show where most density occurs.

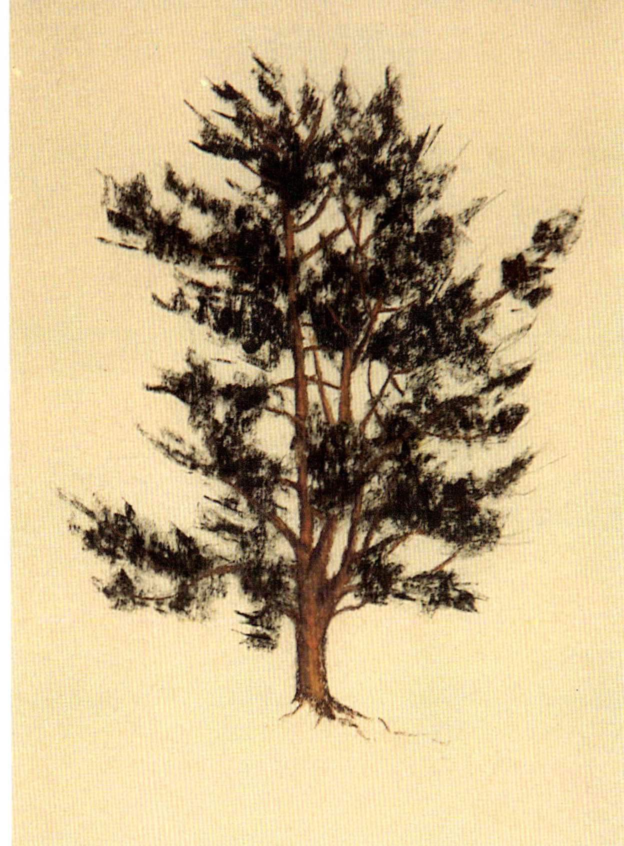

Step 3

Apply color to the visible trunks and branches.

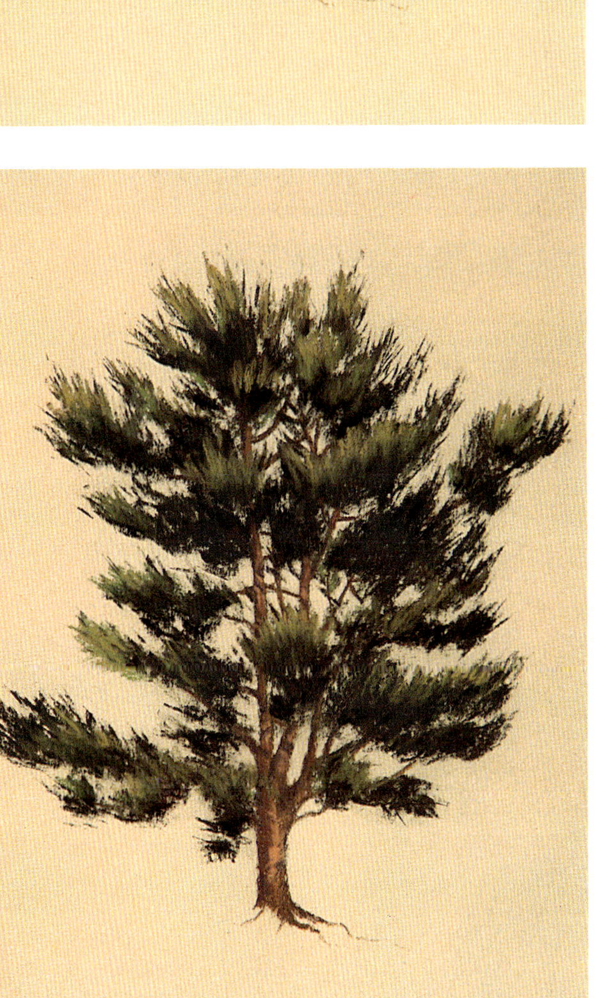

Step 4

Now link up the masses and define the mass edges.

Step 5

Highlights and shadows model the tree.

WHITE PINE
Pastel on sanded paper
12″ × 8″

PAINTING EVERGREENS IN A MASS

Massed evergreens can be used to contribute rich density to a large shape in winter paintings. In this landscape, a mass of evergreens on the far side of the stream provides a contrasting backdrop for the snow-covered rocks. Since such an intense mass of evergreens needs almost no detail, depth is achieved without distraction. The key here is not to think about the delicately needled hemlock branches, but to put in the large, dark area as a singular shape.

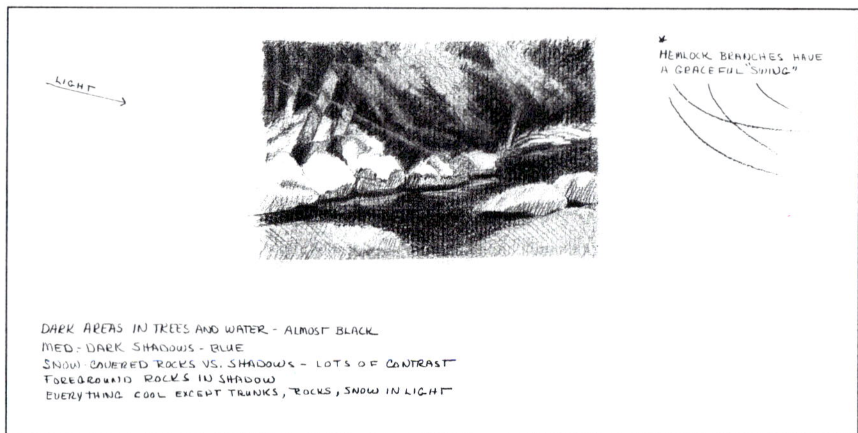

In winter, once I find my subject matter, I frequently try to keep my sketch within a small, blocked-in area on my sketchbook page so that I can get down the information I need before I become too cold. On a pleasant day, however, I would more likely do a larger, more leisurely sketch, allowing it to take its own directions over the page, having in mind the possibility of using parts of the sketch for more than one future painting.

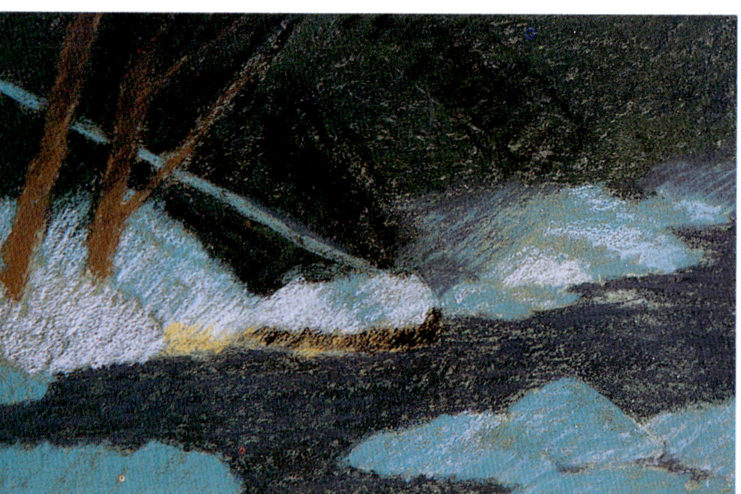

Step 1 The Transition to Color
Referring to the small pencil sketch, I use soft pastels to block in the large masses on my surface. The upper portion of the painting, which consists of dense hemlocks, is treated as a single deep-value mass of green, blue and some brown. This mass divides the surface diagonally and includes a fallen tree in another diagonal position, emphasized here so that I won't lose it.

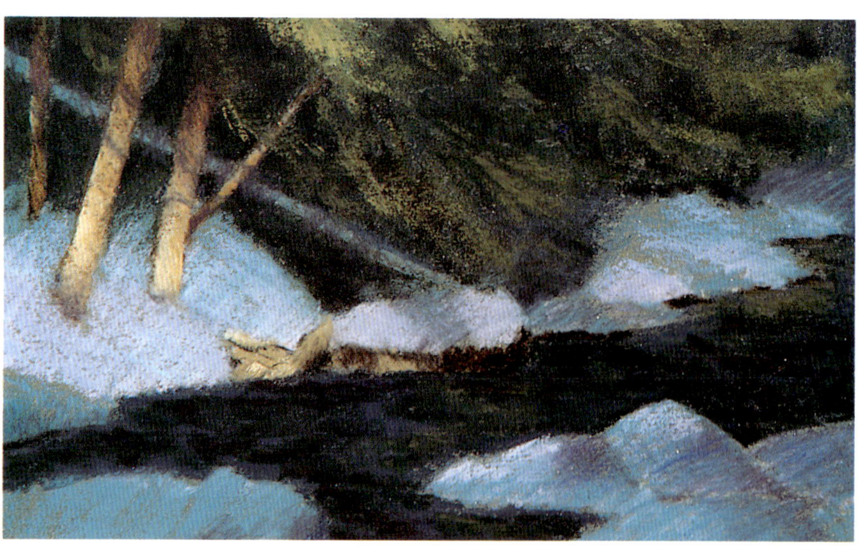

Step 2 Building Up Color
As I build more color into the painting, the shapes become more dimensional and defined. The hemlocks begin to show movement as a result of the direction and swing of the lighter green strokes. Purples, blue and dark greens go into the water, but it still appears flat at this point.

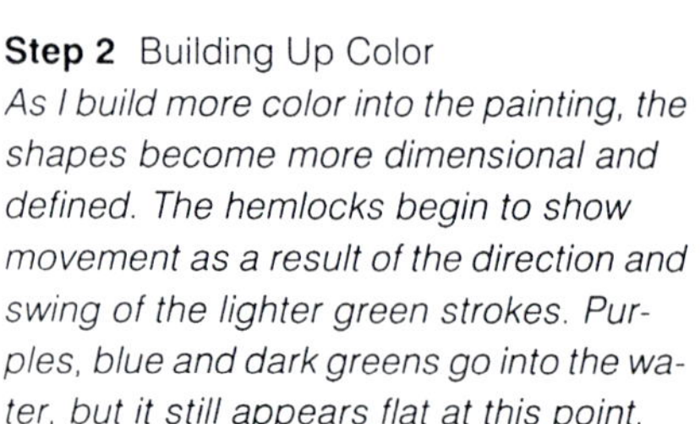

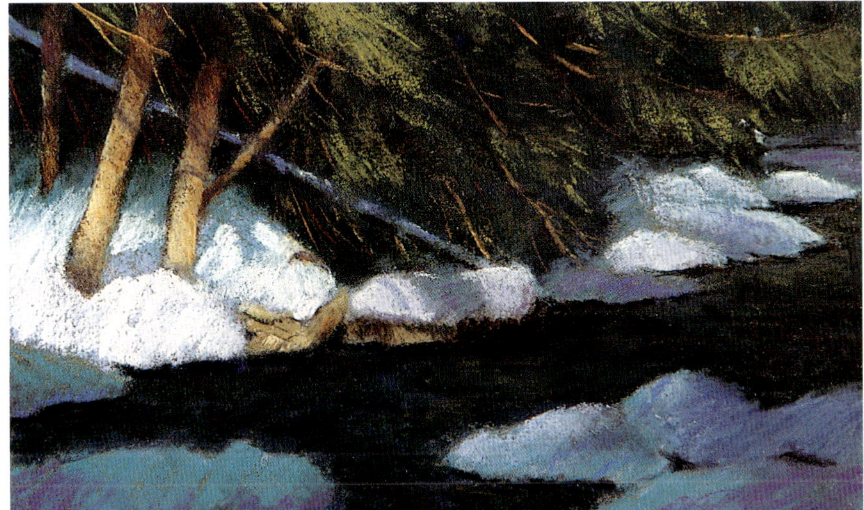

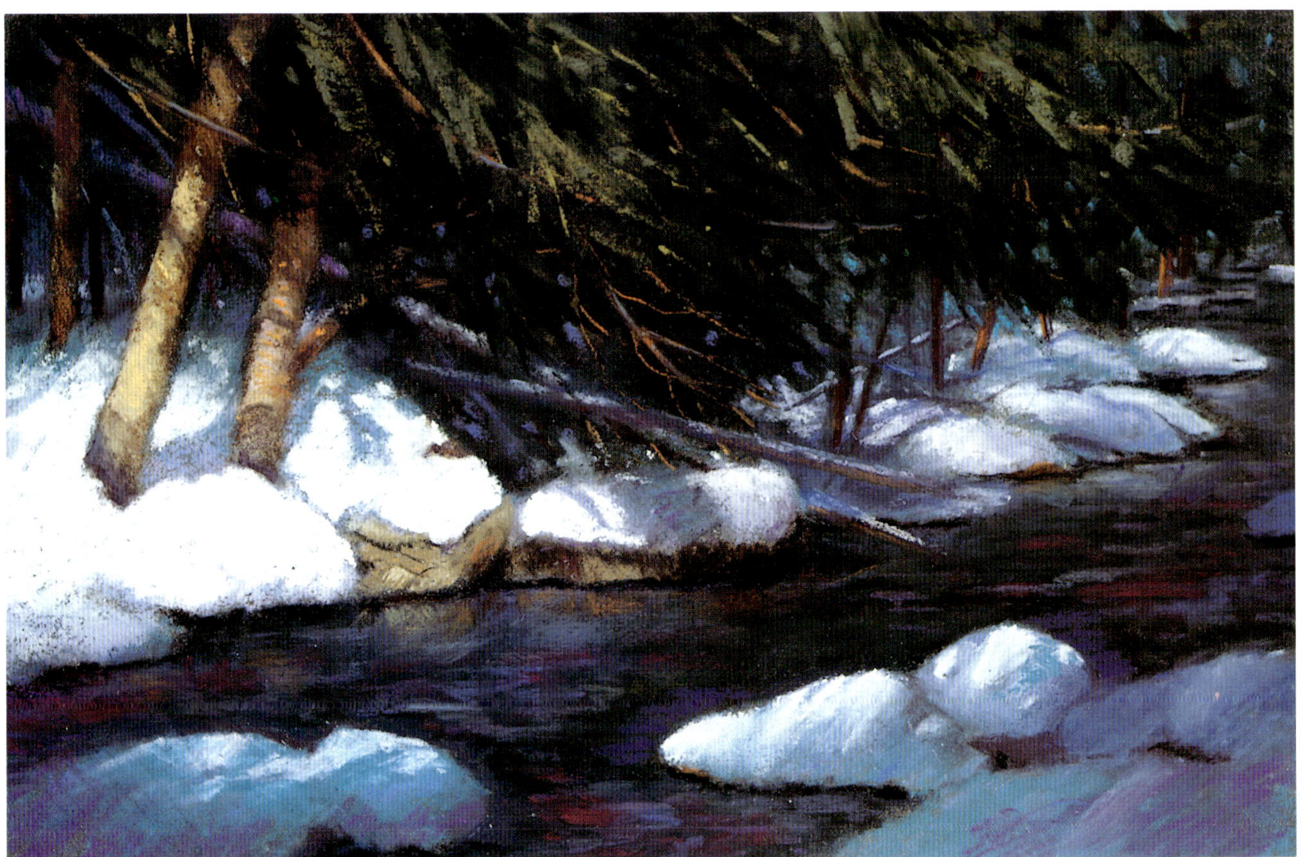

Step 4 Final Adjustments

After a long, critical look, I place some of the branches on the hemlock and the fallen tree back into shadow. There is not much detail, but a feeling of density exists in the trees. I tuck some hints of snow into the deep shadows and suggest several more fallen trees. Lights go in on the tree trunks and on the snow with warm color. Rock reflections and some light blue, directional water strokes get the stream flowing and give it depth.

MINNEWASKA STREAM
Pastel on handmade sanded board
9″ × 14″

LATE WINTER'S TRANSITIONAL PALETTE

Within the woodland's quiet shadows, the reluctant snow holds fast awhile longer, but wherever the sun penetrates, the earth's warm, matted colors begin to appear again. Wet, tangled grasses remain low, broken and decayed. In the clearing, where large ever- greens prevented much of the snow from reaching the ground, the late season's sun changes blue snow shadows to exposed circles of red-brown, sweet smelling needles.

The showiness of early winter is gone, and many people tend to think of the end of winter as dreary. Instead, consider adding ochre and sienna back into your palette, for as soon as the ground softens underfoot and the sap begins to run, new growth is starting. Nature's cycles continue, and spring's new beginning is about to unfold.

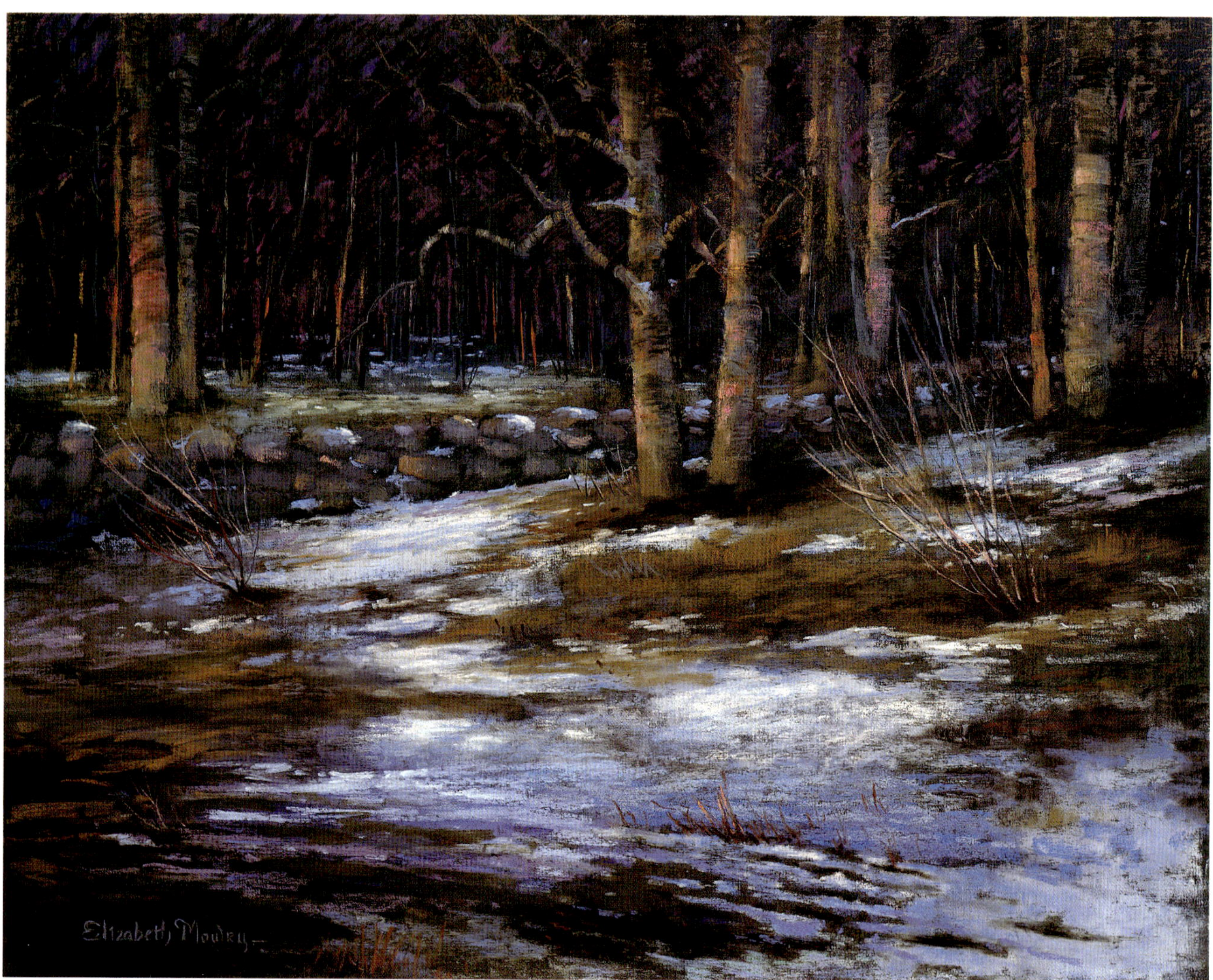

This painting explores winter's transitional palette, in which warm, earth colors temper the coolness of the diminishing snow. The solitude of the woodlands is conveyed here by the absence of life and movement. Soon a single warm and sunny afternoon will uncover the soggy, wet ground, and the signs of a new season will begin.

THE STONE WALL
Pastel on sanded paper
18" × 24"

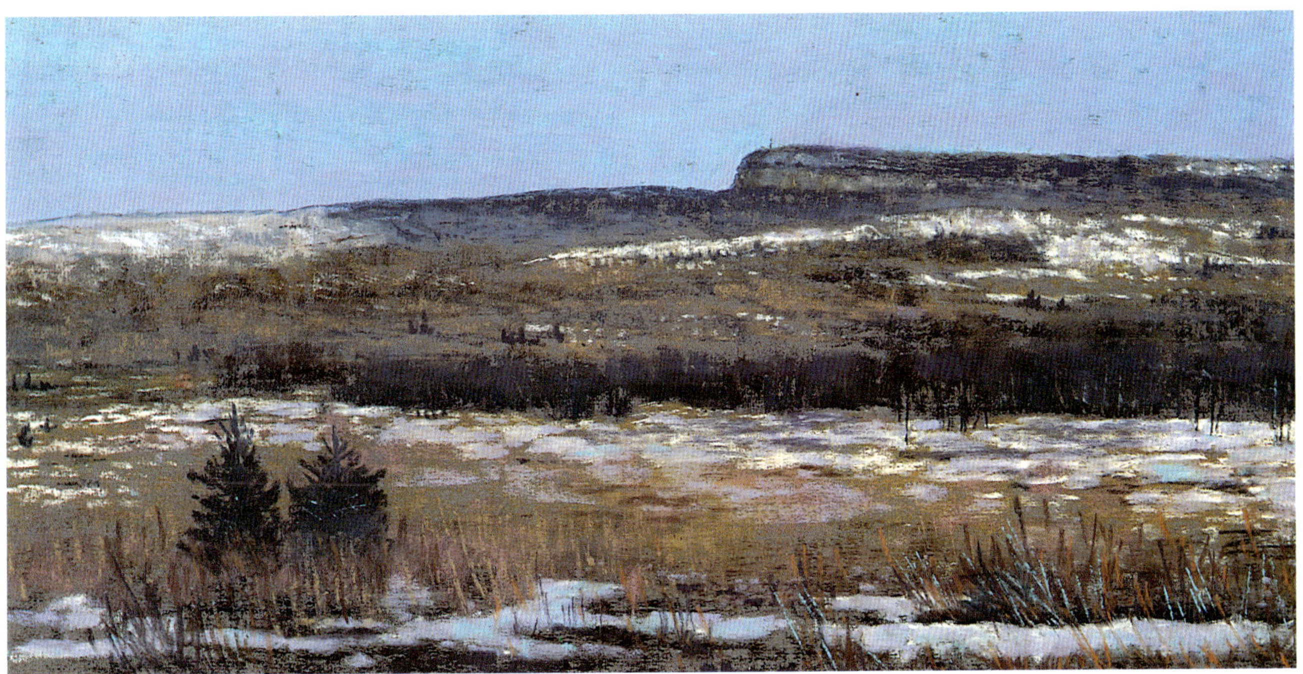

The winter palette used in this painting is not extensive, but quiet strength comes from the way it is used. Sunlit and shadowed snow divides the picture plane horizontally, while cool purple-grays and blues are placed next to complementary ochre grasses.

MOHONK, FEBRUARY
Pastel on sanded paper
9½″ × 22″
Collection of Harry and Marge Phillips

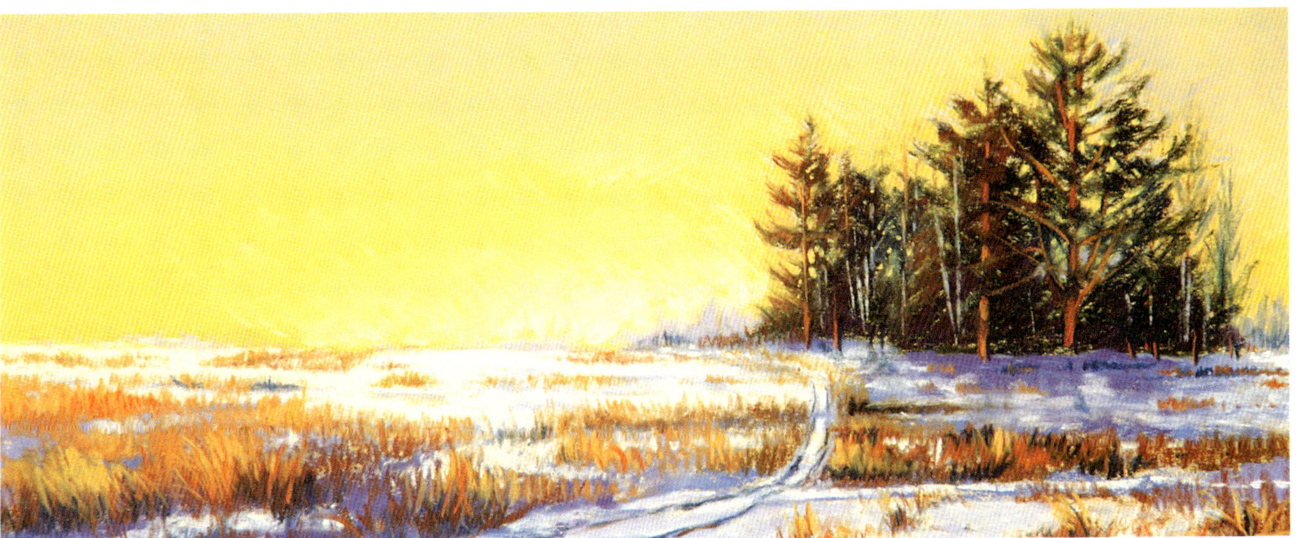

Here, the warmth of an optimistic winter sky is repeated in the foreground by uncovered grasses and weeds. Winter's palette slowly warms as the snow disappears.

TRACTOR PATHWAYS
Pastel on sanded board
5″ × 12″

FIELD BOX PLANS AND INSTRUCTIONS

I. Materials Purchase List
- ¼″ plywood; you will need a piece 18″ × 24″
- one ¼″ × 2¼″ × 8′ pine lattice strip
- two ¼″ × 1⅜″ × 8′ pine lattice strip
- one 1″ × 1″ × 8′ pine stock
- four 10-24 × ¾″ machine screws
- four #10 flat washers
- four 10-24 nuts
- ⅝″ 18-gauge nails
- white carpenter's wood glue

II. Materials Prepared for Construction
- one 12″ × 18″ plywood [FLOOR]
- two ¼″ × 2¼″ × 18″ pine lattice strip [SIDE WALLS]
- four 1″ × 1″ × 7″ pine stock [LEGS]
- two ¼″ × 2¼″ × 14½″ pine lattice strip [END WALLS]
- two ¼″ × 1⅜″ × 14½″ pine lattice strip [FLOOR SUPPORTS]
- one ¼″ × 1⅜″ × approximately 33″ finished size pine lattice strip, bent as noted in Construction Notes [HANDLE]
- one ¼″ × 1⅜″ × 18″ pine lattice strip [INTERIOR DIVIDER]
- four ¼″ × 1⅜″ × 6¾″ pine lattice strip [INTERIOR DIVIDER]
- one ¼″ × 1⅜″ × 5″ pine lattice strip [INTERIOR DIVIDER]
- one 11⅞″ × 17⅞″ plywood [OPTIONAL REMOVABLE LID]

III. Construction Notes
NOTE: Dimensions given here are based on actual lumber dimensions of material obtained from my local lumberyard. Slight variations in finished stock size may be encountered; therefore, I suggest that you measure all pine stock carefully and make necessary adjustments to overall dimensions prior to cutting.

1. Assemble Body
Glue and nail (at about 2″-3″ spacing) the 18″ side walls to long edges of plywood floor. Glue and nail the 14½″ end walls to the remaining edges of plywood floor and the ends of sidewalls, leaving 1″ overhang at each end of the sidewall to accommodate legs. Allow glue to dry (clamp if possible wherever glue is used).

2. Add Legs and Floor Supports
Glue and nail legs to body, nailing through side walls from inside the box, and through end walls from outside the box. Allow glue to dry. Glue and nail floor support to legs, positioning it tightly against the plywood floor.

3. Interior Dividers
Glue and nail from ends and from below plywood floor the 18″ central divider. Allow glue to dry. Install secondary dividers in like manner. Divisions shown may be rearranged to suit individual requirements.

4. Handle
Cut a length of ¼″ × 1⅜″ lattice about 4′ long. Cut two small notches on each end, wide enough to accommodate a sturdy string as shown, pulling string tight enough to create a bow in strip (see Figure III). Immerse in water and leave for twenty-four hours, then shorten string to pull curve tighter. Repeat until distance across string is about 16″. Allow to dry with string on for several days. After string is removed, cut handle to desired length. Position handle against end wall, drill two ³⁄₁₆″ holes, taking care to locate them below the bottom of the removable lid, glue and bolt (see Figure IV). Note: Holes should be placed offset as shown to avoid splitting of wood.

5. Optional Removable Plywood Lid
Lid sits within the exterior walls, supported by the interior dividers, providing a ⅜″-deep shelf above for sketch pad. Small knobs may be screwed onto lid or finger-sized holes drilled through to facilitate easy removal.

SOURCES OF PASTEL MATERIALS

Daler Ingres Pastel Paper, Rowney Pastels, and Perfix Low-odor Fixative
Daler Rowney USA
1085 Cranbury South River Road
Jamesburg, NJ 08831

Larroque Bergerac, La Carte Pastel, Sennelier Pastels
Savoir Faire
P.O. Box 2021
Sausalito, CA 94966

Nupastels
Nupastel
Faber Castell Corporation
Lewisburg, TN 37091

Professional Artists' Pastels (formerly Arc-en-Ciel Pastels) and Townsend Handmade Soft Pastels
Dianne Townsend
385 Broome Street
New York, NY 10013

Stabilo Carb-Othello Pencils
Schwan Stabilo
403 Dividend Drive
Peach Tree City, GA 30269

Windberg Pastel Panel
Windberg Enterprises, Inc.
1111 N I H 35, Ste. 220
Round Rock, TX 78664-4244

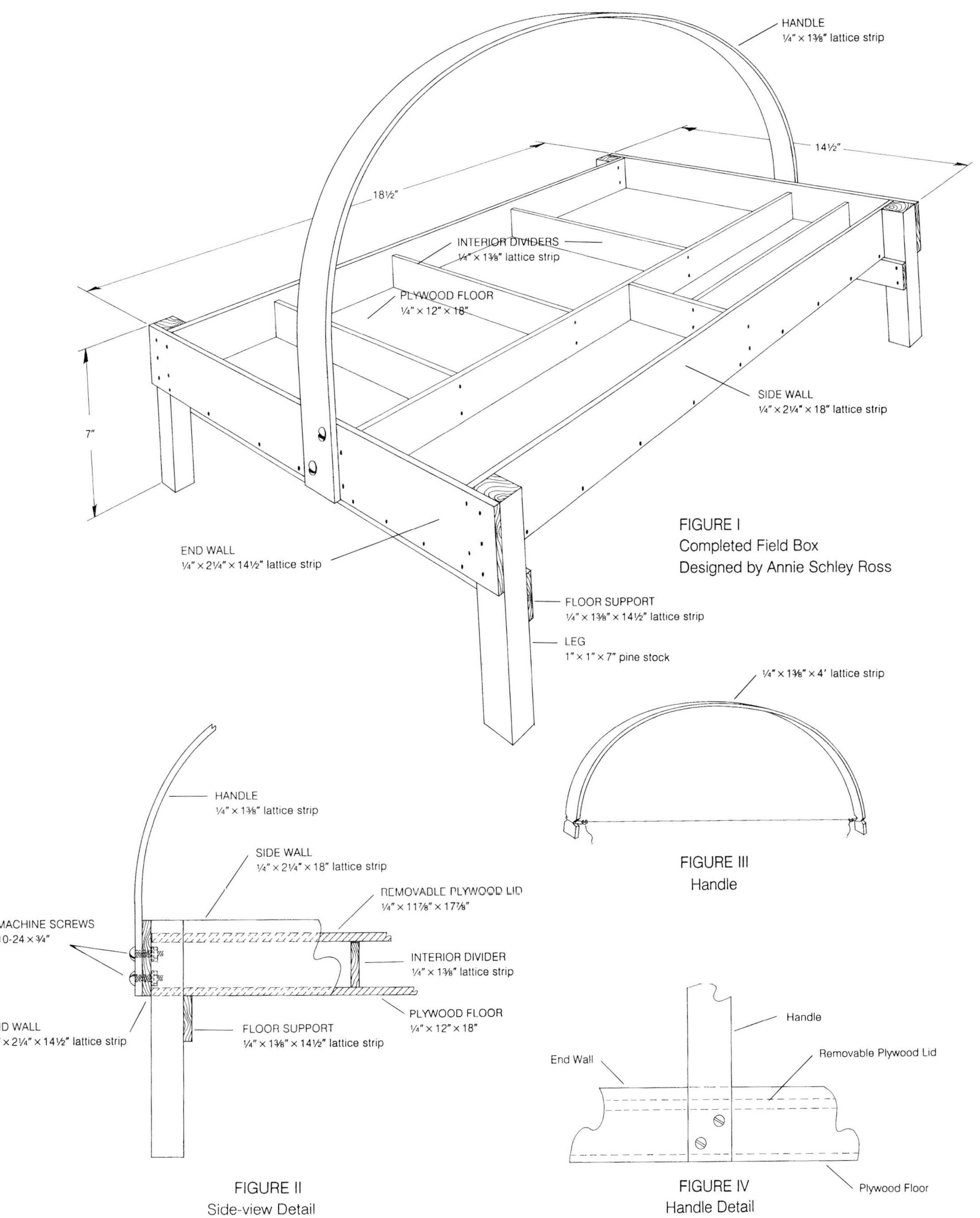

HANDLE
¼" × 1⅜" lattice strip
14½"
18½"
INTERIOR DIVIDERS
¼" × 1⅜" lattice strip
PLYWOOD FLOOR
¼" × 12" × 18"
SIDE WALL
¼" × 2¼" × 18" lattice strip
7"
END WALL
¼" × 2¼" × 14½" lattice strip
FLOOR SUPPORT
¼" × 1⅜" × 14½" lattice strip
LEG
1" × 1" × 7" pine stock
FIGURE I
Completed Field Box
Designed by Annie Schley Ross
¼" × 1⅜" × 4' lattice strip
FIGURE III
Handle
HANDLE
¼" × 1⅜" lattice strip
SIDE WALL
¼" × 2¼" × 18" lattice strip
REMOVABLE PLYWOOD LID
¼" × 11⅞" × 17⅞"
MACHINE SCREWS
10-24 × ¾"
INTERIOR DIVIDER
¼" × 1⅜" lattice strip
END WALL
¼" × 2¼" × 14½" lattice strip
FLOOR SUPPORT
¼" × 1⅜" × 14½" lattice strip
PLYWOOD FLOOR
¼" × 12" × 18"
FIGURE II
Side-view Detail
Handle
End Wall
Removable Plywood Lid
Plywood Floor
FIGURE IV
Handle Detail

INDEX

More Great Books for Pastel Painters!

100 Keys to Great Pastel Painting—Discover how to revitalize overblended colors, tone down bright ones, achieve a variety of special effects, and more! *#30591/$16.95/ 64 pages*

Pastel Interpretations—Explore dozens of techniques as you observe Foster Caddell, Frank Zuccarelli and 16 other artists render their interpretation of the same photo. *#30516/$28.95/144pages/275 color illus.*

The Pastel Painter's Pocket Palette—This handy reference takes the guesswork out of mixing the right colors for more natural fleshtones, greener fields and more! *#30436/$16.95/64 pages/1200 + color illus.*

Pastel Painting Techniques—17 step-by-step projects lead you through the pastel painting process. Plus, you'll get great advice on materials and proven techniques. *#30306/$21.95/144 pages/200 + color illus./ paperback*

Capturing Light & Color with Pastel—Learn how to make shape, value and color work together for beautiful results. *#30319/$27.95/144 pages/175 color illus.*

Creative Painting with Pastel—Delight in the colorful versatility of pastel as 20 outstanding artists reveal their secrets! *#30228/$27.95/144 pages/120 color illus.*

Colored Pencil Drawing Techniques—Explore the versatility of this medium with 18 full-color illustrations. *#07316/$24.95/176 pages/200 color illus.*

The Complete Colored Pencil Book—Discover the many ways the medium can be used to draw rich landscapes, glowing portraits, rugged textures and more! *#30363/ $27.95/144 pages/185 color illus.*

The Colored Pencil Artist's Pocket Palette—Save time! This handy guide lets you see how color blends will look before you mix! *#30563/$16.95/64 pages*

How To Paint Living Portraits—Make your portraits come alive! 24 demonstrations show you great techniques for all mediums. *#30230/$28.99/176 pages/112 illus.*

Painting Vibrant Children's Portraits—Let a master painter, Roberta Carter Clark, teach you how to capture the charm and innocence of children in any medium. *#30519/$28.95/144 pages/200 + color illus.*

North Light Book of Illustrated Painting Techniques—Explore 45 diverse painting techniques and how they apply to specific painting subjects. *#8009/$29.95/208 pages/ 750 + color illus.*

Enrich Your Paintings with Texture—Step-by-step demonstrations from noted artists will help you master effects like weathered wood, crumbling plaster, turbulent clouds, moving water and more—in any medium! *#30608/$27.95/144 pages/262 color illus.*

Enliven Your Paintings with Light—Sharpen your light-evoking abilities with loads of examples and demonstrations. *#30560/$27.95/144 pages/194 color illus.*

Strengthen Your Paintings with Dynamic Composition—Create powerful, memorable paintings with an understanding of balance, contrast, and harmony. *#30561/ $27.95/144 pages/200 color illus.*

Dramatize Your Paintings with Tonal Value—Make lights and darks work for you in all your paintings, in every medium. *#30523/$27.95/144 pages/270 color illus.*

Energize Your Paintings with Color—Create a sense of drama and emotion within your paintings as you master the use of vivid color and brilliant light. *#30522/ $27.95/144 pages/230 color illus.*

Drawing: You Can Do It!—Over 100 fun projects will help you learn to draw (or learn to draw better!) *#30416/$24.95/144 pages/200 + illus.*

The Pencil—Let master artist, Paul Calle, show you the mechanics of various strokes, how to make corrections, draw the figure and more! *#08183/$19.95/160 pages/200 + illus.*

Basic Drawing Techniques—Let Frank Webb, Charles Sovek and others show you how to work successfully in variety of mediums. *#30332/$16.95/128 pages/128 illus./paperback*

How To Write and Illustrate Children's Books—Break into this lucrative market with fresh insight on how to create books and get them published! *#30082/$22.50/ 144 pages/115 illus.*

Foster Caddell's Keys to Successful Landscape Painting—You'll paint glorious landscapes with practical advice from this master painter. Plus, dozens of helpful hints will help you solve (and avoid!) common painting problems. *#30520/$27.95/144 pages/135 color illus.*

Welcome To My Studio: Adventures in Oil Painting with Helen Van Wyk—Share in Van Wyk's masterful advice on the principles and techniques of oil painting. By following her paintings and sketches, you'll learn the background's effect on color, how to paint glass, the three basic paint applications, and much more! *#30594/$24.95/128 pages/146 color illus.*

Timeless Techniques for Better Oil Paintings—You'll paint more beautifully with a better understanding of composition, value, color temperature, edge quality and drawing. *#30553/$27.95/144 pages/175 color illus.*

Splash 3—You'll explore new techniques and perfect your skills as you walk through a diverse showcase of outstanding watercolors. Plus, get an inside glimpse at each artist's source of inspiration! *#30611/ $29.99/144 pages/136 color illus.*

Paint Watercolors Filled with Life and Energy—You'll learn how to use your materials and brushstrokes to create powerfully expressive work—without fear of mistakes. *#30619/$27.95/144pages/275 color illus.*

Learn Watercolor the Edgar Whitney Way—Learn watercolor principles from a master! Excerpts from Whitney's workshops, plus a compilation of his artwork will show you the secrets of working in this beautiful medium. *#30555/$27.95/144 pages/130 color illus.*

Write to the address below for a FREE catalog of all North Light Books. To order books directly from the publisher, include $3.00 postage and handling for one book, $1.00 for each additional book. Ohio residents add 5½% sales tax. Allow 30 days for delivery.

North Light Books
1507 Dana Avenue
Cincinnati, Ohio 45207

VISA/MasterCard orders call TOLL-FREE
1-800-289-0963

Prices subject to change without notice.   Stock may be limited on some books.

Write to this address for information on *The Artist's Magazine*, North Light Book Club, North Light Art School, and Betterway Books.   8548